Lynda Weinman's | Hands-On Training

Includes CD-ROM with Exercise Files and Demo Movies

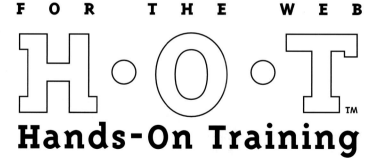

Photoshop®7/ImageReady®

FOR THE WEB

H·O·T™

Hands-On Training

lynda.com/books

By Lynda Weinman
and Jan Kabili

Photoshop 7/ImageReady For the Web | H·O·T
Hands-On Training

By Lynda Weinman and Jan Kabili

lynda.com/books | Peachpit Press
1249 Eighth Street • Berkeley, CA • 94710
800.283.9444 • 510.524.2178 •
510.524.2221(fax)
http://www.lynda.com/books
http://www.peachpit.com

lynda.com/books is published
in association with Peachpit Press,
a division of Pearson Education
Copyright ©2003 by lynda.com

ISBN: 0-321-11276-8

0 9 8 7 6 5 4 3 2 1

Printed and bound in the
United States of America

H•O•T | Credits

Original Design: Ali Karp, Alink Newmedia

lynda.com Director, Publications: Garo Green *(garo@lynda.com)*

Peachpit Project Manager: Suzie Lowey

Peachpit Copyeditors: Jennifer Ashley, Darren Meiss

Peachpit Proofreader: Darren Meiss

Peachpit Production: Myrna Vladic

Peachpit Compositors: Rick Gordon, Emerald Valley Graphics; Debbie Roberti, Espresso Graphics

Beta Testers: Grace Hodgson, Steve Perry, Eleanor T. Culling, Shane Rebenschied

Cover Illustration: Bruce Heavin *(bruce@stink.com)*

Indexer: Emily Glossbrenner

H•O•T | Colophon

The preliminary design for the H•O•T series was sketched on paper by Ali Karp | Alink Newmedia. The layout was heavily influenced by online communication—merging a traditional book format with a modern Web aesthetic.

The text in Photoshop 7 / ImageReady H•O•T was set in Akzidenz Grotesk from Adobe, and Triplex from Emigré. The cover illustration was painted in Adobe Photoshop and Adobe Illustrator.

This book was created using QuarkXPress 4.11, Adobe Photoshop 7.0.1, Microsoft Office 2002, and a Macintosh G4, running Mac OS X and OS 9.2.2.

Photoshop 7/ImageReady | H•O•T_____ **Table of Contents**

Introduction

Photoshop 7/ImageReady

For the Web

A Note from Lynda and Jan

We were motivated to continue this Hands-On Training book series because it's our experience that people buy computer books to educate themselves. Most books and manuals are reference based, and although there is nothing wrong with reference books in general, it seemed that a book with hands-on tutorials would be of great value. We are the type of learners who learn by doing. We enjoy a reference manual or book after we know our way around a program, but those types of materials don't help us get up to speed as quickly as we like. We at lynda.com wrote this series of books with our own learning styles in mind. We know we're not alone in our impatience to get productive in a tool as soon as humanly possible.

In this book, you will find carefully developed lessons and exercises that have been tested in lynda.com's digital arts training center to help you learn Photoshop 7 and ImageReady. If you are new to Photoshop or even if you've owned Photoshop for years, this book will teach you many new things that you didn't know. That's mostly because there are so many new features in Photoshop and ImageReady that even experienced Photoshop users will be on new ground.

This book is targeted toward beginning- to intermediate- level Web developers who are looking for a great tool to create graphics and Web content. The premise of the hands-on exercise approach is to get you up to speed quickly in these programs, while actively working through the book's lessons. It's one thing to read about a product, and an entirely different one to try the product and get measurable results.

Many exercise-based books take a paint-by-numbers approach to teaching by offering instructions that tell you what to do, but not why or when the instruction will apply to your work later. Although this approach sometimes works, it's often difficult to figure out how to apply those lessons to a real-world situation, or understand why or when you would use the technique again. What sets this book apart is that the lessons contain lots of background information for each given subject, which is designed to help you understand the process as well as the particular exercise.

At times, pictures are worth a lot more than words. When necessary, we have also included short QuickTime movies to show any process that's difficult to explain in writing. These files are located on the **H•O•T CD-ROM** inside a folder called **movies**. We approach teaching from many different angles because we know that some people are visual learners, while others like to read, and still others like to get out there and try things. This book combines a lot of teaching approaches so you can learn Photoshop and ImageReady as thoroughly as you want to.

We didn't set out to cover every single aspect of these programs. The manual and many other reference books are great for that! What we saw missing from the bookshelves was a process-oriented book that taught readers core principles, techniques, and tips in a hands-on training format. We've been making graphics for the Web since 1995, and it used to be a lot tougher than it is today. These versions of Photoshop and ImageReady in particular are oriented toward making Web graphics faster to download and easier to make. Additionally, ImageReady even writes JavaScript code and HTML, something that traditional imaging programs have seldom broached.

It's our hope that this book will raise your skills in Web design and digital imaging. If it does, we have accomplished the job we set out to do!

• We welcome your comments at **psir7faq@lynda.com**.

• Please visit our Web site as well at **http://www.lynda.com**.

• The URL for support for this book is **http://www.lynda.com/books/psir7hot**.

–Lynda Weinman
Jan Kabili

How This Book Works

This book has several components, including step-by-step exercises, commentary, notes, tips, warnings, and movies. Step-by-step exercises are numbered, and filenames and command keys are bolded so they pop out more easily. When you see italicized text, it signifies commentary.

• At the beginning of each exercise you'll see the notation **[IR]** if the exercise takes place in ImageReady, or **[PS]** if the exercise takes place in Photoshop.

• Whenever you're being instructed to go to a menu or multiple menu items, it's stated like this: **File > Open**.

• Code is in a monospace font: `<HTML></HTML>`.

• URLs are in a bold font: **http://www.lynda.com**.

• Macintosh and Windows interface screen captures: Most of the screen captures in the book were taken on a Macintosh. Windows shots were taken only when the interface differed from the Macintosh. We made this decision because we do most of our design work and writing on Macs. We also own and use Windows systems, so we noted important differences when they occurred.

Exercise Files and the H•O•T CD-ROM

All of your course files are located inside a folder called **exercise_files** on the **H•O•T CD-ROM**. These files are divided into chapter folders. Please copy the chapter folders to your hard drive because you will be required to alter them, which is not possible if they stay on the CD.

WARNING | Platform Concerns

Windows: Locked Files

Unfortunately, when files originate from a CD-ROM, older versions of the Windows operating system (not Windows XP) default to making them write-protected (read-only). This means that by default you will not be able to alter and resave any exercise files you copy from the **H•O•T CD-ROM** to a Windows hard drive. If you are working on Windows, you must remove the read-only setting from each copied exercise file as follows:

1. Open the **exercises** folder on the **H•O•T CD-ROM**, and copy one of the subfolders (for example, the **chap_05** folder) to your desktop.

2. Open the **chap_05** folder you copied to your desktop, and choose **Edit > Select All**.

3. Right-click on one of the selected files, and choose **Properties** from the pop-up menu.

4. In the **General** tab of the **Properties** dialog box, uncheck **Read-only**. This will unlock all of the files in the **chap_05** folder on your desktop.

Windows: Missing File Extensions

By default, **Windows 98/ME/2000** users will not be able to see file extension names, such as .gif, .jpg, or .html. Don't worry, you can change this setting.

Windows 98/ME Users:

1. Double-click on the **My Computer** icon on your desktop. (**Note:** If you or someone else has changed the name, it will not say **My Computer**.)

2. Select **View > Folder Options** to open the **Folder Options** dialog box.

3. Click on the **View** tab at the top. This will allow you to access the different view settings for your computer.

4. Uncheck the check box inside the **Hide file extensions for known file types** option. This will make all of the file extensions visible.

Windows 2000 Users:

1. Double-click on the **My Computer** icon on your desktop. (**Note:** If you or someone else has changed the name, it will not say **My Computer**.)

2. Select **Tools > Folder Options**. This opens the **Folder Options** dialog box.

3. Click on the **View** tab at the top. This opens the **View** options screen so you can change the view settings for Windows 2000.

4. Make sure there is no checkmark next to the **Hide file extensions for known file types** option. This makes all of the file extensions visible.

Software Files on the CD-ROM

The **H•O•T CD-ROM** includes a Mac and Windows version of Netscape 6, as well as QuickTime 5.0. All software is located inside the CD's software folder (imagine that!).

Troubleshooting FAQ

If you find yourself getting stuck in an exercise, be sure to read the Troubleshooting FAQ in the back of the book. If you don't find your answer there, send an email to **psir7faq@lynda.com** and we'll post an update on the companion Web site for the book (**http://www.lynda.com/books/psir7hot/**) as quickly as we can. Obviously, we can't offer personal technical support for everyone who reads the book, so be sure to refer to this FAQ before you request extra help.

Note: This FAQ is intended to support the exercises in this book. If you have other questions about Photoshop or ImageReady, as a registered owner of the program you can call Adobe's technical support line at 206-675-6203 (Mac) or 206-675-6303 (Windows), or visit their excellent Web site at **http://www.adobe.com.**

Skill Level

This book assumes that you possess a basic knowledge of Photoshop. If you have never used Photoshop before, you should go through the tutorial in the manual before you begin this book. Web design and digital imaging are challenging, somewhat technical, creative mediums. You must have good general computer skills to work with Web applications, because they require that you save and open numerous files and often work in multiple programs at the same time.

RAM, RAM, and More RAM

It's ideal to keep Photoshop, ImageReady, and a Web browser open at the same time. To do this, we recommend that you have at least 128MB of RAM. This book assumes that you can open all these programs simultaneously. If you cannot, you will need to quit whichever program you're in whenever you are requested to enter another. This is possible to do but will grow tiring, we assure you. Photoshop and ImageReady are professional tools and require professional-level systems to run optimally.

System Requirements

Macintosh

• PowerPC® processor (G3, G4, or G4 dual)

• Mac OS software version 9.1, 9.2, or Mac OS X version 10.1.3

• 128MB of RAM (192MB recommended)

• 320MB of available hard-disk space

• 800 x 600 color monitor with 16-bit color or greater video card

Windows

• Intel® Pentium® III or 4 processor

• Microsoft® Windows® 98, Windows 98 Second Edition, Windows Millennium Edition, Windows NT® with Service Pack 6a, Windows 2000 with Service Pack 2, or Windows XP

• 128MB of RAM (192MB recommended)

• 280MB of available hard-disk space

• 800 x 600 color monitor with 16-bit color or greater video card

About lynda.com

lynda.com is dedicated to helping Web designers and developers understand tools and design principles. lynda.com offers training books, CDs, videos, hands-on workshops, training seminars, and on-site training. The Web site contains online tips, discussion boards, training products, and a design job board. Be sure to visit our site at **http://www.lynda.com** to learn more!

*Check out Lynda's other books at **http://www.lynda.com/books**.*

*Check out Lynda's training DVDs and CDs at **http://www.lynda.com/videos**.*

About Lynda

I've been practicing computer design and animation since 1984, when I bought one of the first Macintosh computers. I worked as an animator and motion graphics director in the special-effects industry for seven years before having a daughter in 1989. At that time, I was asked to teach my first workshop in multimedia animation, and eventually became a full-time faculty member at Art Center College of Design in Pasadena, California. I've worked as a beta tester for imaging and animation software packages since 1984, and have worked as a consultant for Adobe, Macromedia, and Microsoft. I've conducted workshops at Disney, Microsoft, Adobe, and Macromedia, and have been a keynote speaker and/or moderator at numerous design, broadcast-design, animation, Web-design, and computer-graphics conferences. With my husband Bruce Heavin (who is responsible for the beautiful covers of all my books!), I cofounded lynda.com, Inc., which specializes in digital arts training via hands-on classes, seminars, training videos, books, Web tips, and CD-ROMs. The list could go on and on, but I basically love teaching and sharing knowledge, and that's what I spend most of my waking hours doing. I hope you'll visit **http://www.lynda.com** to learn more.

About Jan

I'm an author and educator in the evolving world of new media design. As a lead instructor and head of the Adobe training program at lynda.com, I've taught hundreds of students how to design for the Web using Photoshop, ImageReady, GoLive, and other software. I've taught multimedia and Web design at universities and national conferences, written books, articles and teaching curricula, and beta-tested the latest software for Adobe. I recently completed my third book on Photoshop and ImageReady, and am now heading up the teaching with technology program at the University of Colorado School of Law (yes, I'm also a lawyer with a JD from Stanford Law). In my spare time, I'm a digital artist with a masters degree in electronic media. You're welcome to see my digital artwork at **http://www.saga2.com**, and read my latest musings on Web graphics in *Mac Design* magazine.

Lynda and her husband/partner **Bruce Heavin.**   *Lynda* and her beautiful daughter, *Jamie.*

Jan and her great kids, **Ben** (17), **Coby** (12), and **Katie** (11).

Acknowledgments

We could not have written this book without the help of many key people.

Lynda sends special thanks to...

My daughter Jamie–Nothing else comes as close to mattering than you. I love you with all my heart.

Jan Kabili for her dedication to this project, and everything that she touches! Jan, you are da bomb! Your attention to detail and commitment to excellence is inspiring, and it is an honor to work with you.

Garo Green, our Director of Publications, who knows how to wear a lot of hats and still have cute hair! It is a gift to have the opportunity to work with you and to count you as a friend.

Ramey McCullough, our General Manager, who holds our ship together and also wears so many hats so well. It is a gift to know you, and work along your side. Our bike rides are great, too!

The **staff** at lynda.com for helping with everything.

Domenique Sillet, for the rockin' javaco images. You are so good! Hope you get lots of work from this project–check her out at **http://www.littleigloo.com.** You are a great friend as well.

David Rogelberg, my book agent (**http://www.studiob.com**), for helping make the Hands-On Training book series dream a reality.

My husband **Bruce** for his support, humor, art, and patience. I know I am not an easy person to live with, and I'm grateful for your understanding.

Suzie Lowey, **Nancy Ruenzel**, and **Victor Gavenda** at Peachpit for their hard work and commitment to this series.

Adobe, for making software that is just so damn good. To all the engineers and support team who keep making a great tool greater.

You, the reader, for supporting this series. I hope this book is helpful to you, and that you enjoy creating Web graphics in this most amazing tool!

Jan sends special thanks to...

My wonderful family **Ben**, **Coby**, and **Katie Kabili** and **David Van de Water**.

My inspiring friend **Lynda Weinman**.

My indefatigable Mom and Dad, **Barbara Morrison Feldman** and **Seymour Feldman**, and brother **Peter Feldman**.

The many fascinating people with whom I've worked along the way. You know who you are, but to name just a few—**Ellen Norgard Donovan**, **Grace Hodgson**, **Bruce Heavin**, **Garo Green**, **Neil Salkind**, **Alex Sweetman**, **Jo Davies**, and more.

I.

Getting Started

| What You Can Make with Photoshop and ImageReady |

| When to Use Photoshop versus ImageReady |

| New Feature Overview |

chap_01

Photoshop 7/ImageReady
H•O•T CD-ROM

This chapter gives you an overview of what Photoshop and ImageReady have to offer the Web designer. You'll find ideas for the kind of Web graphics you can make with these programs, advice on when to use each program, and an introduction to new Web-related features in Photoshop 7 and ImageReady 7. The information in this chapter builds a foundation for what you'll learn in the hands-on chapters that follow.

Making Web Images in Photoshop and ImageReady

Photoshop and ImageReady can be used for creating a variety of Web graphics. Here are some examples of the kinds of files you can create for the Web in these programs. You'll get a chance to explore projects like these in the chapters to come.

Photographs: You'll learn to optimize photographs for the Web in Chapter 4, "*Optimization.*"

Logos and graphic art: Use the drawing skills you'll learn in Chapter 7, "*Shapes and Layer Styles,*" the coloring skills you'll practice in Chapter 3, "*Color,*" and information about optimizing GIFs that you'll learn in Chapter 4, "*Optimization,*" to make awesome logos and graphic art.

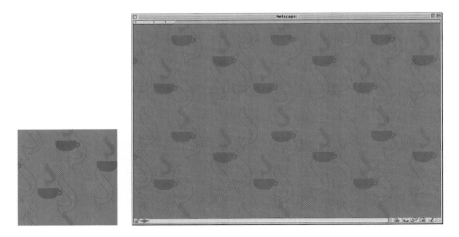

Background images: You can make a small patterned image in Photoshop or ImageReady. Next, you'll need to write HTML code in a Web authoring program, or better yet, have ImageReady write the code for you! The code is what will make the image repeat to fill an entire page background in a Web browser. Background images are covered in depth in Chapter 8, *"Background Images."*

Type: Another kind of useful file to create is text as an image rather than as HTML type. This sort of text is used if you need a Web page headline or logo that requires a fancy font or a special type effect. You'll learn all about creating and editing type in Chapter 6, *"Type."*

Rollovers: You can easily create buttons and other rollover graphics that change appearance when a mouse moves over an image on a Web page. See Chapter 10, *"Slicing,"* and Chapter 11, *"Rollovers."*

Image maps: A single image can be made into an image map that contains multiple links to other Web pages. Learn how to do this in Chapter 12, "*Image Maps.*"

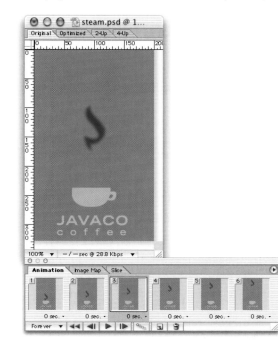

Animated GIFs: Animated GIF files are often used as attention-getting Web graphics or banners. You'll find everything you ever wanted to know about animated GIFs in Chapter 13, "*Animated GIFS.*"

Web Photo Gallery site: Photoshop can generate an entire Web site automatically with the Web Photo Gallery. With this feature, Photoshop will automatically optimize your images, write the HTML code for the site, and even open a Web browser to display your completed site. Learn how easy it is to use the Web Photo Gallery feature in Chapter 14, "*Automation.*"

When to Use Photoshop versus When to Use ImageReady

It's not always clear when you should use Photoshop and when you should use ImageReady. The two programs have many common features, as well as some features exclusive to each. Here are our recommendations about when to use each program:

- **Image editing:** Work in Photoshop when you're doing complex image editing, like retouching a photograph, making a collage, or creating a Web page layout. The reason is simple—Photoshop has more sophisticated image editing tools than ImageReady.

- **Optimizing graphics:** It's convenient to optimize images in whichever program you happen to be working at the time. Photoshop's Save For Web feature is similar to ImageReady's Optimize palette, but ImageReady gives you better access to the original version of the image if you want to make changes while you're optimizing. For this reason, we prefer to optimize graphics in ImageReady, but if you're in Photoshop and it's inconvenient to switch, you don't have to.

- **Slicing for rollovers and animation:** Work in ImageReady when you're slicing an image to make rollovers or animations, because only ImageReady can program these dynamic Web graphics. However, if you're slicing so that you can save some parts of an image as GIFs and other parts as JPEGs, you can use the slicing features in either program.

- **Rollovers:** ImageReady is the program to use when you're creating rollovers. Photoshop does not have a Rollover palette and cannot write JavaScript to make your rollovers work. However, you could use Photoshop to make artwork for your rollovers, and then bring that artwork into ImageReady to program as rollovers.

- **GIF animations:** ImageReady is also the program in which to build GIF animations. Photoshop does not have this capability, although you could use Photoshop (or Illustrator for that matter) to prepare the artwork, and then bring it into ImageReady to animate.

- **Image maps:** ImageReady is the exclusive program for creating image maps.

Don't worry if you're still unsure about which program to use when. You'll get hands-on experience doing all of these tasks in the appropriate program as you work through this book, and you can always glance back at the handy reference chart that follows.

When to Use Photoshop versus ImageReady	
Task	**Program**
Making simple Web graphics, like buttons or graphic backgrounds	Photoshop or ImageReady
Complex photo retouching and manipulation	Photoshop
Optimizing images	Photoshop or ImageReady
Slicing for rollovers and animations	ImageReady
Slicing an image to save part as JPEG and part as GIF	Photoshop or ImageReady
Creating rollovers	ImageReady
Building animations	ImageReady
Making image maps	ImageReady

New Features in Photoshop 7 and ImageReady 7

There are some new features in ImageReady 7 that are directly related to Web work. Photoshop 7 has fewer new features that are aimed specifically at the Web, but there are a couple that deserve mention here, because you may use them as you make Web graphics. For a more complete list of new features, see the Photoshop products section of the Adobe Web site, **www.adobe.com**.

- **Rollovers palette:** ImageReady's Rollovers palette has changed. It now looks a lot like the Layers palette, and it can show information about all of the rollovers, image map hot spots, and animations in an image. You can also choose to show animation frames in the Rollovers palette. You'll learn how to use the new Rollovers palette in Chapter 11, "*Rollovers.*"

- **Matching rollover states:** ImageReady has several new features for matching layer properties across rollover states. These are useful for unifying the position, opacity, or style of a layer across states. These features are addressed in Chapter 11, "*Rollovers.*"

- **Transparent colors:** When you're optimizing an image as a GIF, you can remap any colors in the image to transparency, so that a Web page background will show through those areas. This is a change from the last version of the programs, which would allow you to make a GIF transparent only where the original image was transparent. Learn more about this feature in Chapter 9, "*Transparent GIFs.*"

- **Transparency dither:** This new optimization feature adds dither (small dots of color) to partially transparent pixels at the edge of a graphic. This is designed to help blend the edge of transparent GIF with a patterned Web page background. See Chapter 8, "*Background Images,*" for details.

- **Weighted optimization of type layers:** This feature protects the colors in a type layer when you're choosing a color palette with which to optimize a GIF. You'll try this feature in Chapter 4, "*Optimization.*"

- **Slice options:** There have been a few tweaks to Photoshop's slice options. Settings for changing the appearance of slice numbers and lines have been relocated to **Preferences > Guides, Grid & Slices.** Photoshop's Slice tool has a new option for making slices from guides, and the Slice Select tool has new options for dividing slices and for hiding those slices that the program makes automatically so it's easier to see the slices you make yourself.

- **File Browser:** Photoshop has a new File Browser, which is an image viewer and file manager that is particularly useful for organizing photographs taken with a digital camera. You'll get a chance to work with the File Browser in Chapter 2, "*Interface.*"

- **Custom workspaces:** You can customize arrangements of Photoshop palettes and save them as reusable workspaces, as you'll learn to do in Chapter 2, "*Interface.*" This is a useful feature if you often switch between doing print and Web work, or if you're one of several people who use the same computer.

- **Tool presets:** In Photoshop 7, you can create custom-built, reusable tools by saving sets of options as tool presets. You'll try this new feature in Chapter 2, "*Interface.*"

- **Dynamic data:** You can create templates for data-driven graphics in ImageReady. You'll learn about this in Chapter 15, "*Data Sets*" and Chapter 16, "*Integrating with Other Programs.*"

Now that you've had a taste of what Photoshop and ImageReady have to offer, move on to the next chapter to get what you came for—hands-on instruction in how to use Photoshop and ImageReady for the Web.

2.

Interface

Disabling Color Profiles	Gamma
Preference Settings for the Web	Interface Overview
Photoshop/ImageReady Toolboxes	Jump To	Palettes and Tabs
Options Bar	Tool Presets	Docking to Palette Well
Custom Workspace	Shortcuts	Resetting Tools	File Browser

chap_02

Photoshop 7/ImageReady
H·O·T CD-ROM

Adobe has always been known for the consistency of its interfaces across products, platforms, and versions. The new twist in this version of Photoshop is that the program wears a slightly different look depending on the operating system in which it's running. It looks like the same old Photoshop in Mac OS 9 or Windows 98/2000. But if you run Photoshop in Mac OS X or Windows XP, the program's interface reflects the stylish veneer of those new operating systems. You'll see drop shadows and ice-blue dimensional buttons in Photoshop on Mac OS X, and flat blue borders around Photoshop palettes in Windows XP. This is no obstacle to learning Photoshop 7, because the differences are all cosmetic. Under the hood, the program works pretty much the same way in Mac OS X as it does in Mac OS 9 and in the various versions of Windows. We'll point out any small differences as they come up.

This chapter includes information and advice on color settings, gives an overview of the interfaces of Photoshop and ImageReady, and shows how to set up Photoshop preferences for Web graphics. You'll practice working with the new File Browser, custom Workspace feature, and custom Tool Presets. The overarching principles of the interface are covered here as well as instruction on how to optimize your settings for Web graphics workflow.

Color Profiling in Photoshop 7

Color profiling was introduced into Photoshop with version 5.0 to help Web and print developers manage color consistency between printers, scanners, and computer monitors. Photoshop 7 ships with Color Settings set to Web Graphics Defaults. This effectively turns color profiling off, except for the sRGB setting which will be covered in the next section.

What are color profiles, anyway? Computer color reliability has always been an inexact science. Digital artwork looks different on the computer monitor than it does once it's printed. A number of computer software and hardware vendors, such as Adobe, Apple, Hewlett Packard, and Microsoft, got together to form some standards around computer color, and came up with the concept of color profiles. The premise was that computer files could carry information about where they were created and how they were supposed to look, and that printing devices could read the information and duplicate the intended settings. Sounds good so far, right?

The trouble is, unless there's a receiving device that understands color profiles, they are of little use to anyone, and Web browsers do not understand color profiles. Sadly, that is the case on today's Web, though at some point it will potentially change for the better. Today, if you use color profiles in your Web graphics, not only will no Web browser recognize them, but the result is that your images will look different in Photoshop than they do in other software that does not recognize color profiles.

Although color profiles could ultimately be a great thing, we don't advocate using them for Web work. We believe it will be more damaging to turn them on because you won't have an accurate idea of how your artwork looks in browsers and in other applications. Photoshop's display will be adjusted, actually changing the appearance of pixel colors. Your document will look different in Photoshop than in environments that don't recognize color profiles, effectively ruining Photoshop's capability to integrate with other applications.

sRGB in Photoshop 7

It's great that Adobe chose to leave color profiles turned off in Photoshop 7, allowing advanced print users to turn them on, and leaving those who don't know how to use them less bewildered and frustrated. However, there's still one gotcha for Macintosh users only that requires a change from the way the program ships, and that has to do with sRGB. If you are not on a Macintosh, you can skip this sRGB section, as it will not affect you.

sRGB is the default color setting of Photoshop 7 when you first launch the program. The sRGB color setting emulates the appearance of the average PC monitor, which is generally darker than the average Macintosh monitor. Adobe claims that sRGB is endorsed by many hardware and software manufacturers, and that sRGB is becoming the default color space for many scanners, low-end printers, and software applications. Adobe recommends this color space for Web work, but we do not.

Although choosing this color setting will make your screen emulate a PC while you're in Photoshop, it will not change the way your screen looks in Web browsers and other Web applications, such as ImageReady, GoLive, LiveMotion, Dreamweaver, etc. It's rather disconcerting to choose colors in Photoshop, and then have those colors look different in other applications on the same computer.

It should be noted that Photoshop is not actually changing the colors of the real pixels in sRGB mode. Instead, it is changing the way the colors are previewed in Photoshop. We personally don't see the advantage of having artwork preview differently in Photoshop than in a Web browser or in ImageReady (which uses your monitor's RGB working space, rather than the sRGB working space to display an image on screen). Adobe's thought was that this preview is more accurate to how your Web graphics will be viewed from PCs, which have a higher market share than Macintoshes. In our opinion, there are other, better ways to preview how your artwork will look on different platforms, such as changing your gamma, as explained later in this chapter.

For this reason, the next section will cover how to change the Color Settings in Photoshop 7 from sRGB to Monitor RGB.

I. [PS] _____ Setting Photoshop Color Settings (MAC Users Only)

This exercise is for Macintosh users only. If you are using a Windows machine, skip ahead to Exercise 2! The purpose of this exercise is to disable the sRGB settings, so that the colors you choose in Photoshop will look the same as they do in ImageReady, other applications, and your browser.

1. Launch Photoshop, and choose **Edit > Color Settings** (Mac OS X: **Photoshop > Color Settings**).

2. In the **Color Settings** dialog box, choose **Settings: Color Management Off**. Click OK.

Note that this change sets the RGB field to Monitor RGB, which effectively leaves the appearance of your monitor set to its defaults (just like in browsers, other graphics applications, and HTML editors). The artwork on your screen will appear without any alteration, like it did in the days of Photoshop 4.0 and earlier, before color profiles were introduced. By the way, your Monitor RGB setting may read a little differently than the one in this example–Monitor RGB – Color LCD–depending on what kind of monitor you're using.

Now that you've finished these steps, all the color profile and preview options will be turned off, and your images will look exactly like they will in every other graphics and browser application you use.

TIP | Additional Color Help

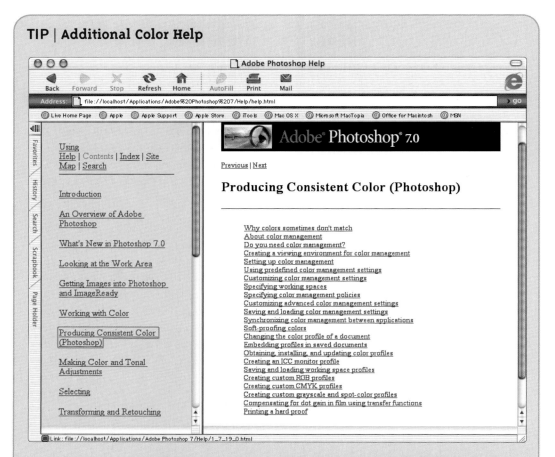

Photoshop 7 ships with additional documentation about color management, which you can access by choosing **Help > Photoshop Help > Contents** and clicking **Producing Consistent Color (Photoshop)**. We're intentionally not bogging you down with all the technical details of this highly complex subject, so that the book stays focused on the Web instead of print. However, if this subject piques your curiosity, be sure to give this **Help** file a read. Additional Color Management information is also available in the **Adobe Photoshop 7 User Guide**.

NOTE | Gamma on Macintoshes

The "gamma" of your monitor sets a midpoint for gray, meaning that it affects not the white point or black point display, but the grays or values between white and black. Windows has a setting of 2.2 gamma, while Macintosh uses a setting of 1.8. This is why Web graphics look darker on Windows than they do on Macintoshes. Many Web developers who work on Macs like to change their gamma setting to match that of Windows. If you make this change, it will affect all applications, not just Photoshop. When designing the **lynda.com** site, we leave our gamma settings alone because we have a large Mac audience. If you think that your site might have a larger Windows audience, this change might save you from potential unanticipated revisions to lighten your graphics so they read better on Windows machines.

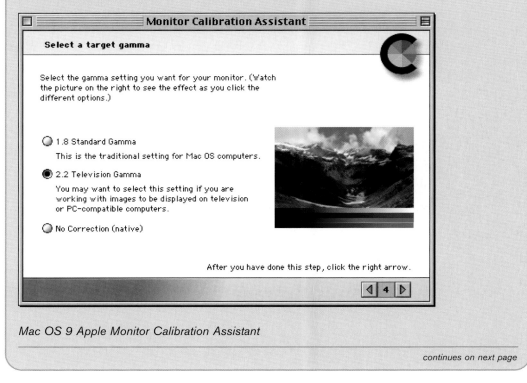

Mac OS 9 Apple Monitor Calibration Assistant

continues on next page

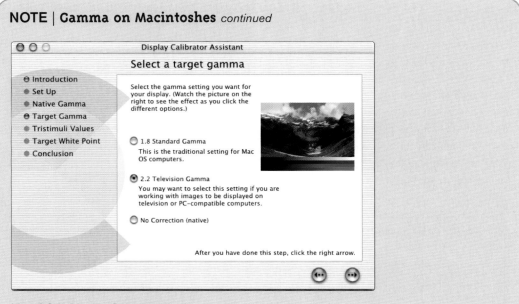

NOTE | **Gamma on Macintoshes** *continued*

Mac OS X Display Calibrator Assistant

Use the calibration utilities that are built into Mac OS 9 and OS X to change your gamma. If you're working in Mac OS 9, access the Apple Monitor Display Calibration Assistant by choosing **Apple > Control Panels > Monitors**, clicking the **Color** icon, and clicking the **Calibrate** button. Click the right-facing arrow to move through the panels to the target gamma window. Choose **2.2 Television Gamma**, which is the setting you want if you do a lot of Web authoring for a Windows audience.

If you're using Mac OS X, you can change your gamma setting by choosing **Go > Applications > Utilities**, and double-clicking **Display Calibrator**. In the **Display Calibrator Assistant**, click the right-facing arrow to move to the target gamma window, and choose **2.2 Television Gamma**. Click the right arrow twice more, name the profile **Windows Gamma**, and click **Create**.

The beauty of changing your system to match a Windows system with either of these utilities is that this change will affect all applications, including Photoshop, ImageReady, GoLive, etc. Before you move on, don't forget to follow these instructions again, choosing **1.8 Standard Gamma** this time, to switch back to the Mac gamma settings.

Previous editions of this book recommended that you use the Adobe Gamma Control Panel to change gamma on a Mac. That recommendation is no longer valid, because there is no Adobe Gamma Control Panel for OS X, and the OS 9 version of that control panel does not automatically install with Photoshop 7. (If you want to install the Mac OS 9 version of the Adobe Gamma Control Panel, you'll find it hidden in the **Goodies > Calibration > Mac Classic Only > Adobe Gamma** folder on the Photoshop 7 application CD-ROM. Follow the instructions for installing and using it in the **About Adobe Gamma** file you'll find there.)

2. [PS] Setting Photoshop Color Settings (Windows Users Only)

This exercise is for Windows users only. If you are using a Macintosh, skip ahead to Exercise 3! The purpose of this exercise is to make sure that color profiles for print graphics are not invoked when you are working on Web graphics.

1. Launch Photoshop 7, and choose **Edit > Color Settings**.

2. In the **Color Settings** dialog box, choose **Settings: Web Graphics Defaults**. Click **OK**.

Even though this setting leaves sRGB active, that's immaterial on a Windows machine. Your colors will still match between Photoshop, ImageReady, and other applications on your Windows screen, since sRGB is the native color space on Windows machines.

3. [PS] _____Setting Photoshop Preferences for the Web

There are numerous **Preference** settings in Photoshop, and many of them are related to general work-flow. The only setting that directly impacts whether you are set up properly for the Web or print is the **Units & Rulers** preference, which you will learn to change in this exercise. For a complete list of preferences and their settings, refer to the **Adobe Photoshop 7 User Guide**.

Preferences

Units & Rulers

Units
Rulers: ✓ pixels
        inches
Type: cm
        mm
        points
Column Size
Width: picas   oints
        percent
Gutter: 12   points

New Document Preset Resolutions
Print Resolution: 300   pixels/inch
Screen Resolution: 72   pixels/inch

Point/Pica Size
● PostScript (72 points/inch)
○ Traditional (72.27 points/inch)

OK
Cancel
Prev
Next

1. In Photoshop, choose **Edit > Preferences > Units & Rulers** (Mac OS X: **Photoshop > Preferences > Units & Rulers**). In the **Preferences** dialog box, click the **Rulers** button and choose **pixels**. Click **OK**.

When you work on the Web you measure everything by pixels and sometimes points, not picas, as you would in print.

Note: *ImageReady is designed for creating Web graphics, so there are no ImageReady preferences to set to prepare for Web work. For example, units and rulers are set to pixels and there is no option to change them.*

Interface Overview

Photoshop 7 and ImageReady 7 are still separate applications that ship together, just as they were in the last version of the programs. The good news is that from an interface standpoint you're in for an easy learning curve. That's because Photoshop's and ImageReady's toolboxes, palettes, and menu items are quite similar, are organized in a very logical way, and support your workflow to a higher degree than just about any other software tool on the market.

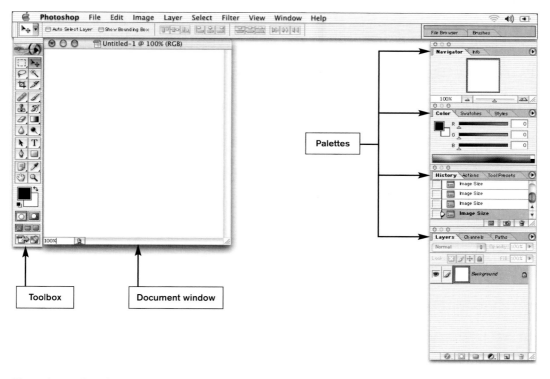

Photoshop 7 interface

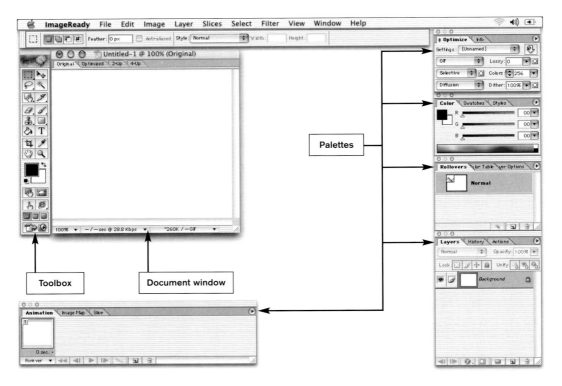

ImageReady 7 interface

When you first open Photoshop or ImageReady, they default to showing the Toolbox and a few
key palettes. The figures above also show an open, untitled document, which you can create by
choosing File > New. Pressing the Tab key toggles all the palettes on and off in either application.
Even though you'll see a few different palettes, it's obvious from first glance that these two programs
have very similar interfaces. If you know Photoshop already, you'll have a huge advantage when
learning ImageReady.

The Photoshop 7 and ImageReady 7 Toolboxes

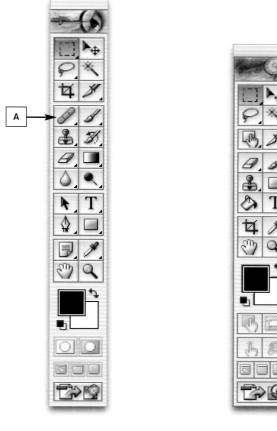

A →

Photoshop Toolbox   ImageReady Toolbox

The Photoshop 7 and ImageReady 7 Toolboxes are almost identical to those in the previous version of these programs. The only changes are that the **Airbrush** has been moved from the Photoshop Toolbox to the Options bar for all the brush tools, and there are two new tools in the Photoshop toolbox—the **Healing Brush** and the **Patch** tool (labeled **A** in the Photoshop Toolbox illustration). The Healing Brush and Patch tool, which are useful for retouching, are similar to the **Rubber Stamp** tool, except that they blend cloned pixels with the area to be repaired. Because this is not a Web technique, the Healing tools will not be covered in this book. Check the **Adobe Photoshop 7 User Guide** for more in-depth documentation.

Fly-Out Menus

Whenever you see a little arrow on the bottom right of a tool in Photoshop or ImageReady (or any Adobe application for that matter), it means there are other tool choices. Simply hold your mouse button down on the tool, and other choices will appear. Sometimes it's hard to find that one tool you're looking for because it's hidden under a fly-out menu icon. These handy illustrations should help you find hidden tools in Photoshop and ImageReady. You'll get a chance to see what a number of the hidden tools do as you work through the exercises in this book.

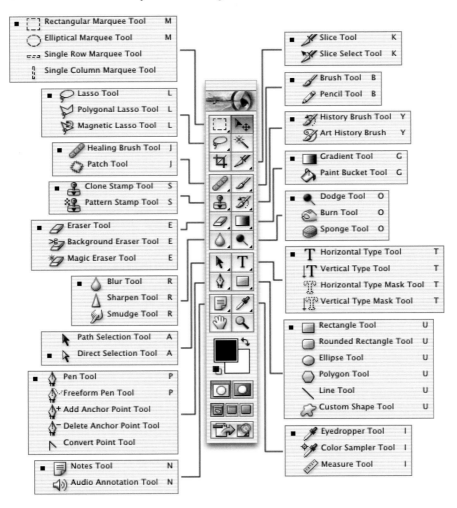

Photoshop 7 fly-out tool menus. The letter to the right of some of the tools is the shortcut key that enables you to access that feature quickly.

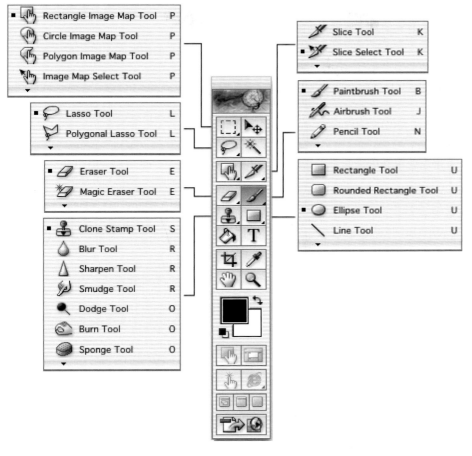

ImageReady 7 fly-out tool menus

Jump To Buttons

The **Jump To** button is located at the bottom of both toolboxes. It lets you switch between Photoshop and ImageReady with a convenient click of a button.

Jump To ImageReady
button in Photoshop

Jump To Photoshop
button in ImageReady

You'll have plenty of opportunities to use the Jump To button throughout this book. When you have an open document and click this button, the same document reopens in the other application. If you don't have a document open, the Jump To button will not work.

4. [PS/IR] _____Using Flexible Palettes and Tabs

Photoshop and ImageReady both allow you to reorganize items by docking or undocking a tab to form a new palette. This is a very convenient thing to do if you find that you are working with only a few palettes that are not grouped together, or if you don't want to crowd your workspace with palettes you don't use.

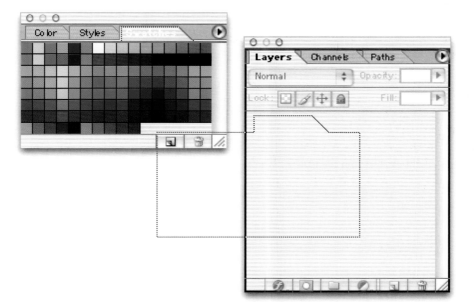

1. In either application, click the **Swatches** tab (if it's not visible, choose **Window > Swatches**), and drag the **Swatches** palette by its tab into the group of palettes that includes the **Layers** palette (if not visible, choose **Window > Layers**).

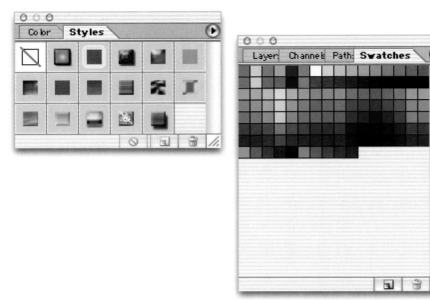

By dragging the Swatches palette by the tab area, you can drag it into another palette group. We do this often when working in Photoshop or ImageReady because we find ourselves using just a few features, and don't want to clutter up the screen with lots of separate palettes.

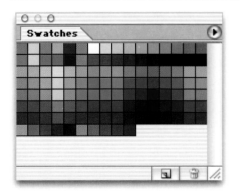

2. You can also create a palette with just one item if you want to, rather than nesting several items into a palette group. Drag the **Swatches** palette out of the **Layers** palette group and it will form its own palette all by itself.

5. [PS] _____Docking Palettes to Each Other in Photoshop

There's another way you can dock palettes in Photoshop, creating a vertical grouped palette. Here's how.

1. The **Swatches** palette should be on its own right now, if you followed the last exercise. If not, drag the **Swatches** palette by its tab away from any palette group in which it might be nested, so that it forms its own single palette.

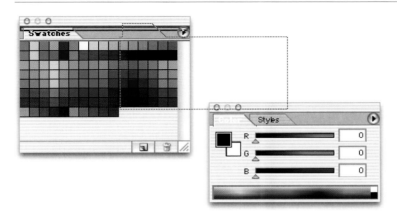

2. Drag the **Color** palette by its tab (not by the title bar of its palette group), and position it so that it is just under the top-most title bar of the **Swatches** palette. When you see a small black outline under the title bar, release your mouse.

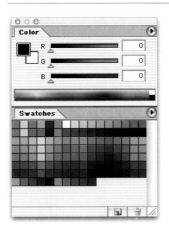

This should result in the palettes being docked to each other in a vertical fashion. We like to do this with palettes like these that relate to one another.

6. [IR] _____ Docking Palettes to Each Other in ImageReady

It's possible to dock palettes to each other in ImageReady as well, but it's done a little differently.

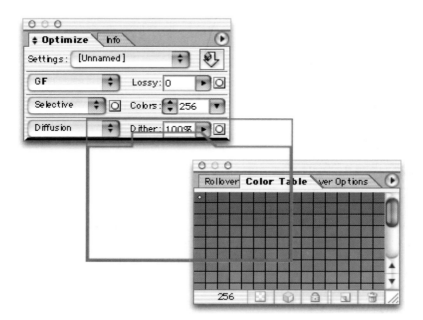

1. Drag the **Color Table** palette by its tab (but not by the title bar of its palette group) onto the bottom of the **Optimize** palette so only the bottom line of the Optimize palette becomes highlighted, as shown above.

Note: Your Optimize and Color Table palettes may not look exactly like this right now, but that doesn't matter for purposes of this exercise. Leave yours as they are for now.

The result is that these two palettes form a vertical docked configuration. We like to consult these two palettes often when we're optimizing images, and find this docking technique very helpful.

NOTE | Returning the Palettes to Default Settings

The fact that you can rearrange palettes and tabs is wonderful until you wish you could set them back to the way Photoshop or ImageReady had them in the first place. The procedure for returning palettes to their default positions is the same in both applications.

In either Photoshop 7 or ImageReady 7, choose **Window > Workspace > Reset Palette Locations**.

7. [PS/IR]_____Using the Options Bar

The **Options** bar, which was introduced in Photoshop 6, contains option settings for each tool in the Toolbox. The Options bar is context sensitive; it changes depending on which tool you've selected. What's nice about the Options bar is that it defaults to opening at the top of the screen so you don't have to hunt for it. The Options bar is not the only source of tool options. Some tools, like the Type tool and the Brush tool, offer options in palettes in addition to the Options bar. This exercise shows you how to access the Options bar, and when necessary, the additional options palettes.

1. Choose **File > New**, and click **OK**.

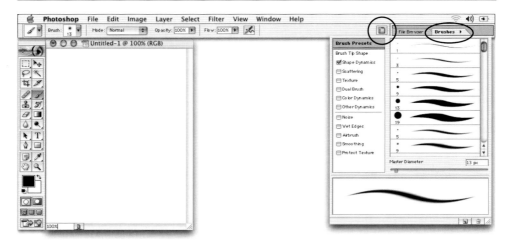

2. Click the **Brush** tool in the Toolbox.

Notice that settings for the Brush tool (Brush samples, Mode, Opacity, Flow, and Airbrush) are visible in the Options bar, which is located at the top of the screen.

3. Click the **Palette** button on the right side of the Options bar. This will open the **Brushes** palette.

The Brushes palette, one of the major new features in Photoshop 7, offers lots of options for creating your own brushes, as well as many new preset brushes. Click on any of the brush properties on the left side of the Brushes palette, and the right side of the palette will display options for that property. This book doesn't give instruction for the new Brushes palette, since it is not a Web-centric feature. We offer an Online Movie Training Library module on Photoshop 7 brushes, available for a nominal fee from the lynda.com Web site.

You'll also find a Palette button that opens the Brushes palette on the Options bar for other tools, like the Pencil tool, Eraser tool, Clone tools, Toning tools, and Focus tools.

4. Click the **Type** tool in the Toolbox.

Notice that the Options bar settings have changed to show the options for the Type tool.

5. Click the **Palette** button in the Options bar.

This brings the Character and Paragraph palettes forward. These palettes also offer Type settings, some of which are not found on the Options bar. You'll get a chance to work with some of these settings in Chapter 6, "Type."

6. Close the file. You don't need to save it.

8. [PS] _____Making a Tool Preset in Photoshop

Photoshop 7 has a useful new feature that allows you to save and reuse custom sets of tool options. This comes in handy if you use a tool to do different kinds of tasks and want to switch easily between the tool options you use for each task.

1. Copy the **chap_02** folder from the **exercise_files** folder on the **H•O•T CD-ROM** to your desktop if you haven't already done so.

2. In Photoshop, open **poster.psd** in the **chap_02** folder now on your desktop.

3. Click the **Zoom** tool, and click anywhere in the open image.

Notice that the image gets bigger, but the document window does not.

4. In the **Options** bar, put checkmarks next to both **Resize Windows to Fit** and **Ignore Palettes**. Click again in the image.

Notice that the document window now expands to fit the magnified image, because you checked Resize Windows to Fit. Depending on the size of your monitor, you'll also see the document window expand under the palettes on the right, because you checked Ignore Palettes. This is a pretty useful setup for the Zoom tool. So you'll save it so that you can use it again on this or other images.

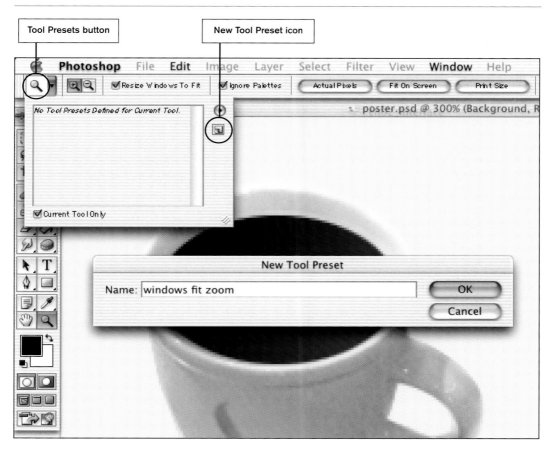

5. Click the **Tool Presets** button at the left of the **Options** bar.

This will open the Tool Presets picker. You'll see that there are no presets yet defined for the Zoom tool, although Photoshop ships with presets for some other tools.

6. Click the **New Tool Preset** icon on the **Tool Presets** picker.

7. In the **New Tool Preset** dialog box, give the preset a name (**windows fit zoom**).

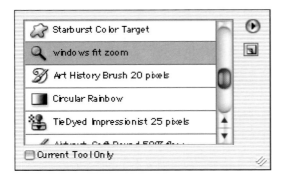

You can reuse this preset with the Zoom tool at any time, by selecting "windows fit zoom" *from the Tool Presets picker or from the Tool Presets palette* (Window > Tool Presets). *If you uncheck* Current Tool *Only in either location, you'll see a list of all of the tool presets, including those that ship with Photoshop and presets you make yourself.*

8. Choose **File > Close**, and close **poster.psd** without saving.

9. [PS] _____ Docking Palettes to the Photoshop Options Bar

There's a spot to the far right of the Photoshop Options bar called the **Palette Well**, where you can dock one or more palettes that you use often. This is useful for keeping often-used palettes within easy arm's reach. For example, you're likely to use the Swatches and the Layers palettes frequently. Because of this, they are great candidates to dock in the Palette Well on the Options bar. Here's a short exercise to show you how.

Note: You won't be able to see or use the Palette Well unless your screen resolution is set to greater than 800x600 resolution and you have a big enough screen (set your working area to Maximize on Windows). Here's how to change resolution so you can see the Palette Well. Choose Apple > Control Panels > Monitors, and change resolution to 1024x768 or higher. (Windows XP: Choose Control Panel > Appearance and Themes > Change the Screen Resolution, and change resolution in the Settings tab.) (Mac OS X: Choose Apple > System Preferences > Displays, and change resolution in the Display tab.)

1. Make sure the **Swatches** and the **Layers** palettes are both open. If they are not on your screen already, choose **Window > Swatches** and **Window > Layers**.

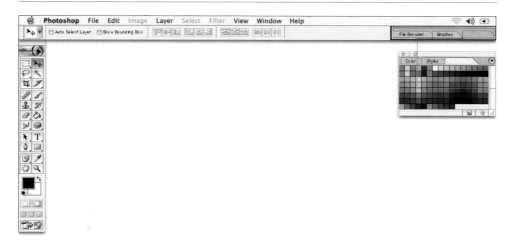

2. Drag the tab of the **Swatches** palette to the **Palette Well** in the upper-right corner of the **Options** bar.

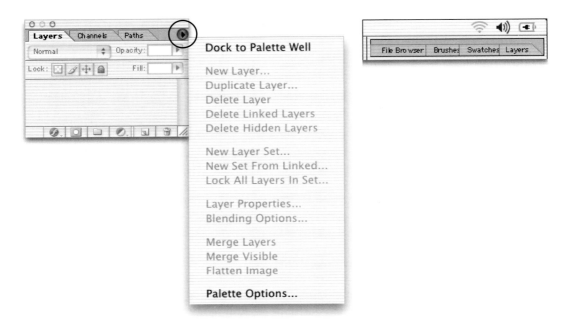

3. Click the arrow on the upper-right corner of the **Layers** palette, and choose **Dock to Palette Well** from the pop-up menu.

All Photoshop 7 palettes have a Dock To Palette Well command in their pop-up menus. **Note:** *If Dock To Palette Well is grayed out in your pop-up menu, it's because your monitor resolution isn't set high enough to display the Palette Well on the far right of your screen. Increase your monitor resolution to at least 1024x768, as explained at the beginning of this exercise.*

Now, both these palettes are docked inside the Options bar, along with the Brushes palette and File Browser palette, which are there by default. This makes these palettes easier to locate than by going to the Window menu to find them. You can click any tab in the docked Options bar location, and the corresponding palette will pop up and become active. To undock a palette from the Palette Well, just click on its tab and drag it out of the Palette Well.

IO. [PS] Saving a Custom Workspace

Another useful new feature in Photoshop 7 is the ability to save and reuse a custom configuration of your workspace. Photoshop will save all of your open palettes, including those in the Palette Well, exactly where you've left them. Use this feature to boost your efficiency when you are doing different kinds of tasks. You can save a custom workspace that best suits each task. You'll try this in Photoshop, but it works the same way in ImageReady 7.

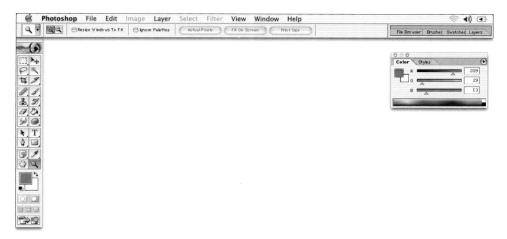

1. Click the **Close** button at the upper-left corner (Windows XP: the upper-right corner) of all the open palette groups except the one that contains the **Color** and **Styles** palettes.

If you did the last exercise, your Layers palette and Swatches palette will be docked in the Palette Well on the Options bar.

2. Choose **Window > Workspace > Save Workspace**.

3. In the **Save Workspace** window that appears, name the workspace **Painting**, and click **Save**.

4. Now change things around as much as you like. Choose **Window** > **Info** to open another palette group; click and drag the **Color** palette to another place on the screen; move the **Layers** palette out of the **Palette Well**.

5. Choose **Window** > **Workspace** > **Painting**. Your workspace will immediately return to the saved configuration. Very neat!

Notice that reusing a saved Workspace does not restore tool choices or tool options.

Keyboard Shortcuts

Next are some of the most useful keyboard shortcuts you can use when doing Web work in Photoshop 7 and ImageReady 7. Here are two big ones:

- The **Tab** key shows or hides all palettes and the Toolbox. To show or hide only the palettes, leaving the Toolbox as is, press **Shift+Tab**.

- To select a tool quickly, press its shortcut key on your keyboard. To see a tool's shortcut key, move your mouse over the tool in the Toolbox.

The two charts below give the keyboard letter shortcuts to tools that are commonly used when doing Web design in Photoshop 7 and ImageReady 7.

Photoshop Shortcut Keys	
Tool	**Shortcut Key**
Eraser	e
Eyedropper	i
Hand	h
Move	v
Switch Background/ Foreground Colors	x
Type	t
Zoom	z

ImageReady Shortcut Keys	
Tool	**Shortcut Key**
Slice	k
Slice Select	k
Hide/Show Slices	q

Resetting Tools in Photoshop and ImageReady

Photoshop's and ImageReady's tool Options bar and tool options palettes are "sticky," meaning they remember the settings that were last used. There's a different procedure in each program for resetting their values back to defaults.

In Photoshop 7, click the Tool Presets button at the left of the Options bar to open the Tool Presets palette. Click the arrow on the top right of the Tool Presets palette, and choose Reset All Tools. Click OK.

In ImageReady 7, choose Edit > Preferences > General, *and click* Reset All Tools. *(Mac OS X: Click the* Tool Presets *button at the top left of the Options bar, choose* Reset All Tools, *and click* OK.*)*

II. [PS] _____Managing Image Files with the File Browser

One of the most useful new features in Photoshop 7 is the File Browser (an environment in which you can view, sort, and arrange folders full of images. This feature is very useful for handling source images from a digital camera, which often come into your computer with meaningless names, without image previews, and turned the wrong way. The File Browser is just as great for organizing any folder of image files. In this exercise you'll explore the general features of the File Browser.

1. Click the **File Browser** tab in the **Palette Well** of the **Options** bar to open the **File Browser** window.

Note: If you can't see the Palette Well because of your monitor resolution, you can open the File Browser by choosing File > Browse *or* Window > File Browser.

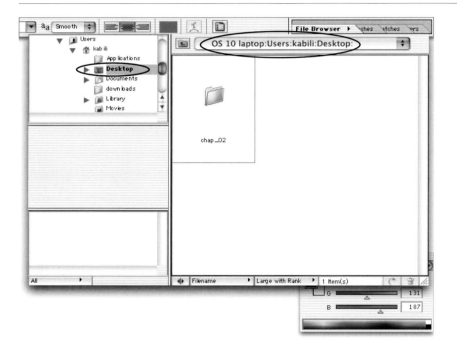

2. Use the navigation bar at the top of the **File Browser** to navigate to your desktop. The preview pane on the right side of the File Browser will display all the files and folders on your desktop, including the **chap_02** folder you transferred to your hard drive from the **H•O•T CD-ROM** in a previous exercise.

Alternatively, you can use the navigation tree in the top-left pane of the File Browser to navigate through your file system to the desktop.

3. In the preview pane of the **File Browser**, double-click on the **chap_02** folder. Then double-click on the **images** folder inside the **chap_02** folder.

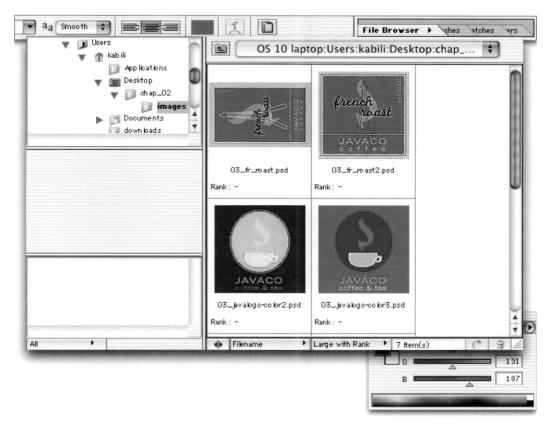

The File Browser will display thumbnails of all of the images in the images folder.

---

4. Click the **File Browser** tab and drag the **File Browser** out of the **Palette Well**.

While the File Browser is open in the Palette Well, it covers any palettes beneath it. But when the File Browser is dragged out of the Palette Well to become a separate window, palettes float on top of it, making them easier to access if you need them.

---

5. Click the diagonal lines at the bottom right of the **File Browser** window, and expand the window so you can see all of the image thumbnails.

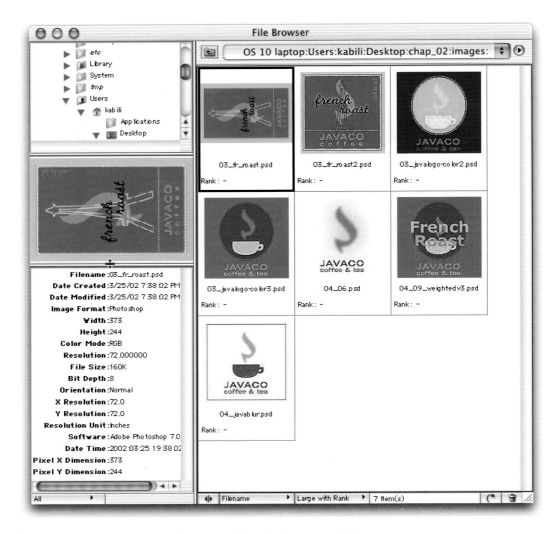

6. Click on the image thumbnail at the top left, which is rotated 90° counterclockwise.

7. Notice the detailed information about the selected image that now fills the file information section at the bottom left of the **File Browser** window. A preview of the image appears above the file information.

If you can't see all of the image information, click on the line separating the information pane from the image preview and drag up to expand the information pane.

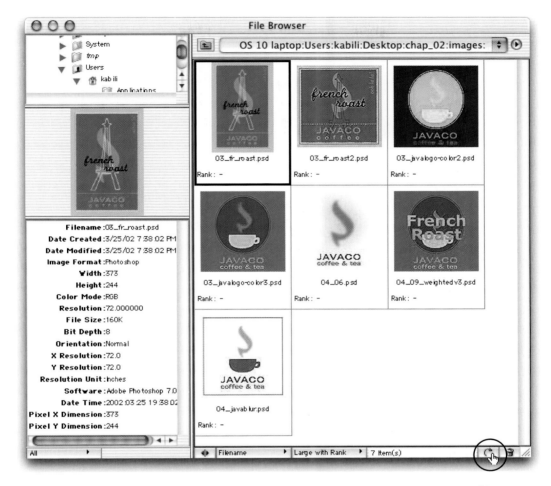

8. Click the **Rotate Image** icon at the bottom right of the **File Browser** window, and click **OK** at the prompt.

This rotates the selected thumbnail 90° clockwise. Holding the Option key while clicking the Rotate Image icon would rotate the thumbnail 90° counterclockwise. More rotation options are available by clicking the arrow on the top right of the File Browser to display a pop-up menu of commands.

9. Double-click the same thumbnail to open the full image in Photoshop. This causes the image itself, which was originally 90° counterclockwise, to rotate to a vertical format, based on your rotation of the thumbnail in the **File Browser**.

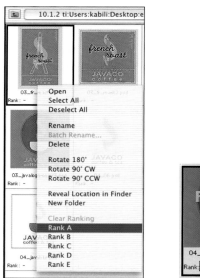

10. Ctrl+click (Mac) or right-click (Windows) on each thumbnail, and choose a ranking for that image from the pop-up menu. Click the **Rank** field under the thumbnail with the yellow words **French Roast**, and type **throw away**.

You can use the letter ranks in the menu, or type in your own rankings. You can base your rankings on any subjective criteria that's useful for your purposes. For example, you might rank images on the basis of image quality or relevance to your subject matter.

11. Click the double-pointed **Sort By** arrow at the bottom of the thumbnail display, and choose **Rank** from the pop-up menu. This causes the thumbnails to reorder themselves in the **File Browser** according to the Ranks you assigned to each thumbnail.

Sorting is done numerically if you've given thumbnails numerical ranks, and then alphabetically. Alternatively, you can sort thumbnails by any of the criteria listed in the pop-up menu.

12. Click the arrow at the top right of the **File Browser** window, and choose **New Folder** from the pop-up menu. An untitled folder icon will appear in the preview pane.

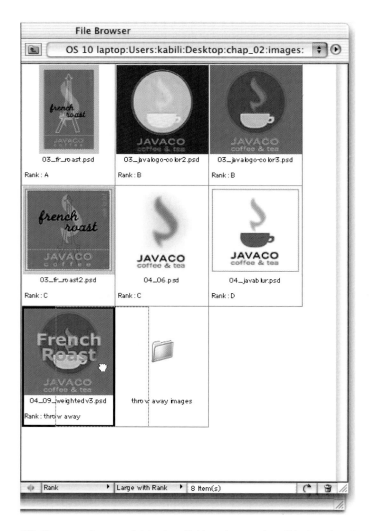

13. Rename the new folder by clicking the word **untitled** and typing **throw away images** as the new name.

14. In the **File Browser** window, click the thumbnail you ranked with the phrase **throw away**, and drag that thumbnail into the **throw away images** folder.

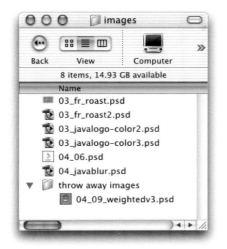

15. On your desktop, double-click the **images** folder inside the **chap_02** folder. Notice that there is now a folder there labeled **throw away images**, which contains the file that corresponds to the thumbnail you moved in the File Browser.

16. Click the arrow at the top right of the **File Browser** window, and choose **Dock to Palette Well**.

Unlike a palette, you can't drag the File Browser window into the Palette Well. Instead, you have to use this command.

17. Close any open files without saving.

Now that you understand the Photoshop 7 and ImageReady 7 interfaces, you're ready to begin making some Web graphics. In the next chapter, "Color," you'll learn about choosing and using color in your Web images.

3.
Color

| Decline of Web-Safe Color |
| Color Picker | Custom Swatches |
| Lock Transparent Pixels | Copy HTML Color |

chap_03

Photoshop 7/ImageReady
H•O•T CD-ROM

Photoshop and ImageReady offer great tools for working with color. In this chapter you'll learn our favorite tips for picking, editing, and changing colors. First you'll explore the color-picking capabilities of Photoshop's Color Picker and Swatches palette. Then you'll learn how to recolor existing artwork with colors you choose.

You'll find less emphasis on Web-safe color in this chapter than you may have come to expect in our **lynda.com** series of books. That's because today there's less reason to limit yourself to designing with a browser-safe palette, as 8-bit (256 color) computer display systems become obsolete. You'll read about the demise of Web-safe color in this chapter, but you'll also learn how to access Web-safe colors when you need them. Along the way, you'll learn how to limit the Color Picker to Web-safe colors, load a special **lynda.com** swatch of Web-safe colors, create your own custom color swatch, and copy color values to HTML.

The Decline of Web-Safe Color

If you've been around the Web for a while, you might have heard the term Web-safe color. Perhaps you've heard other terms, too, such as browser-safe palette, Web palette, 216 palette, Netscape palette, or 6 x 6 x 6 color cube. These all refer to the same 216 colors. What's special about these colors is that they are the only colors that a Web browser on an 8-bit computer system can display without causing color shifts or dithering. (8-bit color actually refers to 256 colors, but 40 of those colors are reserved for non-Web purposes.)

The only reason to limit your color choices to the browser-safe palette is if you think your Web site will be viewed on an 8-bit system. Just a few short years ago, almost all computers had 8-bit video cards. In the beginning, when Web design first emerged as a design medium, it was important for designers to understand Web-safe color and know how to create Web graphics in that limited palette. That was no picnic, because the browser-safe palette is not very visually exciting. (It contains mostly highly saturated colors of medium value, and not many light or dark colors, nor many muted or tinted tones.)

The good news is, in most cases it is now safe to design for the Web without the browser-safe palette. Today only a minority of computer users have machines with 8-bit video cards—most computer users can see any color that you design with. If you're unsure when to use the Web-safe palette, the answer depends on your audience, clients, and maybe even the employer for whom you're designing.

If you are designing sites for alternative online publishing devices, like cell phones, PDAs, or Internet applicances, you may still need to use a browser-safe palette. Most of those devices currently display only 8-bit color, and some are still 1-bit (black and white) systems. The advent of these alternative devices does not guarantee continued life for the browser-safe color palette, but it might extend it a bit longer!

Some companies that hire designers and developers still feel it's a badge of Web design honor to work with browser-safe colors, so you might want to know how to use them if you have to. As you'll learn in this chapter, the Web palette is built into Photoshop's and ImageReady's color picking tools, so it's easy to create or recolor a Web graphic in browser-safe colors.

Keep in mind that there's no harm in using the browser-safe palette. It simply limits your choices to 216 colors. If you don't have a lot of experience or confidence picking colors that work well together, you might find it easier to work with a limited number of color choices. There's no right or wrong about using browser-safe colors, as long as you're able to combine them in pleasing and effective ways.

The upshot is that the need to stick to a browser-safe palette is on the decline. We realize that it may be difficult to let go of the notion that you should design with Web-safe colors, particularly if you've put effort into developing that skill. Try to look at it like we do—as a sign of the great progress that's been made so quickly in the development and marketing of personal computers, and as a liberating step forward for online design!

What Happens on an 8-bit System If You Don't Use Web-Safe Color?

It's still useful to know what your site will look like if you don't design with Web-safe colors and the site is ever viewed on an 8-bit system. Two problems will occur.

The first problem is that colors you set in the HTML code, like the colors of page backgrounds, text, and links, will shift in the 8-bit viewer's browser. The danger of such unpredictable color shifts is that they can cause text or links to become unreadable against a similar colored background.

Graphic viewed in 24-bit

Same graphic viewed in 8-bit

Close-up 24-bit

Close-up 8-bit

The second problem has to do with color in images. If you make flat art (like illustrations or cartoons) with non-Web-safe colors, those colors will appear dithered (made up of tiny dots) when the image is viewed on an 8-bit system. The unwanted dithering is the result of the viewer's 8-bit display system trying to simulate colors that it can't display. Above are some examples of what that looks like. The examples here illustrate why you'll want to use Web-safe colors in your flat art Web graphics in the rare event that you are designing for an 8-bit audience. However, the opposite is true for photographic content. If you're preparing photographs for the Web, never force them to Web-safe colors. When an 8-bit browser displays photographic images, it converts them to 8-bit on the fly and does a better job than if you'd converted them yourself.

In the next few exercises you'll learn how to select Web colors when you want them, and how to use the color picking tools Photoshop and ImageReady offer. In Exercise 5, you'll pull it all together as you learn a quick and easy way to recolor layered artwork.

I. [PS]   Setting the Color Picker to Only Web Colors

In the early versions of Photoshop, it was difficult to choose a Web-safe color from the **Color Picker** without manually typing in Web-safe RGB values. This hassle has been removed since Photoshop 5.5, because the **Color Picker** can now be set to display **Only Web Colors**. ImageReady has a Color Picker that's almost identical to the Photoshop Color Picker you'll learn about in this exercise. The only differences are that ImageReady's Color Picker lacks some print-oriented features—feedback about L.a.b. and CMYK color, and an out-of-print-gamut warning. This is because Photoshop has a dual purpose—it can be used for print or the Web; but ImageReady was developed specifically for making Web graphics.

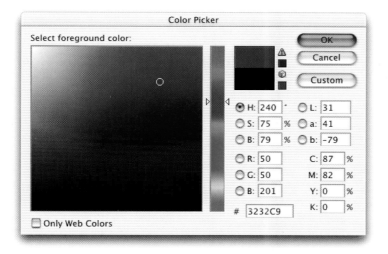

1. Click on the **foreground** color swatch in the Photoshop Toolbox. This will open the **Color Picker**.

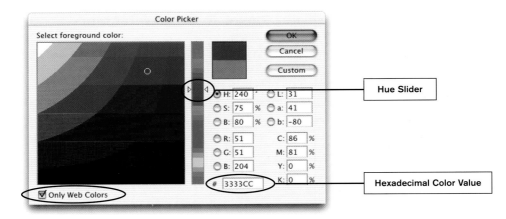

Hue Slider

Hexadecimal Color Value

2. Check **Only Web Colors** in the lower-left corner of this dialog box.

Notice the hexadecimal readout at the bottom of the Color Picker? If you move the arrows up the vertical hue slider you'll see these readout numbers and the colors on the screen change.

H, S, and B stand for Hue, Saturation, and Brightness. The above Color Picker is set to view by hue. All the different radio buttons offer different ways of seeing and picking colors. You may find that these different choices help you find colors that go together more quickly. It's very interesting to see how Web colors spread across the spectrum if you actively move the slider when exploring these different settings of H, S, B, R, G, B, or L, a, b.

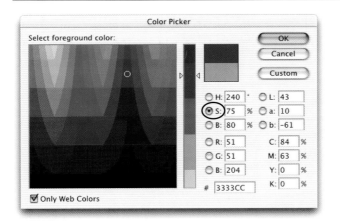

3. Click **S** to view the **Color Picker** by saturation. **Saturation** is the measure of color intensity. Try moving the vertical slider or clicking on a different color in the rainbow area to view Web-safe colors by this criterion. Move the slider arrows up to view more highly saturated Web colors, and down to view the desaturated ones.

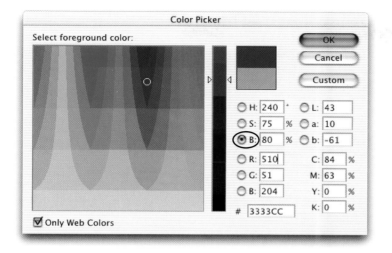

4. Click **B** to view the **Color Picker** by brightness. **Brightness** is the measure of light to dark values. Try moving the brightness slider or clicking on a different color in the rainbow area to view Web-safe colors by this criterion. Move the slider arrows up to view brighter Web color values, and down to view darker ones.

Try clicking on the R, G, and B buttons as well. These stand for Red, Green, and Blue. Click on the L, a, and b buttons next. These stand for Lightness, a Axis (green to magenta), and b Axis (blue to yellow). Aside from the psychedelic color experience, these methods offer some other interesting color formations from which to view or pick Web colors.

5. Click **Cancel** to get out of color-picking mode, and move on to the next exercise to learn more about Web-color-picking options.

2. [PS] _____Snapping to Web Colors

The thing about Photoshop is that there are often numerous ways to achieve the same goal. Instead of viewing Only Web Colors, you can use the standard **Color Picker** and then snap a non-Web-safe color to a safe one. This feature is also available in ImageReady.

1. Click on the foreground color swatch in the Photoshop Toolbox again to access the **Color Picker**.

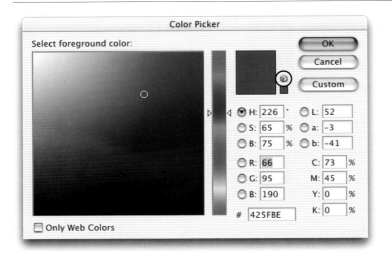

2. Uncheck the **Only Web Colors** box and click on the **H** button to display the **Hues** view. Move and click your cursor around inside the color area on the left. Notice the cube icon that appears to the right of the color preview. The cube alerts you when you've selected a color that's not safe for the Web. If you click on the cube, the color selection will jump to the closest Web-safe color and then the cube will disappear.

3. Click **OK**, and the Web-safe color will appear in the foreground color swatch of your Toolbox.

Note: This feature works identically in ImageReady. If you decide to try it out in ImageReady now, be sure to return to Photoshop for the next exercise.

3. [PS] ——————Creating a Custom Swatch

Another way to set foreground colors is with the Swatches palette. Photoshop 7 ships with some prebuilt swatches (which you'll learn how to load in the next exercise), but there are going to be times when you have a custom color scheme, and you'd rather limit the Swatches palette to contain only those colors. In this exercise, you'll learn to make custom swatches for the Swatches palette two ways—by selecting colors from an existing swatch, and by sampling colors from an image. You'll work in Photoshop's Preset Manager, because there you can delete multiple colors at once. You can also make a custom swatch in ImageReady, but it's more tedious because you have to add and delete colors one by one in the Swatches palette.

1. Choose **Edit > Preset Manager**.

Photoshop's Preset Manager is a command center from which you can control libraries of preset color swatches as well as brushes, gradients, styles, patterns, and other items.

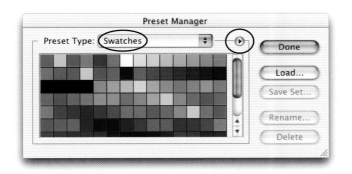

2. In the **Preset Manager** window, choose **Preset Type: Swatches**.

3. Click the arrow on the top right of the Preset Manager and choose **Web Hues** from the menu. At the prompt, choose **OK**.

This will replace the currently loaded swatch in the Preset Manager (and in the Swatches palette) with a swatch that contains all the Web-safe colors. The Web Hues swatch is one of a number of prebuilt swatches that ship with Photoshop.

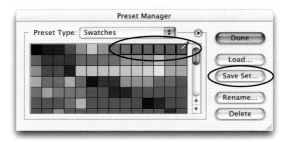

4. Shift+click on some red and orange colors in the palette displayed in the Preset Manager.

Holding the Shift key while you click allows you to select multiple colors.

5. Click the **Save Set** button in the Preset Manager.

6. In the **Save** window, type a name for your new swatch—**warmweb.aco**—in the **Save As** field.

Be sure to add the .aco extension, which identifies the file as a color swatch.

7. Navigate to your **Photoshop applications folder > Presets > Color Swatches**, and click **Save**.

8. Back in the **Preset Manager**, click **Done**.

9. Close and then relaunch Photoshop.

You have to close and reopen Photoshop (or just wait until the next time you open the program) in order to see your new swatch listed in the Swatches palette pop-up menu.

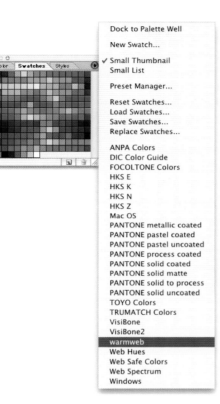

10. Click the arrow in the upper-right corner of the **Swatches** palette. You'll see that your custom swatch has been added to the list of swatch presets! Choose **warmweb** from the pop-up menu, and click **OK** when prompted.

Your new warmweb custom swatch will replace the current Swatches palette.

Next, you'll make a reusable custom swatch from the colors in an existing image. This is a good way to build a collection of pleasing palettes for use on your own images.

11. Copy the **chap_03** folder from the **exercise_files** folder on the **H·O·T CD-ROM** to your desktop, if you haven't already done so.

12. Open the **french.psd** file from the **chap_03** folder you copied to your desktop.

At this point you could delete the existing colors from the Swatches palette one by one, by dragging each to the Trash icon on the Swatches palette. But it's quicker to delete all of the colors at once, as you'll do in the next two steps.

13. Click the arrow in the upper-right corner of the **Swatches** palette, and choose **Preset Manager** from the pop-up menu.

The Preset Manager opens with your warmweb swatch showing.

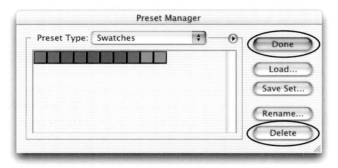

14. Click **Cmd+A** (Mac) or **Ctrl+A** (Windows) to select all the colors in the **warmweb** swatch in the Preset Manager. Click the **Delete** button in the Preset Manager to delete all of those colors. Then click the **Done** button to close the Preset Manager.

The loaded swatch now displays no colors, leaving you free to create a custom swatch from scratch.

15. Select the **Eyedropper** tool in the Toolbox.

16. Click on a color in the open image, and then click the **New Color** icon at the bottom of the **Swatches** palette.

This will add the color you selected in the image to your custom swatch. Repeat this step until you have all the colors you want in your swatch.

17. Click the arrow at the top right of the **Swatches** palette, and choose **Save Swatches**. Navigate to the **Photoshop application folder > Presets > Color Swatches**, name your new swatch **frenchblue.aco**, and click **Save**.

The next time you launch Photoshop, your custom frenchblue swatch will appear in the pop-up list of preset swatches. You can load that custom swatch and use it to build a new image or recolor an existing image.

18. Close the image without saving.

4. [PS] _____Loading the lynda.com Swatch

Lynda Weinman and Bruce Heavin wrote a book together in 1997 called *Coloring Web Graphics*, which is now out of print. Bruce developed a series of Web color swatches for that book, which he organized aesthetically for picking Web colors. One of those swatches is included inside the **chap_03** folder of the **H•O•T CD-ROM** for you to try. This exercise takes place in Photoshop, but it works just the same way in ImageReady.

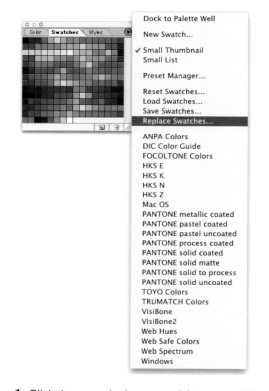

1. Click the arrow in the upper-right corner of the **Swatches** palette and choose **Replace Swatches**. Navigate to the **chap_03** folder that you transferred to your hard drive from the **H•O•T CD-ROM** and choose **color.aco**. Click **Load** (or **Open** in ImageReady).

Note: *If you choose to Replace Swatches, the former swatch will disappear. Or, you can choose to Load Swatches if you want to append one swatch set to another.*

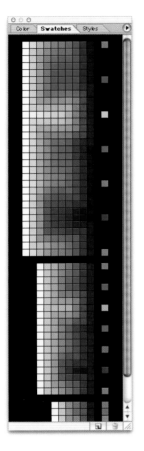

2. Drag the **Swatches** palette window down as long as it will go, and then use the scroll bar to view the entire swatch document. This swatch is organized by hue (up and down), by value (right to left), and saturation (up and down).

Note: Many of the colors are repeated for the sole reason of presenting an array that is organized efficiently for color picking. It's nice to see all the hues together. If you want to pick a red, for example, you can view the choices easily. It's also helpful to easily see all the dark colors and/or colors of equal saturation together. Once you use this swatch set, you will likely never remove it from the Swatches palette because it is so useful.

3. You can leave the Swatches palette set up this way. Next time you open Photoshop, it will still be set.

5. [PS] _____Recoloring Layered Documents

Now that you've learned how to view and pick colors in a variety of different ways within Photoshop, how do you make images that use these colors? You could use a brush and paint with any of these colors at any time. You could also use fill tools to color artwork. This next exercise focuses on how to recolor an existing Photoshop document. The exercise gives you a chance to work with the **Lock Transparent Pixels** feature, which allows you to easily recolor layered documents with any color you want. This exercise takes place in Photoshop but will work in a similar fashion in ImageReady.

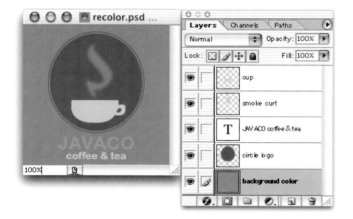

1. Open **recolor.psd** from the **chap_03** folder on your hard drive.

Look at the Layers palette (Window > Layers), and you'll notice that this document is composed of multiple layers. It's helpful to set up your files with separate layers like this and give the layers meaningful names, so you can color each layer separately and keep track of it.

2. Select the layer at the bottom of the **Layers** palette called **background color**.

Right now, this document is colored using blues and greens. To change this color scheme to reds and yellows (or any other color choices you'd prefer), you'll be working on a layer at a time, starting with the background color layer.

3. Make sure the **Swatches** palette is visible (**Window > Swatches**) (Mac OS X: **Window > Swatches**). The **color.aco** swatch is still loaded from Exercise 4 in this chapter. Use the **Eyedropper** tool to pick a dark red from the **Swatches** palette.

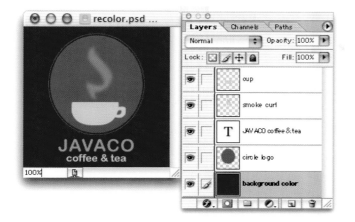

4. To fill the **background color** layer with this dark red, press **Option+Delete** (Mac), or **Alt+Backspace** or **Alt+Delete** (Windows).

This is one of our favorite shortcuts for filling a layer with a color, because it is faster than using the menu command Edit > Fill *or the Paint Bucket tool.*

5. Next, select the layer called **circle logo** that contains the circle. Pick a gold color from the **Swatches** palette, and use the fill shortcut again by pressing **Option+Delete** (Mac), or **Alt+Backspace** or **Alt+Delete** (Windows).

Notice that the entire layer filled with this color. In order to recolor the circle, and not the entire contents of the layer, there's a valuable trick you'll learn in the following step.

6. Undo the fill you just created by using the shortcut key **Cmd+Z** (Mac) or **Ctrl+Z** (Windows).

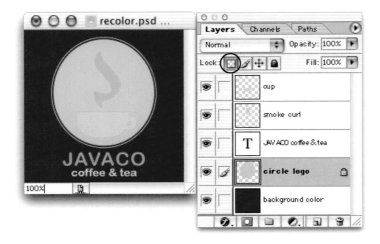

7. Click the **Lock Transparent Pixels** button on the **Layers** palette, and press **Option+Delete** (Mac), or **Alt+Backspace** or **Alt+Delete** (Windows). This time, only the contents of the selected layer fill with yellow.

Tip: The shortcut key to toggle Lock Transparent Pixels on or off is the / (forward slash) key.

Lock Transparent Pixels means that Photoshop will protect the transparent areas of this layer. When you fill the layer with a new color, Photoshop fills only the area of the layer that contains an image, and preserves the transparent areas. We can't tell you how many students we watch try to use the magic wand or other selection tools to select shapes on layers in order to fill them. The technique we give you here works much better because it's easier, it fills only areas of the layer that contain information, and it doesn't leave rough edges on color fills.

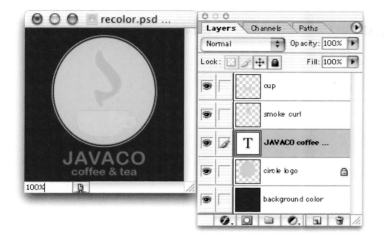

8. Next, select the editable type layer (signified by the letter **T** on the layer). Choose an orange color from the **Swatches** palette, and press **Option+Delete** (Mac) or **Alt+Backspace** or **Alt+Delete** (Windows).

Note that the Lock Transparent Pixels check box is active, even though it's dimmed out. This is a default behavior for an editable type layer.

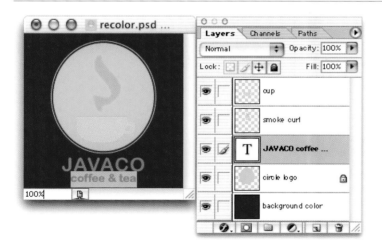

9. Click the **Type** tool from the Toolbox. Select the words **coffee & tea** in the type layer by clicking and dragging over them. Select a bright red color from the **Swatches** palette. Once you deselect the type by clicking on a different layer, you'll see that only the words **coffee & tea** on the type layer changed color.

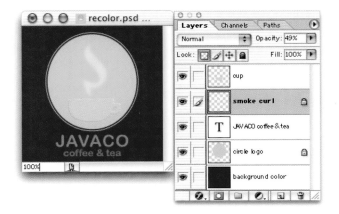

10. Select the layer called **smoke curl**. Choose white from the **Swatches** palette. Click the **Lock Transparent Pixels** check box and use the shortcut keys **Option+Delete** (Mac) or **Alt+Backspace** or **Alt+Delete** (Windows) to fill with the new color.

What's really cool about this step is that the artwork in this layer is slightly blurry. There's no other way to make a clean selection of blurry artwork than activating Lock Transparent Pixels.

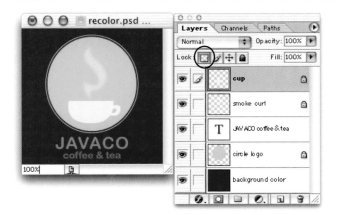

11. Select the layer called **cup**. Click the **Lock Transparent Pixels** check box and use the shortcut keys **Option+Delete** (Mac) or **Alt+Backspace** or **Alt+Delete** (Windows) to fill with white.

12. Close the file without saving.

The skills covered in this exercise will help you recolor artwork that is on layers at any point in your Web design or Photoshop design life. You'll probably use this technique more than most others in the book. Many students have told us it was worth the price of admission to a class for the time it saved.

NOTE | Lock Check Boxes in Photoshop 7

You might have noticed a few other check boxes in the **Layers** palette. There are four: **Lock Transparent Pixels**, **Lock Image Pixels**, **Lock Position**, and **Lock All**. Here's a handy chart to explain what these terms mean, and when to use locking features.

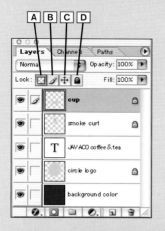

Lock Check Boxes in Photoshop 7 and ImageReady

A. Lock Transparent Pixels	Protects the transparent pixels on a layer. Use this feature on layers that have transparency when you want to edit only the colored pixels and mask the transparent ones.
B. Lock Image Pixels	Prevents you from editing any pixels in a given layer. This is good to check when you don't want anyone changing the content of a layer.
C. Lock Position	Prevents you from moving a layer.
D. Lock All	Does all of the above, preventing you from moving or editing a layer. It's good to use when you want to lock the content and position of a layer.

6. [PS] _____ Copy Color as HTML

Suppose you are making an image in ImageReady or Photoshop, and want to use a color from that image inside your HTML code so you can color a background, link, or some other element in HTML to match the image. In this scenario, you will find the **Copy Color as HTML** feature useful.

When you specify color in HTML code, as you must for elements like background color, text, and links, you have to use values from a numbering system that's different than the decimal numbering system you are used to. That numbering system is called the **hexadecimal system**. In a nutshell, the hexadecimal numbering system is based on 16 digits, and uses letters as well as numbers to identify colors. You don't have to worry about knowing any more than that about hexadecimal numbers when you're working with Photoshop and ImageReady, because they take care of the math for you. The **Copy Color as HTML** feature converts any **RGB** (red, green, blue) color value (for example, the shade of blue called **153 153 204** in RGB parlance) to a string of hexadecimal digits (**#9999CC** in this example). The command also puts that hexadecimal color value into your computer's clipboard so you can paste it as text into other applications. This is a handy feature if you are writing HTML from scratch and want to quickly and easily get a color value from Photoshop into your code in an HTML or text editor.

1. In Photoshop, open **french.psd** from the **chap_03** folder that you transferred to your hard drive.

2. To copy the hexadecimal color of an image so you can paste it into an HTML editor, select the **Eyedropper** tool from the Toolbox (the shortcut is the letter **I** on your keyboard). **Ctrl+click** (Mac) or **right-click** (Windows) on a color in a document, and choose **Copy Color as HTML** from the contextual menu.

If you're working in ImageReady, first click on a color in the document with the Eyedropper *tool; then* Ctrl+click *(Mac) or* right-click *(Windows) anywhere in the document, and choose* Copy Foreground Color as HTML. ***Note:*** *The Eyedropper tool must be selected for this to work in either program.*

3. When you go to paste this color into a text editor or HTML program, it will look like this:

`COLOR="#9999CC"`

4. Close the file. You won't need it again.

Now you know how to use the flexible color picking features in Photoshop 7 and ImageReady and how to apply your color choices quickly and efficiently to a layered image. These programs make choosing and using color fun and creative by offering the best color picking tools around.

4.
Optimization

GIF and JPEG	Bit Depth	Palette Descriptions
Optimizing in Photoshop	Optimizing in ImageReady
Matte Color on JPEG	Previewing and Writing HTML

chap_04

Photoshop 7/ImageReady
H•O•T CD-ROM

Anyone who has ever used the Web has surely been frustrated by slow-loading Web pages. There's never been a design medium before in which the file size of your artwork translates into the speed at which someone can view it. Making small Web graphics is both an art and a science. Fortunately, Photoshop and ImageReady are the ideal tools with which to master this craft.

Prepare for a long chapter, because optimization is a fairly complex subject that both Photoshop and ImageReady handle with great detail. If terms like dither, adaptive palettes, bit depth, JPEG, and GIF are unfamiliar to you, they won't be for long. Even if you're a pro at optimizing Web graphics, you will be impressed by Photoshop's and ImageReady's superb optimization capabilities.

What Affects Speed on the Web?

Unfortunately, just making your file sizes small in Photoshop or ImageReady does not guarantee fast Web site performance. There are more factors involved than just the file size of your images. Here are some of the other factors that slow down Web sites:

• Slow Web-server connection speed.

• Clogged arteries in the Information Highway (otherwise known as router problems "somewhere" in the system).

• Large service providers, such as AOL, Earthlink, or GeoCities, sometimes have so much traffic that your site's performance might slow down during heavy usage hours.

• Sometimes small local providers can't offer fast connections either, because they don't have the resources to handle their heaviest traffic periods.

Solutions? Make sure that you run your Web site off of a fast connection or that you hire a hosting company that guarantees a fast connection. If you have a serious business site, get a dedicated hosting service instead of a large consumer-based Web service. If the Web is slow because of router problems, it affects everyone. Such is life. The best thing you can do is to control the things that you can (like file size) and accept that you can't control everything. The only predictable thing about the Web is that it won't always perform in a predictable manner. You can make your mark on speed by making images that are small in file size, which is what this chapter is going to get to as soon as some of the background information is out of the way.

GIF or JPEG?

GIF stands for **G**raphic **I**nterchange **F**ormat and **JPEG** stands for Joint **P**hoto**g**raphic **E**xperts **G**roup. The words "graphic" and "photographic" are intentionally bolded here to point out what each file format handles best. It isn't that GIF is better than JPEG or JPEG better than GIF, but that each of these compression schemes is best suited for certain types of images.

• GIFs are best for flat or simple graphic images that contain a lot of solid areas of color, including logos, illustrations, cartoons, line art, etc.

• JPEGs are best for continuous-tone images, including photographs, glows, gradients, drop shadows, etc.

Some images don't fall into either category because they are hybrids of line art and continuous-tone artwork. In those cases, you have to experiment with GIF and JPEG to see which gives you the smallest file size and the image quality you want.

GIF Transparency and Animation

Whether a graphic contains line art or continuous tone is not the sole deciding factor for whether to choose GIF or JPEG. The GIF format can do a couple of things that the JPEG format cannot: transparency and animation. This book has a chapter devoted to each, but we've provided a brief explanation of these terms in this chapter, too, because these capabilities may factor into your optimization strategy.

GIF Definitions	
GIF transparency	All digital image files are rectangular. To prove it to yourself, take a look at any image in the Photoshop document window. The space defined by the window is always a rectangle or square. What if you have a button design that's circular instead of square or rectangular and is intended to be viewed on a patterned background? You would need to use transparent pixels to mask out parts of the image, leaving a shape that would appear circular in a Web browser. The GIF file format supports 1-bit masking, meaning that the image can be turned off in specified areas, making it possible to create artwork that appears to be irregularly shaped. Because the file format supports only 1-bit transparency, there are no degrees of opacity except on or off (visibility or no visibility for each pixel). For more information, check out Chapter 9, "*Transparent GIFs.*"
GIF animation	A single GIF document can contain multiple images and display them in a slide-show fashion. GIF files that contain multiple images are called animated GIFs. For more information on how the GIF file format supports animation, check out Chapter 13, "*Animated GIFs.*"

Lossy or Lossless?

There are two categories of file compression—**lossy** and **lossless**. Lossy means that the compression scheme reduces file size by discarding information, and lossless means that compression reduces file size without throwing away information. JPEG is a lossy compression method. Traditionally, GIF was a lossless method, but in Photoshop and ImageReady you have the option to add lossiness to GIF compression as a tool for reducing file size.

WARNING | Don't Recompress a Compressed Image

Recompressing a JPEG or a lossy GIF can erode the quality of the image. That's because you throw away image information each time you apply lossy compression to a lossy file format. The result can be visible, unwanted compression artifacts that cause the image to look distressed. If you need to make a change to an image that's already been compressed as a JPEG or lossy GIF, find the original, uncompressed version of the image, make your changes there, and compress that file as a fresh JPEG or lossy GIF to keep your image quality is good as it can be. This is one reason we recommend that you always save the original PSD (Photoshop Document format) files of images you create for the Web in Photoshop or ImageReady.

How Can You Make Small JPEGs?

The JPEG file format best compresses images that are continuous tone. Here is a handy chart that shows what can be done to compress an image most effectively in this format. You'll practice these techniques in Exercises 1, 10, and 11 in this chapter.

JPEG Compression	
What to Do	**Why Do It**
Start with an image that has tonal qualities, such as a photograph, continuous tone graphic, or image that incorporates effects like glows, drop shadows, etc.	The JPEG file format looks for the type of data it's best at compressing: areas of low contrast, subtle variation, and slight tonal shifts. It can't compress areas of solid color well at all, and it doesn't work well for graphic-style artwork.
Add blur	Unlike GIF, the JPEG format compresses blurry images well. Adding a little blur to a JPEG can decrease its file size.
Add more JPEG compression	The more JPEG compression you add, the smaller the file size becomes. Too much JPEG compression can cause unwanted compression artifacts to appear. It's your job to find the balance between making the file small and making it look good.
Decrease the saturation	The JPEG format has an easier time compressing images with low color saturation than images with highly saturated colors. Decreasing saturation usually results in a JPEG with smaller file size.
Decrease the contrast	The JPEG format also favors low contrast images. Decreasing the contrast in an image usually results in a smaller-sized JPEG.
Use an alpha channel	Compressing different areas of a single image with two different levels of JPEG compression sometimes lowers the overall file size of the image. The two areas are delineated by a mask that's stored in an alpha channel. You'll learn to do this later in the chapter.

How Can You Make Small GIFs?

The principles for making a small GIF are almost opposite to those you'd use to make a small JPEG. The GIF file format works best on areas of solid color—and that's why it's best for line art, logos, illustrations, and cartoons.

GIF Compression	
What to Do	**Why do It**
Start with an image that has large areas of solid color	The GIF file format looks for patterns in artwork, such as large runs of a single color in a horizontal, vertical, or diagonal direction. **Note:** Areas of color change in an image cause file size increases in GIF format.
Reduce the number of colors	Reducing the number of colors in a GIF image also reduces the file size. At some point during the color reduction process the image won't look right, and that's when you'll have to back up and add some colors. The objective is to find that exact threshold where the image looks good but contains the fewest number of colors.
Reduce the amount of dithering	**Dithering** is a process in which the computer adds different-colored pixels in close proximity to each other to simulate secondary colors or smooth gradations of color. A dithered image often looks noisy or has scattered pixels. Some images have to contain dithering to look good, but it's best to use the least amount of dithering necessary in order to see better file-size savings.
Add lossy compression	Adding a little lossy compression to a GIF file will often reduce its file size.
Add an alpha channel	You've been able to use an alpha channel mask to weight the choice of colors and the amount of dither applied to different areas of a GIF during compression since the last version of Photoshop. A new twist In Photoshop 7 allows you to apply these techniques to a type or vector layer. You'll see how this works when you try out weighted GIF optimization later in this chapter.

> **NOTE | Recompressing Non-Lossy GIFs**
>
> Compression artifacts are not an issue with non-lossy GIFs, as they are with JPEGs and GIFs to which lossy compression has been added. You can recompress a non-lossy GIF with no ill compression effects, though it's sometimes preferable to begin with a clean original PSD, PICT, or BMP format than to recompress an already compressed GIF. If, for example, you recompressed a GIF that had been set to six colors, you wouldn't be able to introduce any more colors even if you wanted to. You would have more latitude with your choices if instead you compressed a GIF from an original image source.

What Is Bit Depth?

Bit depth has to do with the number of colors in a graphic file. GIF is an 8-bit file format and JPEG is a 24-bit file format. We're not suggesting that you memorize these numbers, but if you ever need to refer to a chart that lists bit depth, here you go.

Bit-Depth Chart	
32-bit	16.7 million colors plus an 8-bit masking channel
24-bit	16.7 million colors
16-bit	65.6 thousand colors
8-bit	256 colors
7-bit	128 colors
6-bit	64 colors
5-bit	32 colors
4-bit	16 colors
3-bit	8 colors
2-bit	4 colors
1-bit	2 colors

JPEG and GIF Photoshop Options

In the upcoming exercises, you'll use Photoshop 7's **Save For Web** window to prepare images for compression as GIFs and JPEGs. When you open the Save For Web window, you'll see lots of options in the GIF and JPEG settings area. Here's a quick reference guide to those settings. You'll try out the majority of these features in the exercises that follow. You'll also find similar settings in the ImageReady 7 Optimize palette, as you'll learn shortly.

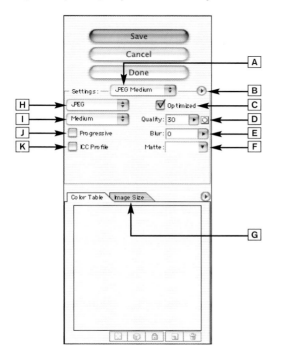

JPEG Context-Sensitive Properties		
A	**Settings menu**	Settings contain preset compression values. You can choose from the ones that ship with Photoshop, or you can make your own by choosing **Save Settings** in the **Optimize** menu (B).
B	**Optimize menu**	To see this menu, hold your mouse down on the arrow. This is where you are able to save and load settings for the **Settings** menu (A).
C	**Optimized**	Highly recommended for making the smallest possible JPEG files.

continues on next page

	JPEG Context-Sensitive Properties *continued*	
D	**Quality**	Enter the quality value in this field. You can type it in manually— or, if you hold your mouse down on the arrow, a slider will appear, which you can then drag to the desired value. Click the small circle to access a window in which you can use channels to modify quality in different parts of the image.
E	**Blur**	Blurry images compress better as JPEGs than sharp images. This value field allows you to blur the image by typing a value or by holding your mouse down on the arrow to access a slider. We prefer using the slider because it's easier to make small incremental changes to the blur, which is usually what you'll want to prevent the image from appearing too blurry.
F	**Matte**	If you begin with an image that is against a transparent background, choosing a matte color sets the color that will replace the transparency when an image is saved as a JPEG. Later in this chapter you'll learn how to set the matte color for a JPEG.
G	**Image Size**	You can change the physical dimensions of your image if you click on this tab and change the pixel or percent values.
H	**File Format**	This controls whether you're going to apply JPEG, GIF, or PNG compression to an image.
I	**Quality Presets**	Preset quality values for the JPEG format. You can also enter values into the **Quality** setting (D).
J	**Progressive**	Progressive JPEGs, like interlaced GIFs, appear chunky and come into focus as they download.
K	**ICC Profile**	ICC (**I**nternational **C**olor **C**onsortium) profiles work with some printing devices, but not with Web browsers. They add file size to a compressed image. We don't recommend them for Web images at present. However, there might come a day when browsers recognize this setting.

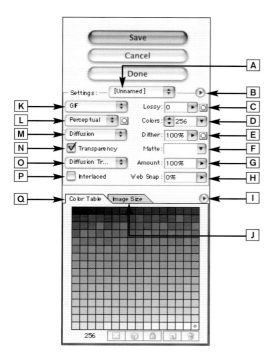

	GIF Context-Sensitive Properties	
A	**Settings menu**	Settings contain preset compression values. You can use the ones that ship with Photoshop, or you can make your own by choosing **Save Settings** in the **Optimize** menu (B).
B	**Optimize menu**	To see this menu, hold your mouse down on the arrow. This is where you can save and load settings for the **Settings** menu (A).
C	**Lossy**	Changing the value in this field will add lossy compression to your GIF images. We often find that small values of lossy decrease the file size of a GIF. This works best on continuous-tone GIF files (such as photographs). The channel symbol to the right of this field allows you to use alpha channels to vary lossy in different parts of the image.
D	**Colors**	Reducing the number of colors in a GIF image always results in file size savings. The trick is to find the threshold where it has the fewest colors but still looks good.

continues on next page

		GIF Context-Sensitive Properties *continued*
E	**Dither**	This setting controls the amount of dither. Adding dither to a GIF always increases file size, but is sometimes necessary for the color of the image to look best. The channel symbol to the right of this field allows you to use alpha channels to vary the amount of dither in different parts of the image.
F	**Matte**	Changing the matte color of an image with transparent areas can help blend the image into a Web page background. You'll get a chance to do this in Chapter 9, "*Transparent GIFs.*"
G	**Transparency Dither Amount**	This setting controls the amount of dither added to the partially transparent pixels at the edges of a transparent GIF. Transparency dither sometimes helps blend an image with a patterned Web page background.
H	**Web Snap**	If an image contains non-Web-safe colors, you can set a threshold so that colors within the threshold will "snap" to become Web safe. It's usually preferable to change colors to Web safe one at a time, rather than with this slider, so that you retain control over which colors shift.
I	**Color Palette menu**	This menu allows you to sort the colors in your palette, to load and save color palettes, and to create new colors in your palette.
J	**Image Size**	You can change the physical dimensions of your image if you click on this tab and enter changes to the values.
K	**File Format**	This menu controls whether you're going to apply JPEG, GIF, or PNG compression to an image.
L	**Color Reduction Palette**	The Adobe engineers give you a lot of options as to which type of algorithm (palette) to use for best compressing your GIF images. You'll try them out in several upcoming exercises. The channel symbol to the right of this field allows you to use alpha channels to influence the palette applied to different parts of the image.
M	**Dither Algorithm**	Bet you didn't know that your dithering could have algorithms! This is just a fancy way of saying that there are a few types of dithering options. You'll get to try these out in this chapter, too.

continues on next page

	GIF Context-Sensitive Properties *continued*	
N	**Transparency**	Check this box when you want to make transparent GIF images. You might find that it won't work, and that is most likely because your image doesn't contain any transparent areas. You'll learn all about how to make perfect transparent GIFs in Chapter 9, "*Transparent GIFs.*"
O	**Transparency Dither Algorithm**	Use this setting to choose whether and what type of dithering to apply to the partially transparent edges of a transparent GIF to help blend it with a Web page background. You'll try out this technique in Chapter 9, "*Transparent GIFs.*"
P	**Interlaced**	Check this box if you want your GIFs to be interlaced, which means they will look chunky until they finish downloading. Interlaced GIFs work on all browsers, so you don't have to worry about backwards compatibility. We suggest you don't use interlacing on text because it can be frustrating to wait for an image to appear in focus when you have to read it. If you're ever going to use interlacing, it might be on graphics that contain no text; but the truth is we don't ever use interlacing because we don't like the way it looks. To each his or her own preference.
Q	**Color Table**	This area displays the colors that are being assigned to the GIF image. You'll explore this feature in this chapter.

I. [PS] _____ Saving For Web Using JPEG

This first exercise will walk you through saving a JPEG. It will introduce you to Photoshop's **Save For Web** feature. The Save For Web feature gives you control over so many options that you will be able to make the smallest possible Web graphics once you master its nuances.

1. Copy the **chap_04** folder to your hard drive from the **H•O•T CD-ROM** if you haven't already done so.

2. Open **javapress.psd** from the **chap_04** folder that you transferred to your hard drive.

3. Choose **File > Save For Web**.

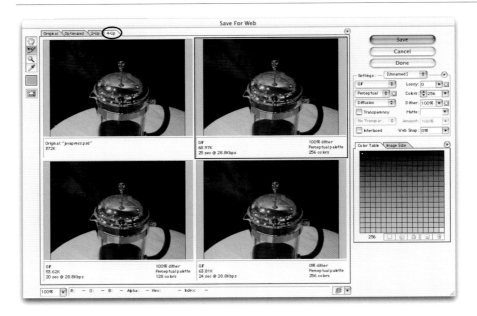

4. Click on the **4-Up** tab in the **Save For Web** window. The multiple previews in this tab will let you compare different compression settings.

Notice that the upper-left tab has the term "Original" in it? This allows you to compare the way the image looks in its original, uncompressed state to the other previews, which show how the image would look with different combinations of compression settings.

If you have already used the Save For Web feature, your copy of Photoshop might default to different compression settings than you see here. That's because Save For Web memorizes whatever compression settings you used when you last saved an optimized image.

5. You'll probably see a black border around the preview on the upper right of the Save For Web window, indicating that is the active preview. If not, click on the **upper-right** image.

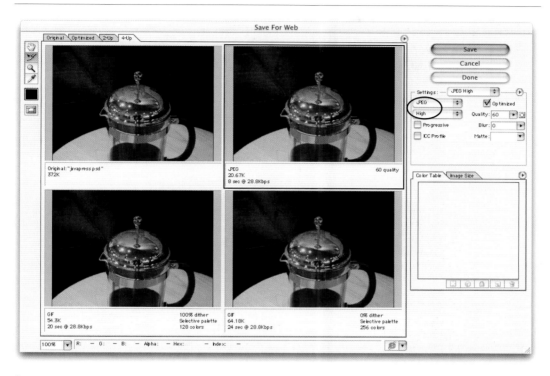

6. Take a look at the **File Format** field on the right side of the window. If it reads **JPEG**, leave it as it is. If it reads **GIF**, click the **File Format** button and choose **JPEG** from the pop-up menu. Then click the **Quality Presets** button and choose **High**. This will set the quality of the selected preview to 60.

Notice that the JPEG is better looking than any of the other previews that are GIFs? This illustrates the point we made earlier that continuous-tone images, such as photographs, always compress better as JPEGs than as GIFs.

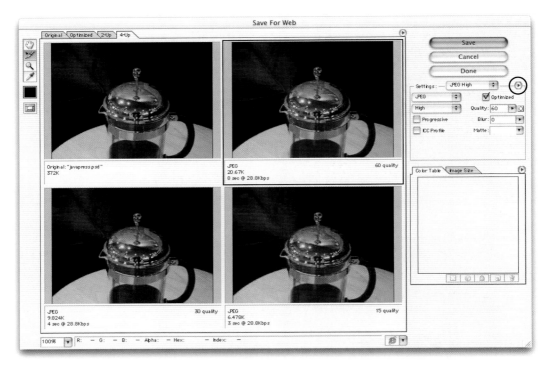

7. Click on the **arrow** circled above to access the **Optimize** pop-up menu, and choose **Repopulate Views**. This will change the other previews in the two frames at the bottom of the window to the same file format—JPEG in this case—as the selected preview.

Notice the readout below each preview? It tells you the JPEG quality and file size of each preview. Photoshop also estimates how long this graphic will take to download over a slow connection. Note that this is a theoretical estimate of speed, and it might not be accurate due to other factors such as server speed and bottlenecks in the Internet. Your readouts may have different numbers than those in the example above, because Photoshop remembers the compression levels from the last time you saved for Web with JPEG settings.

Judging the relative image quality and file sizes of all of the previews in the example above, it looks like the best choice for the JPEG quality setting would lie between 60 and 30. The higher the quality setting, the larger the file size will be. The lower the quality setting, the more artifacts you'll see in the preview. Every image that you optimize will have a different balance of quality versus size.

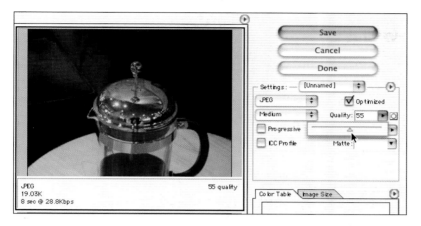

8. With the upper-right preview selected, click on the arrow next to the **Quality** field, and move the Quality **slider** to **55**. **Note:** You must release the slider for the results of the new setting to take effect.

The slider is useful because it lets you experiment easily with settings that are between the default numbers used by the Quality Presets button.

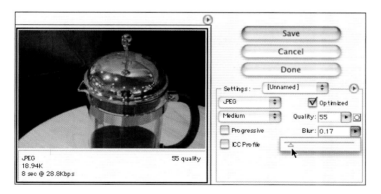

9. Click the arrow next to the **Blur** field, and use the Blur **slider** to add a tiny amount (around 0.17) of blur to the image.

This will result in a slight file savings, but you should avoid adding too much blur or you will adversely affect the quality of the image.

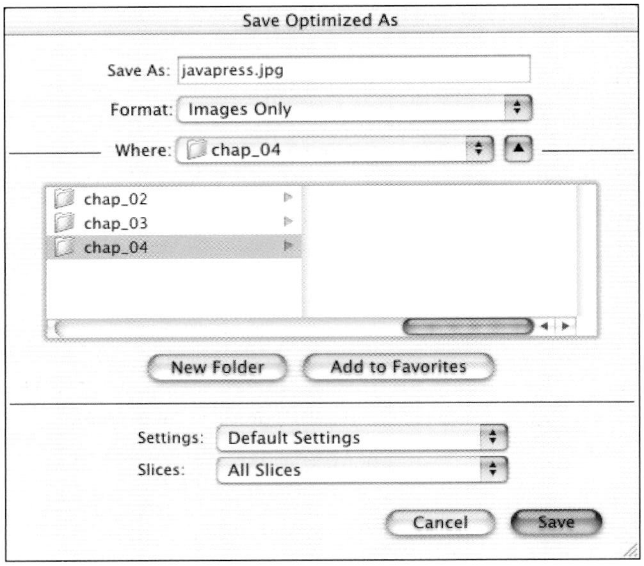

10. When you are satisfied with all of your optimization settings, click **Save**. The **Save Optimized As** window will open.

The program automatically puts a .jpg suffix on the filename for you. It also generates a filename, which you can change, based on the name of the original image.

---

11. Navigate to the **chap_04** folder on your hard drive, and click **Save**.

Notice that the original, uncompressed javapress.psd file remains open in Photoshop. You haven't altered the original a bit. When you choose Save For Web, Photoshop saves an optimized copy of the file on your hard drive and does not harm the original file.

---

12. Close the original **javapress.psd** image without saving.

---

2. [PS] _____Selective JPEG Optimization with Alpha

An alpha channel is a type of mask that Photoshop stores in the Channels tab of the Layers palette. If you create and use an alpha channel mask on an image, you can compress the masked area of the image with a different JPEG quality setting than the rest of the image. This selective optimization technique often will reduce the overall file size of a JPEG. This exercise walks you through how to do this in Photoshop. You can do the same thing in ImageReady using controls in the ImageReady Optimize palette, except that you'd have to create the alpha channel in Photoshop before bringing the image into ImageReady, because you can't create channels in ImageReady.

1. Open **javapress_layers.psd** from the **chap_04** folder on your hard drive.

This is the same image you used in the last exercise, except that the table and its contents are on a separate layer from the background to make it easier for you to make a perfect mask in the following steps.

2. Hold down the **Cmd** key (Mac) or **Ctrl** key (Windows) and click on the **table** layer in the **Layers** palette. This will cause the cursor to change to a hand with a rectangle on top of it (as seen above), and a selection marquee to appear around the content of the table layer only.

This is our favorite shortcut for creating a perfect selection around artwork on a layer. It's much better than using the magic wand or any of Photoshop's other selection tools, because it always gives you a perfect selection. Any time you have a layer with content and transparency, this is the best method for making a selection. However, if you are working with an image that does not have transparent layers, you can use any of Photoshop's selection tools to create a selection to use with the optimization technique taught in this exercise.

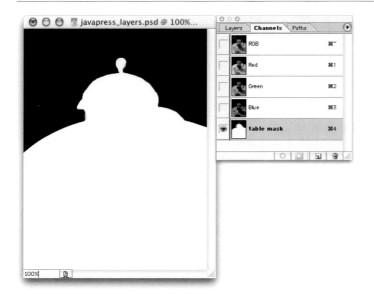

3. Choose **Select > Save Selection**. The **Save Selection** dialog box will appear. In the **Name** field, type a name for your new alpha channel (like **table mask**), and click **OK**. That's all there is to turning an ordinary selection into a mask stored in an alpha channel.

4. Press **Cmd+D** (Mac) or **Ctrl+D** (Windows) to deselect the contents of the **table** layer.

If you want to see the mask you just created, click on the Channels *palette, which is next to the* Layers *palette. In the* Channels *palette, click on your new table mask channel to display the grayscale alpha mask in the document window. If you notice any substantial holes in the mask, you can set the foreground color in the Toolbox to white or black, and use a* Brush *tool to touch up those holes. When you're done viewing the alpha mask, click on the* RGB *channel in the* Channels *palette, and return to the* Layers *palette. This is all optional. You do not have to view the alpha channel for it to work; this was simply a suggestion if you've never seen one before.*

5. Choose **File > Save For Web**. In the Save For Web window, click on the **2-Up** tab so that you can see more of the image preview than in the 4-Up tab, and make sure **File Format** is set to **JPEG**.

6. Set the **Quality** slider to the lowest level at which there are no noticeable artifacts in the most important items in the image—the coffee press and other foreground items. (**Hint:** Try setting the quality slider at **55**. With the entire image compressed at that quality the file size will be 19.11K.)

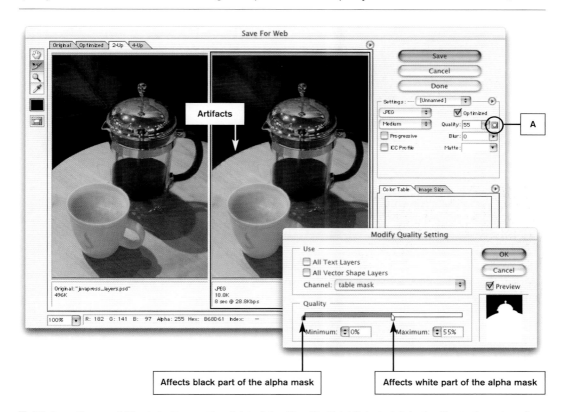

7. Click on the small **Mask** button to the right of the **Quality** field (labeled **A** in the illustration above). This will open the **Modify Quality Setting** dialog box. Select **Channel: table mask**. Notice the black and white preview of your alpha mask and the two sliders in the Quality area. The white slider (on the right) sets the level of quality for the content that is inside the white alpha mask (the table, the coffee press, and the cup). The black slider sets the level of quality for the content that is outside of the white mask.

8. Leave the white slider set to its default of **55%**. In the preview image, notice the artifacts around the outer edge of the table (shown in the previous illustration). That area is covered by the black area of the mask. Move the black slider up to around **30%** to eliminate those artifacts. Click **OK**.

With the white and black sliders set to their defaults, 55% and 0% respectively, the overall size of the file (reported at the bottom left of the preview window) is less than it was when you had the quality of the entire image set to 55, back in step 6. As you move the black slider to the right, increasing the quality of the image covered by the black part of the mask to around 30, the file size increases slightly, but it's still less than when the quality of the whole image was set to 55.

Applying relatively high compression (low quality) to the area outside of the white alpha mask, without sacrificing the higher quality necessary for the more important areas inside the mask, resulted in a small reduction in overall file size. The amount of file size you can save with this technique varies from image to image and mask to mask. In most cases, it's worth experimenting with this technique to see if you can lower file size while applying optimal compression to different areas of an image.

9. Click **Save** in the **Save For Web** window, and you will be prompted in the **Save Optimized As** window to save this image as **javapress_layers.jpg**. Click **Save**.

10. Close the **javapress_layers.psd** file, without saving.

3. [PS] _____Saving For Web Using GIF

Optimizing an image as a GIF is more complex than optimizing as a JPEG, because there are so many more GIF settings that affect file size. The next few exercises will expose you to the key settings for optimizing a GIF: lowering the number of colors, adjusting the dither options, and choosing a palette.

1. Open **frenchlogo.psd** from the **chap_04** folder you copied to your hard drive, and choose **File > Save For Web**.

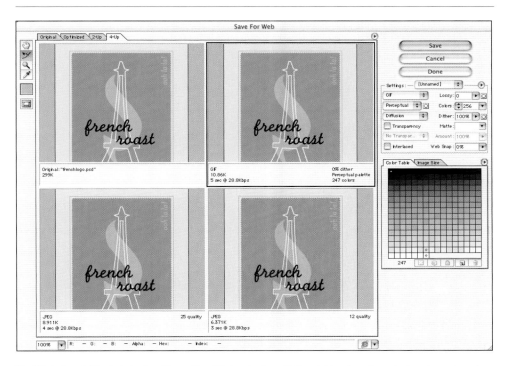

2. Click the **4-Up** tab in the **Save For Web** window, if the 4-Up view is not showing already. All three previews should be set to JPEG as a result of the last exercise. Select the **upper-right preview**, click the **File Format** button, and choose **GIF** from the pop-up menu. Change any of the settings on the right side of your Save For Web window that do not match those in the illustration above (**GIF, Perceptual, Lossy: 0, Colors: 256, Diffusion Dither: 100%**).

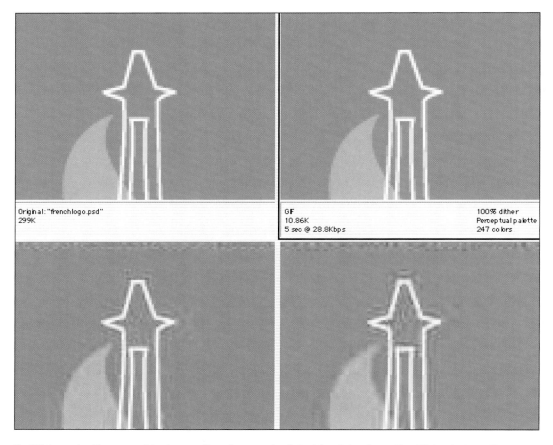

Original: "frenchlogo.psd"
299K

GIF
10.86K
5 sec @ 28.8Kbps

100% dither
Perceptual palette
247 colors

3. Click on the **Zoom** tool in the small toolbox on the left side of the **Save For Web** window. Click twice in whichever preview pane is selected to change the magnification in all of the views to **300%**. Select the **Hand** tool in the small **Save For Web** toolbox. Click and drag in any of the view panes to move the image to match the illustration above. Notice that the two JPEG previews on the bottom contain artifacts that make them look distressed, but the the GIF preview on the upper right looks more like the original on the upper left. As we mentioned before, flat-style graphics like this are better suited for the GIF than the JPEG format.

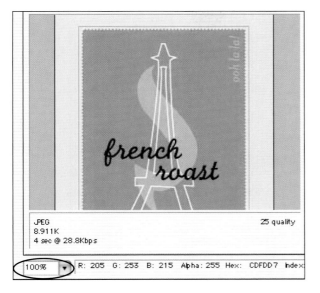

4. Click the **arrow** next to the size readout on the bottom left of the **Save For Web** window, and choose **100%** from the pop-up menu to return all of the previews to normal size.

No one will ever see your Web images at anything other than 100%, so don't fuss too much with an image at a high magnification. We asked you to zoom in so you could see the artifacts we were describing, but when you're actually optimizing an image, it's best to judge image quality at 100% magnification.

5. Click on the JPEG preview on the **bottom left**, and then back on the GIF preview on the **upper right**, keeping your eye on the settings at the far right of the Save For Web window. As you switch from JPEG to GIF, notice that the optimization settings in this context-sensitive window change, and that there are more and different options available for GIF than for JPEG.

Notice that when a preview is set to GIF there is a Color Table, but when it's set to JPEG there is not. That's because the GIF file format supports a maximum of only 256 colors. So all of the colors in the original image have to be converted (sometimes called mapped) to a limited palette of colors, which you'll learn to select in the next exercise. The Color Table displays the colors in the currently selected palette to which this GIF preview is mapped. The JPEG format supports millions of colors, so a JPEG doesn't need to map to a limited palette.

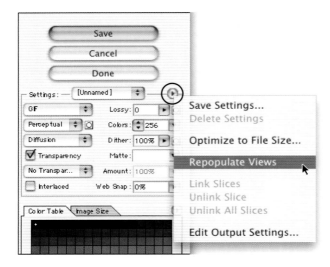

6. With the **upper-right** GIF preview selected, click the arrow circled above and choose **Repopulate Views** from the pop-up **Optimize** menu. This changes all the views to the same format as the selected preview—GIF.

You can choose to use Repopulate Views whenever you want to see variations on one compression format.

7. Leave this file open in the **Save For Web** window for the next exercise.

Note: If you press Cancel, the Save For Web window will not remember all of these settings. If you have to take a break and can't leave the Save For Web window open, click Done to save these settings so that they appear the next time you open any image in the Save For Web window. The Done button is a useful new addition to Photoshop 7.

4. [PS] ——————Choosing the Right Palette

GIF palette settings are the most difficult to understand of the optimization controls. This exercise is designed to shed light on these mysterious palette settings, and help you get through the hardest part of optimizing GIFs.

1. The image **frenchlogo.psd** should be open in the **Save For Web** window from the previous exercise. Make sure the **upper-right preview** is selected. Click on the **2-Up** tab.

You'll see the original image on the left and a single preview on the right (although the illustrations that follow include only the preview so that you can see the optimization settings in detail too).

2. With the preview on the right selected, change the **Color Reduction Palette** setting from **Perceptual** to **Selective**, then **Adaptive**, and then **Web**, just to see the effect that these settings have on the file size and the appearance of the selected preview.

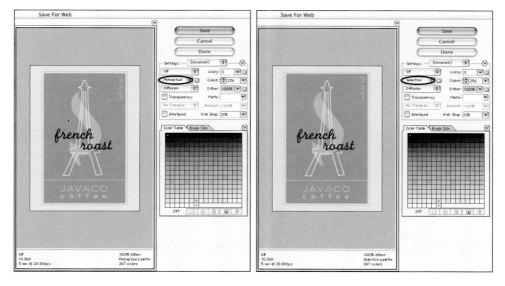

Perceptual   Selective

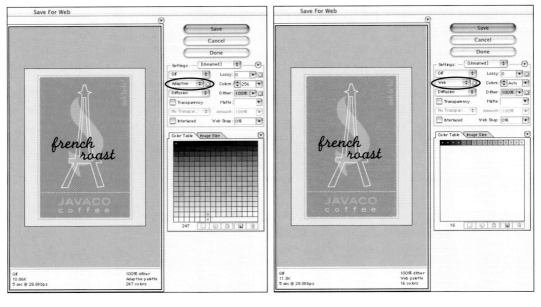

Adaptive   *Web*

Notice that the Color Table, file size, and image appearance are almost identical for the Perceptual, Selective, and Adaptive palettes. That's because all three of these palettes are derived from the colors in this particular image, each by means of a slightly different algorithm. The Web palette resulted in a preview that had fewer colors and didn't look very good. That's because the Web palette is independent of the colors in any image, and tries to force the colors in an image into its set palette. For this reason, we almost always use the Adaptive, Perceptual, or Selective palette instead of the Web palette.

3. Once you've looked at all of these palette choices, change the **Color Reduction Palette** setting in the upper-right preview back to **Perceptual**, and make sure that the **Dither method** is set to **Diffusion**, the **Dither amount** is set to **100%**, and the number of **Colors** is set to **256**. There's nothing magical about these particular settings. They're just the settings you should return to so your settings match those in the rest of these GIF optimization exercises.

---

4. Leave the **Save For Web** window as it is and move to the next exercise. If you have to quit Photoshop right now and start the next exercise later, be sure to click **Done** so that the next time you enter the Save For Web window, your last settings will be remembered.

NOTE | When to Use Which Palette

Use either the Adaptive, Selective, or Perceptual palette whenever you're optimizing a GIF. Each will result in a GIF whose colors are similar to those in the original image, because each of these palettes is based on colors in the original image. To choose between them, apply each of the three palettes to an image preview, as you did above. Select the one that results in a relatively small file size and an image whose color and appearance are as close to the original as possible.

The only time to use the Web palette is if you need a quick-and-dirty way to convert an image made with non-Web-safe colors to one that's Web safe. As mentioned above, the disadvantage of using the Web palette is that it has no relationship to the original image, and so might adversely affect your image. If you do have to convert to Web-safe colors, we suggest you do so selectively, as described in the following note.

There's no reason to use any of the other available palettes when you're optimizing an image for the Web.

NOTE | Changing Selected Colors in a Palette to Web Safe

If you ever run into a situation in which you must convert a non-Web-safe image to a Web-safe one, we recommend that you change only those colors that fill large, solid-color areas of your image. This will eliminate the most noticeable dithering in an 8-bit browser, while keeping the GIF as true as possible to the colors of the original image. Avoid the Web palette or the Snap To Web slider, because both are wholesale solutions that don't let you control which colors will be changed to Web safe. Instead, do the following.

Select the **Eyedropper** tool at the top left of the **Save For Web** window. Click in the image preview on the color you want to change. The corresponding color chip will become highlighted in the **Color Table** on the bottom right.

continues on next page

NOTE | Changing Selected Colors in a Palette to Web Safe *continued*

Save For Web

Save

Cancel

Done

Settings : [Unnamed]

GF   Lossy: 0

Perceptual   Colors: 256

Diffusion   Dither: 100%

Transparency   Matte:

No Transpar...   Amount: 100%

Interlaced   Web Snap: 0%

Color Table   Image Size

246

Shifts/Unshifts selected colors to Web palette

GF   100% dither
10.85K   Perceptual palette
5 sec @ 28.8Kbps   246 colors

Click the **Shift to Web-safe Color** icon at the bottom of the **Color Table**. This shifts the color in the image preview to the nearest Web-safe color from the palette you chose. That color chip in the Color Table now contains two small icons. The diamond indicates that it's a Web-safe color, and the square indicates that it's locked. (The lock means that this color will be retained in the Color Table even if you reduce the number of colors in the image. You'll learn how the lock works in Exercise 6.)

If you don't like the Web-safe color that the program chose and want to change to a different one, double-click the highlighted color in the Color Table. This will open the **Color Picker**, from which you can choose a different Web-safe color.

5. [PS]_____Reducing the Colors

Minimizing the number of colors in a GIF is the most significant thing you can do to limit GIF file size. Your goal is to reduce the number of colors until you arrive at the fewest that are necessary to keep the image looking good. This exercise teaches how to reduce colors in the Photoshop Save For Web window.

1. The file **frenchlogo.psd** should still be open in the Photoshop **Save For Web** window from the preceding exercise. Make sure the **upper-right preview** is selected and the optimization settings for that preview are the same as they were at the end of the last exercise (**GIF, Perceptual, Colors: 256, Diffusion, Dither: 100%**).

Notice that although the number in the Colors field is set to 256, the notes at the bottom of the selected preview tell you that there are only 239 colors in the optimized image. That's because this particular image was originally made with less than 256 colors. The 256 in the Colors field is just the maximum number of colors to which an image could be mapped with this setting.

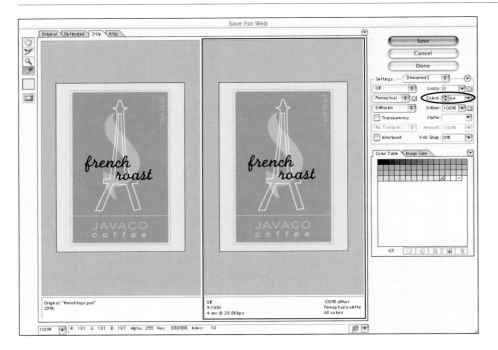

2. With the **Color Reduction Palette** set to **Perceptual** from the previous exercise, change the number of colors from **256** to **64** by clicking the arrow next to the **Colors** setting to access the pop-up menu. You'll see the file size get smaller right away. Compare this preview to the original, and you'll see that the preview still looks great. Try smaller values until the image stops looking good.

We're satisfied with this image at 32 colors, which results in a file size of about 8.1K. When we tried taking this image down to 16 colors, the edges of the text looked too rough for our taste. We still think this image can be coaxed to go smaller, though.

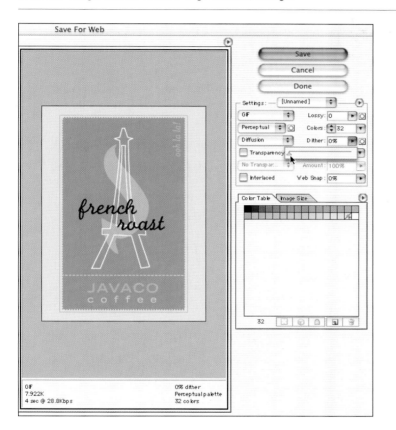

3. With the number of colors set to 32, move the **Dither** slider to **0%**.

Notice that the file size is now slightly smaller—7.922K. Different types of images realize different amounts of file saving with dithering set to zero, but lowering or omitting dither almost always results in some file savings.

4. Click **Save** to save the GIF, and close the original **frenchlogo.psd** without saving.

NOTE | What Is Dither?

When you limit the number of colors available in the Color Table, you might make it impossible to exactly reproduce some of the colors from the original image in the GIF image preview. So Photoshop takes two colors that are in your Color Table and places small dots of each right next to one another to try to simulate the original color. Photoshop offers three patterns of dither dots—diffusion, pattern, and noise—which differ mainly in the way the dither dots are arranged. You can apply any of these to an image preview by clicking the **Dither Algorithm** button and choosing one from the pop-up menu. The Diffusion dither pattern also offers the opportunity to regulate the amount of dither applied, by using the Dither slider, as you did in this exercise.

In most cases, your best bet is to avoid dither, because it adds to file size and gives the image a dotted look. However, if your image has a large area of gradient, glow, or shadow, adding dither can sometimes improve its appearance. When you have items like that in an image, try out each of the dither patterns and the Diffusion dither slider to see if dither improves the appearance of the image without increasing the file size too much.

6. [PS] _____ Locking Colors

One of the great features of Photoshop and ImageReady is the fact that you can influence which colors are included in a GIF, even when you greatly reduce the number of colors in the Color Table.

1. Open **oohlala.psd** from the **chap_04** folder you copied to your hard drive. Choose **File > Save For Web**.

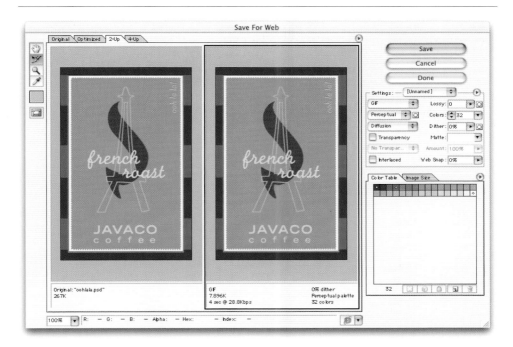

2. Click the **2-Up** tab, and change the settings to **GIF, Perceptual, Diffusion, Lossy: 0, Colors: 32, Dither: 0%**. You may already see these settings, because they are the Save For Web settings you used at the end of the preceding exercise.

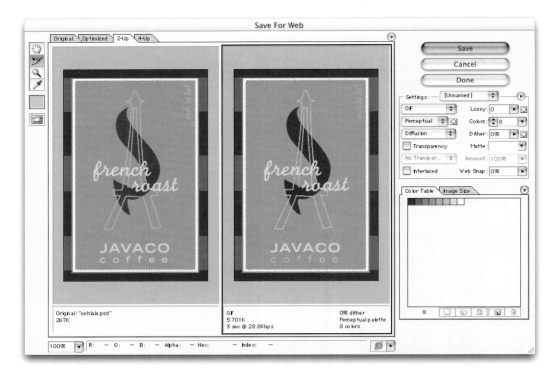

3. Reduce the number of colors to **8**. Notice that this causes some of the central colors to change in the preview.

Some unanticipated colors changed in the preview because Photoshop made the decision about which colors to throw away without your input.

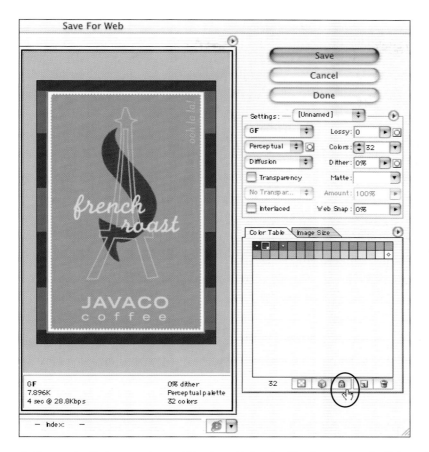

4. Return the **Colors** setting to **32** colors. Using the **Eyedropper** tool, click on the **purple** color in the steam graphic. Its corresponding color chip in the **Color Table** will be highlighted. Click on the **Lock** symbol at the bottom of the Color Table to lock the highlighted color. Once the color has been locked, a small white square will appear in the lower-right corner of the color chip.

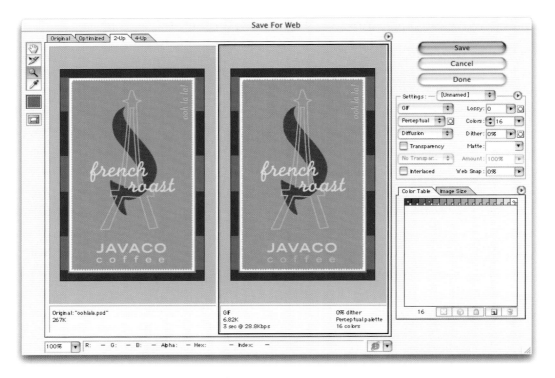

5. Go through the image with the **Eyedropper** and lock all the colors that you want to preserve. Once you have all the colors locked, reduce the **Colors** setting to **16** colors.

This time all the important colors in the image were preserved. Being able to lock colors is a very useful feature in the Save For Web window.

6. Leave the file open in the **Save For Web** window for the next exercise.

7. [PS]_____Changing the Dimensions of a Graphic

There is only one more thing that can make this image smaller: changing its dimensions. The cool thing is that you can change the dimensions without leaving the Save For Web window. Aside from convenience, another advantage of changing image dimensions this way is that it leaves the original untouched and resizes only the Web version of the graphic.

1. With **oohlala.psd** still open in the **Save For Web** window from the previous exercise, click on the **Image Size** tab to the right of the **Color Table** tab.

2. Enter **Percent: 75**, click the **Apply** button, and watch the file size shrink along with the image dimensions.

3. Click **Save** to save this image as a **GIF**, and close the original **oohlala.psd** file without saving. This will cause the GIF to be 75%, with no change in size to the original.

8. [PS] _____ Selective GIF Optimization with Alpha

Earlier, you learned how to selectively optimize parts of an image using alpha channels in the JPEG file format. You can also apply selective optimization to GIF files. In this context , you can control color reduction, dither, and lossy compression via an alpha channel mask. Photoshop 7 has a new twist on selective optimization. It will automatically create an alpha mask for you based on the content of all type layers or vector shape layers in your image. This exercise will show you how to create an automatic alpha channel based on a type layer, and how to use it for selectively optimizing color reduction, dither, and amount of lossy compression.

NOTE | When to Use Selective GIF Optimization

The purpose of selective GIF optimization is to protect important areas of an image from degradation while reducing the file size of the whole image. One situation in which this comes in handy is when you're trying to reproduce a logo for the Web that matches the colors in the original. Logos are often composed of text or vector-based images. The new automatic alpha masks for text and vector shapes will help you protect these parts of a logo without having to build your own alpha mask. You can use these automatic masks to favor the colors from the protected areas of your logo in the Color Table, and to protect the appearance of those areas from negative effects of dither or lossy compression.

You can also use selective GIF optimization on a file composed entirely of bitmap imagery, in which some parts of the image are more important than others. For example, if you're creating an animated GIF, you might want to favor a character in the foreground over the background illustration. In that case, you can create your own alpha mask by selecting the character and storing the selection in an alpha channel, just as you learned to do back in Exercise 2, "Selective JPEG Optimization with Alpha."

1. Open **weighted.psd** from the **chap_04** folder on your hard drive. If your **Layers** palette isn't open, choose **Window > Layers**. Notice that this file has one type layer containing the words **French Roast**.

2. Choose **File > Save For Web**. Click the **2-Up** tab, and set the **File Format** to **GIF**. Choose a **Perceptual** palette, **Diffusion**, **Dither: 100%**, and **64** colors, as shown above.

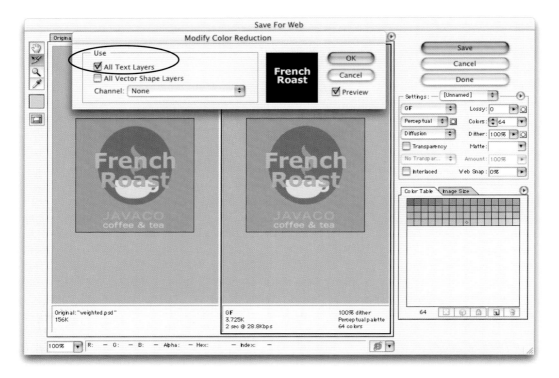

3. Click the **Mask** button to the right of **Perceptual**. This will open the **Modify Color Reduction** dialog box.

---

4. Put a checkmark next to **All Text Layers** in the **Modify Color Reduction** dialog box, keeping an eye on the colors in the Color Table as you do.

Notice that when you do this, the colors in the Color Table change to primarily yellows. The Color Table is now weighted toward the yellow colors in the Type layer, rather than uniformly representative all of the colors in the image. Notice that there's a white mask over the words French Roast *in the Modify Color Reduction dialog box. Photoshop automatically created that mask when you checked All Text Layers. The white area of the mask determines what part of the image has the most influence on the selection of colors in the Color Table.*

---

5. Remove the checkmark from **All Text Layers**. This eliminates the mask and unweights the Color Table. Now you'll see more blues in the Color Table representing the nontext areas of the image. Click **OK** to close the **Modify Color Reduction** dialog box.

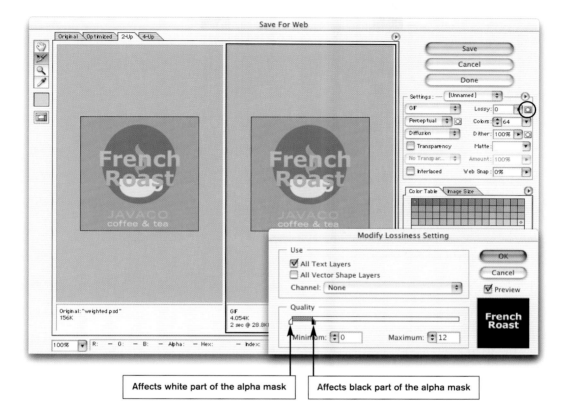

Affects white part of the alpha mask   Affects black part of the alpha mask

6. Click the **Mask** button to the right of the **Lossy** field. This will open the **Modify Lossiness Setting** dialog box. Put a checkmark next to **All Text Layers**, This automatically creates a white alpha mask defined by the content of the type layer: the words **French Roast**.

7. Use the sliders to apply a different amount of lossy compression to the text than to the rest of the image. Leave the **white slider** at **0**, and move the **black slider** to the left until the nontext area in the preview looks good to you (try around **12**). Click **OK**.

The white slider controls the amount of lossiness applied to the text in the white area of the mask. The black slider controls the amount of lossiness applied to the rest of the image, which is in the black area of the mask.

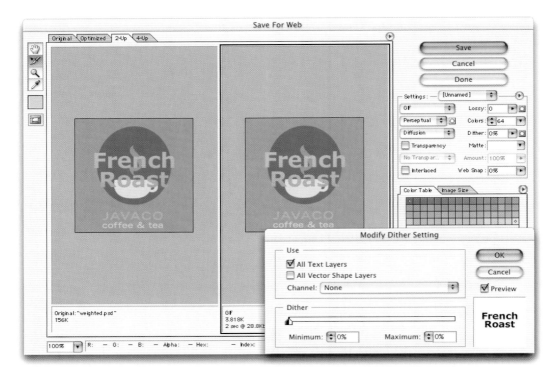

8. Click the **Mask** button to the right of **Dither**. This will open the **Modify Dither Setting** dialog box. Put a checkmark next to **All Text Layers**.

You could use the sliders to apply different amounts of dither to the text and nontext areas of the image. However, there's no reason to do that in this case because none of the areas of this image stands to benefit from dithering. So either push both sliders all the way to 0% in the Modify Dither Setting *dialog box and click* OK, *or close this dialog box and move the* Dither *slider on the right of the* Save For Web *window to 0%.*

9. Leave this file open in the **Save For Web** window for the next exercise.

9. [PS] _____ Previewing in a Browser

You can preview your images in a Web browser as you're optimizing them in Photoshop's Save For Web window.

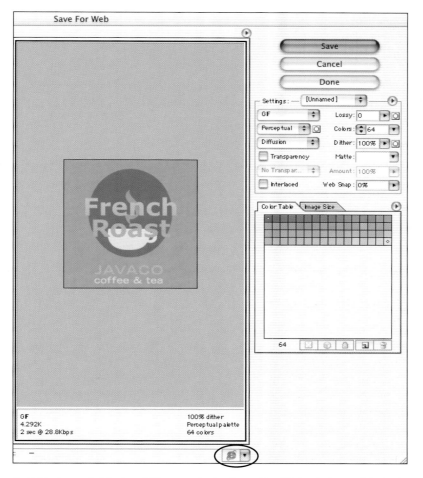

1. With the **weighted.psd** file open in the **Save For Web** window, click the **Preview in Browser** icon at the bottom of the Save For Web window to preview the optimized image in the default browser, Internet Explorer. Or, click the **arrow** to the right of the Preview in Browser icon to access a pop-up menu of other browser choices.

The preview that is highlighted in the Save For Web window will be the image that is displayed in the browser.

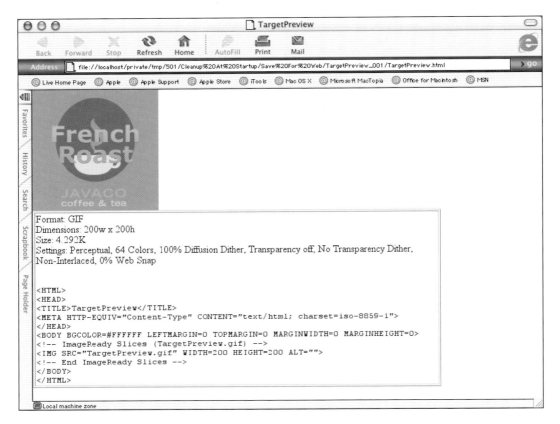

The information and HTML code in the preview browser window is just temporary and used for preview purposes only. If you want to use HTML that Photoshop generates in final form, you have to save an HTML file when you save an image file. You'll learn to do this in future exercises.

2. Return to Photoshop to click the **Save** button at last. You'll be prompted to save this image as **weighted.gif**. Save it into your **chap_04** folder.

3. Close the **weighted.psd** image without saving.

ImageReady Palettes and Preference Settings

The following exercises show you how to do some of the same optimization tasks in ImageReady that you just learned in Photoshop, so you will know how to optimize in either application.

You might wonder *why* you would optimize a graphic in ImageReady when you can do it in Photoshop. There are two reasons. First, if you're already working in ImageReady, it's more convenient to optimize there. We find that we do lots of optimizing in ImageReady because we're often using that program to do Web-oriented tasks, like making rollovers or animations, that can't be done in Photoshop. Second, it's easier in ImageReady than it is in Photoshop to make changes to the original image while you're in the process of optimizing. In Photoshop, you have to exit the Save For Web window to change anything in the original image. In ImageReady, there is no separate Save For Web environment, so it's easier to access the original version of the image at any time.

Don't worry about the results being different in these two programs; the underlying code is identical. The only true differences are in the two interfaces. In Photoshop, when you choose **Save For Web**, a single window appears. In ImageReady, the optimization settings are spread across several palettes.

To prepare for optimizing in ImageReady, we suggest you dock your **Optimize** and **Color Table** palettes together, as you learned to do in Chapter 2, "*Interface.*" That's because you'll need access to the Color Table whenever you're optimizing a GIF, and this way you won't have to go searching for it. If you don't see either of these palettes on your screen, choose **Window > Optimize** or **Window > Color Table**.

We also recommend that you change one ImageReady optimization preference:

Choose **Edit > Preferences > Optimization**. (Mac OS X: **ImageReady > Preferences > Optimization**). In the **Preferences** dialog box, change the **Default Optimization** setting to **Auto Selected GIF or JPEG**.

This instructs ImageReady to make a best guess as to which type of compression format (GIF or JPEG) to select for each image. You can override its guess, but why not have ImageReady offer a starting point?

| 115 |

IO. [IR] _____ Optimizing a JPEG in ImageReady

Everything in this exercise should be pretty familiar to you. The optimization process is almost identical in ImageReady and Photoshop. We'll show you a few new tricks along the way, which you can try in either application.

1. Make sure you are in ImageReady, not Photoshop. Open **sign.psd** from the **chap_04** folder on your hard drive. Notice that it opens in the main document window, which has tabs that read **Original**, **Optimized**, **2-Up**, and **4-Up**.

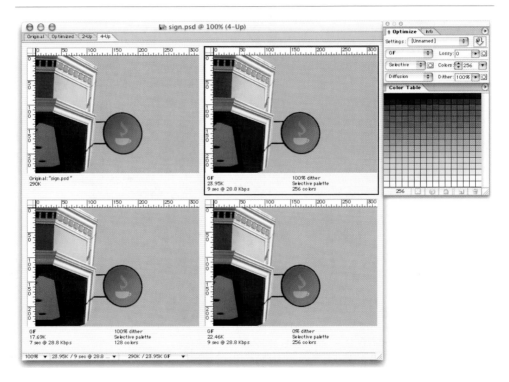

2. Click on the **4-Up** tab and the image should appear in four small preview windows.

3. Move the **Optimize** palette to position it where you want on the screen. (It should bring the Color Table along with it if you docked those two palettes as we suggested.)

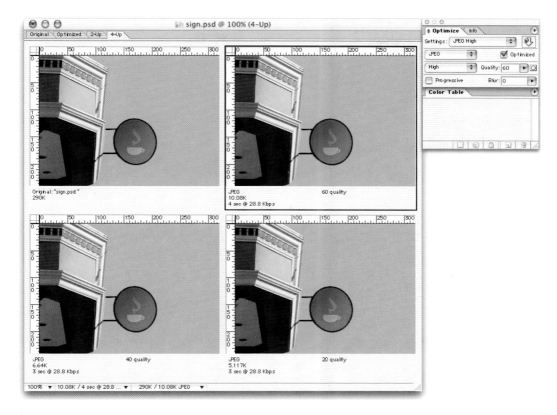

4. Make sure the **upper-right preview** is selected. In the **Optimize** palette, change the **File Format** to **JPEG** and the **Quality Preset** drop-down menu to **High**. Click the **arrow** on the top right of the **Optimize** palette, and choose **Repopulate Views** to set all of the previews to **JPEG**. JPEG is the format to use here, because this image has photographic elements and a continuous-tone gradient, and therefore will look better and be smaller when optimized as a JPEG than as a GIF.

---

5. Try all of the things you learned in the Photoshop section of this chapter. Change the **Quality** setting, add **Blur**, and see what makes the smallest file size.

You already know how to use this program, because most of it is identical to Photoshop.

---

6. When you're ready to save this JPEG, choose **File > Save Optimized**. The **Save Optimized** window will appear with the name **sign.jpg** already filled in. Leave the other settings at their defaults for now. Save the optimized file, and leave **sign.psd** open for the next exercise.

Whenever you want to save a file in a Web format, choose Save Optimized or Save Optimized As. Whenever you want to save the original PSD file, choose Save or Save As.

II. [IR] Using a Matte Color on a JPEG in ImageReady

One major difference between Photoshop and ImageReady is that you can edit this image easily in ImageReady, which was not true of the Save For Web feature in Photoshop. You would have had to click Cancel in the Save For Web window to return to Photoshop's image-editing environment. Here in ImageReady, you can edit whenever you want. It's best to click on the Original tab, or else ImageReady will try to optimize the graphic while you're working, which can take a long time. In this exercise you will edit the image by erasing the background and inserting a new color by using the **Matte** feature.

1. With **sign.psd** still open from the previous exercise, click back on the **Original** tab. This will cause the 4-Up view to collapse into a single view of just the original.

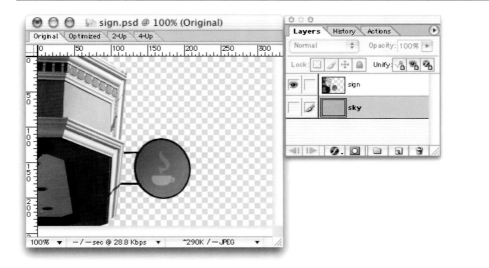

2. Choose **Window > Layers** if you cannot locate the Layers palette. Click the **Visibility** icon (the **Eye**) on the layer named **sky** to turn off the visibility of that layer. This should cause the checkerboard pattern to appear behind the sign, indicating transparency.

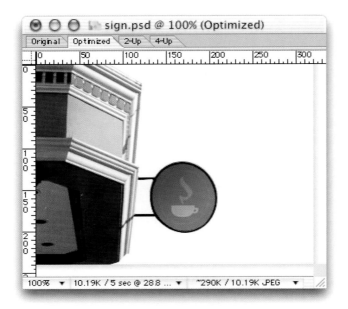

3. Click on the **Optimized** tab.

Notice that the checkerboard background disappeared and turned white? That's because the JPEG format doesn't support transparency. So ImageReady replaces the transparent pixels of the original image with a solid (matte) color in this JPEG preview. You didn't specify a matte color, so ImageReady defaulted to using white. You'll learn how to assign a different matte color in the next few steps.

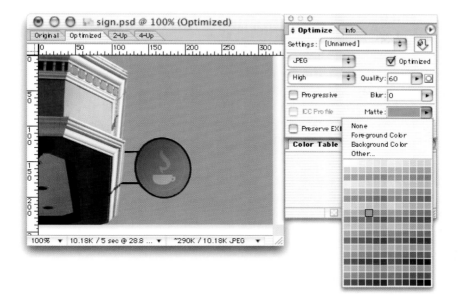

4. In the **Optimize** palette, click on the arrow next to the **Matte** field, and select a color from the pop-up color palette.

Note: If you don't see the Matte field, click the arrow on the top right of the Optimize *palette, and choose* Show Options *from the pop-up menu.*

5. The sign will now have behind it whichever color you chose. Keep the file open for the next exercise.

If you click back on the Original *tab, you'll see the matte color disappear. It is only a function of the JPEG that the matte color exists. You have not permanently altered the file except to turn off the visibility of the* sky *layer.*

12. [IR] _____ Previewing and Writing HTML in ImageReady

If you're an experienced Photoshop user, you might be wondering why you would choose to use the Matte color to insert a background color into a JPEG. You could have easily made a new layer in ImageReady, filled it with this color, and achieved the same effect. The advantage is that because you used the Matte feature, ImageReady can write this same color into the background color element of an HTML page, so that the the image blends into the HTML page background. This is a way to fake transparency in a JPEG, which doesn't support real transparency. This exercise will show you how to set the background color of a Web page to match the Matte color in ImageReady.

Warning: There are times when the JPEG Matte color will not perfectly match your HTML background color. If this happens to you, it would be better to create a transparent GIF, which you will learn about in Chapter 9, "*Transparent GIFs.*"

1. With **sign.psd** still open from the last exercise, choose **File > Output Settings > Background**. In the **Output Settings** dialog box, make sure that **View Document As** is set to **Image**, and **BG Color field** is set to **Matte**. These are the default settings in ImageReady 7. Click **OK**.

2. Choose **File > Preview In** and select the browser of your choice.

Notice that ImageReady creates a preview in the browser and puts a white box below the image that displays temporary HTML code. You can select, copy, and paste this code into an HTML editor, if you want. Better yet, you can have ImageReady write a full HTML file for you. You'll learn to do that next.

3. Return to ImageReady and choose **File > Save Optimized As**.

4. In the **Save Optimized As** window, create a folder for this artwork named **shopsign** by clicking **New** (Mac OS 9), **New Folder** (Mac OS X), or the yellow **Create New Folder** button (Windows). **Note:** Windows users should open the new folder **shopsign** after you create it.

A separate folder is not required, but it helps to keep your files organized.

5. In the **Save Optimized As** window, change the **Format** field (Mac) or **Save as type** field (Windows) to **HTML and Images**, and click **Save**.

6. Look on your hard drive for the folder **shopsign** or for the directory where you chose to save your optimized files. Notice that there are two items there—an HTML file called **sign.html**, and a folder labeled **images** that contains the JPEG file **sign.jpg**.

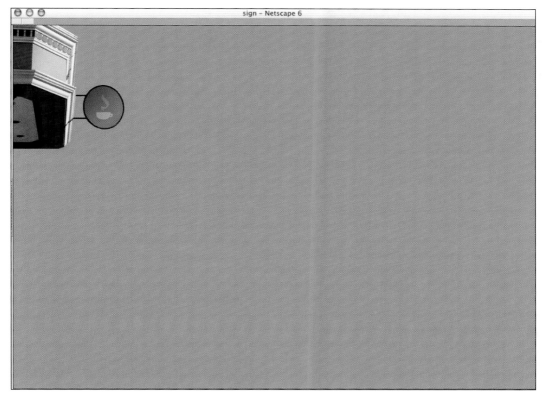

7. Double-click on **sign.html**, and you'll see the page open in your browser without the white information box that the preview generated before.

This page can be opened in any HTML editor or uploaded directly to the Web. If you wanted to format it differently, for example to center the picture or put a headline at the top, you could add to the HTML in an editor if you know how.

8. Return to **ImageReady**, and choose **File > Save** to save the original PSD file with its changes, and close the file.

You should congratulate yourself for doing so much in this chapter! Knowing how to optimize images is one of the most valuable skills a Web designer can have, and is well worth the time and effort you put in here.

5.
Layers

Layer Basics	Linking and Aligning Layers
Layer Sets	Solid, Gradient, and Pattern Layers
Adjustment Layers	Clipping Groups
Knockout Layer Option

chap_05

Photoshop 7/ImageReady
H·O·T CD-ROM

Understanding layers is one of the most important cornerstones of mastering Photoshop, because when you use layers, you can separate elements of your artwork so they can be independently edited. With layers, you can isolate image areas and apply special effects, or change the image's location, color, or opacity without affecting the rest of your art on the other layers. Photoshop 7 offers a few new layers features—some new layer blending modes, and an easier way to name layers. Otherwise, layers work as they did in the last version of Photoshop. Layers are powerful and sometimes complex, but by the time you work through these exercises, you should be comfortable with most layering tasks.

What Are Layers?

When the **Layers** palette was introduced in Photoshop way back in 1996, it revolutionized the way that digital artists created, edited, and saved their work. Prior to that, pixels in an image would be canceled out if other pixels were placed on top of them. This changed when layers came along. Suddenly, by separating areas of an image into layers, you could have stacks and stacks of bitmap images on separate layers that could be changed or moved without altering the pixels in the image areas below them. As long as you didn't "flatten" your layers, each one of them would remain independent of the others to allow you to make your changes. Although layers were introduced originally to help artists edit specific areas of artwork, they have grown to be more powerful with each new version. Now, layers not only isolate artwork, but they can contain special types of artwork, such as masks, patterns, gradients, solid fills, and vector shapes. It all might seem a bit abstract now, but the following exercises should make these concepts come to life for you.

I. [PS] _____Layer Basics

If something doesn't work as expected in Photoshop, one of the first things to check is whether you're on the correct layer. Even seasoned Photoshop users get mixed up about which layer they're working on sometimes. This first exercise teaches the stacking order of layers, how to alter that order, how to rename a layer, and how to change the Background layer from being fixed to being flexible. **Note:** Everything you learn in this chapter is applicable in ImageReady as well.

1. Transfer the **chap_05** folder to your hard drive from the **H•O•T CD-ROM**.

If you're working on a Windows computer, and you're having trouble unlocking files from the CD-ROM or viewing the file extensions, go back to the Introduction for instructions on how to solve those problems.

2. In Photoshop, open **shop.psd** from the **chap_05** folder that you transferred to your hard drive.

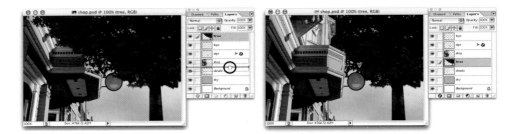

3. In the **Layers** palette, click on the **tree** layer and drag it below the **shop** layer. Your cursor will change to a closed **fist** icon as you drag. Release your mouse when you see a double line under the **shop** layer.

This is the way to change the stacking order of a layered Photoshop document. You don't touch the image at all; you just move the layers around via the Layers palette. At this point, the tree should appear to be behind the coffee shop. Notice that the stacking order goes from the background to the foreground of the image as you move from the bottom of the Layers palette to the top.

4. Click on the **clouds** layer in the **Layers** palette, and drag it to the top of the layer stack, above the **logo** layer.

In the image, the clouds look out of place in front of the tree. In the next step you'll learn how to fix this problem by making the clouds layer invisible.

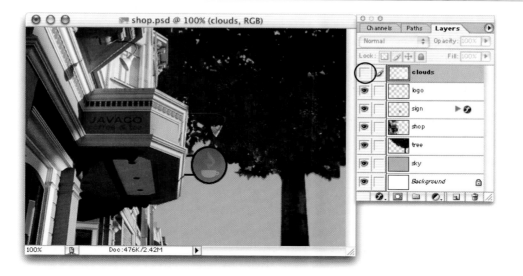

5. In the **Layers** palette, click the **Visibility** icon (the **Eye**) on the **clouds** layer to make that icon disappear. Notice that you don't see the artwork that's on the **clouds** layer in your document window any longer. Clicking the Eye icon toggles the visibility of that layer on and off.

6. Click on the **Background** layer and try moving it above the **clouds** layer. You will discover that this layer cannot be moved.

That's because a Background layer, which is generated automatically when a new document is created with a non-transparent background, has some different properties than a regular layer. For one thing, it's immovable unless you convert it to a regular layer by renaming it, as you'll do in the next step.

7. Double-click the **Background** layer to open the **New Layer** dialog box. You can leave the default name **Layer 0** in the **Name** field and click **OK**.

8. Now move **Layer 0** above the **sky** layer, and it will move just like the **tree** layer did in step 3.

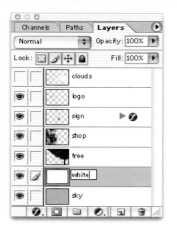

9. Layer 0 isn't a terribly descriptive name for the white layer. To rename it, double-click the layer name in the **Layers** palette. A bounding box will appear around the words **Layer 0**. Type a new name—**white**—and press **Return** or **Enter**.

Be careful to double-click directly on the layer name. If you click anywhere else on the layer, you'll inadvertently open the Layer Style dialog box and you won't have the opportunity to rename the layer. This technique of renaming a layer is new to Photoshop 7 and is a very welcome change from the more complicated method in the last version of Photoshop. Notice that the technique for renaming a regular layer is different than that for renaming a Background layer, which you did in step 7.

10. With the **white** layer selected, click the **Layer Blending Mode** pop-up menu (which is set to Normal by default), and choose **Multiply** from the pop-up menu.

Layer blending modes control the way the color and tone of pixels on a selected layer interact with pixels on the layers below. The Multiply mode blends layers to produce a darker color, turning the white sky to blue in this case. There are 22 Layer blending modes in Photoshop 7, including some new ones since the last version of Photoshop (Linear Burn, Linear Dodge, Vivid Light, Linear Light, and Pin Light). Experiment with Layer blending modes on different images when you get a chance. That's the best way to get a sense of what each one does.

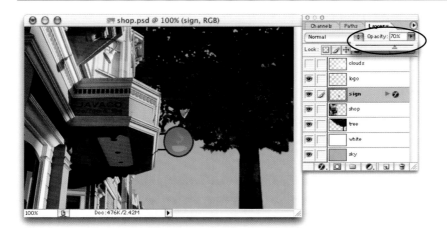

11. Select the **sign** layer, and lower the **Opacity** slider to **70%**. Notice that everything on this layer—the sign and the black border around it—becomes less opaque (more see-through). The sign border looks unnaturally faded, so return the Opacity slider to 100%.

Lowering the opacity of a layer makes the artwork on that layer more translucent, so that the layers beneath it show through. The sign on this layer is artwork. The black border is a special effect called a stroke layer style. You'll learn all about layer styles in Chapter 7, "Layer Styles." For now, focus on the fact that the Opacity slider affects everything on a layer, including layer styles.

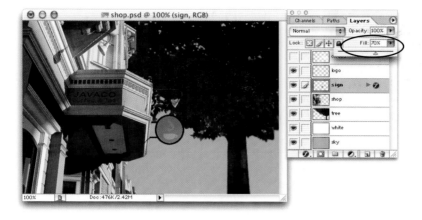

12. With the **sign** layer still selected, lower the **Fill** slider to **70%**. Notice that the sign becomes less opaque, but the black border around the sign, which is a layer style, does not.

The Fill slider, unlike the Opacity slider, does not affect everything on a layer. It makes the artwork on a layer less opaque, but does not affect any layer styles on that layer. Fill opacity was available in the last version of Photoshop, but it was hidden away in the Layer Style dialog box. Photoshop 7 is the first version of the program to put this additional fill opacity control in an easy to reach location on the Layers palette.

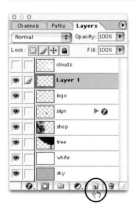

13. Click on the **logo** layer to select it. Click the **New Layer** icon at the bottom of the **Layers** palette. Notice that a new empty layer appears in the Layers palette just above the logo layer, but nothing has changed on your screen inside the document window.

When you add a new layer, by default the layer is empty and transparent. Next, you'll draw on the empty layer. The benefit to drawing on this layer, as opposed to drawing on any of the other layers, is that it can be isolated on its own—turned on or off, opacity lowered or raised, reordered, etc.

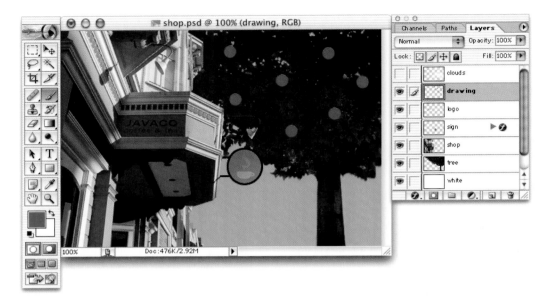

14. Make sure that the new empty layer is selected. Using the **Brush** tool from the Toolbox, select a color, and start drawing dots on the tree. Rename the layer **drawing**, using the technique you learned in step 9.

The benefit to drawing on this new empty layer is that it can be turned off if you don't like what you draw. Whew!

15. Experiment more with the techniques you just learned. Turn the **Visibility (Eye)** icons on and off, move layers around, reduce opacity and fill opacity, and change layer names. The more you play with this document, the more you'll build your layer skills.

16. Close and save the file.

NOTE | Flattening Photoshop Files

In Photoshop, the term "flattened" means that the document's layers have been compressed into a single layer. There are times when you might want to flatten a Photoshop document—to send it to a client, or to make the file size smaller. If you plan to do this, it's always best to save a non-flattened version as well as a flattened one. You never know when having access to the layers will be important. It's possible to flatten all the layers, or just flatten certain layers to simplify a layered document that has grown to be very complex.

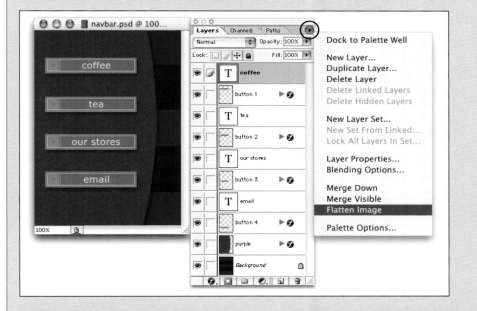

To flatten an image or layer, hold down the arrow button on the upper-right corner of the Layers palette and select one of the following items from the pop-up Layers palette menu:

Merge Down: Combines (flattens, to use Photoshop's terminology) the selected layer and the layer directly below it.

Merge Visible: Combines all layers that have the Eye icons turned on. This is a great method to selectively flatten layers that aren't next to each other in the Layers palette.

Merge Linked: Combines layers that are linked to one another, which you'll learn about in Exercise 3 later in this chapter. This is another way to merge non-consecutive layers. You won't see the Merge Linked choice in the Layers palette menu unless you select a linked layer.

Flatten Image: Combines all layers in the document.

2. [PS] _____Moving and Linking Layers

In the last exercise, you learned to move the stacking order of layers from front to back, but what if you want to move a layer's position on the screen? This next exercise will teach you how to link layers together so they can be moved and aligned.

1. In Photoshop, open **navbar.psd** from the **chap_05** folder on your hard drive. Notice that there are four buttons in the image, which are represented by eight layers of button artwork and text in the Layers palette.

If you are wondering what the f symbol means to the right of most of the layers, it shows that a layer style is in use. You'll learn more about the new layer styles feature in Chapter 7, "Layer Styles."

2. Select the **Move** tool from the Toolbox. It's worth memorizing the keyboard shortcut for the Move tool, because this is a tool that is used often in Photoshop work. Just press the letter **V** on your keyboard, and this tool will become selected.

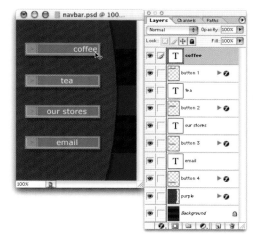

3. Click on the **coffee** layer in the **Layers** palette to select it. Move your mouse to the document window and click and drag. The word **coffee** should move with your movements.

You've just hit one of the biggest hurdles of being adept in Photoshop. A layer must be selected before it can be moved in an image. This is a difficult concept for most new Photoshop users, because there's a disconnect between wanting to move a piece of art in an image and having to think first about which layer contains that artwork. Photoshop can help you with this if you instruct it to auto-matically select layers, as you'll learn to do in the next step.

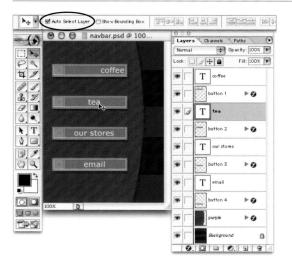

4. Make sure the **Move** tool is still selected. Click the **Auto Select Layer** checkbox in the **Options** bar at the top of your screen to put a checkmark in that box.

5. Click on different areas of your screen and watch the layer selections in the **Layers** palette change automatically. When you're done, uncheck **Auto Select Layer**.

Using the Auto Select Layer option is usually an easier way to select a layer than going to the Layers palette and selecting a layer manually. Photoshop selects the topmost layer in the Layers palette that contains artwork at the spot you've clicked in the image. Unfortunately, if you leave Auto Select Layer checked and forget about it, you'll have trouble selecting a layer manually down the road. So its best to deselect this option after you've used it.

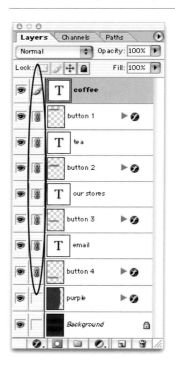

6. To move more than one layer at a time, you'll need to link your layers using the **Link** icon. In the **Layers** palette, select the **coffee** layer. Click inside the **Link** region, located directly to the left of the layer thumbnail, on all the layers except the purple and Background layers at the bottom of the stack.

Notice that your active layer (the coffee layer) has a Paintbrush icon instead of a Link icon in the Link region. This means that all the other layers in which you've put a Link icon are linking to the coffee layer.

7. With the **Move** tool selected, click and drag on your screen. You'll see the artwork on all the linked layers move together.

8. Click in the **Link** region of the **button 1** layer and drag down through the Link regions of all of the linked layers to remove the **Link** icon from these layers and unlink them.

Tip: It's smart to unlink layers when you're done with the task for which you linked them. Otherwise, you might inadvertently affect more than one layer when you working on another task in the future.

9. Close and save this file. The next exercise will show you how the Link icon is helpful when aligning layers.

This exercise works identically in ImageReady.

3. [PS] Aligning Layers with the Link Icon

The link function in Photoshop is useful for more than just moving your layers as a group. You can also use it to align linked layers to one another by left, center, or right axes, and to distribute distances between layers.

1. Open **align.psd** from the **chap_05** folder you transferred to your hard drive from the **H•O•T CD-ROM**.

If you get a message that your text layers need to be updated, click the Update *button in the message.*

2. First, you'll align the buttons by their left edges. Select the **button 1** layer in the **Layers** palette.

You'll see a Paintbrush icon in the Link region that confirms this is your active layer.

3. In the **Layers** palette, click in the **Link** region on the **button 2**, **button 3**, and **button 4** layers to link all of the buttons together.

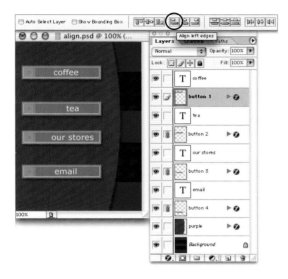

4. Click the **Align left edges** button in the **Options** bar to align the buttons vertically. You'll see all the button shapes line up to the left.

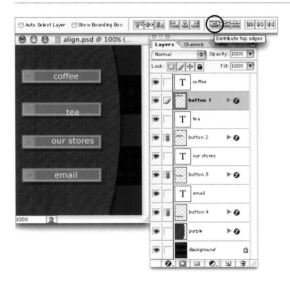

5. Click the **Distribute top edges** button in the **Options** bar to distribute the buttons vertically. All the button shapes will be evenly spaced.

With the Move tool selected, you can move these four perfectly aligned and spaced buttons around and they'll stay grouped this way.

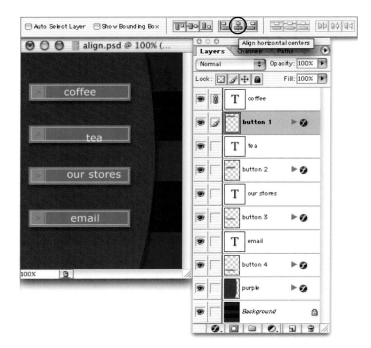

6. Now you'll align the text to the buttons. First, unlink all the layers you linked to **button 1** in the preceding steps. Select **button 1** in the **Layers** palette and link the **coffee** layer to it.

7. Click the **Align horizontal centers** button. The word **coffee** will be centered on the first button. See if you can get the other labels to align to the horizontal center of their buttons.

Hint: Select the button artwork first, then link the lettering to it before you align. Alignment is always based on the selected layer as the starting point, as indicated by the Paintbrush icon. If you select the text first and then the button layer, your button will move instead.

8. Close and save the file.

This exercise works exactly the same way in ImageReady.

What Are Layer Sets?

A **layer set** is a group of layers stored inside a folder in the Layers palette. Layer sets are a useful organizing tool, particularly if you have lots of layers in an image. They can make layers more manageable by grouping them in a meaningful way, and minimizing the stack in the Layers palette. Putting layers in a layer set also allows you to change the visibility, opacity, layer blending mode, and position of multiple layers at once. You'll get to work with layer sets in the upcoming exercise. The following chart summarizes what you can do with layer sets, comparing them to individual layers.

What Are Layer Sets Good For?

Using Individual Layers	Using Layer Sets
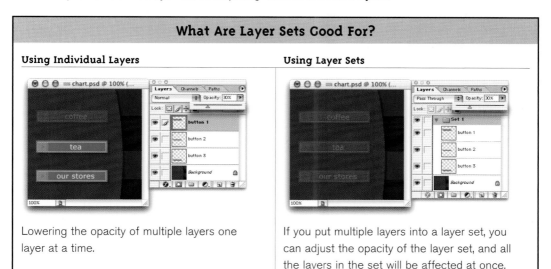	
Lowering the opacity of multiple layers one layer at a time.	If you put multiple layers into a layer set, you can adjust the opacity of the layer set, and all the layers in the set will be affected at once.
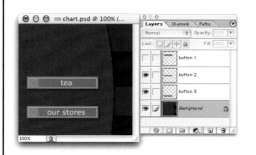	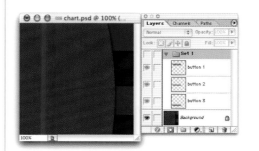
Turning the visibility of multiple layers on and off layer by layer.	Using a layer set, you can affect the visibility of multiple layers at the same time by toggling the Eye icon on the layer set on or off.

continues on next page

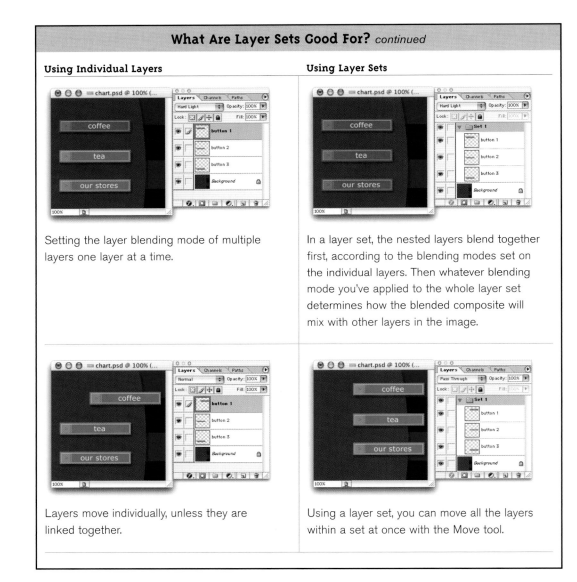

What Are Layer Sets Good For? *continued*

Using Individual Layers

Setting the layer blending mode of multiple layers one layer at a time.

Using Layer Sets

In a layer set, the nested layers blend together first, according to the blending modes set on the individual layers. Then whatever blending mode you've applied to the whole layer set determines how the blended composite will mix with other layers in the image.

Layers move individually, unless they are linked together.

Using a layer set, you can move all the layers within a set at once with the Move tool.

4. [PS] _____Layer Sets

In this exercise, you'll practice creating layer sets and changing the opacity, visibility, position, alignment, and blending mode of layers nested in a layer set. This exercise also works in ImageReady.

> **1.** Open **layersets.psd** from the **chap_05** folder you copied to your hard drive.

> _If you get a warning to update text layers, click Update._

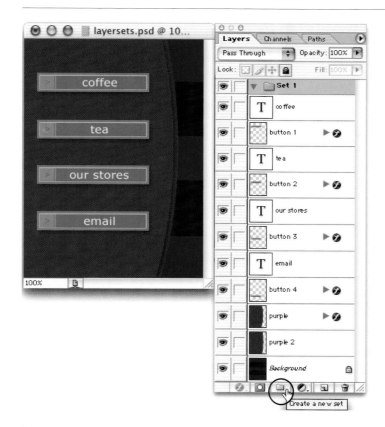

> **2.** In the **Layers** palette, select the **coffee** layer. Click the **New Set** icon at the bottom of the Layers palette. A folder called **Set 1** will appear above the selected layer.

> _**Tip:** Before you create a new layer set, click on one of the layers that you plan to put into that layer set. This ensures that the layer set will be created right above that layer, which will make it easier to drag the appropriate layers into the set._

3. Move the **coffee** layer, and then the **button 1** layer into **Set 1** by clicking and dragging those layers onto the Set 1 layer set in the Layers palette.

Your cursor will change to a closed fist, and Set 1's folder icon will open when you move the cursor over the layer set.

Tip: A layer set can be moved in the stacking order just like any other layer.

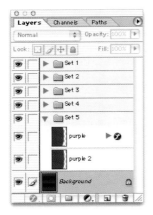

5. Twirl up the arrow on layer sets **1** through **4** to hide their contents.

This makes the Layer palette shorter and more manageable, especially when you have lots of layers in an image.

Tip: *You can shorten your Layers palette by clicking on the bottom-right corner (Windows: any corner) and dragging. Mac OS X users have a shortcut: Move your cursor over the three buttons at the top left of the Layers palette to cause those buttons to turn color. Click on the button that turns green to automatically shrink the Layers palette to its contents.*

6. Double-click on **Set 5** in the **Layers** palette, and type **navbar** to give this layer set a more meaningful name.

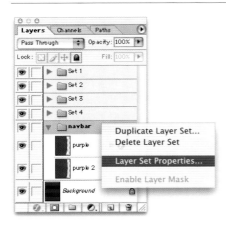

7. Ctrl+click (Windows: **right-click**) on the name of the **navbar** layer set to display a contextual menu. Choose **Layer Set Properties** from the menu.

Layer Set Properties

Name: navbar

Color: ☐ Violet

Channels: ☑R ☑G ☑B

OK

Cancel

8. In the **Layer Set Properties** dialog box, click the **Color** button and choose a color for **Set 5**. Click **OK**.

The navbar layer set and each of its nested layers is now identified with the same color in the Layers palette. This is another tool for identifying and organizing related layers. You can twirl up the arrow on the navbar layer set when you're done looking at it.

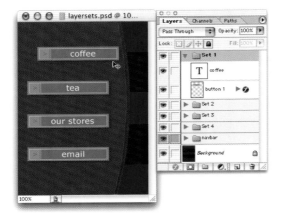

9. Twirl down the arrow on **Set 1** in the **Layers** palette so you can see its layers. Select **Set 1**. Click and drag in the document with the **Move** tool (**V**), to move the coffee button and its text together.

Layer sets can be used to group layers with related artwork (like a button and its text), and can provide an alternative to using the Link icon for moving multiple layers.

Note: *If you're having trouble with this step, take a look at the Auto Select Layer option in the Options bar. It has to be unchecked when you're working with layer sets.*

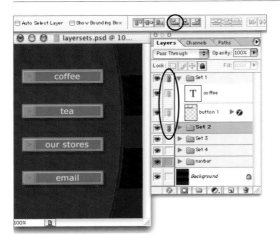

10. Select **Set 2** in the **Layers** palette. Click in the **Link** region next to **Set 1**. Click the **Align Left Edges** button in the **Options** bar to align Set 1 (the coffee button and its text) to Set 2.

Notice that there are active Link icons next to Set 1 and Set 2, but the Link icons next to the individual layers are grayed out. That's because aligning layer sets to each other is a separate operation from aligning layers to one another. In the next step, you'll align layers that are nested in separate layer sets.

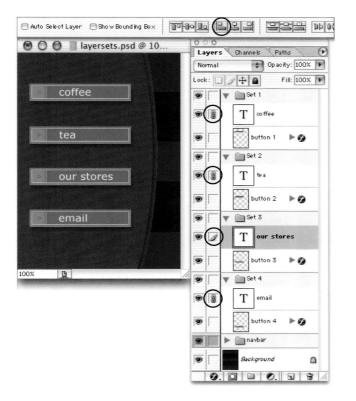

11. Twirl down the arrows next to **Sets 2**, **3**, and **4** in the **Layers** palette. Select the **our stores** layer. Click in the **Link** regions next to the **coffee**, **tea**, and **email** layers. Click the **Align Left Edges** button in the **Options** bar. This will align these type layers, which are in separate layer sets, to one another.

When you're done, you can twirl up the arrows on all of the layers sets except Set 1. (Most of the operations you'll do on layer sets will work the same way whether the arrows on the layer set are twirled up or down. We've asked you to twirl them up here just to shorten the layer stack.)

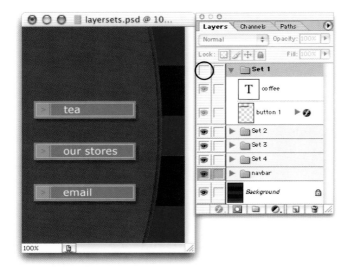

12. Turn off the **Visibility** (Eye) icon for **Set 1** in the **Layers** palette, and you'll see both the coffee button and its text disappear. Click again to make Set 1 visible. Layer sets are useful for changing the visibility of multiple layers at once.

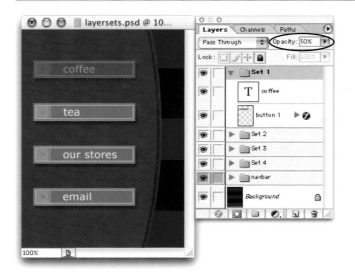

13. With **Set 1** selected, change the **Opacity** slider to **50%**. This will affect the opacity of both layers in Set 1. Change the **Opacity** back to **100%** once you've seen this.

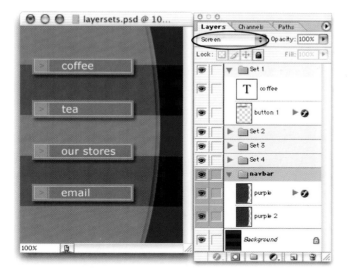

14. Select the **navbar** set and twirl down its arrow. Click the **Layer Blending Mode** button at the top of the **Layers** palette and choose **Screen**.

This changes how the whole layer set interacts with the layer below. (The Screen mode blends the navbar layer set and the Background layer, creating a lighter mix.) If you click on the purple *or* purple 2 *layer, you'll see that each has its own blending mode–Normal. Layers in a layer set blend together first, using their own blending modes. The result of that blend is then blended with the layers below the Layer Set, using the blending mode assigned to the Layer Set.*

Note: *The default blending mode for a layer set is pass through. This means that only the blending mode of the layers nested in the layer set has an effect.*

15. Close and save this file.

5. [PS] _____ Solid Color Layer

This exercise will show you how to quickly generate a **solid color layer** in Photoshop, which is useful for changing backgrounds on images. You can't create a solid color layer in ImageReady, but ImageReady will recognize a solid color layer in an image that was created in Photoshop.

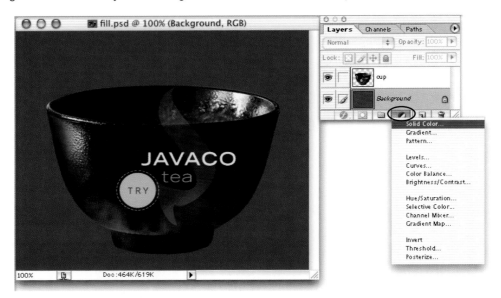

1. Open **fill.psd** from the **chap_05** folder, and select the **Background** layer. Click the black-and-white circle icon at the bottom of the **Layers** palette to display the **Create New Fill or Adjustment Layer** menu. Choose **Solid Color** from that menu. This will open the **Color Picker**.

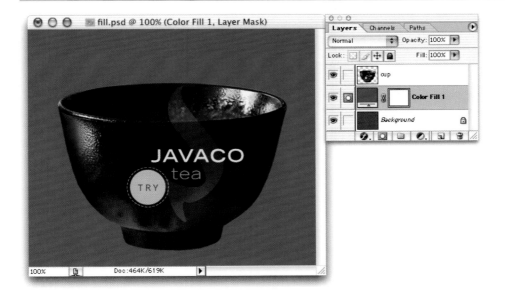

2. Select a color in the **Color Picker**, and click **OK**.

Notice that a new layer, Color Fill 1, that has two thumbnails and a link symbol associated with it, has been added to the Layers palette. The thumbnail on the left is a solid color fill. The white thumbnail on the right is a layer mask. You can see the solid color fill through the mask because the mask is set to white. The reason for using a solid color layer is that it gives you the flexibility to easily change a solid fill. The next step will show you how easy it is to change your mind about a color when using a solid color layer.

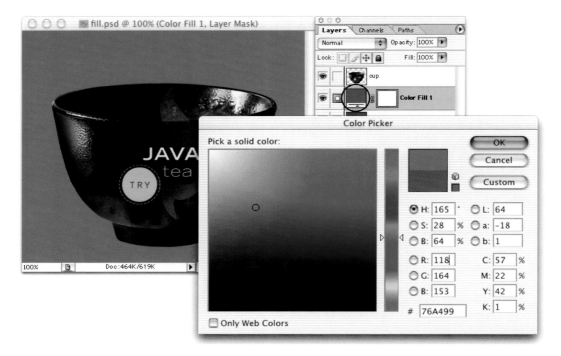

3. In the **Layers** palette, double-click on the thumbnail on the left side of the **solid color** layer. This will open the **Color Picker**. Choose a new color and notice the live preview of the color changes to the layer. Click **OK**.

4. Leave this image open for the next exercise.

6. [PS] _____ Gradient Layer

Next, you'll create a **gradient layer**. Gradient layers are one of several ways to make a gradient in Photoshop. The advantage of using a gradient layer to create a background is that this feature is quick to use and is very flexible if you ever want to change the colors or blend of the gradient. Like solid color layers, gradient layers cannot be created in ImageReady, but ImageReady will support gradient layers made in Photoshop.

1. In the **Layers** palette, select the **Color Fill 1** layer that you created in the last exercise. This ensures that the gradient layer you're about to make will appear above this layer in the stacking order.

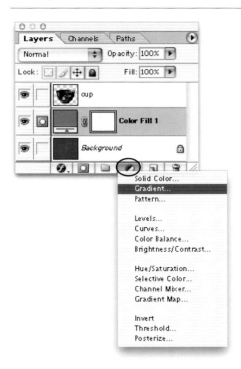

2. Click the black-and-white circle icon at the bottom of the **Layers** palette to create a new fill layer, and from the pop-up menu, select **Gradient**. This will open the **Gradient Fill** dialog box.

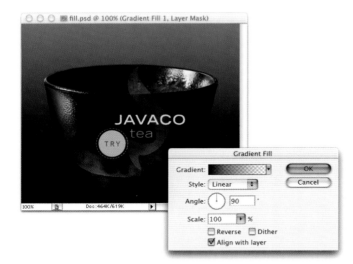

Your initial gradient may look different the one in this illustration, depending on the gradient you last used. The gradient you see here is black to transparent (which lets the color of the layer beneath the gradient show through). Notice the live preview in the document window.

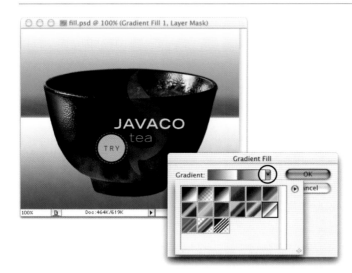

3. Click the **arrow** to the right of the **Gradient** field to open the default **Gradient** library. Click on some of the gradient presets in this library, and you'll see them update automatically in your image. Once you've chosen a gradient from this library, click back inside the **Gradient Fill** dialog box and your choice will be accepted.

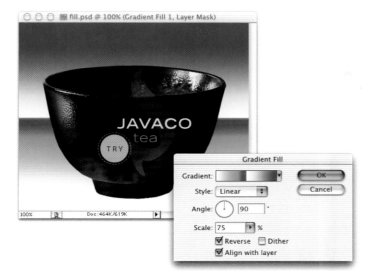

4. Change the **Style**, **Angle**, **Scale** options in the **Gradient Fill** dialog box to see different effects. (In this illustration, a checkmark was put in the Reverse field to flip the gradient.) Click **OK** once you've explored this dialog box.

What if you want to make your own custom gradient? That's possible too, as you'll learn from the following steps.

5. Double-click on the **gradient** thumbnail on the far left of the **Gradient Fill 1** layer to re-access the **Gradient Fill** dialog box.

If you look at the Layers palette, you'll see that like the solid color layer, the gradient layer also has two thumbnails: a gradient thumbnail and a layer mask thumbnail.

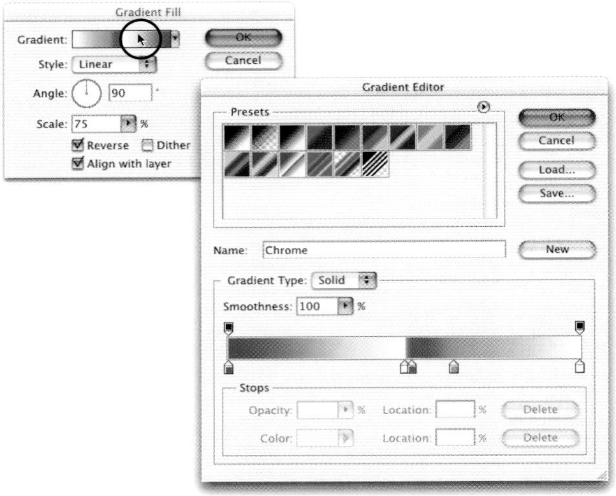

6. In the **Gradient Fill** dialog box, click inside the **Gradient** bar, as shown here, to reopen the **Gradient Editor**.

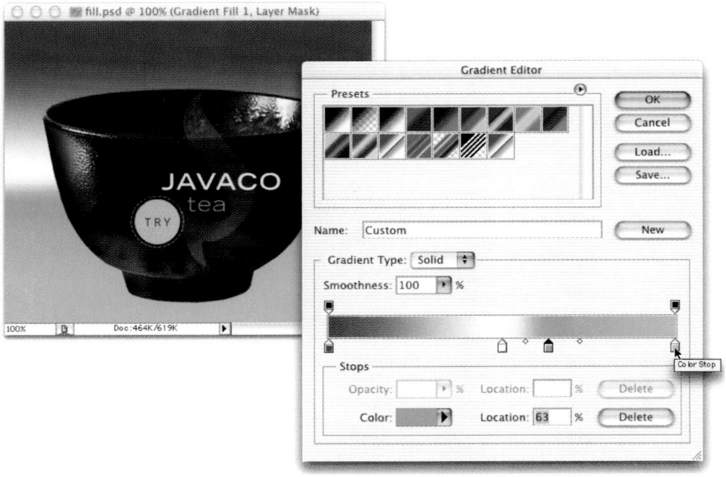

7. Experiment with changing and moving the colors on the gradient bar in the Gradient Editor.

The Color Stops under the gradient bar control the colors in the gradient. Try clicking on one of the Color Stops and moving your mouse into the image to sample a color from there for the Stop. Or double-click one of the Color Stops to open the Color Picker, and choose a color for the Stop from there. Omit a Color Stop by clicking and dragging it off the gradient bar. Add a Color Stop by clicking just beneath the gradient bar.

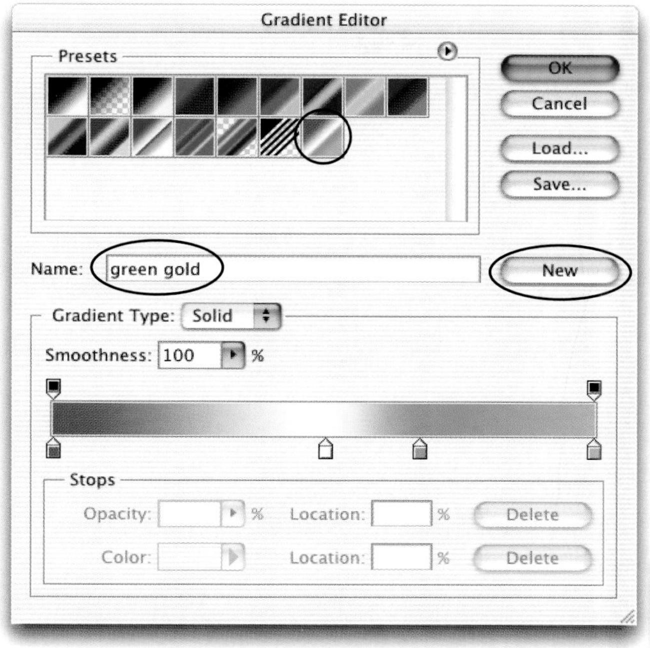

8. When you're satisfied with your custom gradient, click in the **Name** field, and type a meaningful name for the new gradient. Then click **New**. You'll see your new gradient in the **Presets** library, at the top of the Gradient Editor.

9. Click **OK** in the **Gradient Editor**, and click **OK** in the **Gradient Fill** dialog box.

10. Save the file and leave it open for the next exercise.

7. [PS] _____Pattern Layer

A **pattern layer** allows you to fill a layer with ... you guessed correctly, a pattern! This exercise introduces you to pattern layers. Later in Chapter 8, "_Background Images_," you'll learn more about patterns—how to make a seamless pattern tile for a Web page. A pattern layer is another kind of layer that is supported by but cannot be created in ImageReady.

1. In the **Layers** palette, select the **Gradient Fill 1** layer that you created in the last exercise. This ensures that the pattern layer you're about to create will appear above this layer in the stacking order.

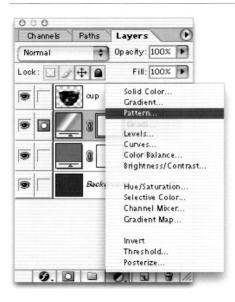

2. Click the **New Fill or Adjustment Layer** icon at the bottom of the **Layers** palette, and from the pop-up menu, choose **Pattern**. This will open the **Pattern Fill** dialog box.

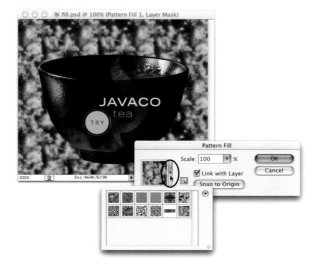

3. Click the **arrow** to the right of the **Pattern** thumbnail, which will access the **Pattern** library.

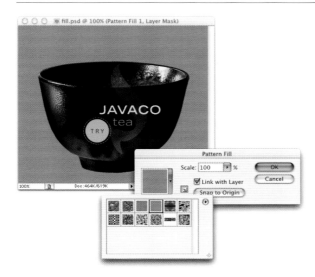

4. Click and try different patterns until you're ready to accept one by clicking **OK**.

Chances are, you'll be wondering right about now if you can create and add your own patterns. The answer is yes. First, create a pattern (you'll learn all about creating patterns in Chapter 8, "Background Images"). Next, select the pattern and choose Edit > Define Pattern. *Give the pattern a name and click* OK. *Your custom pattern will then show up in the* Pattern Fill *menu.*

NOTE | Pattern Features and When to Use Them

You may be wondering when to use a pattern layer, and when to use the other pattern features—the offset filter, which you'll learn about in Chapter 8, "*Background Images*," and the Pattern Maker, which is new to Photoshop 7. Here's a small chart to guide you.

Pattern Feature When to Use It	
Pattern layer	Use a pattern layer when you want to fill the entire background of a layered image with a pattern, as you learned to do in this exercise. You might use an image like this as a foreground image on a Web page. A pattern layer becomes part of the image, and can't be separated to be reused to create a repeating background image in HTML. You will learn all about background images in Chapter 8, "*Background Images*."
Pattern Maker	Use the Pattern Maker as one way to generate content for custom patterns you can insert into a pattern layer. This feature isn't covered in this book, but refer to the **Photoshop 7 User Guide** if you want to make custom patterns to use within Pattern Layers.
Offset filter	Use the offset filter when you're making small tiles that will repeat themselves over and over in the background of a Web page. The offset filter helps arrange a pattern so that a tile appears seamless when it repeats. This may sound confusing here, but you'll learn all the nuances of making this kind of patterned tile in Chapter 8, "*Background Images*."

5. You're finished learning about fill layers. Save and close the file.

8. [PS] _____Adjustment Layer

Adjustment layers allow you to make image adjustments that are nondestructive, preserving the original image. They are great for changing contrast, hue, or color balance levels of an image. You'll learn how to implement them in this exercise.

1. Open **colorize.psd** from the **chap_05** folder you transferred to your hard drive.

2. Select the **tea collage** layer, and click the **New Fill or Adjustment Layer** icon at the bottom of the **Layers** palette. Choose **Hue/Saturation** from the pop-up menu.

3. In the **Hue/Saturation** dialog box, put a checkmark in the **Colorize** box, and watch the image change. Experiment with the **Hue**, **Saturation**, and **Lightness** sliders to change the effect. When you're satisfied, click **OK**.

4. Notice the new **Hue/Saturation** layer that appeared in the **Layers** palette? You can re-access the Hue/Saturation settings at any point by double-clicking on the **layer** thumbnail on the left side of this layer.

5. Add a different **adjustment layer** to the **tea collage** layer. Try **Color Balance**, **Levels**, **Hue**, **Saturation**, **Posterize**, and any others that make you curious. After you've added an adjustment layer, you can always change your mind and modify it, or turn off its visibility to return to the original image. This is the great advantage of nondestructive editing!

6. Close the file and move on to the next exercise.

Adjustment layers are recognized by ImageReady, but they cannot be created there. You can go back and forth between the two applications, however, and the adjustment layers will not be disturbed or altered.

9. [PS] _____ Clipping Groups

You've probably seen type on the Web and elsewhere that contains a photographic image inside the letters. This technique can be achieved in Photoshop and ImageReady by using **clipping groups**. This technique consists of artwork on a layer that is used as a mask and content on another layer that goes into that mask. In this example, we're using type as the mask, but you can use other kinds of artwork for clipping groups, too.

1. Open **beans.psd** from your **chap_05** folder.

If you get a warning about updating type, click Update.

2. Move the **beans** layer above the **Javaco coffee** type layer in the **Layers** palette by clicking and dragging the beans layer to the top position. This will temporarily obscure the type layer in the image.

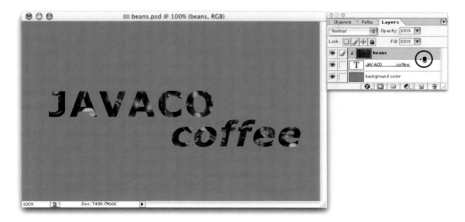

3. Hold down the **Option** (Mac) or **Alt** (Windows) key and move your cursor to the line that divides the **beans** and type layers. The cursor will change from a hand to the clipping groups icon. When your cursor is directly over the line, click, and the photograph will appear inside the type in the image.

When you create a clipping group by clicking on the line that divides the layers, an arrow will appear to the left of the layer thumbnail on the masked layer (the top-most layer), indicating that the clipping group is in effect.

4. Make sure that the **beans** layer is selected and that the **Move** tool from the Toolbox is active. Click on the screen, and notice that you can move the **beans** layer independently from the type. Position the **beans** layer where you like it.

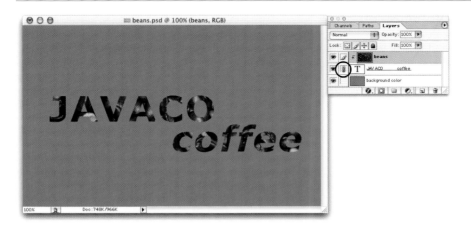

5. If you want to move the type and the photo together, select the **beans** layer and click on the **Link** region (circled above) in the type layer. Now if you use the **Move** tool to move the artwork, both items will move together.

check

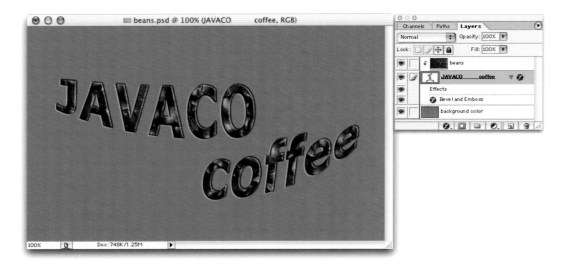

Because the type is editable, you can still change the font, the size, or the style even though the clipping group is in effect. This allows experimentation with numerous variations. Here the type layer has been warped, and has a bevel and emboss layer style added to it. You'll learn about these special effects in later chapters.

This feature works identically in ImageReady. In the next exercise, you'll learn how to get the same effect another way in ImageReady—by using the knockout layer option.

MOVIE | clippinggroup.mov

To learn more about setting up clipping groups, check out **clippinggroup.mov** from the **movies** folder you copied from the **H•O•T CD-ROM**.

IO. [IR]_____Layer Knockout Option

The layer **knockout option** is another way to achieve a look similar to the one you had with a layer clipping group in the last exercise. The knockout feature uses artwork on a top layer to mask out artwork on underlying layers, allowing you to see through to a lower layer. You'll work in ImageReady in this exercise, because it's easier to do a knockout in ImageReady than in Photoshop. ImageReady's knockout settings are in the easily accessible Layer Options palette, but similar controls in Photoshop are buried in the Layer Styles palette. You'll be pleased by how simple it is to produce a knockout effect.

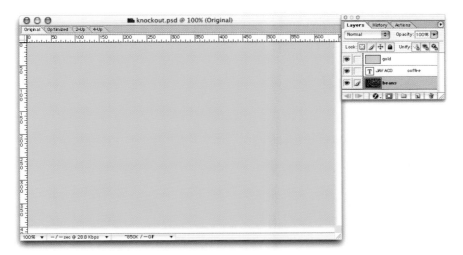

1. Launch ImageReady if it's not already open. Open **knockout.psd** from the **chap_05** folder on your hard drive.

2. In the **Layers** palette, select the **beans** layer on the bottom of the stack. Choose **Layer > New > Background from Layer**.

This converts the beans layer into a special background layer that stops the knockout. Without an official background layer, the knockout feature will drill down through the bottom-most layer to reveal the transparency checkerboard.

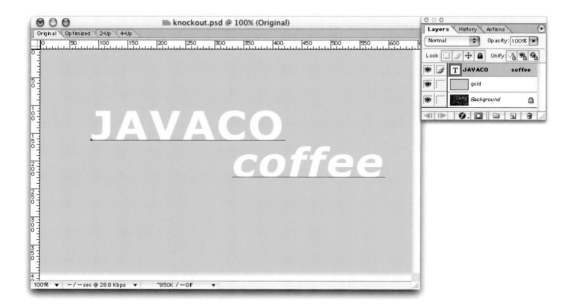

3. Click on the type layer in the **Layers** palette, and drag it to the top of the layer stack.

The layer you're using to knock out underlying layers always should be at the top of the stack.

4. Choose **Window > Layer Options/Style** to open the **Layer Options** palette if it's not visible on your screen. Click the **double-pointed arrow** on the **Layer Options** tab to expand the Layer Options palette if you don't see all of the options in this illustration.

The double-pointed arrow cycles through several levels of expansion. If you shrink the palette by mistake, just keep clicking until all of these options appear.

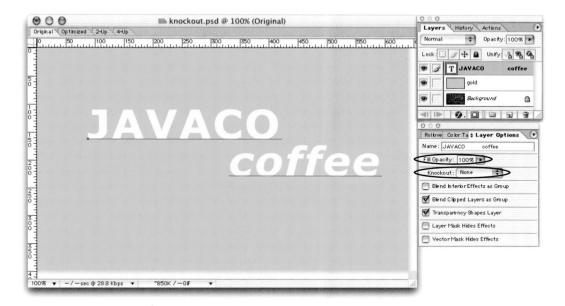

5. With the type layer selected in the **Layers** palette, click the **Knockout** button in the **Layer Options** palette and choose **Deep**, and drag the **Fill Opacity** slider to **0%**.

This knocks out the gold layer in the middle of the stack wherever there is type on the top layer. Now you can see through to the beans image on the background layer. That's all there is to it!

6. Save and close this file.

You've completed another long chapter. Now that you've seen how powerful layers are, put them to work to boost your creativity and efficiency as you make Web graphics in Photoshop and ImageReady. In the next chapter, you'll learn how to use another important feature—the Type tool and its options.

6.

Type

Options Bar Settings	Character Palette
Paragraph Text	Spell Checking	Finding and Replacing Text
Warp Text	Rasterizing Text	Transforming Text

chap_06

Photoshop 7/ImageReady
H•O•T CD-ROM

Text on the Web can be a frustrating subject for professional designers, because HTML affords very little typographic control. Many Web designers avoid the limitations of HTML type by embedding text in GIF or JPEG files instead of relying on code. Photoshop and ImageReady offer unsurpassed controls for editing and formatting text, making it easy to create typographic artwork for the Web. There were some major changes to type in the last version of Photoshop and ImageReady, including the introduction of vector-based type you can add directly to an image, and paragraph type you can format as a block. Photoshop 7 and ImageReady 7 add a few new type features—a Spell Checker, an additional anti-aliasing mode, and some cosmetic changes to the Type tool and the Character palette. But for the most part, type features haven't changed much in this release.

This chapter covers many aspects of type in Photoshop and ImageReady, including anti-aliasing, coloring, changing fonts, warping, and using paragraph text. The techniques you'll learn in this chapter will add great visual appeal to the sites you design.

Comparing Type in Photoshop and ImageReady

Photoshop and ImageReady handle type pretty much the same way. In both programs, type is entered directly into the document window and is vector-based, which means that it's defined mathematically rather than by pixels. As a result, type layers remain editable, and you can scale, rotate, skew, or warp text without degrading its appearance.

The only noticeable difference in the way type works in Photoshop and ImageReady is that a tiny blue line, which is the baseline on which the type rests, appears under text in ImageReady. If you are an Adobe Illustrator user this might be a familiar sight. If you find the blue line distracting, make it disappear by pressing the keyboard shortcut **Cmd+H** (Mac) **Ctrl+H** (Windows).

In ImageReady, a tiny blue line appears under editable text.

To make the blue line disappear, click off the type layer in the Layers palette, choose View > Show > Text Baseline, *or use the keyboard shortcut* Cmd+H *(Mac) or* Ctrl+H *(Windows).*

I. [PS] Type Options Bar

The next few exercises show you how to enter and edit type in Photoshop, using the Type tool, the Options bar, and the Character and Paragraph palettes. ImageReady has an identical type Options bar and Character and Paragraph palettes.

1. Copy the **chap_06** folder from the **H•O•T CD-ROM** to your hard drive if you have not already done so. In Photoshop, open **coupon.psd** from the **chap_06** folder on your hard drive. If you get a warning that Type layers need to be updated, click Update.

In the Layers palette, you'll see that this image has one layer that has a T icon, which means it is an editable type layer of vector-based text. There is another layer, labeled javaco, that seems to contain text, but has no T icon. This is a layer that started out as a type layer, but was rasterized, so that its text is now just pixel-based artwork. You'll learn how and why you would rasterize type later in this chapter.

Note: *The type in coupon.psd was created in the Verdana font, which is a font that is easy to read on the Web and ships with current Windows and Mac operating systems. If you do not have Verdana installed in your computer, other fonts will be substituted in Photoshop. You can download Verdana for free from the Microsoft Web site (http://www.microsoft.com/ typography/fontpack/default.htm) if you'd like, or work with whatever fonts are automatically substituted for you.*

2. Select the **green** layer, and click the **Lock All** button at the top of the **Layers** palette. This will make it impossible to inadvertently move or edit that underlying layer, so that you can focus on editing the type.

Lock All is a great technique to use when you don't want to accidentally move or edit a layer. When you click the Lock All button, you'll see a dark gray lock icon in the green *layer, and all of the layer lock buttons will be grayed out, meaning that they all are activated. If you want to review what each of the locks does, turn back to Chapter 3, "Color." Locks are activated by buttons in Photoshop 7, rather than by check boxes as they were in the previous release. Notice that the* Background *layer already has a light gray lock icon, meaning that it is partially locked. One of the special characteristics of a real Background layer is that it can't be moved.*

3. Click on the **Horizontal Type** tool in the Toolbox. Notice that the **Options** bar changes to display settings for type.

A minor change in Photoshop 7 is that horizontal type, vertical type, horizontal type mask, and vertical type mask are no longer options on the Options bar. They are now separate Type tools, all accessed from a fly-out menu in the Toolbox.

4. In the **Options** bar, click the arrows next to the **Font** field, the **Font Style** field, and the **Font Size** field to set the font for the text you're about to type. (We chose Verdana, bold, and 30 pt. for this illustration.)

5. Click inside the document window. Be careful not to click too close to the text at the top of the image to avoid typing into the same layer as the text that's already there. Type **1 free coffee!** Select the **Move** tool in the toolbox, and click and drag to move the new text to the middle of the image.

In the Layers palette, Photoshop automatically made a separate layer for the new text. That's how easy it is to create type in Photoshop 7!

6. With the **1 free coffee!** layer selected in the **Layers** palette, select the **Type** tool, and click in the **Type Color** field in the **Options** bar. This will open the **Color Picker**. Choose a medium blue, and click **OK**.

This changes the color of all of the text on the layer. You can also change the color of selected text on a type layer, as you'll do in the next steps.

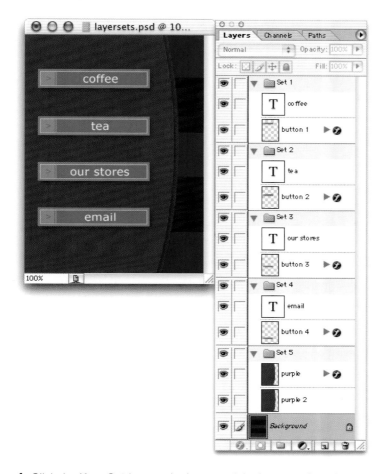

4. Click the **New Set** icon at the bottom of the Layers palette four more times to create a total of five sets. Move the **tea** and **button 2** layers into **Set 2**, the **our stores** and **button 3** layers into **Set 3**, the **email** and **button 4** layers into **Set 4**, and the **purple** and **purple 2** layers into **Set 5**.

Note: Another special property of a Background layer is that it cannot be moved into a layer set. Try it and you'll see.

7. With the Type tool still selected, click and drag your cursor across the phrase **come visit us and receive**, which is just part of the text on the other type layer in this image. Click in the **Type Color** field on the **Options** bar to access the **Color Picker**. Choose a blue, and click **OK**.

This process colors only the selected text in this type layer. Notice that the color change is hard to see accurately while the type is still selected? That's because the highlight on the type selection area causes the type color to reverse. There's a good trick to fix this problem. After you've selected type, press the shortcut key–Cmd+H (Mac) or Ctrl+H (Windows) to hide the highlighting. This command key is easy to remember because H stands for "hide."

8. Using the **Cmd+H** (Mac) or **Ctrl+H** (Windows) shortcut to hide the highlighting on the selected text, click in the **Type Color** field on the **Options** bar again, and change the type to green. This time, you can see what you're picking! Click **OK**.

9. Click the arrow next to the **Font Size** field to select **14 pt** from the pop-up menu in the **Options** bar.

This changes the size of only the selected text on this type layer. The text is still selected, even though you can't see it because the highlighting is gone.

---

10. Click the big checkmark on the right side of the **Options** bar to accept the changes you made to the selected type on this type layer.

You have to accept or cancel type edits in order to move out of type edit mode so that you can perform other operations in Photoshop. This is pretty painless because there are lots of ways to accept a type edit other than clicking on the big checkmark. You can accomplish the same thing by clicking on another layer in the Layers palette, selecting another tool in the Toolbox, clicking in another palette, choosing a menu command, or pressing Enter on a numeric keypad. If you want to cancel a type edit, click the circular icon next to the checkmark in the Options bar.

---

11. Click anywhere in the three lines of type at the top of your screen to make an edit to the entire type layer. Click on the pop-up menu next to the **Anti-Alias** button (the button marked **aa**) on the **Options** bar, and choose from **Crisp, Strong, Smooth,** or **Sharp**.

Sharp is a new anti-alias option in Photoshop 7. It's most useful for really small text that is likely to run together and be hard to read onscreen in the other anti-aliasing modes. None aliases the type. Use Sharp or None If you ever use type that is smaller than 14 points in artwork for the Web (which will probably be rare), and experiment with Crisp, Strong, and Smooth for larger type.

12. Save the image and leave it open for the next exercise.

NOTE | What Is Anti-Aliasing, Anyway?

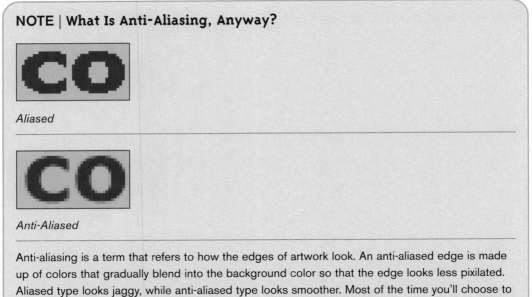

Aliased

Anti-Aliased

Anti-aliasing is a term that refers to how the edges of artwork look. An anti-aliased edge is made up of colors that gradually blend into the background color so that the edge looks less pixilated. Aliased type looks jaggy, while anti-aliased type looks smoother. Most of the time you'll choose to anti-alias the type in your Web graphics, though sometimes on very small point sizes aliased type is more readable.

2. [PS] _____Using the Character Palette

So far, you've learned to edit type with the Options bar at the top of your screen. There are two other type-related palettes: **Character** and **Paragraph**. These palettes have some of the same features as the Options bar, and some features not found in the Options bar. You'll work with some of the exclusive Character palette settings in this exercise. The Paragraph settings will be covered in a later exercise.

1. With the Type tool selected, click the **Palettes** button on the Options bar to display the Character palette and Paragraph palette.

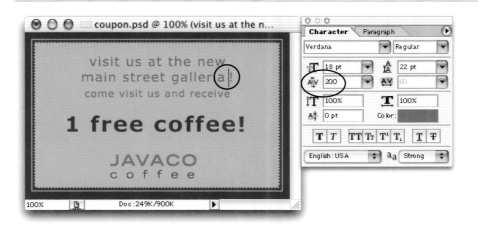

2. Position your cursor between the letter **a** and the exclamation point in the word **galleria!** in the second line of type, and click so the insertion bar appears. Hold down the **Option** (Mac) or **Alt** (Windows) key and press the right or left arrow on your keyboard. Notice how the space between the two characters expands and contracts? That's known as kerning. Alternatively, you can adjust the kerning in the **Character** palette. In the field for **kerning**, change the setting to **200** so your document and palette match the example above.

3. Highlight the third line of type in the image, **come visit us and receive**, and enter **160** in the **Tracking** field in the **Character** palette.

Notice how all the letters in the highlighted text expand. Kerning affects the space between two characters, while tracking affects the space between all selected characters.

4. With the same line of type still highlighted, enter **36** in the **Leading** field. When you're done, click the big **checkmark** in the Options bar to accept the edits to the highlighted type.

Notice that the selected line of type moves so there is more vertical space between it and the preceding line. Leading affects the space between lines of type. The term refers to the olden days of typesetting, when typesetters would use actual pieces of lead to physically separate each line of type. Do you wonder whether some old typesetters are turning in their graves watching this process?

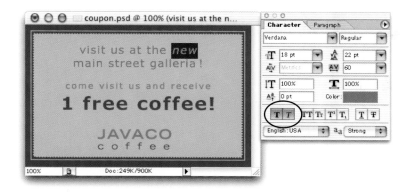

5. Highlight the word **new** in the first line of text in the image. In the **Character** palette, click the **Faux Bold** and **Faux Italic** buttons.

The faux italic and faux bold features have moved to this more visible location in Photoshop 7 and are now controlled by buttons. They allow you to apply italic and bold effects to fonts that don't otherwise include those styles. (Even though Verdana does have bold and italic font styles, we wanted to take this opportunity to show you where these features are now located.)

6. Select the **1 free coffee!** layer in the **Layers** palette.

Selecting this layer in the Layers palette has the same effect as clicking the checkmark in the Options bar. It accepts your type edits on the other type layer.

7. Highlight the word **free** in the image, and click the **All Caps** button in the **Character** palette.

This converts the selected word to uppercase letters. Experiment with the other buttons and settings in the Character palette. For example, try out the baseline adjustment that allows you to move one or more characters above or below the baseline of a line of type to create a superscript or a footnote. When you're done, click the big checkmark or the cancel icon in the Options bar.

NOTE | Simulating HTML Type with System Layout

visit us at the *new*
main street galleria!

visit us at the *new*
main street galleria!

Default 12 pt. type   *12 pt. type with System Layout on, simulating HTML type*

You'll find more type settings by clicking the arrow at the top right of the Character palette to access an options menu. For example, the **System Layout** feature, which is new to Photoshop 7, is useful when you're mocking up a Web page in which you plan to include some HTML type. Click System Layout in this menu to modify a layer of type so that it looks more like HTML type. Photoshop accomplishes this by aliasing the type and turning off the Fractional Widths option so that each character appears like it will on the Web.

8. Save and close the file.

The Character Palette

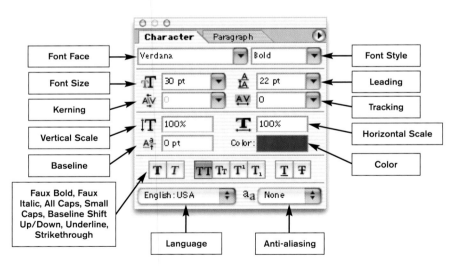

The Character palette contains many settings. This chart briefly describes each feature.

Character Settings	
Feature	**Function**
Font Face	Applies a font
Font Size	Adjusts the size of type
Kerning	Adjusts the spacing between two individual characters
Vertical Scale	Distorts type by scaling it on a vertical axis
Font Style	Applies italic or bold styles
Faux Bold, Faux Italic	Applies styles to fonts that don't come with them
All Caps	Applies uppercase
Small Caps	Applies small cap case
Underline	Underlines characters
Strikethrough	Puts a horizontal line through characters
Baseline	Adjusts the baseline of type to create subscript or superscript
Leading	Adjusts the amount of space between lines of type
Tracking	Adjusts the amount of space equally between selected characters in a word or paragraph.
Horizontal Scale	Distorts type by scaling it on a horizontal axis
Color	Changes the color of a selected character, word, or line of type
Anti-aliasing	Blends and smoothes edges
Language	Changes the dictionary referenced by the spell checker.

3. [PS] _____Using Paragraph Type

The last release of Photoshop introduced a new kind of type called **Paragraph** type, which you'll also find in Photoshop 7. Paragraph type is different from regular type because it's confined in a bounding box, which allows you to rotate, scale, or skew a whole paragraph of text. You can also reshape a paragraph of text, controlling how it flows, aligns, justifies, and indents inside its bounding box. The Paragraph palette contains settings that are fantastic for controlling the formatting of Paragraph text. You'll get to try these features firsthand in this exercise.

1. Open **paragraph.psd** from the **chap_06** folder that you copied to your hard drive from the **H·O·T CD-ROM**.

This image contains regular type, just like the kind you've been using until now. It was typed directly into the document window, and Enter or Return was pressed at the end of every line to create a hard return. If you were to expand or contract a line using the Character options you just explored, the lines would stay separated as they are, rather than rewrapping in the document window. As you'll see in the following steps, Paragraph type behaves differently.

2. Select the type layer in the **Layers** palette. Then choose **Layer > Type > Convert to Paragraph Text**.

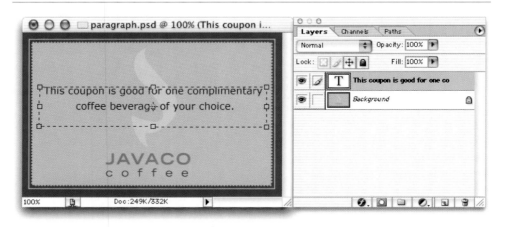

3. Using the **Type** tool from the Toolbox, click on the text. You'll see a bounding box around the text.

This is how you convert regular text to Paragraph text. You can also create Paragraph text from scratch by selecting the type tool, clicking and dragging inside the document to make a bounding box, and typing inside the box, as you'll do later in this exercise.

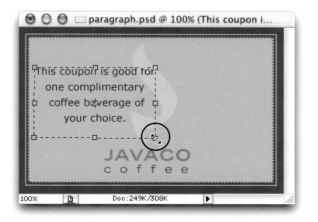

4. Move your mouse over one of the corners of the bounding box, and you'll see an arrow appear. Click and drag with this arrow to reshape the bounding box. Notice that the text reflows to fit the new shape of the bounding box!

If you see a cross in the bottom-right corner of the bounding box, it means that the box is too small to contain all of the text. Click an anchor point and drag some more to expand the box and reveal the missing text.

5. Move your mouse outside one of the corners of the bounding box, and you'll see the cursor change to a rotate symbol. Click and drag to rotate the text in the bounding box.

6. Move the mouse over one of the corners of the bounding box, and **Shift+Cmd+drag** (Mac) or **Shift+Ctrl+drag** (Windows) to scale the type proportionately along with the bounding box.

You can also move the entire bounding box and its contents by holding down the Cmd key (Mac) or the Ctrl key (Windows), clicking inside the bounding box, and dragging.

7. Once you're happy with these changes, click the big **checkmark** on the right side of the **Options** bar to accept your edits.

Now that you've reshaped and transformed this Paragraph text, you'll practice formatting it using options in the Paragraph palette.

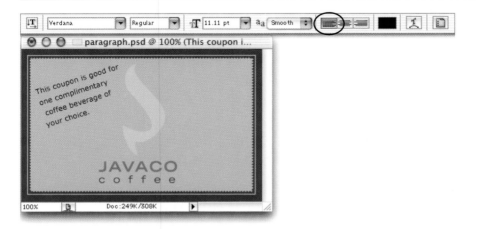

8. With the **Type** tool still selected in the Toolbox, and the type layer selected in the **Layers** palette, click the **left align** icon on the **Options** bar to align the type to the left edge of its bounding box, which is invisible at this point.

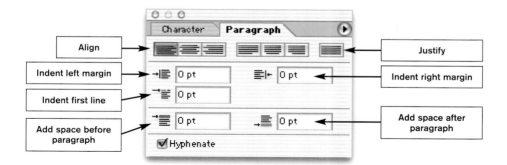

9. Click the **Palette** button on the **Options** bar, and then click on the **Paragraph** tab to bring the Paragraph palette forward and make it active.

The Paragraph palette contains the same text alignment buttons as the Options bar, as well as spacing and justification settings. Try some of these settings, and watch the paragraph type move around.

In the next step you'll make another paragraph of this special kind of text from scratch.

10. With the **Type** tool selected from the Toolbox, click and drag in the image to create a new bounding box. Start typing **Try our espresso, cafe au lait, FrostBlend or specialty drinks**, and your type will appear and become constrained by the shape of the box. Don't like the shape of the box? Move your mouse over one of the corners to drag it out to a new shape and the type will rewrap to fit the new shape. Experiment with rotating and aligning the text as you learned to do in this exercise. We're sure you'll agree that these features are pretty cool.

11. Save and close this file.

Note: You can create and edit Paragraph text in ImageReady too. If you don't see the bounding box in ImageReady, choose View > Show > Text Bounds.

4. [PS] _____ Spell Checking and Replacing Text

Photoshop 7 adds more word-processing functions with the addition of a spell checker and a find and replace text feature for type layers. Check them out in this exercise. ImageReady does not have either of these new features.

1. Open **spell.psd** from the **chap_06** files you transferred to your hard drive from the **H•O•T CD-ROM**.

2. Choose **Edit > Check spelling**.

This opens a Check Spelling *window. By default, Photoshop will check spelling on all type layers. If you want to limit spell checking to the selected layer, uncheck the* Check All Layers *box at the bottom of this window.*

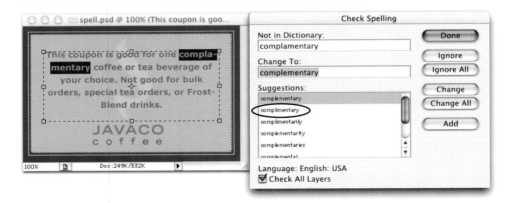

3. The spell checker identifies **complamentary** as a misspelled word, offers a preferred spelling, and suggests some other spellings. Select the word **complimentary** in the **Suggestions** area of the **Check Spelling** dialog box, and click **Change**.

This automatically corrects this word in the image using the spelling in the Change To *field.*

4. The spell checker stops next on the proper name **FrostBlend**, because it is not in the English: USA dictionary that ships with Photoshop. Click **Ignore** to leave this word spelled as it is in the image.

Alternatively, you can click Add to add this word to the active dictionary so that it won't be identified as misspelled again. Photoshop ships with dictionaries in various languages. You can change the spell checker's active dictionary by clicking the Language button at the bottom of the Character palette and choosing from a menu of languages.

5. Click **OK** when you see a message that spell checking is complete, to close the **Check Spelling** window.

Next, you'll try the new feature that finds and replaces text in type layers.

---

6. Choose **Edit > Find and Replace Text**.

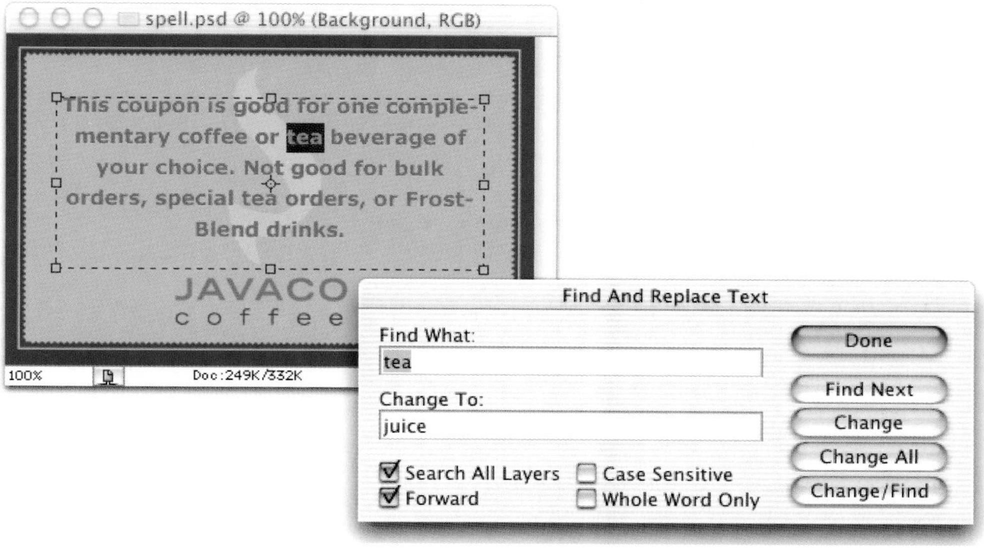

---

7. In the **Find and Replace Text** window, enter **tea** in the **Find What:** field, and **juice** in the **Change To:** field.

---

8. Click **Find Next** to identify the first instance of the word **tea** in the image. Click **Change** to change that instance of **tea** to **juice**.

---

9. Click **Done** to close the **Find and Replace Text** window.

---

10. Save and close the image.

5. [PS] _____ **Warped Text**

You can also create **warped text** in Photoshop. This is an effect that we doubt you'll use often, but it's fun to learn, so you can take it for a test spin in this exercise.

1. Open the file **banner.psd** from the **chap_06** folder that you copied from the **H•O•T CD-ROM** to your hard drive.

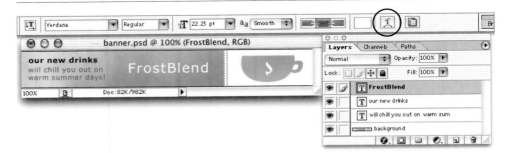

2. Select the **Type** tool in the Toolbox, and select the **FrostBlend** layer in the **Layers** palette.

3. Click the **Warp Text** button on the **Options** bar.

The Warp Text *dialog box will open. This window contains all of the options for warping the selected text.*

4. Click on the **Style** menu in the **Warp Text** dialog box, and choose **Flag**. Move the sliders and watch the type distort. When you like what you see, click **OK**.

Warped type can be edited and even undone after the file is saved. Try changing what the type says and notice how it keeps the warp effect. Try undoing the warp effect by reopening the Warp Text *dialog box and choosing* None *from the* Style *menu. This is an interesting novelty effect, but one that could be easily abused. Have fun with this tool, but don't mistake its gimmick for a concept or high art.*

5. When you're finished experimenting with Warp Text settings, save and close the file.

6. [IR] _____Rasterizing Type

It's wonderful that type is editable in ImageReady and Photoshop, because you can change your mind at any time. There are certain Filter effects, however, that cannot be applied to editable type. As well, there might be times when you want to share a Photoshop file with another person who doesn't own the font you've chosen to use. Or you might want to distort text or paint it, which you can't do to editable type. That's when you'll need to rasterize a type layer. Rasterizing converts editable type to an image of the type, so that it's no different from regular artwork. This makes it possible to distribute files that use specialty fonts to others, to use a plug-in filter on a layer of text, and to treat text like any artwork.

1. Make sure you're working in ImageReady, rather than Photoshop for this exercise. Open **clickme.psd** from the **chap_06** folder that you copied from the **H•O•T CD-ROM** to your hard drive.

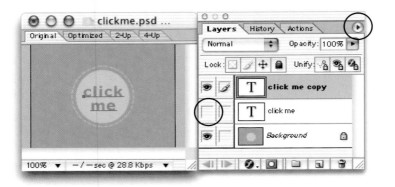

2. Select the **click me** type layer in the **Layers** palette. Click the **arrow** at the upper-right corner of the Layers palette, and choose **Duplicate Layer**. Click the **Eye** icon to the left of the **click me** layer to turn off the visibility of that layer, and make sure the **click me** copy layer is selected.

It's wise to make a copy of any type layer you're going to rasterize, because once a type layer is rasterized it can no longer be edited. This way you'll have an editable type layer to go back to if you have to make any changes.

3. Choose **Filter > Blur > Gaussian Blur**.

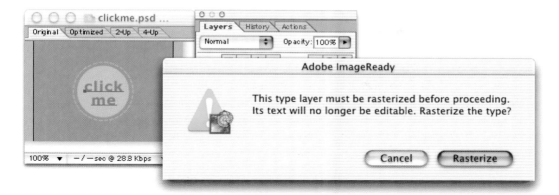

4. A dialog box will appear with a warning that the type must be rasterized before the Filter effect can be applied. Click **Rasterize** (Mac) or **Yes** (Windows) to render the layer as fixed pixels instead of editable type.

Choosing to render a type layer converts the type from editable text to non-editable text. It freezes the type into pixels, so that it is no longer editable as type but is now fully editable as an image. This enables the features that are disabled when the type is editable. Once type is rasterized, you can do things like apply filters, paint inside the type with the Paintbrush tool, or distort the shape of type (as you'll do in the next exercise).

NOTE | Rasterizing Type Manually

When you're applying a filter to a type layer, Photoshop/ImageReady will rasterize the type for you, as you've seen in this exercise. However, if you're rasterizing type for another reason, like sharing the file with a user who doesn't have a particular font, you'll have to rasterize type manually. To do that, select the type layer in the **Layers** palette, and choose **Layer > Rasterize > Type**.

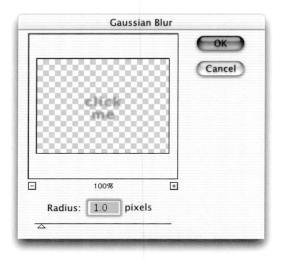

5. In the **Gaussian Blur** dialog box, change the slider to adjust the amount of blur, and click **OK** when you're happy with the preview.

6. Choose **File > Save As** and name the file **clickme2.psd**. Close the file, and leave ImageReady open for the next exercise.

Note: *This exercise would work identically in Photoshop. Saving the file as* clickme2.psd *saves a copy with your changes and leaves the original* clickme.psd *untouched, so you can try this exercise in Photoshop if you want to.*

7. [IR]_____Transforming Type

One of the most common things that you'll want to do with type is to change its size, rotate it, or skew or distort it. You learned how to change type size using the Options bar, how to rotate and transform Paragraph text, and how to distort using the Warp Text feature. There are some alternate ways to achieve some of these same functions using **Transform** commands.

1. In ImageReady, open the file **sale.psd** from the **chap_06** folder that you transferred to your hard drive from the **H·O·T CD-ROM**.

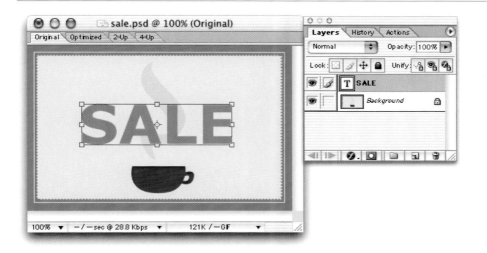

2. Click on the **SALE** type layer. Then press **Cmd+T** (Mac) or **Ctrl+T** (Windows). This is the keyboard shortcut for using the **Free Transform** feature, which allows you to scale or rotate. A bounding box will appear around the text in the image.

What is a Free Transform, you might wonder? It means that you can scale or rotate artwork by any value (as in freedom of movement).

3. Click on one of the anchor points with your mouse and drag to transform your text in the direction that you want. Click the **checkmark** icon on the **Options** bar when you're finished.

The following chart describes your options when you manipulate objects using the Free Transform tool and your mouse.

Using Free Transform with Your Mouse	
Feature	**Function**
Stretch Vertically	Click top or bottom anchor point with your mouse, and drag
Stretch Horizontally	Click a side anchor point with your mouse and drag
Scale Uniformly	Hold **Shift** key down, click a corner point, and drag with your mouse
Rotate	Move your mouse outside one of the corners of your object. When the cursor turns into a rotate symbol, click and rotate the selection into place.

Don't be afraid to scale the type larger. Editable type in ImageReady and Photoshop is made of vectors, meaning that it is based on mathematical instruction rather than fixed pixels. Unless you've rasterized your type, if you scale it up in size its edges will still be crisp and beautiful. You can also transform rasterized artwork using the Free Transform feature, but your images will tend to get fuzzy if they are scaled larger.

4. You can also transform objects using the **Options** bar. Press **Cmd+T** (Mac) or **Ctrl+T** (Windows) to display transform settings in the Options bar. Enter values into any of the fields on the **Transform Options** bar, as shown in the illustration above. When you're satisfied with your transformations, press **Return** or **Enter**, or click the **checkmark** icon on the **Options** bar.

5. If you want to add distortion or perspective, you must first rasterize the type, because these effects are not available for editable type. Choose **Layer > Rasterize > Type**. Then choose **Edit > Transform > Distort** or **Edit > Transform Perspective**. Click and drag on the anchor points to achieve the Perspective or Distort transformations. Once you're satisfied with the result, click the **checkmark** on the **Options** bar, or press **Return** or **Enter** on your keyboard.

6. Save and close the file.

Congrats, you've completed another chapter and got another notch on your Photoshop belt!

7.
Shapes and
Layer Styles

| Bitmapped versus Vector |

| Shapes, Shape Tools, and Shape Layers |

| Work with Custom Layer Styles | Create Layer Styles |

| Save Custom Layer Styles | Apply Styles |

chap_07
———————————————
Photoshop 7/ImageReady
H•O•T CD-ROM

Making button art is one of the most common tasks in a Web graphics workflow. Several features introduced in the last release of Photoshop (shape tools, shape layers, and layer styles) make it easier than ever to create button art with unique shapes and special effects.

Photoshop's shape tools create graphics that are vector-based, rather than pixel-based. This means that you can use the shape tools to make button shapes that have crisp edges, and that remain scalable and editable in a layered Photoshop file. Drawing with a shape tool creates a special kind of layer called a shape layer. In this chapter, you'll get a chance to use shape tools and shape layers to create a navigation bar of buttons for a Web page. Layer styles offer special effects that will make your buttons unique. A layer style can be a simple effect, like a drop shadow or bevel, or it can be a mix-and-match combination of layer-based features. You'll find layer styles easy to implement and fun to explore when you try them later in this chapter.

Bitmapped Images and Vector Graphics

This chapter introduces you to shapes, shape tools, and shape layers, which are all vector-based. Before you get to the exercises in which you'll use these features, take a minute to read this explanation of what "vector" and "bitmapped" mean.

For a long time, Photoshop was known exclusively as an editor of bitmapped images. What you may not know is that Photoshop also supports vector-based objects in the form of shapes, paths, and type. Bitmapped images are created pixel by pixel, with each pixel assigned a specific color and location on the screen. Vector objects, on the other hand, are created as mathematical instructions. For example, a bitmapped circle is composed of a collection of pixels in a circular arrangement on an invisible grid. A vector circle consists of a number of mathematical instructions, like "radius=100." You might have worked with some vector drawing programs, such as Illustrator, CorelDraw, FreeHand, or Flash.

Photoshop's documentation draws a distinction between "painting" and "drawing." In this context, painting means using pixels to create a bitmapped image (sometimes called a rasterized image), and drawing means using mathematical instructions to create a vector graphic (sometimes called an object-oriented graphic). For example, Photoshop's Brush tool paints with pixels; its shape tools draw with vector objects.

All this behind-the-scenes explanation helps you understand the theoretical differences between the terms "bitmapped" and "vector," but in real terms, how and when should you use a bitmapped image versus a vector graphic? Here's a chart to help you with these practical questions.

Bitmapped Versus Vector		
	Bitmapped Images	**Vector Graphics**
When to use	Bitmapped images are best for continuous tone content, such as photographs, glows, soft edges, and blurs.	Vector graphics are best for graphic content, such as shapes, type, and objects that require sharp edges.
How to create	Create a bitmapped image by using Photoshop's painting tools or fill commands.	Make vector graphics with the shape tools, the pen tools, or the Type tool.
How to edit	Bitmapped images are edited by modifying individual pixels.	Vector graphics are edited by manipulating points and handles around the object.

About Shape Tools

The shape tools were introduced in Photoshop 6, and haven't changed much in Photoshop 7, except for the addition of more prebuilt custom shapes and a few changes to the Options bar, which you'll see as you go through these exercises. Here's a chart that describes what each of the shape tools does:

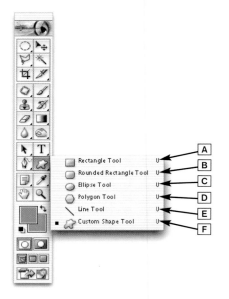

Shape Tool Functionality	
Tool Name	**Functionality**
A. Rectangle tool	Draws squares and rectangles.
B. Rounded Rectangle tool	Draws squares and rectangles with rounded corners. The radius of the rounded corner can be controlled via the Options bar.
C. Ellipse tool	Draws ellipses and circles.
D. Polygon tool	Draws multi-sided shapes, including stars. The number of sides can be set on the Options bar when this tool is active.
E. Line tool	Draws straight lines and arrows.
F. Custom Shape tool	Draws shapes that are stored in a library, accessed via the Options bar. You can use any of the prebuilt shapes that come with Photoshop 7 or create your own custom shapes and store them in the custom shape library.

About Shapes

Shapes you create with Photoshop's shape tools are object-oriented. Therefore, you can select, edit, and move them separately from one another even if they are on the same layer. A shape is defined by a smooth outline called a path, which you can modify after it's been drawn. A shape also has attributes, like fill color and fill style, that can be changed at any time. Unlike bitmapped graphics, shapes are resolution-independent, so that they can be resized without degrading the image. However, when you save an image as a GIF or JPEG for the Web, shapes are rasterized and lose all of these vector qualities.

About Shape Layers

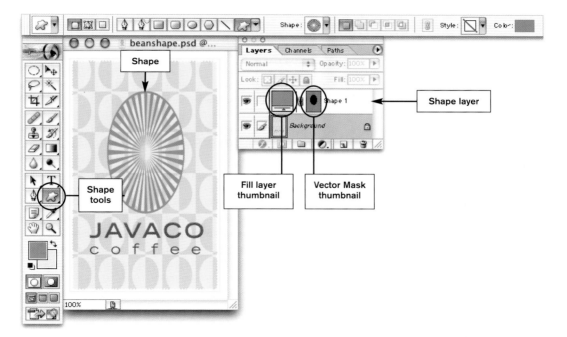

A shape layer is created automatically when you use any of the shape tools. This special kind of layer combines a fill layer (which you learned about in Chapter 5, "*Layers*"), with a vector mask that contains an outline of the shape. A vector mask is a black and white image that's linked to a layer and hides or reveals the contents of that layer. In a shape layer, the vector mask is represented by a thumbnail that is stored to the right of the fill layer thumbnail. The fill layer and vector mask work in tandem to produce a shape layer.

I. [PS] _____Shape Tools and Shape Layers

You've read all about shapes, shape tools, and shape layers; now it's time to try them out on your own. In this exercise, you'll learn to draw a shape and edit its outline and color.

New		
Name: Untitled-1		OK
Image Size: 176K		Reset
Preset Sizes: Custom		
Width: 300	pixels	
Height: 200	pixels	
Resolution: 72	pixels/inch	
Mode: RGB Color		
Contents		
⦿ White		
◯ Background Color		
◯ Transparent		

1. Choose **File > New** and enter the settings above. Click **OK**.

Note: If you set Width *and* Height *to pixels, it doesn't matter what number you enter in the* Resolution *field. That field, which measures pixels per inch, is relevant only for print work measured in inches. There is no need to worry about the resolution—always keep it set at 72 because that's the way it will display on the Web. Any other resolution adjustments are used only for print and are something we don't address in this text because this is a book about Web design.*

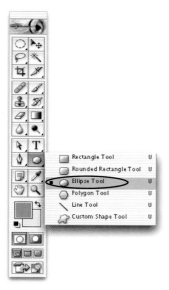

2. Select the **Ellipse** tool from the Toolbox. If it isn't visible, hold your mouse button down on the Toolbox as shown above to reveal the tool choices.

Notice that the Options bar displays an icon for each of the shape tools. You can use these to switch quickly between shape tools. New to Photoshop 7 is the appearance of the Pen tool and the Freeform Pen tool icons on the shape tools Options bar. You can use these pen tools to draw your own vector shape from scratch, but it's often quicker and easier to start with one of Photoshop's shapes and modify it, as you'll learn to do in this exercise.

3. In the **Options** bar, click the **Options** arrow to the right of the shape icons. In the **Ellipse Options** box, put a checkmark next to **From Center**. Click anywhere inside the **Options** bar to close the **Ellipse Options** box.

The From Center *option allows you to draw an ellipse from the center out, which you may find easier than drawing from an edge of the ellipse. You'll find that each shape tool has different options accessible from the* Options *arrow.*

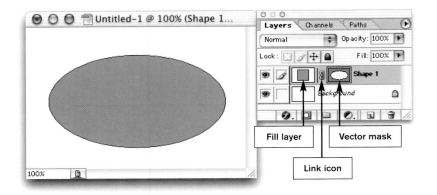

4. Click in the middle of the document window and drag to draw an ellipse shape. You need to be sure the **Shape Layers** icon is selected in the **Options** bar. If **Paths** or **Fill Pixels** is selected, a new layer will not be created in the **Layers** palette.

You control the shape and size of the ellipse as long as you keep your mouse pressed down.

This automatically creates a shape layer in the Layers *palette called* Shape 1. *(If the* Layers *palette isn't visible, choose* Window > Layers.*) The shape layer has three components (a fill layer, a vector mask, and a link between the two:*

- *The left thumbnail image on the* Shape 1 *layer represents a fill layer. The default fill layer is a solid color (the Foreground Color in the Toolbox). You can change the solid color fill to a gradient or pattern fill by choosing* Layer > Change Layer Content > Gradient or Pattern. *Try this if you like, but then chose* Edit > Step Backward *as many times as necessary to undo your changes.*

- *The thumbnail on the right represents a vector mask. It contains an outline of your ellipse shape, and it masks out (or hides) any part of the fill layer outside of that outline. The shape outline is smooth because it's vector-based.*

- *The* Link *icon connects the shape's fill and outline so that one moves with the other. For example, if the fill were a pattern, and you clicked the* Link *icon to unlink the fill and the outline, you could move the pattern around independently with the* Move *tool, so that a different part of it showed inside the outline.*

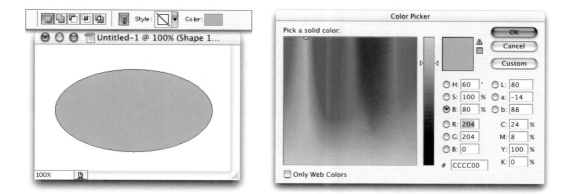

5. Click inside the **Color** field on the **Options** bar to open the **Color Picker**. Choose an **olive green** color, and click **OK**.

This is Photoshop 7's new and improved method of recoloring a shape. In the last version of the program, the only way to do it was to double-click the fill layer thumbnail. You can still do that in Photoshop 7, but using the Color *field is more intuitive.*

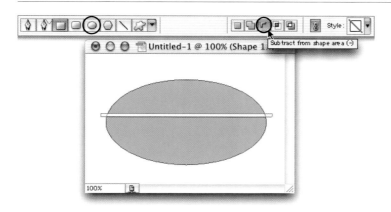

6. Click the **Rectangle Shape** tool icon on the **Options** bar to switch shape tools. Click the **Subtract from shape area** button on the **Options** bar. Click in the document window and drag out a narrow rectangular shape that cuts through the ellipse horizontally.

The Subtract from shape area *option allows you to use the rectangle shape like a cookie cutter to cut out a piece of the ellipse shape on the same layer. There are several shape combination options on the Options bar that allow you to combine multiple shapes on a single layer in different ways. This is a departure from Photoshop's default behavior, which is to automatically create a new layer for each shape you draw, so that shapes don't usually affect one another.*

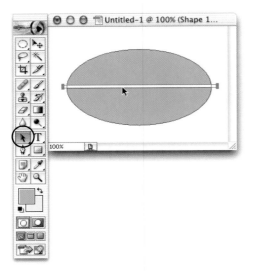

7. Select the **Path Selection** tool (the black arrow) in the Toolbox. Click on the rectangle shape in the document and move the rectangle to the vertical center of the ellipse shape.

You can move shapes independently on a shape layer because they are vector-based.

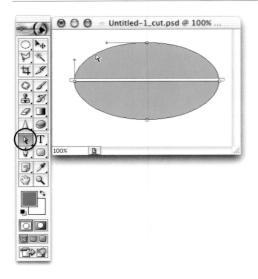

8. Click the **Path Selection** tool in the Toolbox to reveal a fly-out tools menu. Select the **Direct Selection** tool (the white arrow) from that fly-out menu. Click on the black outline of the ellipse shape in the document. You'll see small square anchor points and handles for editing the shape.

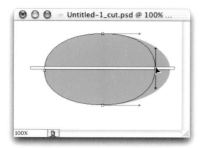

9. Click on the anchor point on the left side of the ellipse and move it slightly towards the center of the ellipse to change the shape. Do the same on the right side of the ellipse, squeezing the shape in towards its center. The ellipse should now be slightly rounder and fatter, as in this illustration.

You can change the outline of a vector shape as much as you want, without harming the image in any way.

---

10. With the shape still selected, choose **Edit > Define Custom Shape**. In the **Save** dialog box, name the shape **coffee bean**, and click **OK**.

The coffee bean shape will now appear in the menu of custom shape tools that you'll explore at the end of this exercise, and it will be available for you to add to other documents.

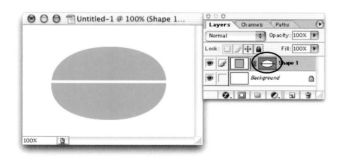

11. Click on the **vector mask** thumbnail on the **Shape 1** layer to deselect the thin outline around this shape in the document window. This allows you to see your shape without the distraction of the blue outline. Notice that the shape has very smooth edges.

---

12. Save and close the file. You can give the file any name you want.

Artwork built with Photoshop's shape tools offers more flexibility than bitmapped artwork. Shapes on shape layers can be recolored and edited, have crisp edges, and are perfect for buttons, icons, and Web graphics based on simple forms. Shapes work similarly in ImageReady, except that there are no polygon shape tools or custom shape tools, there are no options for combining multiple shapes on one layer, and shapes can be edited only with the Transform command.

NOTE | Custom Shapes

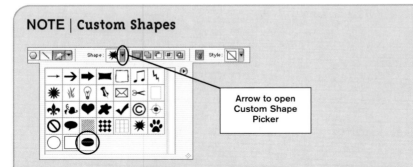

Arrow to open Custom Shape Picker

You can use the Custom Shape tool to add one of Photoshop's prebuilt custom shapes to an image, or to create and save a custom shape of your own. Photoshop 7 comes with lots more custom shapes than the last version of the program. You can explore Photoshop's libraries of shapes by clicking on the **Custom Shape** tool in the Toolbox or Options bar. Then click on the small **arrow** in the shape field on the Options bar to open the **Custom Shape Picker**. Notice your custom coffee been shape at the bottom of the current shape library.

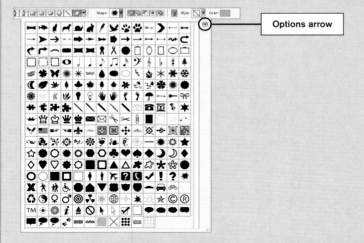

Options arrow

Look under the options arrow (circled above) in the **Custom Shape Picker**, choose **All**, and click **OK** to replace the default shapes with all of the prebuilt custom shapes. (Choosing one of the other menu items, such as Animals or Music, will display a subset of all of these shapes.) Click on the **bottom-right corner** of the **Custom Shape Picker** and drag to see all of the many icon, tile, border, and frame shapes that ship with Photoshop 7. To close the **Custom Shape Picker**, click anywhere in the **Options** bar.

If you're tempted to experiment with these shapes, open a new image (**File > New**). Draw a shape by selecting it in the **Custom Shape Picker**, and clicking and dragging inside the image. When you're done playing with shapes, close the image without saving.

2. [PS]_____Creating Layer Styles

Next, you'll turn a shape like the one you just made into original button artwork using layer styles. Layer styles are a combination and embellishment of some features that have been around since older versions of Photoshop—layer effects, styles, and layer blending modes. Photoshop 6 pulled all of these features together into one big, easy-to-access menu called the Layer Style dialog box, which hasn't changed much in Photoshop 7 except to offer more prebuilt styles and patterns. You can use layer effects to embellish flat artwork with shadows, glows, bevels, textures, patterns, gradients, colors, and stroked outlines, combined in almost limitless ways.

Many of the effects now available through layer styles used to require learning complicated steps and combining filters, which resulted in changes to the underlying artwork that couldn't be edited. Layer styles, on the other hand, do not destroy the original artwork and are easy to create and edit. You can always go back to a layered PSD file, and change the color of a drop shadow or the height of a bevel that's applied as a layer style. Another great thing about layer styles is that if you create a layer style on one layer, you can automatically apply the same layer style, with all of its custom settings, to other layers or files. This makes it easy to set up an efficient production process for your navigation buttons. You'll be enthralled by all the creative possibilities layer styles offer.

1. Open **button.psd** from the **chap_07** folder that you transferred to your hard drive from the **H·O·T CD-ROM**. This is a replica of the button you made in the last exercise, with a type layer called **french roast**.

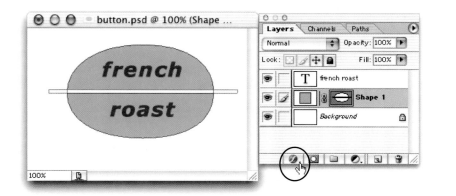

2. With the **Shape 1** layer selected, click the *f*-shaped layer style icon at the bottom of the **Layers** palette. Choose **Bevel and Emboss** from the drop-down menu.

This opens the Layer Style dialog box.

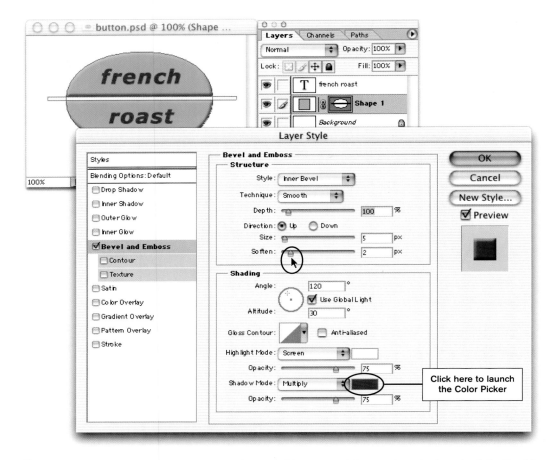

3. In the **Layer Style** dialog box, drag the **Soften** slider to the right to soften the bevel a little. Double-click on the **Color** field (circled above) next to the **Shadow Mode** button. This opens the **Color Picker**. Choose a **dark green** to change the color of the bevel's shadow from the default black. (This will make the bevel look more realistic, because most shadows aren't really black.) Click **OK** to close the **Color Picker**. Do not click OK in the Layer Style dialog box yet; you'll need it open for the next step.

4. Experiment with some of the other settings. When you're done, match the settings to those in the illustration on step 3, and click **OK** to close the Layer Style dialog box.

You should see changes appear in the image as you are making changes in the Layer Style dialog box. As you explore the settings, you'll see terms that may be new to you, such as choke, contour, and jitter. For descriptions of some of these terms, turn to the chart at the end of this exercise.

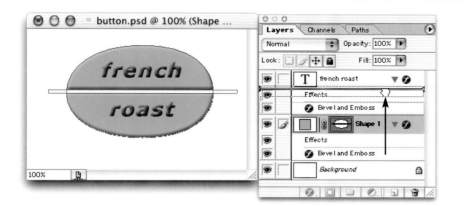

5. In the Layers palette, drag the **Bevel and Emboss** layer style from the **Shape 1** layer to the line below the **french roast** type layer, and release your mouse.

The text looks beveled, just like the button! You can copy any layer style to another layer by simply dragging it there. You can move multiple layer styles one at a time to another layer. This is a lot simpler than re-creating the settings for each layer, isn't it?

Notice that there are blue outlines around all of the elements of the button in this illustration. These are the vector outlines of the ellipse and rectangular shapes that make up the button. If you find these lines distracting, you can hide them by clicking on the vector mask thumbnail *on the* Shape 1 *layer and moving your mouse off of that layer.*

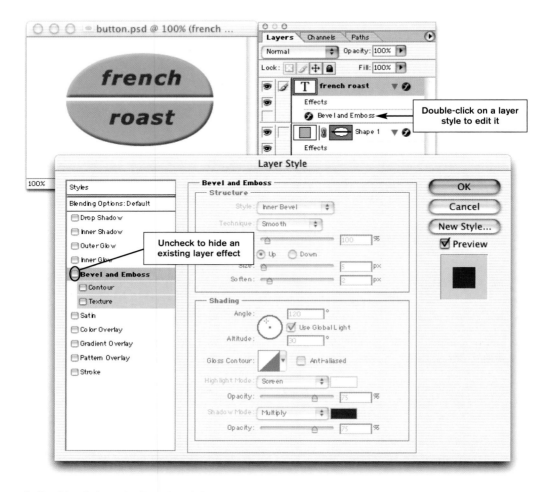

6. Double-click on the **Bevel and Emboss** layer style on the **french roast** type layer. The **Layer Style** dialog box will open. Uncheck the box next to **Bevel and Emboss** on the left side of the dialog box to hide the bevel and emboss on the **french roast** type layer. This turns the visibility of the Bevel and Emboss layer off without discarding the layer.

You can reactivate the bevel and emboss on the text layer at any time by going to the Layers *palette and clicking inside the* Visibility *box to the left of the* Bevel and Emboss *sublayer under the* french roast *layer.*

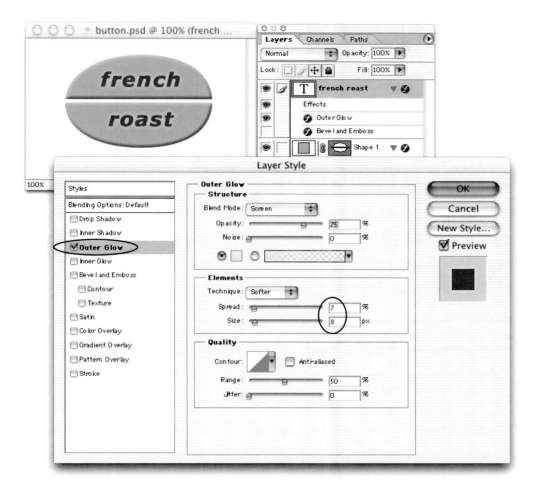

7. Click on the phrase **Outer Glow** in the **Layer Style** dialog box to display options for that layer style. Experiment with any of the settings for this layer style. (Try changing the **Spread** to 7% and the **Size** to **8%** to make the glow more visible.) Click **OK** when you're ready. You'll see a new Outer Glow layer style on the french roast layer in the Layers palette and in the image.

Note: *You have to click on the name of an effect in the* Layer Style *dialog box to edit its settings. Adding a checkmark just activates the effect. You can add new layer styles from the* Layer Style *dialog box, as you did here, or from the menu that drops down from the ƒ icon on the Layers palette.*

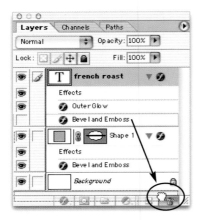

8. Since we're not going to suggest that you reactivate the bevel and emboss on the **french roast** layer, drag that **Bevel and Emboss** sublayer to the **Trash** icon at the bottom of the **Layers** palette.

If you ever have multiple effects on a layer and want to throw them all away at once, drag the word Effects *to the* Trash*, and all the sublayers below it will be deleted.*

9. Save your file as **mybuttonstyles.psd**, and leave it open for the next exercise.

Layer Style Dialog Box

The Layer Style dialog box has enough settings to make anyone's head spin. As you try different layer styles (Drop Shadow, Inner Shadow, Outer Glow, Inner Glow, Bevel and Emboss, etc.), you'll see that the options in the dialog box will change. Some of the terms are probably foreign to you, such as Spread, Contour, or better yet… Gloss Contour! Here's a handy chart that describes what some of these strange-looking terms mean.

Layer Style Terms	
Term	**Definition**
Blend Mode	Determines how the layer style blends with underlying layers. Uses all the standard Photoshop blending modes, such as Multiply, Screen, etc.
Opacity	Changes the opacity of the layer style only.
Color	Specifies the color of the layer style, such as the drop shadow or glow color.
	continues on next page

	Layer Style Terms *continued*
Term	**Definition**
Angle	Determines the lighting angle.
Spread/Choke	Determines the intensity of some effects, such as glows or strokes. The spread setting increases the glow outward to make it actually bigger; the choke setting reduces the glow inward.
Noise	Adds dithering to soft edges.
Contour	Allows you to sculpt the ridges, valleys, and bumps that are used in some effects, such as bevels and embosses.
Anti-Alias	Affects how the edges of an effect blend with underlying artwork.
Depth	Affects the dimensional appearance of effects like bevel and emboss.
Gloss Contour	Adds a glossy, metal-like appearance to bevel or emboss.
Gradient	Allows you to select from a gradient editor.
Highlight or Shadow Mode	Determines the blending mode of a highlight or shadow, such as Multiply, Screen, etc.
Jitter	Varies the gradient color and opacity.
Layer Knocks Out	Controls the drop shadow's visibility or invisibility on a semi-transparent layer.
Drop Shadow	Controls the drop shadow's visibility or invisibility on a semi-transparent layer.
Soften	Blurs the effect.

NOTE | Layer Styles Are Non-Destructive

The beauty of layer styles is that they are non-destructive, meaning you can edit them at any time and the original document is never harmed. Try turning the Visibility icons (the Eye icons) on the layer styles on and off in the Layers palette. You'll see that with layer styles turned off, the original button art is still there! Be sure to turn them all back on for the next exercise. You'll need them turned on to learn how to make reusable styles.

3. [PS] _____Saving a Custom Layer Style

Let's say that you're totally happy with the effects you applied to a layer in the file you just worked on. Wouldn't it be great if you could save the resulting layer style in a library so it could be applied to other layers or documents? Luckily, it's easy to save a custom layer style for reuse. This exercise shows you how.

1. Your image **mybuttonstyles.psd** should still be open from the previous exercise. (If it's not, open and use the prebuilt **buttonstyles.psd** file, which you'll find in the **chap_07** folder you copied to your hard drive from the CD-ROM.)

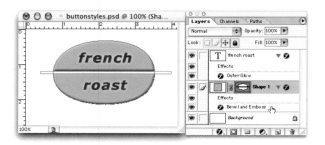

2. Double-click the **Bevel and Emboss** layer style on the **Shape_1** layer in the **Layers** palette to open the **Layer Style** dialog box.

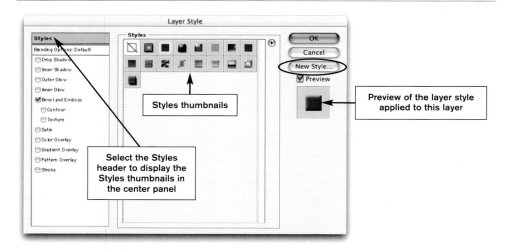

Styles thumbnails

Select the Styles header to display the Styles thumbnails in the center panel

Preview of the layer style applied to this layer

3. Click on the **Styles** header on the left side of the **Layer Style** dialog box. You'll see a collection of Styles thumbnails in the center panel. Make sure the **Preview** box on the right side of the dialog box is checked, so you can see a thumbnail preview of the layer style you created in the last exercise for the **Shape_1** layer. Click the **New Style** button.

4. The **New Style** dialog box will open. Make sure **Include Layer Effects** is checked. (You didn't include any special layer blending settings in this layer style, so you don't need a checkmark next to **Include Layer Blending Options**.) Enter **coffee button** in the **Name** field, and click **OK**.

A thumbnail of your new style will appear in the Styles *panel of the* Layer Style *dialog box. Move your cursor over that thumbnail, and you'll see the name* coffee button.

Notice that the thumbnail for your new style is gray. That's because it contains only the bevel and emboss layer style, which is colorless (unlike some other layer styles such as Color Overlay and Gradient Overlay). This means that you can apply your coffee button style to any graphic without changing the color of that graphic.

5. Click **OK** to close the **Layer Style** dialog box.

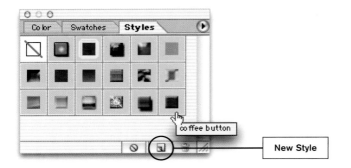

New Style

6. Choose **Window > Styles** to open the **Styles** palette. Drag the window by the lower-right corner to stretch it larger. You should see a thumbnail of the style you just created! If you move your mouse over the thumbnail, the name **coffee button** will appear.

Next, you'll learn another way to make a style in Photoshop 7, right from the Styles palette.

7. Select the **french roast** type layer on the **Layers** palette. Click the **New Style** button at the bottom of the **Styles** palette. This will open the **New Style** dialog box, in which you can name this style **coffee text**, and click **OK**.

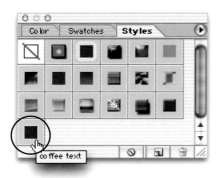

A thumbnail of the new coffee text *style you just created will appear. This thumbnail is gray with a pale yellow glow, because it contains only the Outer Glow layer style. The* coffee text *style contains no other information about color, font, or any other property, so it can be applied to any graphic (not only text) without changing anything other than adding a glow.*

8. Close **buttonstyles.psd**. You don't need to save the file again, because you've made no changes to it since the last exercise.

4. [PS] _____ Applying Styles from the Styles Palette

Now that you've designed a button and created some custom styles from layer styles, it's a snap to apply those styles to other artwork and quickly create a collection of buttons with a consistent appearance.

1. Open **navbar.psd** from the **chap_07** files you transferred from the CD-ROM to your hard drive.

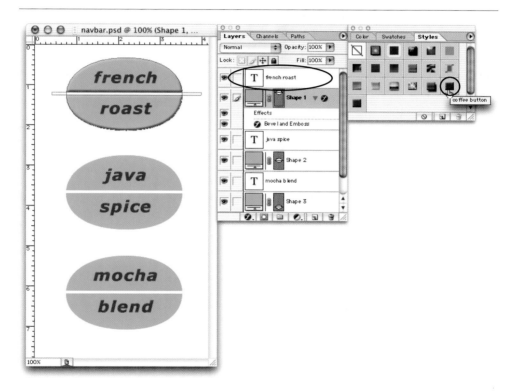

2. Select the **french roast** layer, and click the **coffee button** style thumbnail on the **Styles** palette. The button should magically change, and a **Bevel and Emboss** layer style should appear as a sublayer to the **french roast** layer.

3. Select the **Shape 2** layer on the **Layers** palette and click the **coffee button** thumbnail from the **Styles** palette. Do the same for the **Shape 3** layer.

You should now see three similar looking buttons on your screen, and three Bevel and Emboss layer styles should be visible as sublayers inside the Layers palette. Pretty simple and fast to make these buttons look consistent, is it not? Now you'll do the same for the text on each button.

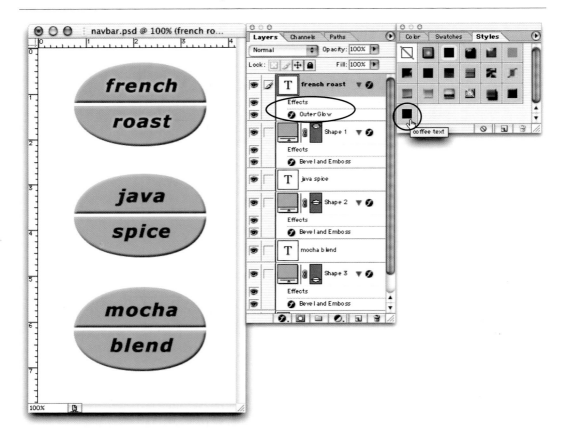

4. Select the **french roast** type layer, and click the **coffee text** thumbnail from the **Styles** palette.

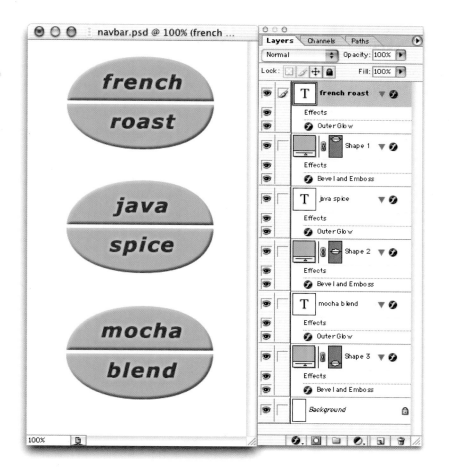

5. Repeat the last step on the other type layers, **java spice** and **mocha blend**.

See how fast and easy it is to create similar buttons using layer styles and the Styles palette? Imagine how much you would love these features if you had a zillion buttons on one screen that had to look consistent? OK, maybe not a zillion, but even if you had a few buttons to standardize, this feature would save you time and trouble.

6. Save and close the file.

Congrats, you've finished this chapter! Now you know how great shape layers and layer styles are for making Web graphics.

8.

Background Images

Size Relationships	Previewing Backgrounds
Saving Backgrounds	Seamless Backgrounds
Tile Maker Filter	Full-Screen Backgrounds
Directional Backgrounds

chap_08

Photoshop 7/ImageReady
H•O•T CD-ROM

Designing for HTML is challenging because standard HTML is capable of displaying only two layers—a background layer and a foreground layer. By contrast, it's possible to work with unlimited layers in just about every digital design program, including Photoshop, InDesign, QuarkXPress, Illustrator, FreeHand, etc. Because HTML restricts you to only two layers, knowing how to create a variety of appearances for the background layer is particularly important. This chapter will help you learn how to deal with these limitations by teaching numerous techniques for creating images that work well as Web page backgrounds.

You can work around the two-layer limitation by using style sheets instead of standard HTML. But this book is about making Web artwork, not about writing code or using a Web page editor. For that reason, this chapter focuses on the challenges of and solutions for making effective background images that work with standard HTML. There are two core issues to think about when you're making a background image: the speed with which it will download (which you learned about back in Chapter 4, "*Optimization*"), and its appearance, which involves the imaging techniques you'll learn in this chapter.

What Is a Background Image?

A background image appears in the background layer of a Web page. By default, it will repeat to fill the size of a browser window. The number of times that a background image will repeat (or tile, as it's also called) is dictated by the size of the original image and the size of the particular browser window in which it is being viewed at the moment. This means that a background image can appear differently on different monitors. The challenge is to design one piece of art that can look different on different monitors and still look good everywhere. Not easy! This chapter will offer some concrete examples and solutions to this common challenge.

Regardless of how many times a background image tiles in a browser window, it downloads to the viewer's computer only once. Each time the image appears on a Web page it is called out from the cache in the viewer's computer, rather than downloaded again. This means that as a designer, you can get a lot of mileage from a background tile. If you create a tile that is relatively small in file size, you can fill an entire browser window for a very small penalty in download time.

The other important property of a background image is that you can put other images on top of it. In fact, in standard HTML, a background image is the only kind of image on which you can place another item that's in a graphic format. So if you want an illustration, a photograph, or text you've made as a graphic to float on top of an image, you'll have to identify the underlying image as an HTML background, as you'll learn to do in this chapter.

A background image begins life no differently than any other GIF or JPEG. The thing that makes it a background is the HTML code inside the **BODY** tag. The HTML for a tiled background is simple. Here's the minimum code required to transform an image (**small.jpg** in this example) into a tiled background in an HTML document.

```
<HTML>
<BODY BACKGROUND="small.jpg">
</BODY>
</HTML>
```

> ## NOTE | Vocabulary: Background Tile and Tiling
>
> In this chapter, you'll run into the terms **tiling** and **background tile**, both of which are used in a technical sense. **Tiling** refers to the horizontal and vertical repetition of an HTML background image in a Web browser. **Background tile** is used interchangeably with the term **background image** to mean a GIF or JPEG that repeats in an HTML background.

TIP | Design Tips for Readability

When you are creating artwork for background tiles, it's especially important to pay attention to contrast and value. Try to use either all dark values or all light values. If you combine darks and lights in a single background image, your background might look great on its own, but neither light nor dark type will work consistently against it, and your image won't read well.

Light background   *Dark background*

If you are wondering how to pick colors for backgrounds in relation to foreground type, here are some basic guidelines:

- If you're using a light background, use dark type.

- If you're using a dark background, use light type.

- Avoid using a medium value for a background image, because neither light nor dark type will read well on top of it.

- Avoid using contrasting values in a background image, because they will interfere with type of any value.

Background Image Sizes

Artwork that is used for a background image can be any dimension, large or small. The size of a background tile will determine the number of times its pattern will repeat inside a Web browser.

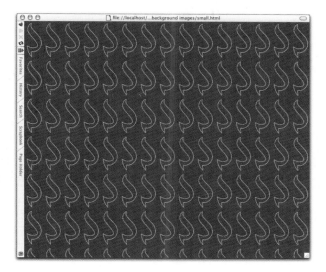

Small   *Result in browser*

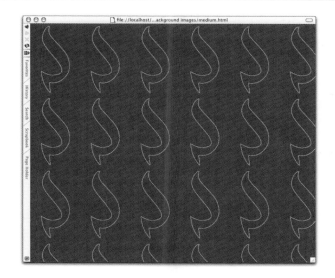

Medium   *Result in browser*

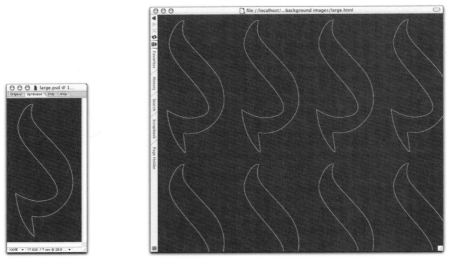

Large   Result in browser

As you can see in these examples, a background tile with larger dimensions is going to repeat less often than a smaller tile. A tile that measures 40 × 40 pixels will repeat 192 times (16 times across and 12 times down) in a 640 × 480 browser window. A tile that measures 320 × 240 pixels will repeat four times (two times across and two times down) in a 640 × 480 browser window. You can create an image so large that it's going to repeat only once in a standard-size browser window. Basically, the size of the image you choose to make depends on the effect you want to create.

Enlarging the dimensions of a background tile will enlarge its file size as well. If you create a background tile that is 50K, it is going to add that much file size to your Web page and adversely affect download speed. (One formula that some designers use, though it is not scientifically accurate or measurable, is that each kilobyte of file size represents one second of download time for the average viewer.) Therefore, it is just as important to practice good optimization skills with background images as it is with other types of images.

I. [IR]____Defining, Editing, and Previewing a Background Image

Once you've created or opened an image in ImageReady, the program's **output settings** make it easy to define your image as a background image. You can then use the preview feature to see how the image will look in a browser as a tiled Web page background. In this exercise, you'll learn to define, edit, and preview artwork as a background image in ImageReady. You can also perform these functions in Photoshop from the Save For Web window, but it's easier to make background images in ImageReady, because the Output and Preview settings are more accessible from ImageReady's main program interface.

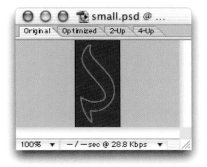

1. In ImageReady 7, open **small.psd** from the **chap_08** folder that you transferred to your hard drive.

The first step in previewing an image as a background tile is to identify it as an HTML background, as you'll do in the next two steps. This lets ImageReady know that when you preview this image, you want to see it as a tiled background image, rather than as a single foreground image.

2. Choose **File > Output Settings > Background**. This will open the **Output Settings** dialog box to its **Background** settings.

Output Settings

Settings: Background Image

Background

View Document As
○ Image   ⦿ Background

Background Image
Path: Choose...

BG Color: Matte ▶

OK
Cancel
Prev
Next
Load...
Save...

3. In the **Output Settings** dialog box, choose **View Document As: Background** to identify this image as an HTML background, and click **OK**.

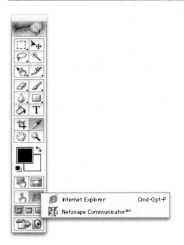

Internet Explorer   Cmd-Opt-P
Netscape Communicator™

4. Click the **Preview In Default Browser** button in the Toolbox to open Internet Explorer. If you'd rather use a different browser, click and hold the Preview In Default Browser button to display a pop-up menu of potential browsers, and select the browser of your choice.

All browsers that were on your computer when you installed ImageReady should appear in the Preview In Default Browser *pop-up menu. If you want to select another browser, choose* File > Preview In > Other, *and navigate to the file in the browser's application folder that launches that browser.*

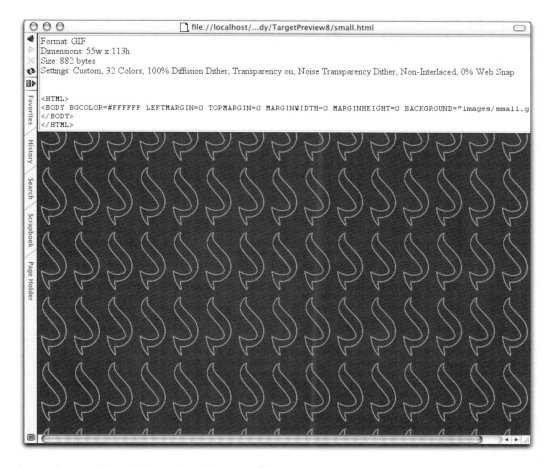

ImageReady will launch the selected browser (if it isn't already open), and will display a preview of this document as a repeating background image. Notice that the preview includes a white text box that contains details about how the image was optimized, as well as the HTML used to define this image as a background. In the next exercise, you'll learn how to have ImageReady write this file as a final HTML document that will not include the text box that appears in this preview.

5. The size and content of this image affect its appearance in a browser. Return to ImageReady. Choose **Image > Canvas Size**. Set the canvas size to **150** pixels by **150** pixels. Make sure the center square in the **Anchor** diagram is selected, and that **Relative** is unchecked, and click **OK**. This will change the size of the canvas around the image to be larger than the image itself.

NOTE | Relative Canvas Size—New to Photoshop and ImageReady 7

The Relative checkbox in the Canvas Size dialog box is new in Photoshop and ImageReady 7. It's just another way of measuring increases or decreases in canvas size—relative to the existing dimensions of the canvas. Here's how it works: If you put a checkmark next to **Relative** and entered **50** pixels in the **Width** field, the resulting canvas would be 50 pixels wider than its current size, regardless of what the current size is. This saves you from having to do the math.

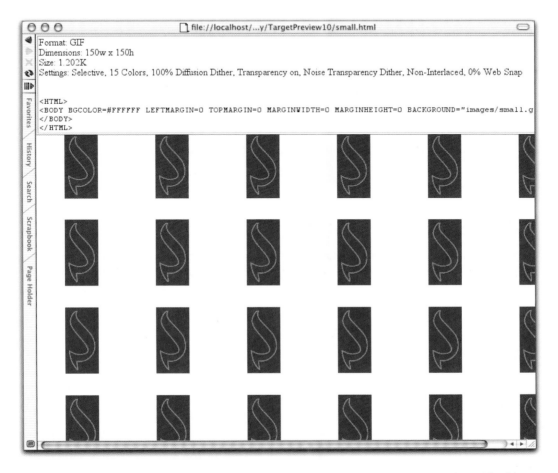

Format: GIF
Dimensions: 150w x 150h
Size: 1.202K
Settings: Selective, 15 Colors, 100% Diffusion Dither, Transparency on, Noise Transparency Dither, Non-Interlaced, 0% Web Snap

```
<HTML>
<BODY BGCOLOR=#FFFFFF LEFTMARGIN=0 TOPMARGIN=0 MARGINWIDTH=0 MARGINHEIGHT=0 BACKGROUND="images/small.g
</BODY>
</HTML>
```

6. Click the **Preview in Default Browser** button, and choose a browser again to see how this change in dimensions will affect the appearance of the tiled background.

Notice that in the browser, the areas of the exposed canvas that were transparent appear as a white background around the designs. That's because ImageReady will substitute a white color for any transparent pixels unless you specify otherwise. In order to change the color of the areas around the shape, you'll need to fill in the transparent pixels with another color.

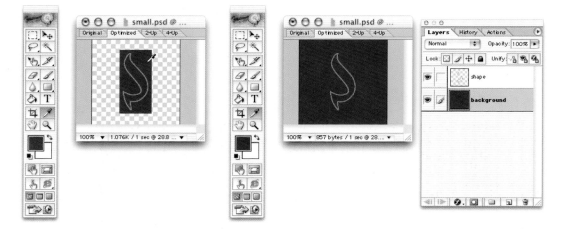

7. To fill the transparent pixels with the same green that is already in the image, select the **Eyedropper** tool from the ImageReady Toolbox, and click on the green in the document to sample that color. Select the **Background** layer from the **Layers** palette (if it's not visible, choose **Window > Layers**). Press **Option+Delete** (Mac) or **Alt+Backspace** (Windows) to fill the entire Background layer with green.

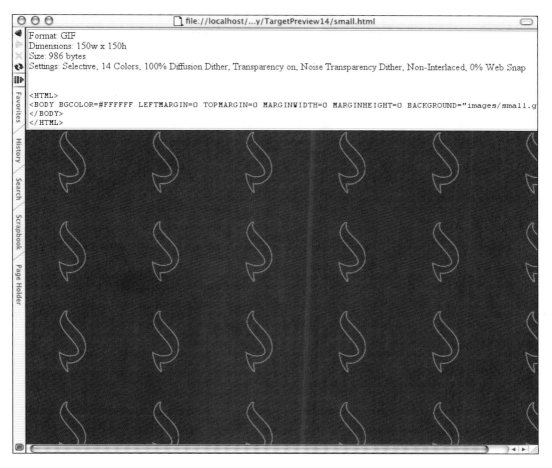

8. Click the **Preview in Default Browser** button, and select a browser of your choice to see how the change will affect the repeating background image. The shape should now be on a green field.

9. Return to ImageReady, choose **File > Save**, and leave the file open for the next exercise.

It's great that ImageReady previews the image as a background so easily. This allows you to try different dimensions, color treatments, or other image qualities before you commit to the design of your background tile.

2. [IR] _____Saving a Background Image

In this exercise, you'll learn to save a background image as a final document, instead of just previewing it from ImageReady as you did in the last exercise. When you're working on your own Web projects, this is what you'll do when you've finished experimenting with the look of your background tile. The image will still be in PSD format, so you'll need to optimize it in order for it to function properly on the Web. The resulting GIF file will be no different than any other GIF image. The only thing that will make it a background image is the code inside the HTML file that tells the browser to display that GIF as a background image. Fortunately, ImageReady saves images and the necessary HTML code to make this happen! Alternatively, you could save just the optimized image without HTML, bring the resulting GIF into the HTML editor of your choice, and code it as a background tile in an HTML editor.

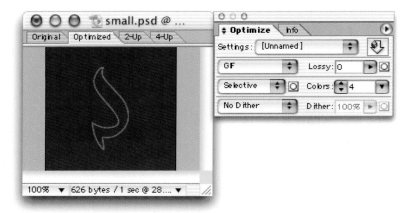

1. With **small.psd** still open from the last exercise, click on the **Optimized** tab in the document window. If the **Optimize** palette isn't open, choose **Window > Optimize**. Match your **Optimize** settings to the ones shown above.

Because the image is composed of flat colors, it is going to look and compress best as a GIF.

2. Choose **File > Save Optimized**. In the dialog box, choose **HTML and Images** from the **Format** menu (Mac) or **Save as type** menu (Windows). Click the **new folder** button (OS X: click the large arrow to the right of the **Where** field, and then click the **New Folder** button), and create a new folder called **chap_08_exercises**. Click **Save**.

When ImageReady saves the file, it will generate a GIF (small.gif) inside an images subfolder, as well as an HTML document (small.html) containing the **BODY BACKGROUND** *tag that identifies this GIF as a background image. ImageReady will know to include this tag in the HTML code it writes, because you designated this image as a background image in Step 3 of the previous exercise.*

Tip: The Settings field in the Save Optimized window is another place from which you can set your image to become a tiled background. In the last exercise, you accessed the Output Settings dialog box from the File menu in order to set your image so that you could preview it as a tiled background. If you had not done that, you could have waited until now and chosen Background Image in the Save Optimized window to have ImageReady save your image as a background tile.

When you save the file, the Name field defaults to the name of your original image file with the extension .html. You can rename the HTML file, along with the accompanying GIF if you like, or keep their default names. Navigate to the chap_08_exercises *folder to see the image and HTML file that were just generated. Next, you'll get to check out the final results by opening the newly created HTML document in a browser.*

NOTE | Save HTML or Not?

Some designers do not use the HTML file that ImageReady generates for background images, because they prefer to use an HTML editor like GoLive or Dreamweaver to assemble Web pages. One reason for using an HTML editor over ImageReady is that a dedicated HTML editor allows more precise control over placement of foreground images on top of the background than ImageReady does. However, it is useful to save the image and the HTML out of ImageReady so that you can view the background image without the white preview text readout.

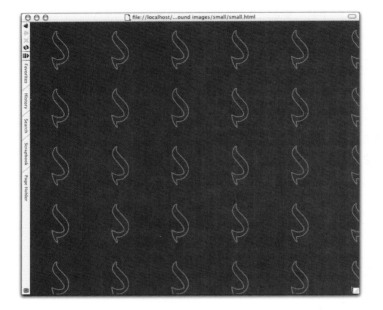

3. Double-click on the HTML file ImageReady just created (**small.html**) in the **chap_08_exercises** folder to open that file in your computer's default browser. If you prefer to view the file in a different browser, launch that browser, choose **File > Open**, and navigate to **small.html** on your hard drive.

```
<html>
<body BGCOLOR=#FFFFFF LEFTMARGIN=0 TOPMARGIN=0 MARGINWIDTH=0 MARGINHEIGHT=0 BACKGROUND="images/small.gif">
</body>
</html>
```

4. If you choose **View > Source** (Internet Explorer) or **View > Page Source** (Netscape Navigator), you will see the HTML code that ImageReady generated. Return to ImageReady, and save and close the source file, **small.psd**.

3. [IR] _____Seamless Background Tiles

The background images you've created so far have produced patterns that very obviously repeat when previewed in a browser. In the following exercises, you'll learn how to use ImageReady's **Offset** filter to create the illusion of a seamless (nonrepeating) background.

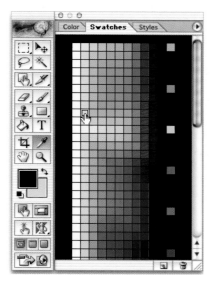

1. In ImageReady, **Cmd+click** (Mac) or **Ctrl+click** (Windows) on a color in the **Swatches** palette to select a background color for a tile.

2. Create a new document that is **150 x 150** pixels. This is just a recommended size; you can make the canvas larger or smaller if you like. In the **New Document** dialog box, select **Background Color** as the contents of first layer. Leave the file untitled for now. Click **OK**.

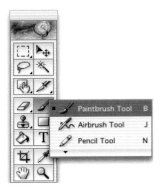

3. Select the **Paintbrush** tool from the Toolbox. If it is not visible, click the **Pencil** or **Airbrush** tool (whichever is showing in the Toolbox), and choose the **Paintbrush** tool from the fly-out menu.

4. Select a hard-edged or soft-edged brush from the pop-up **Brushes** palette, which is accessible from the **Options** bar in ImageReady 7.

Note: One of the new features in Photoshop 7 is a new Brushes palette with lots of preset brushes and many brush options that allow you to create artwork that looks more natural than in past releases. ImageReady doesn't share this new Brushes palette. If you want to take advantage of it, you can paint a tile in Photoshop 7 and then jump to ImageReady to create a background tile for a Web page.

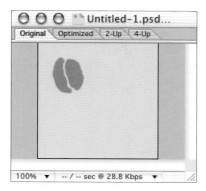

5. Select a foreground color that is different than the background color from the **Swatches** palette, and draw an image on the **Background** layer of your canvas. Make sure that you do not draw to the very edge of the canvas, and that your image does not touch the edge of the document window. You may want to draw the artwork in one corner, so that you can easily see where you last drew shapes as you apply the Offset filter.

6. Choose **Filter > Other > Offset**. In the **Offset** dialog box, enter **Horizontal: 20** and **Vertical: 40**. Click **OK**.

It helps to pick irregular values other than the defaults (which are 50 × 50 percent) in order to create a non-symmetrical background. Because a seamless tile should look organic and not predictable, it is better to use irregular numeric values so the offset is less predictable.

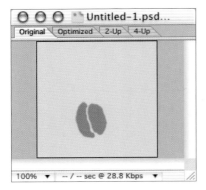

The Offset filter shifts your original image to the right and down, leaving more room to draw other objects.

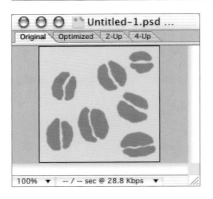

7. Continue to draw inside the blank areas of the image.

Make sure that your artwork doesn't touch any edges. If it does, be sure to undo the drawing and redraw! The object of this exercise is to not touch the edge, and to use the Offset filter to create more free space in which to draw.

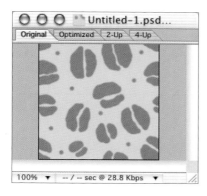

8. Press **Cmd+F** (Mac) or **Ctrl+F** (Windows) to apply the **Offset** filter again.

Note: This keyboard shortcut will reapply whichever filter you last applied. This will again shift the pixels and wrap them around the image, opening some blank area on the canvas. Continue to draw, filling in the blank areas without touching the edge of your canvas.

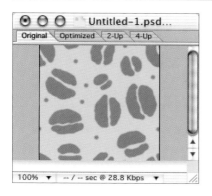

Notice that there is no large unfilled area in this image.

9. Press **Cmd+F** (Mac) or **Ctrl+F** (Windows) to apply the **Offset** filter again. You may need to repeat the Offset filter process several times until no large areas of background color are visible.

10. To see what this image looks like in the browser, you must first identify it as an HTML Background. As you did in Exercise 1, choose **File > Output Settings > Background**, then select **View As: Background** and click **OK**.

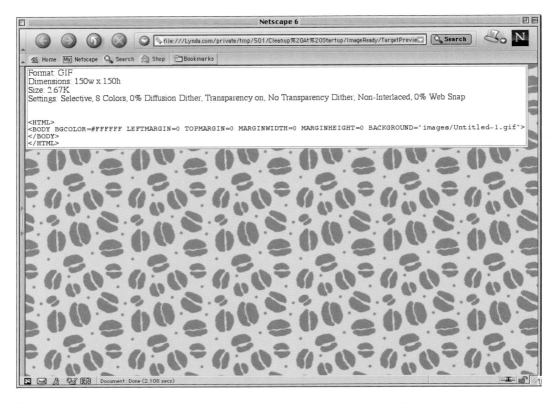

11. Next, click the **Preview in Default Browser** button on the ImageReady Toolbox to preview your tiling image in a browser. *Notice that it's hard to tell where the smaller background image begins or ends? That is the power of this technique! Don't worry if your compression settings are different from mine; ImageReady has "sticky" settings that stay stuck until the next time you change them.*

12. Return to ImageReady and choose **File > Save** to save the original file. Name the file **tilebg.psd** and save it inside your **chap_08_exercises** folder.

It's always a good idea to save both a Photoshop document (PSD) and an optimized graphic, so that you can go back to the original Photoshop document to re-edit the image if you have to.

13. With the **Optimized** tab selected in the document window, check the **Optimize** palette to make sure the controls are set to **GIF** and the number of colors is low (this design looked good with eight colors; yours may require more or less, and you should experiment to see which setting is best). These are the best settings for this image because it is made up of flat colors and is not continuous tone like a photograph. If you need a refresher on how to make the smallest possible GIF, revisit Chapter 4, "*Optimization.*"

14. Choose **File > Save Optimized** to save the optimized file as a GIF. Choose **Images Only** if you plan to use an HTML editing program, instead of ImageReady, to write the code to make your image tile in an HTML background. The application will offer to name it **tilebg.gif** for you. Click **Save**, and close the file.

MOVIE | offset.mov

To learn more about how to use the Offset filter to create a seamless background, check out **offset.mov** from the **movies** folder on the **H•O•T CD-ROM**.

Save Options in ImageReady

There are many different Save options in ImageReady. Here's a handy chart that explains them.

Save Options	
Function	**Result**
Save Optimized	Saves the file with its current optimization settings and file name.
Save Optimized As	Saves the file with its current optimization settings and enables you to change the file name. It can also overwrite an old file if you save it with the same name.
Update HTML	Allows you to overwrite HTML that ImageReady generated. You will get to try this out in Chapter 16, "*Integration with Other Programs.*"
Save	Saves the file as a PSD.
Save As	Saves the file as a PSD and enables you to change the name. It can also overwrite an old file if you save it with the same name.
Export Original	Offers other file format options, such as Photoshop, BMP, PCX, PICT, Pixar, QuickTime Movie, Targa, and TIFF. **Note:** Photoshop, unlike ImageReady, has no Export Original option. To save a file in another format from Photoshop, choose **File > Save As.**

4. [IR] _____Copying and Pasting with Offset

There's another way to create a seamless background tile in ImageReady. In this exercise, you'll apply the Offset filter after you've copied and pasted existing artwork into a new document. This exercise, like the preceding exercise, could be done in Photoshop, but is easier in ImageReady where the Output and Preview settings are accessible from the regular Toolbox.

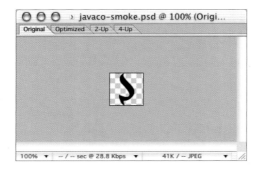

1. Open **javaco-smoke.psd** from the **chap_08** folder you copied to your hard drive from the **H•O•T CD-ROM**.

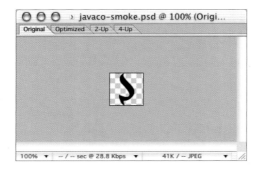

2. Choose **File > New** and create a new document that is **200 x 200** pixels against a white background. Type **seamless_tile** into the **Name** field and click **OK**.

When you try this on your own without canned artwork, you can make the canvas larger or smaller if you like. The key is to make this document larger than the artwork you're using as the repeating pattern (which in the case of this exercise file, javaco-smoke.psd, is 50 × 50 pixels). The relationship between the size of the tile you're creating and the size of the source artwork will determine the spacing of the logo on the background tile.

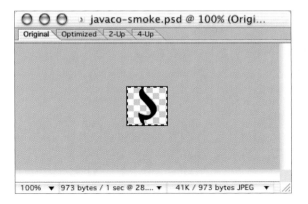

3. Click **javaco-smoke.psd** to make that file active. Then press **Cmd+A** (Mac) or **Ctrl+A** (Windows) to select the entire image area.

4. Press **Cmd+C** (Mac) or **Ctrl+C** (Windows) to copy the logo. Click on your new, empty document **seamless_tile.psd** to make it active, and then press **Cmd+V** (Mac) or **Ctrl+V** (Windows) to paste the logo into the new document.

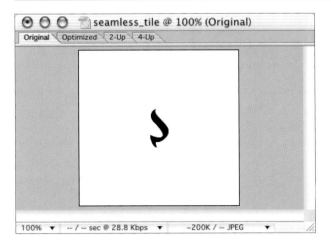

The logo appears in the center of the document. Whenever you paste an element into a document, ImageReady automatically centers it. With the logo in place, you're ready to apply the Offset filter.

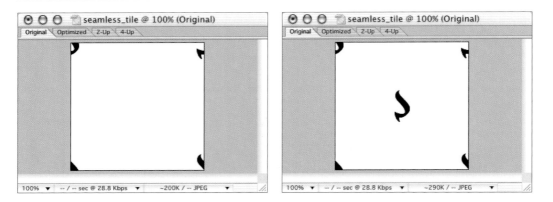

5. Choose **Filter > Other > Offset**. In the **Offset** dialog box that appears, match the settings to what you see above, and click **OK**.

In this instance, you will be making a symmetrical repeating tile, so leaving the default settings at 50 percent by 50 percent is desirable.

6. The logo looks like it's split into four quarters, which are now positioned at the four corners of the tile. Press **Cmd+V** (Mac) or **Ctrl+V** (Windows) again to paste another copy of the logo into the center.

7. Choose **File > Output Settings > Background** to identify this image as an HTML background, then select **View As: Background** and click **OK**.

Now you're ready to preview your seamless background tile in a browser to see the results of your labor.

8. Click the **Preview in Default Browser** button in the Toolbox, and select a browser.

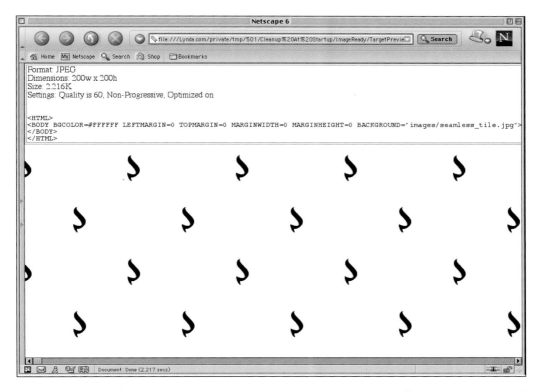

Here are the results of the preview. The first logo you pasted, which was offset by 50 percent and split to the four corners of the tile using the Offset filter, is flawlessly reassembled in the browser window when the image is tiled as a background.

This background effect is very symmetrical and formal. Each repeat of the logo is an equal distance from all the others. That's because you started with a square image, pasted both logos to the document's center, and set both the Horizontal and Vertical offset values to 50 percent. You can also use the Offset filter to create less symmetrical effects by adjusting the offset percentages.

Now that you've previewed this document, you can go back and experiment with adjusting the Offset filter settings or try doing the exercise over with a tile of smaller or larger dimensions. You could also recolor the logo or the background, using the techniques you learned in Chapter 3, "Color."

---

9. When you're finished playing, save the file. See if you can remember how to save it as both a GIF and a PSD.

Tip: Use File > Save Optimized *and* File > Save. *When you've saved the file, close it because it won't be needed again in this chapter.*

Ways to Access the Offset Filter in ImageReady

You might have noticed that there are three different ways to access the Offset filter in ImageReady. Here's a chart to explain the differences.

Offset Filter in ImageReady	
Option	Result
Filter > Other > Offset	This is the way to access the Offset filter the first time you apply it to an image, or when you are reapplying it and you want to enter new settings.
Filter > Offset	This is another way to reapply the Offset filter with an opportunity to change its settings.
Filter > Apply Offset	This is the way to access the Offset filter when you want to reapply it with the same settings as before.

NOTE | The Offset Filter in Photoshop

Offset

Horizontal: 0   pixels right   OK

Vertical: 0   pixels down   Cancel

☑ Preview

Undefined Areas
- ○ Set to Transparent
- ○ Repeat Edge Pixels
- ● Wrap Around

If you want to use the **Offset** filter in Photoshop, it can be accessed by choosing **Filter > Other > Offset**. Photoshop uses a slightly different interface than ImageReady for the Offset filter. It doesn't have a percent option and it offers non-wraparound options (such as **Set to Transparent** and **Repeat Edge Pixels**). You can make seamless tiles in Photoshop using the **Wrap Around** setting. The major drawback to creating background images in Photoshop is that they cannot be identified as HTML backgrounds nor previewed in the browser from the main program interface. To do either of those operations, you have to be in the **Save For Web** interface, which involves extra steps.

5. [IR]_____Seamless Photographic Background Images

Seamless background images are not limited to graphics. With ImageReady's **Tile Maker** filter, photographs can be the source of perfect seamless background images, too. This filter overlaps and blends the edges of an image, which creates a convincing seamless pattern effect. Consider this approach if you are looking for ways to incorporate photographic backgrounds into your Web design while keeping file sizes down. This technique works best with abstract images because they are least likely to reveal easily discernible repeating patterns. This exercise only works in ImageReady; Photoshop does not have a Tile Maker filter.

1. In ImageReady, open **beans.psd** from the **chap_08** folder you copied to your hard drive.

2. Click on the **Optimized** tab in the document window. In the **Optimize** palette, choose **JPEG** as the file format at **medium** quality. Choose **File > Output Settings > Background**. In the **Output Settings** dialog box, set **View As:** to **Background**, then click **OK**.

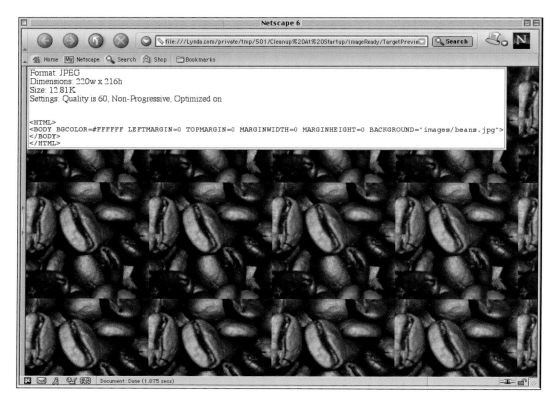

3. Click on the **Preview in Default Browser** button, and select a browser.

Notice the obvious edges from the seams of the source image? The Tile Maker filter will fix those in a snap.

4. Return to ImageReady and choose **Filter > Other > Tile Maker**.

```
                    Tile Maker
  ◉ Blend Edges                      ╭──────────╮
      Width: [ 10 ] percent          │    OK    │
      ☑ Resize Tile to Fill Image    ╰──────────╯
  ◯ Kaleidoscope Tile                ╭──────────╮
                                     │  Cancel  │
                                     ╰──────────╯
```

5. The **Tile Maker** dialog box will appear. Match the default settings you see above: **Blend Edges** selected, **Width: 10 percent**, and **Resize Tile to Fill Image** checked. Click **OK**.

Tip: Kaleidoscope Tile can also give you some beautiful abstract effects, so you might want to experiment with it later.

Here's what the image will look like after you apply the filter. You can see it's a little magnified, but the true difference is easier to see when you preview it.

6. Click the **Preview in Default Browser** button again.

In a browser, the background has become a little softer and the edge blending has hidden the sharp edges where the coffee beans run off the background tile.

Tip: If you want to preview just the background without the HTML information box displayed, generate an HTML document by choosing File > Save Optimized, *and in the Save Optimized dialog box choose* Save HTML and Images *from the pop-up Format menu (Mac) or* Save as type *menu (Windows). If you need a refresher on saving and previewing, revisit Exercise 2.*

Although this image is attractive and has no seams, it contains too much contrast to read with text over it. The next step will show you a useful method for modifying the brightness and hue of an image.

7. In ImageReady, choose **Image > Adjustments > Hue/Saturation**. Try the settings that you see here or pick some you like better. If **Colorize** is checked, the image will appear monochromatic, rather than full color. You can uncheck it if you want to retain the natural colors of the image. Click **OK**.

8. Click the **Preview in Default Browser** button to preview the results. This background image would be much easier to work with than the unadjusted version if you were trying to layer it with readable text.

9. Close the file. If you want to save it, revisit the previous exercises that have described how to save original and optimized background images. Keep ImageReady open for the next exercise.

6. [IR] _____Full-Screen Graphic Background Images

Using a full-screen graphic as a background image can produce an impressive effect. If optimized properly, a full-screen graphic doesn't have to be too large to download efficiently, particularly if you limit your colors and use large areas of flat color. Make all your full-screen background images at least **1024 x 768**, even if you are designing your site to work at a smaller resolution. This will avoid the problem of a background image that's intended to fill an entire screen repeating itself in a browser window that's bigger than the dimensions of the graphic. It's important that the background looks good when viewed at all sizes, from **640 x 480**, to **800 x 600**, all the way up to **1024 x 768** (and for some target audiences even beyond that).

Feature film directors face this problem when they shoot a wide-screen film that will also come out on video. Most directors try to frame their shots to look good in both the wide-screen theatrical screen size and your home TV. You can use the same idea to design a flexible full-screen graphic background that looks good in a variety of browser windows.

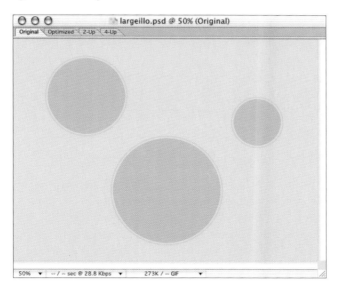

1. This exercise can be done in ImageReady or Photoshop, but because most of these background exercises are done in ImageReady, you'll stick with that program here. So in ImageReady, open **largeillo.psd** from the **chap_08** folder you copied to your hard drive.

It's a big file—1024 × 768 pixels—but when optimized as a GIF with four colors its file size is less than 4K. Images with large areas of solid colors like this optimize unbelievably well. Download speed won't be an issue with an image like this. The issue will be how this graphic will look on different viewers' browsers when cropped by their different resolutions.

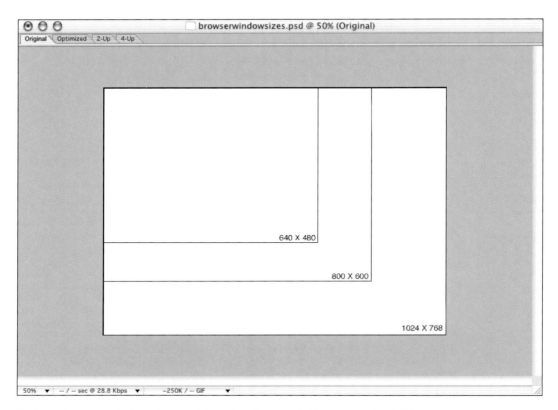

2. Open **browserwindowsizes.psd** from the **chap_08** folder on your hard drive.

This PSD file can be used as an overlay for full-screen background images. Its measurements are an approximation of how much your viewers will be able to see at different resolutions. It will help you to understand how the image will appear to different viewers, depending on the resolution to which a viewer's computer system is set. For example, a viewer whose system is set to 640 × 480 pixels will see only that portion of the background image (and any foreground elements you place on top of it) that fits within the box at the upper left of browserwindowsizes.psd that is marked 640 × 480.

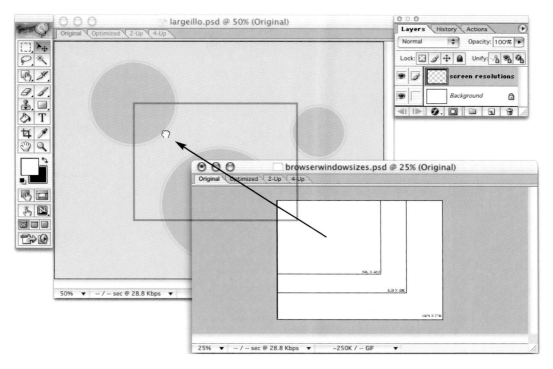

3. Select the **Move** tool from the Toolbox, make sure the layer labeled **screen resolutions** is selected, and click and drag that layer from the **browserwindowsizes.psd** file into the open **largeillo.psd**.

4. Align the upper-left corners of the layers, using the **Move** tool and the arrow keys on your keyboard. These are rather large images, so you might want to zoom in to fine-tune the alignment.

Tip: *To get the two aligned just so, you might want to go back and forth between the letters Z and V (the Zoom tool and the Move tool). Remember that to zoom back out, you'll need to hold down the* Option *(Mac) or* Alt *(Windows) key and click on the image again. We move this overlay document into our full-screen background images all the time at lynda.com to visualize how background images will look at different sizes.*

MOVIE | dragginglayer.mov

To learn more about how to drag a layer from one document into another, check out **dragginglayer.mov** from the movies folder on the **H•O•T CD-ROM**.

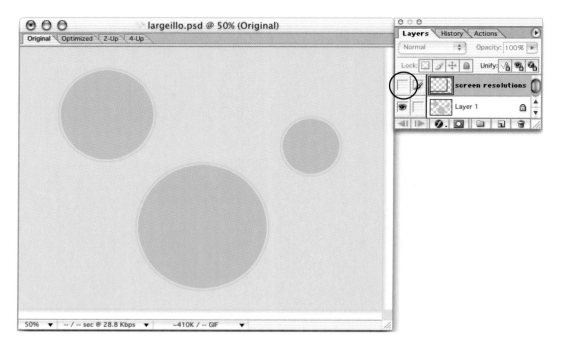

5. When you're ready to create a GIF of the background image, be sure to turn the **screen resolutions** layer off by toggling off the **Visibility** icon on that layer in the **Layers** palette. You don't want this layer to become part of the final optimized image, because it is just a design guide.

If you need a refresher on how to optimize this image as a GIF, revisit Chapter 4, "Optimization."

6. Close both files.

The point of this exercise was to show you how to use an overlay to visualize how a large image would look in smaller browsers. You don't actually want to publish the graphic with the overlay; it's there for your reference only. Feel free to steal this overlay and use it to design all your large background images.

7. [IR]   Large-Screen Photographic Background Images

Full-screen backgrounds are not limited to flat color graphics, like the one used in the last exercise. If you optimize a large photograph carefully, you can use it as a full-screen background. The key is to compress the photograph so that it's small enough to download at a reasonable speed on most browsers. This exercise will allow you to explore some of the optimization options for large-screen photographic images.

1. In ImageReady, open **largephoto.psd** from the **chap_08** folder on your hard drive. Click on the **Optimized** tab in the document window. Click on the **Optimize** palette, and choose the **JPEG** format. With the settings above, we were able to reduce the image size to around 36K.

Tip: If you recall, there are a few other ways to make a photograph smaller. One thing that would make a photograph smaller in file size would be to reduce its contrast and saturation using ImageReady image adjustments. This would offer the added benefit of making it easier to read text placed on top of the photographic background. Be sure to click back on the Original tab before making these adjustments. If you're in the Optimized tab, the program will slow down because it will try to optimize the image with each change you make.

2. Choose **Image > Adjustments > Hue/Saturation**. Match the settings shown above or experiment with your own. Click **OK** when you're happy with the results.

3. Click on the **Optimized** tab again, where you can check the **File Size Information** field to see if the file size got smaller. The changes made brought the image down to around 22K.

4. When you are ready to preview the image, choose **File > Output Settings > Background**, click **View As: Background**, and click **OK**. Then click the **Preview in Default Browser** button. Once you're happy with the results, you can choose to **Save Optimized**, which will save a JPEG version of this document, or **Save**, which will save a PSD file. Either way, close the file.

8. [IR] _____ Directional Tiles

A wonderful trick that's widely used on the Web is to make what are called **directional tiles**—graphics that are narrow and tall or wide and short before you preview them, but that expand into full-screen images when repeated as background images. You can create the illusion of a big full-screen graphic background with a tiny tile. A tall, skinny directional tile like the one below will repeat from left to right across the browser window and create a background of broad horizontal stripes.

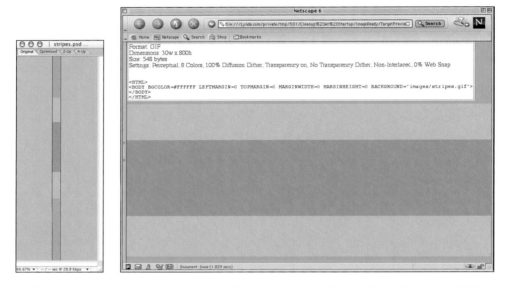

1. Open **stripes.psd** from the **chap_08** folder on your hard drive, and identify it as an HTML background (choose **File > Output Settings > Background**, choose **View As: Background**, and click **OK**). Click the **Preview in Default Browser** button, and select a browser. Notice the effect of the long and narrow tile—it repeats in a horizontal fashion.

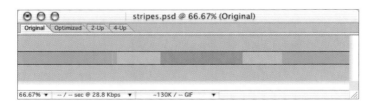

2. Return to ImageReady and rotate the artwork by choosing **Image > Rotate Canvas > 90°CW**.

The CW stands for clockwise, so this will rotate the image to the right. CCW stands for counterclockwise.

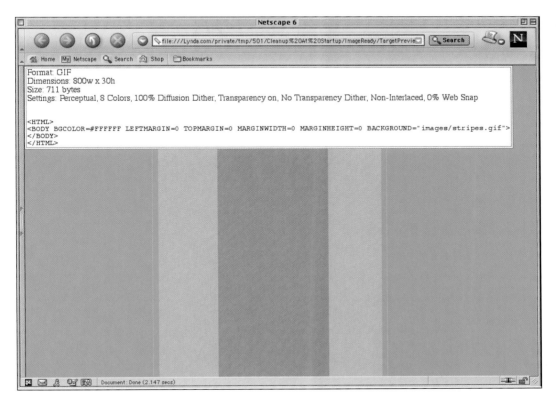

3. Click the **Preview in Default Browser** icon one more time, and select a browser from the list.

This ought to give you an idea of how these directional tiles work. Try changing the image inside this graphic, and watch the results. Fill it with a different color scheme or select and fill a new area for a new stripe. The sky's the limit, now that you know how images repeat inside browsers and you have ImageReady's great preview options at your disposal!

4. Save and close the file.

You've finished another chapter, folks! Making tiles is one of the most fun parts of Web design. With what you've learned here, you should be able to create any kind of background that you or your clients want.

9.
Transparent GIFs

Problems with GIF Transparency	Transparency Terminology
Creating and Previewing Transparency	Fixing Bad Edges
Pitfalls of Backgrounds	Saving Transparent GIFs
Transparent Layers

chap_09

Photoshop 7/ImageReady
H·O·T CD-ROM

By default, all images made on the computer are in the shape of a rectangle or square. This is the reason you see so many rectangular graphics on the Web, causing many sites to have a similar look. We refer to this in our classes as "rectangle-itis." You can eliminate rectangle-itis in your designs by using the GIF transparency techniques covered in this chapter.

At the moment, GIF is the only format in wide use for the Web that supports transparency. Unfortunately, GIF transparency settings are very limited and can produce an unwanted halo around a graphic. As you'll see, both Photoshop and ImageReady have excellent tools for countering the problems that are inherent to transparency in the GIF format. This chapter's exercises are designed to help you master these tools.

Problems with GIF Transparency

Any time you create artwork in Photoshop or ImageReady that contains soft edges (like a drop shadow, a glow, a feathered edge, or an anti-aliased edge), you are using what is called 8-bit or 256-level transparency. This kind of transparency is built into Photoshop, and it means that the program can create many different levels of partially transparent pixels at the edges of your graphic. Edges are given a smooth and natural appearance with 8-bit transparency, making artwork in shapes other than rectangles look so natural that you would never even give it much thought.

Photoshop anti-aliased edge   Photoshop glow

Photoshop and ImageReady use up to 256 levels of opacity when layering artwork. This makes anti-aliased edges, glows, and other soft edges look natural.

Sadly, the GIF file format supports only 1-bit masking, rather than the more sophisticated 8-bit masking that is native to Photoshop. 1-bit masking does not support partially transparent pixels. Instead, each pixel in an image with 1-bit masking is either fully transparent or fully opaque (either on or off). This limitation of 1-bit masking is the cause of the unattractive halo (sometimes called a fringe or matte) of colored pixels that you may have seen around some images on the Web. You'll learn how to control this problem in the following exercises.

GIF anti-aliased edge   *GIF glow edge*

The GIF file format is limited to 1-bit masking. Notice the halos around the edges of these transparent GIFs when they are displayed against a colored HTML background. You'll learn why this happens and how to fix it in this chapter. Yay!

What Is Anti-Aliasing?

The term **anti-alias** describes an edge of a graphic that blends into a surrounding color. The advantage of anti-aliasing is that it hides the otherwise jagged nature of color transitions in computer-based artwork. Most computer graphics programs offer the capability to anti-alias. In Photoshop and ImageReady, there's an anti-aliasing option available for most of the graphics-creation tools, including the selection tools, the Type tool, and the brushes and erasers.

An anti-aliased edge

A blurry graphic uses anti-aliasing, too.

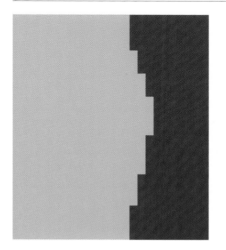

An aliased edge

How to Recognize a Transparent Layer

One way to create transparent GIF files in Photoshop or ImageReady is to first create your artwork on, or convert it to, a transparent layer. How can you tell if your document is using a transparent layer? The checkerboard pattern in Photoshop or ImageReady is the visual cue to let you know that transparent pixels are present.

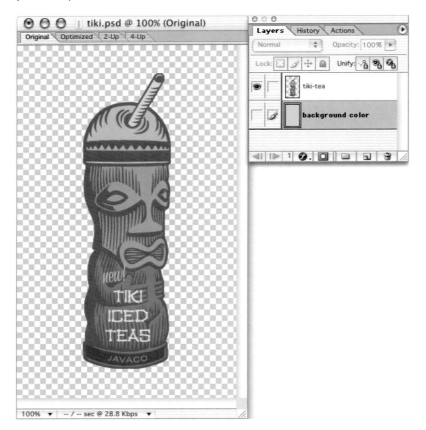

Whenever a Photoshop or ImageReady document is stored on a transparent layer, you will see a checkerboard pattern in the background. If you have other layers turned on that prevent you from seeing the checkerboard background, turn them off before you save the image as a transparent GIF. You'll find this process described in detail in this chapter.

Transparency, Masks, and GIFs

Here's a helpful chart to explain some of the terminology used in this chapter.

Transparency Terminology	
Term	**Definition**
Mask	A mask hides parts of an image from being visible. In the case of a transparent GIF file, the mask is what hides the transparent areas of the image, but the mask itself is not visible to the end user.
Transparent	The checkerboard pattern on a Photoshop layer indicates that a mask is in effect. When you draw a shape on a new layer in Photoshop, an invisible mask (called the *transparency channel*) is invoked.
Transparent GIF	A transparent GIF includes an invisible mask and is displayed by the Web browser in shapes other than squares or rectangles. This chapter shows you how to mask out parts of GIF images.
GIF	A GIF can be transparent or not. To make it transparent, you simply turn on the *Transparency* setting in the Photoshop Save For Web dialog box or the ImageReady Optimize palette.

Offset Problems in Browsers

You might wonder, why the fuss with all this transparency stuff? Couldn't you simply make a foreground image with the background image incorporated and position it over the same background image? Unfortunately, due to constraints within the HTML authoring language, foreground and background images don't line up in browsers, You'd end up with an unwanted offset, as shown below.

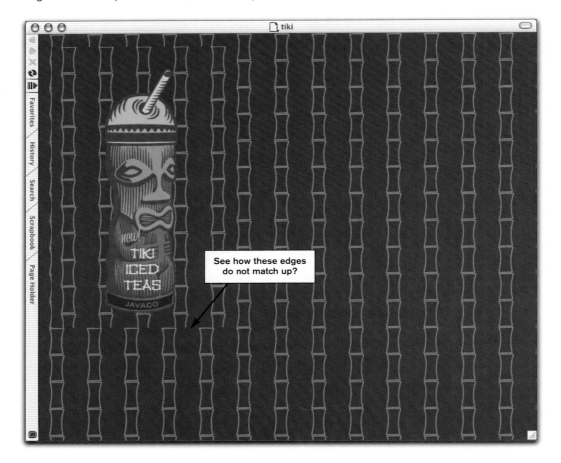

You can't forgo making a foreground GIF transparent, because if you just place the foreground and background images together, they don't necessarily line up in browsers. You can do much better than this by using the methods described in this chapter.

I. [IR] _____Creating and Previewing GIF Transparency

You can create transparent GIF files in either Photoshop or ImageReady. We've chosen to show this process first in ImageReady, because you can define background and foreground images and preview the results in a browser more readily from ImageReady than from Photoshop's Save For Web interface. This first exercise will teach you how to set GIF transparency and how to preview the results in a browser.

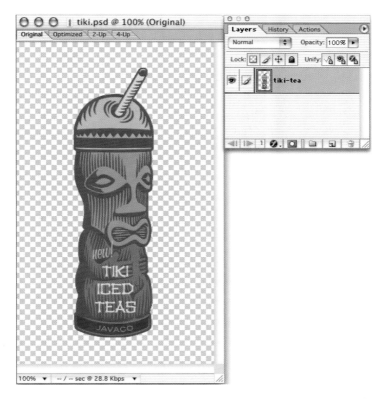

1. From ImageReady, open **tiki.psd** from the **chap_09** folder that you copied to your hard drive from the **H•O•T CD-ROM**.

2. Click on the **Optimized** tab in the document window and make sure that the **Optimize** and **Color Table** palettes are visible. If either palette is not visible, choose **Window > Optimize** or **Window > Color Table**.

3. In the **Optimize** palette, make sure that the compression settings match what you see in this example: **GIF**, **Adaptive**, **Colors: 64**, **No Dither**. Make sure that you can see the **Transparency** check box on the palette, and that it is checked.

Tip: If you don't see the Transparency check box, expand the Optimize *palette to display all its options by clicking on the* double arrows *next to the word* Optimize *(circled above).*

4. Choose **File > Output Settings > Background**. In the **Output Settings** dialog box that appears, choose **View Document As: Image**.

This lets ImageReady know that when you preview this image, you want to see it displayed as a foreground image.

5. Click the **Choose** button in the **Output Settings** dialog box, and navigate to the **chap_09** folder you copied to your hard drive from the **H•O•T CD-ROM**. Select **thinbamboo.gif**, and click **Open**. You will be returned to the **Output Settings** dialog box, where the path name to the file should appear inside the Background Image field. Click **OK**.

This tells ImageReady that when you preview your transparent foreground image, you want thinbamboo.gif *to appear behind it as a background image.*

6. Click and hold the **Preview in Default Browser** button in the Toolbox, and select a browser from the pop-up menu.

From the Preview in Browser pop-up menu, you can set any of the Web browsers installed in your computer as a default browser for previewing your ImageReady files in progress.

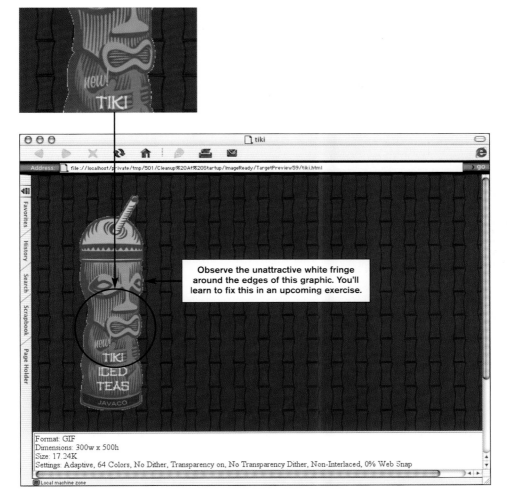

Observe the unattractive white fringe around the edges of this graphic. You'll learn to fix this in an upcoming exercise.

Format: GIF
Dimensions: 300w x 500h
Size: 17.24K
Settings: Adaptive, 64 Colors, No Dither, Transparency on, No Transparency Dither, Non-Interlaced, 0% Web Snap

The browser will open and display the tiki image on top of the background image you selected in step 5. You can see that the transparency settings are working, but notice the white fringe around the edges of the tiki image. You'll learn to eliminate that problem in the next exercise.

Tip: *The white box with HTML text is a product of the preview. To see the page without the text box in a browser, choose* File > Save Optimized As, *save the images and the HTML, and open the HTML file in a Web browser. You learned how to do this in Chapter 8, "*Background Images.*" You may want to revisit it for a refresher on saving HTML.*

7. Return to ImageReady, and leave this document open for the next exercise.

2. [IR] _____Fixing Bad Edges

In the last exercise, you learned to specify transparency in the GIF optimization settings and to preview the results against a patterned background. This resulted in an unwanted edge that is commonly referred to as a fringe, halo, or matte. This exercise shows you how to eliminate this unwanted edge, so that the edges around the image will look good.

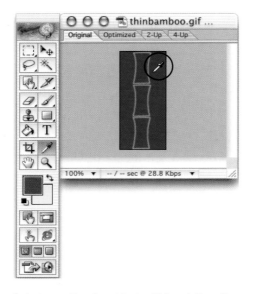

1. In ImageReady, with the **tiki.psd** file still open, choose **File > Open**, and browse to **thinbamboo.gif** in the **chap_09** folder on your hard drive. Select the **Eyedropper** tool from the Toolbox, and click on the green background in **thinbamboo.gif**. This will cause the same green color to appear in the Foreground Color swatch in the Toolbox.

The reason we asked you to sample the color from thinbamboo.gif _is so that you could specify it easily as the matte color for your transparent GIF. You'll learn how to do this in the next step, but it's important first to get the color into the Foreground Color swatch._

2. Switch to the **tiki.psd** image, which you should still have open from the last exercise. (If it's hidden behind other windows on your screen, choose **Window > Documents > tiki.psd**.) Make sure the **Optimize** tab in the document window is selected. In the **Optimize** palette, click on the down-pointing arrow to the right of the **Matte** field to open a pop-up color menu. Choose **Foreground Color** from the pop-up menu.

The same green color that you just put in the Foreground Color swatch of the Toolbox will appear in the Matte field of the Optimize palette. Look closely at the edge of the tiki image on the screen, and you should see that the same green color now appears under the anti-aliased edge of the graphic.

MOVIE | setting_mattecolor.mov

To learn more about setting matte color, check out **setting_mattecolor.mov** inside the **movies** folder you transferred to your hard drive from the **H•O•T CD-ROM**.

3. Check this out in a browser by clicking the **Preview in Default Browser** button in the Toolbox.

Clicking the Preview in Default Browser *button, instead of selecting a browser from its pop-up menu as you did before, will open your file in the default browser you set in the last exercise.*

Format: GIF
Dimensions: 300w x 500h
Size: 16.71K
Settings: Adaptive, 64 Colors, No Dither, Transparency on, No Transparency Dither, Non-Interlaced, 0% Web Snap

The background image is still set from the last exercise. So in the browser you will see the foreground tiki image laid over the thinbamboo.gif *background again, except that this time you won't see a distracting white halo around the tiki image. Instead, the tiki image will have a green matte around the edge that blends in with the background. With a fine-toothed background pattern like this, even though the background is busy, the matte color produces a nice, clean edge.*

4. Return to ImageReady, and leave **tiki.psd** open for the next exercise. You won't need **thinbamboo.gif**, so close it.

3. [IR] _____ Adding a Drop Shadow

Changing the matte color to match the color in the background image did the trick of eliminating the unattractive halo on a simple, anti-aliased foreground image. What if the edge of your foreground image contains a very soft edge, like a drop shadow or a glow? As you'll see in this exercise, the matching technique you just learned can camouflage even a soft drop shadow, as long as you place it over a certain kind of background image—one that has a fine-toothed pattern (as opposed to a pattern with big bold elements).

1. With **tiki.psd** still open in ImageReady, click on the **Original** tab of the document window. In the **Layers** palette, you can add a drop shadow layer effect to this image by clicking on the **layer effect** icon and choosing **Drop Shadow** from the pop-up menu. You can leave this layer effect at its default settings in the **Drop Shadow Options** palette for this exercise.

Tip: Again, we recommend that you edit images when you're in the Original *tab of the document window. Otherwise ImageReady tries to optimize the graphic as you're editing it, which slows things down. When you're in the* Original *tab, it's also possible to perform editing tasks (such as drawing or typing) that are not allowed when the document is set to the* Optimized *tab.*

2. Click on the **Optimized** tab of the document window. The image will appear with an unattractive green border around it because of the matte color you assigned to it in the last exercise.

Although the image looks extremely yucky here, it will look just fine against the background image in a browser, which you'll get to preview in the next step.

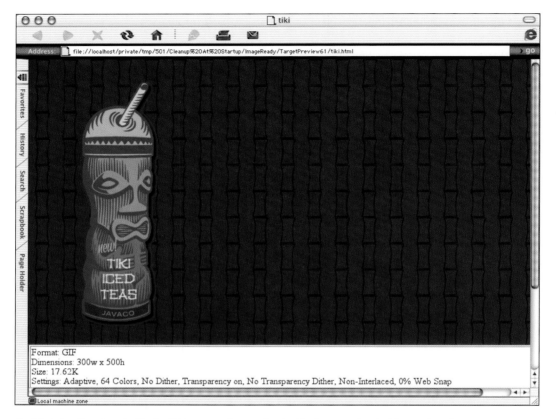

Format: GIF
Dimensions: 300w x 500h
Size: 17.62K
Settings: Adaptive, 64 Colors, No Dither, Transparency on, No Transparency Dither, Non-Interlaced, 0% Web Snap

3. Click the **Preview in Default Browser** button in the Toolbox to check this out in a browser.

If you look closely, you can see the green matte showing in spots. Regardless, it sure beats having unwanted colored edges around the entire image.

---

4. Return to ImageReady and leave the file open. Don't worry about saving it just yet. The next exercise will show you a situation in which the technique you just learned won't work.

---

4. [IR] The Pitfalls of Broad Backgrounds

The reason the green matte worked so well in the previous exercises is that the specified background image had a fine-toothed pattern that contained the same green you assigned as the matte color. This technique does not work in every scenario, as you'll see when you switch to a background image with a broad pattern in this exercise.

```
┌─────────────────────── Output Settings ────────────────────────┐
│                                                                  │
│   Settings: [ Custom                              ▲▼]   ( OK )    │
│                                                                  │
│   ┌ Background                           ▲▼┐─────   ( Cancel )    │
│       ┌ View Document As ──────────────────────┐                │
│       │ ◉ Image            ○ Background         │    ( Prev )     │
│       └────────────────────────────────────────┘    ( Next )     │
│       ┌ Background Image ───────────────────────┐                │
│       │ Path: [chap_09_thickbamboo.gif   ] (Choose...)│ ( Load... )│
│       └────────────────────────────────────────┘    ( Save... )  │
│   BG Color: [ Matte ▶]                                           │
│                                                                  │
│                                                                  │
└──────────────────────────────────────────────────────────────── ┘
```

1. With **tiki.psd** open, choose **File > Output Settings > Background**. In the **Output Settings** dialog box, click **Choose**, and select **thickbamboo.gif** from the **chap_09** folder you copied to your hard drive. Click **Open**. Back in the **Output Settings** dialog box, click **OK**.

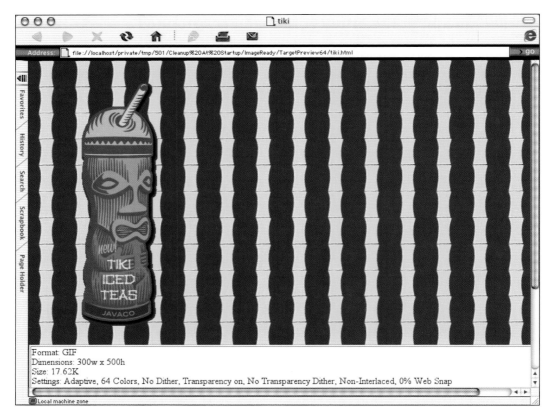

2. Preview this in a browser by clicking the **Preview in Default Browser** button in the Toolbox. Ugh... the results are not pretty.

This is a case when matching the matte to the background image will not work, because the areas of different colors in the background image are too broad and the color changes between them too extreme. When you set the matte to green, it shows up in the yellow areas, as you can see in this exercise. If you changed the matte color to yellow, it would show up against the green areas of the background. The best solution is to remove the soft edges created by the drop shadow effect and the anti-aliasing of the graphic, and also to remove the matte altogether, creating a hard-edged, aliased, nonmatted image, as you'll do in the next steps.

3. Return to ImageReady, and click on the **Original** tab. Turn off the layer effect that you added in the last exercise by clicking on the **Eye** icon to the left of that effect in the **Layers** palette.

4. In the **Optimize** palette, click on the down-pointing arrow to the right of the **Matte** field, and choose **None** from the pop-up menu.

This will remove all the anti-aliasing from the outside edge of the tiki graphic. The nice thing about using Matte: None *is that it removes anti-aliasing from only the outer edges of the graphic. Any anti-aliasing that exists in the interior of the image (like the anti-aliasing around the blue on top of the tiki's head) is preserved.*

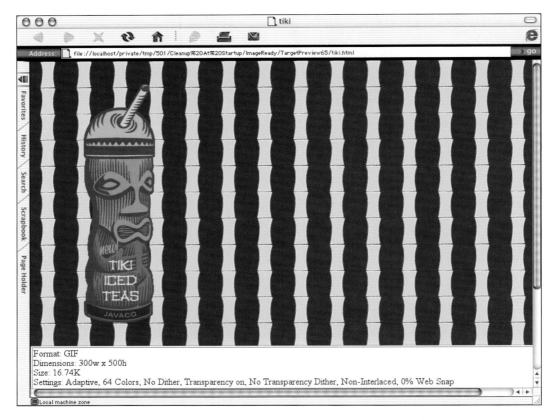

5. Preview the image in a browser. It doesn't look so bad anymore, but it doesn't contain the drop shadow either.

Actually, there is nothing you can do to save the drop shadow except to use a different background, like the fine-toothed pattern you used before. On broad backgrounds, you can't use any matte color because the illusion will be broken over the changing colored image. This is a limitation of the GIF file format, rather than a flaw in ImageReady or Photoshop.

6. Return to ImageReady and keep the same image open.

5. [IR] _____Saving Transparent Images

So far, you've learned how to create a transparent GIF image and how to preview it over different background images, but you haven't yet learned how to save a transparent GIF, alone or with its corresponding background. This exercise will focus on saving techniques in ImageReady.

1. Click on the **Optimized** tab of the **tiki.psd** document window. Check the **Optimize** palette to ensure that the optimize and transparency settings are configured the way you want them to be. Assume that the tiki is going to appear against a broad background, like the one in the previous exercise. Remembering what you've learned about different kinds of backgrounds, set the **Matte** field to **None**.

Save Optimized As
Save As: tiki.gif
Format: Images Only
Where: chap_09
Settings: Custom
Slices: All Slices
Cancel   Save

2. Choose **File > Save Optimized As**. ImageReady will take the first part of the file name from the original image and will insert the **.gif** extension at the end of the file name (**tiki.gif**). Click on the pop-up menu in the **Format** field (Mac) or the **Save as type** field (Windows), and choose **Images Only**. Navigate to the **chap_09** folder on your hard drive and click **Save**.

Note: *The GIF file you are saving will carry all of the settings that are in the Optimize palette. If you want to save the HTML, which specifies the background image as well, choose* HTML and Images *from the* Format *(Mac) or* Save as type *(Windows) pop-up menu. This choice depends on whether you would like ImageReady to build your page, or whether you prefer to build pages within an HTML editor such as GoLive, FrontPage, or Dreamweaver. Either way, click the* Save *button.*

3. Close the **tiki.psd** file.

6. [IR] _____Diffusion Transparency Dither

New to ImageReady and Photoshop 7 is a feature called **Diffusion Transparency Dither**. This odd-sounding term is useful when dealing with broad backgrounds and glows. In Exercise 4, you worked with a broad background and an image with a drop shadow. In essence, we gave up on making it look good because there was no way to see through the drop shadow to the broad background. Diffusion Transparency Dither is an alternative to giving up and setting the **Matte** to **None** as you did in Exercise 4. Not everyone likes the effect Diffusion Transparency Dither creates, but it's worth learning about so you can know all the possible options with GIF transparency. If you're still wondering what the heck we're talking about, try the exercise and you'll soon see.

1. Open **tikiglow.psd** from the **chap_09** folder. Notice its glow? This exercise will work only with artwork that contains a soft edge like this.

2. Choose **File > Output Settings > Background**. The **Output Settings** dialog box will appear. Click on the **Choose** button and navigate to the **chap_09** folder you copied to your hard drive. Select **thickbamboo.gif** and click **Open**. Click **OK**. This sets up the file **thickbamboo.gif** to appear as the background image for this document.

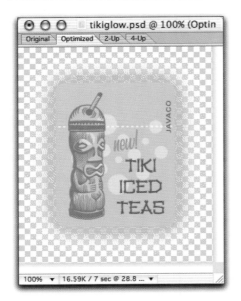

3. Click the **Optimize** tab. In the **Optimize** palette, choose the following settings: **GIF, Adaptive, Colors: 64, No Dither**. Make sure the **Transparency** check box is checked. Click where it says **No Transparency** and choose **Diffusion Transparency Dither** from the drop-down menu.

4. When you do this, the glow around the image will suddenly look very pixellated. This is the effect that some people like and some people don't like. The best way to test whether you're pleased with the results of this setting is to preview it in the browser. Click the **Preview in Default Browser** button on the ImageReady Toolbox.

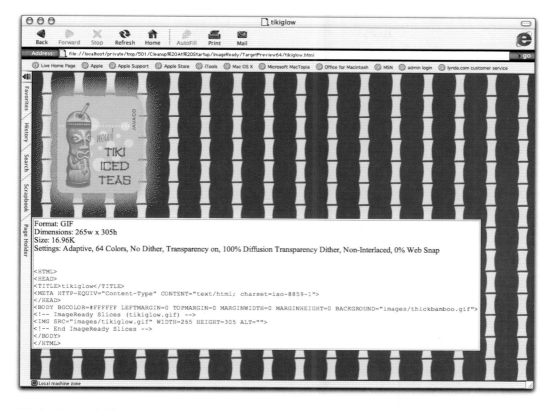

This is the result. You see through the background, but the glow looks pixellated. Because GIF transparency is either on or off, and it can't produce smooth transitions like Photoshop transparency, the only way to see through the GIF is to convert the glow to lots of little dots. As we said, some people like this effect, and some don't!

---

5. Return to ImageReady. Close the file without saving it. You won't be needing it again for this chapter.

NOTE | What Does Dither Mean?

At this point you've probably noticed the term "dither" bantered about in the ImageReady and Photoshop interfaces. Dither means to reduce smooth color transitions so they can be represented by fewer colors, and it always results in the appearance of dots or individual pixels. In the Optimize palette, there are two different locations for dither settings.

In both circled instances, ImageReady is letting you set the dither algorithm. The top instance sets dithering to the picture itself. The bottom instance sets dithering to the edge of the picture. There are three general choices: *Diffusion*, *Noise*, or *Pattern*. *Diffusion* dither is the most natural looking, in that the pixellated dots are matched to the content. For example, the dots in the glow when set to *Diffusion* gradually taper off. *Noise* is a random texture of dots, and *Pattern* produces an obvious patterned series of dots. Feel free to try these different choices. Most people prefer *Diffusion* as the setting when they choose *Dither* in either location.

7. [PS] ————————Transparency in Photoshop

Though we've shown how to create GIF transparency in ImageReady so far, there are going to be times when it's simply more convenient to do so in Photoshop. This first exercise will walk you through the basic steps of establishing preview and transparency settings in Photoshop.

1. Open Photoshop. Open **tiki.psd** from the **chap_09** folder on your hard drive. Open **thinbamboo.gif** as well. With **thinbamboo.gif** selected, choose **File > Save For Web**. Use the **Eyedropper** from the Save For Web Toolbox and click on the green background of **thinbamboo.gif** to sample its dominant green color. Click **Cancel**. You did this step to capture the green color from the image.

Note: Unlike in ImageReady, you must sample the green color in the Save For Web *interface, not in the main Photoshop interface. This is one of the hassles of working in Photoshop that we alluded to earlier. The only reason that you did step 1 was to capture the color in the* Save For Web *interface.*

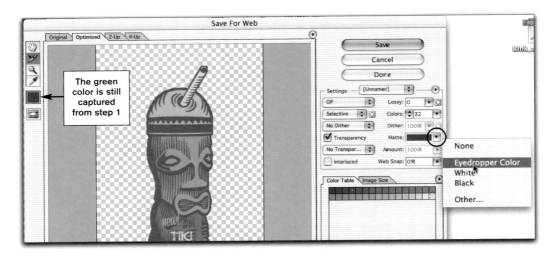

2. Choose **Window > Documents > tiki.psd** to make the ice tea image active. Choose **File > Save for Web,** and the file will open inside the **Save For Web** dialog box. Notice that the green color you sampled in step 1 is still in the color well? Change the settings to what you see above: **GIF, Selective, No Dither, Colors:32**. Select **Eyedropper Color** from the **Matte** menu. Don't click Save yet!

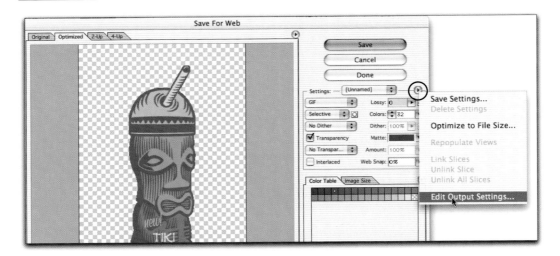

3. Still in the **Save For Web** dialog box, click the arrow to the far right of the **Settings** field, then choose **Edit Output Settings** from the pop-up menu. This will open the **Output Settings** dialog box.

4. In the **Output Settings** dialog box, click on the pop-up menu below the **Settings** field and choose **Background** from the menu. This will cause the **Background** options to appear in this dialog box.

5. Choose **View Document As: Image**. Click the **Choose** button to the right of the **Path** field, browse to **thinbamboo.gif** in the **chap_09** folder on your hard drive, and click **Open**. In the **Output Settings** dialog box, click **OK**.

This lets Photoshop know that you want the tiki image to be viewed in the foreground, over the tiling background image thinbamboo.gif.

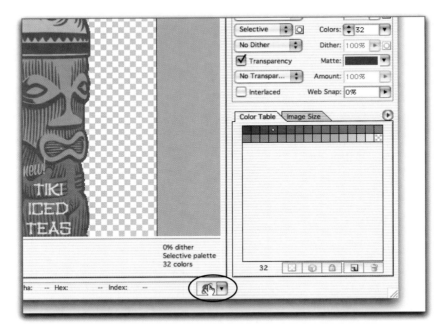

6. Back in the **Save For Web** dialog box, click the **Preview in Default Browser** button. This will open the Photoshop default browser, so you can preview your transparent GIF on top of the background image you specified in the last step.

7. Return to the **Save For Web** dialog box. If you were satisfied with the browser preview, click **Save**. This will open the **Save Optimized As** dialog box.

Note: When you click Save, *you will have a chance to rename the file, if you'd like to preserve your original image.*

8. In the **Save Optimized As** dialog box, click on the **Format** field (Mac) or the **Save as type** field (Windows), and choose **HTML and Images**. Change the **Save As** field to **tiki2.html**, navigate to the **chap_09** folder on your hard drive, and click **Save**.

Photoshop will save a transparent GIF called tiki2.gif, as well as the HTML file tiki2.html that identifies the background image. If you'd rather build your Web page and add a background manually in an HTML editor, choose Images Only from the Format menu, and change the Save As field to tiki2.gif. This is a personal choice that depends on the workflow you prefer.

9. That's all there is to creating a transparent GIF in Photoshop! Close the file.

Note: *Photoshop 7 has an Assistant that will walk you through the steps of creating a transparent GIF, but we don't recommend using it because it doesn't allow you to set or preview a background image. You'll have a lot more control over creating and saving your transparent GIFs in Photoshop if you follow the steps you've learned in this exercise. If you just have to have a look at the Assistant, go to the Photoshop Help menu and choose Export Transparent Image.*

8. [PS]_____What to Do with No Transparent Layer

Although you've worked on **tiki.psd** in this chapter, you might not realize that it was created on a Photoshop transparent layer before you made it into a transparent GIF. Why is this important for you to know? Because ImageReady and Photoshop were able to tell where the edges of the graphic were because they were on a transparent layer. Let's say that your original graphic wasn't on a transparent layer—how would you define where you wanted the transparency for the transparent GIF? You'll learn a technique in this exercise that is new to Photoshop 7. This technique works only in Photoshop, not in ImageReady.

1. In Photoshop, open **banner.psd** from the **chap_09** folder on your hard drive. Choose **File > Save for Web**. Click the **Transparency** check box on and off.

Notice that nothing happens. Since this is a flattened file and there is no Photoshop layer transparency in this document, Photoshop doesn't know what part of the image you want to become transparent. It's essential that the Photoshop layer transparency (indicated by a checkerboard pattern) be visible for Photoshop to understand what to do.

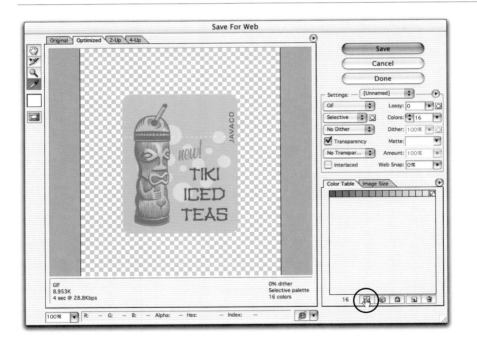

2. Match the settings to what you see above: **GIF, Selective, Colors: 16, No Dither**. Use the **Eyedropper** and click on the white background. Click the **Transparency** check box. The last, most important step is to click on the **Map Transparency** button (circled above). This instructs Photoshop to knock the color out that you selected with the **Eyedropper**.

This feature is new to Photoshop 7 and is very useful when you have to work with an image that doesn't have a transparent layer to begin with. Unfortunately, this feature is only in Photoshop, and not in ImageReady. Go figure!

3. Click **OK** when you've arrived at the settings you like, and save the optimized file. Close the **PSD** file without saving it.

Congratulations! You are now prepared to create transparent GIFs against a variety of backgrounds in ImageReady or Photoshop. This was a long chapter because GIF transparency is a lot more complex than it seems at first glance.

10.
Slicing

What Are Slices?	Slice Types	Slicing and Selecting
Slice Preferences	Optimizing Slices
Previewing and Saving Slices	Slice Options

chap_10

Photoshop 7/ImageReady
H•O•T CD-ROM

Slicing offers the ability to cut apart a single image into multiple images in order to reassemble them inside an HTML table. You might wonder why anyone would want to do such a thing. For starters, you can optimize different parts of an image with different compression settings and file formats in order to reduce the file size. You'll learn to do that in this chapter. Later chapters will show other uses for slices, such as producing rollovers and animations and setting parts of a sliced document to contain HTML links for graphical buttons.

Slicing is simple and complex at the same time. It's easy to cut apart the image, but managing all the resulting files takes practice and the ability to go under the hood to set HTML preferences. This chapter walks you through a slicing example that will help you learn the nuances of making slices and generating table code from Photoshop. You can create slices in ImageReady as well, and you'll learn how to do so in Chapter 11, "*Rollovers*."

What Are Slices?

Slices are the result of cutting up an image into multiple pieces. A single document is sliced into smaller pieces, and those pieces are reassembled to look like a single image again using an HTML table.

When you create slices in Photoshop and save the optimized file, the program generates multiple images (one for each slice) and HTML table code. The table allows the browser to assemble all the separate images seamlessly so they look like one document again.

In the following exercises, you'll learn to use Photoshop to cut a document into several pieces and reassemble them inside an HTML table. The program's settings will affect how the code is written and how the slices are named and saved.

Slice Types

Once you start to make slices, Photoshop will display clues that show what type of slice each is. **User slices,** which are the slices you draw yourself, have bright blue numbers and icons and are surrounded by solid lines. **Auto slices,** which are the slices that Photoshop generates to fill in all the regions where you haven't drawn a slice, have gray numbers and icons and are bordered by dotted lines. You may have noticed that different slices have different-looking icons. You'll learn about the other kinds of slice icons and what they mean in Chapter 11, "*Rollovers.*"

Slice Types	
User slice `02` ⊠	A user slice is created when you create a rectangle or square with the Slice tool.
Auto slice `01` ⊠ `8`	An auto slice is created by Photoshop or ImageReady when you create a slice, and other slices are needed to fill in the resulting spaces. The link symbol indicates that this type of slice will inherit the same optimization settings as other auto slices in the same document. You'll have a chance to work with this kind of slice in this chapter and Chapter 11, "*Rollovers.*"

I. [PS]   Slicing and Reshaping

When slicing artwork manually in Photoshop, you will use two tools—**Slice** and **Slice Select**. This first exercise will demonstrate how to slice up an image and reshape your slice using the Slice tool. Why would you cut this image into slices? You'll see how creating different optimization settings for the right and left sides of this image will not only reduce the file size, but will also make the graphics look better. You'll learn to slice in this exercise and to optimize in the next.

1. In Photoshop, open **comingsoon.psd** from the **chap_10** folder you transferred to your hard drive from the **H•O•T CD-ROM**.

You may see the slice number 01 and a slice icon in the upper-left corner of the image, because Photoshop automatically treats every newly opened document as if it had one all-inclusive slice. If you don't see the slice number and icon, it's because slice visibility is turned off in your copy of Photoshop. To turn it on, choose View > Show > Slices.

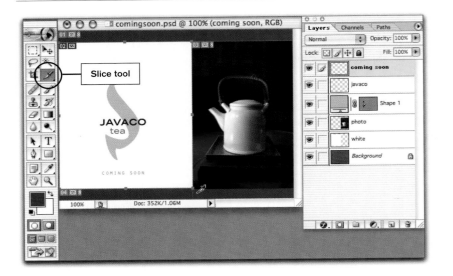

2. Select the **Slice** tool, and drag a slice around the white region of the image, stopping short of the bottom to match what you see in the figure above.

Tip: It doesn't matter what layer is selected in the Layers palette. Slices cut through all layers.

Notice that the slice you drew has been marked with a bright blue icon and a solid line, while other slices have appeared without you even defining them. The slice you create (indicated by the bright blue icon) is called a user slice because you—the user—defined it, and the rest are called auto slices. Photoshop creates slices for all the areas the user doesn't define, so that all of the areas are divided into slices.

Why are all those slices numbered, you ask? When Photoshop creates the user slices and the auto slices, it keeps track of them by assigning numbers to them. **Important note:** *Your numbers might not perfectly match the ones shown here if you do not slice your document identically. If that's the case, you should still be able to do the exercise, but realize that your numbered slices might be different from those we describe.*

3. With the **Slice** tool, create another slice around the teapot photograph, as shown above. There should now be a total of four slices, and Slices 02 and 03 should be blue, indicating that they are user slices.

Note: *If you don't draw the slice properly, move your mouse over one of the edges of any user-based slice, and the tool shape will change to an up/down or right/left arrow tool shape. If you click and drag with this tool shape, you can reshape the slice region. You cannot do this procedure to auto slices (indicated by gray numbers).*

NOTE | Deleting Slices

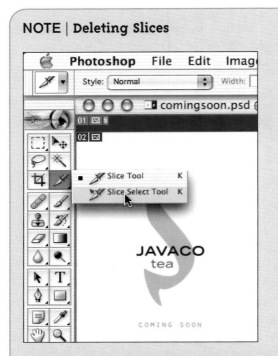

If you ever want to delete a slice, you'll have to first select it. This is done with the Slice Select tool. Click your mouse on the **Slice** tool, and hold it down. You'll see the Slice Select icon. With the mouse still depressed, select the **Slice Select** tool.

Select the slice and delete it by pressing the **Delete** key. The user slice will disappear. Sometimes, an auto slice will take its place, depending on how the document is sliced.

4. You might be wondering if there's a way to turn slices off so you can see the image without the interference of slice borders and icons. You can toggle the preview of slices on and off by choosing **View > Show > Slices**. When you're finished trying this command, leave slices toggled on so you'll be able to see them for the rest of this exercise.

As long as slices are toggled on in the View > Show menu, another way to turn slice visibility on and off is with the View > Show Extras *command, or with the shortcut key* Cmd+H *(Mac) or* Ctrl+H *(Windows). The slice visibility toggles are hard to find in Photoshop 7. In the next chapter, you'll see that it's easier to turn slices on and off in ImageReady, because that program has Show and Hide Slices buttons right in the Toolbox.*

5. Save this file and leave it open for the next exercise.

NOTE | Slice Preferences

You can choose to have your slices snap to the edges of other slices. You'll find that this helps align slices and avoid overlap. Turn this feature on and off by choosing **View > Snap To > Slices**.

You might like to have rulers showing as you draw your slices. Choose **View > Rulers** and make sure you set your ruler preferences to pixels if you haven't already done so (**Photoshop > Preferences > Units and Rulers > Rulers: Pixels**).

2. [PS]_____Optimizing Slices

One reason to cut apart a document is to optimize different sections appropriately. The image you sliced in the last exercise has areas of solid color that would compress better as GIF, as well as areas of continuous-tone photographic content that would compress better as JPEG. In this exercise, you'll apply different optimization settings to these areas to get the best overall file size and quality. This is where slicing comes in really handy.

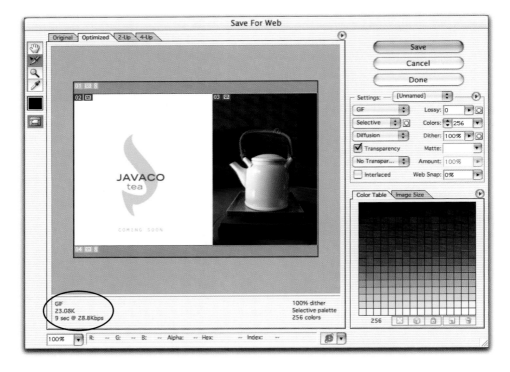

1. With **comingsoon.psd** still open from the last exercise, choose **File > Save for Web**. In the **Save For Web** dialog box, select the **Optimized** tab. In our screen above, you'll see that the overall compression has been set to GIF. Click in the gray area to deselect any selected slices. This allows you to see the file size of the entire image, not an individual slice. Look to the readout near the lower-left corner to see that the file size is currently 23K. Note, this may vary depending on how your settings are defaulting. Do not worry if your settings are different!

The circled file size shown above represents the entire document and all its slices. You can optimize this image much better by compressing each region with settings that best suit the slice images. You'll do this next.

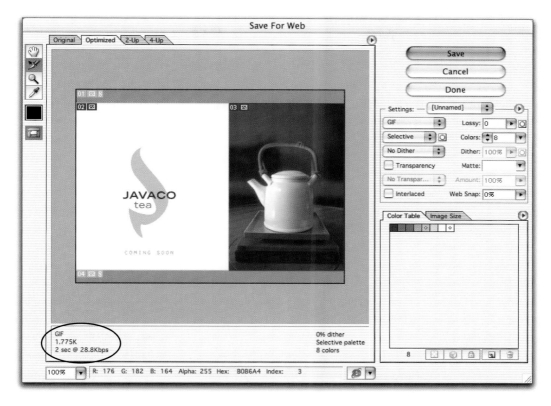

2. Click on the **Slice Select** tool on the left of the dialog box, and select the **javaco** slice (Slice 02) in the image preview. Choose the following settings: **GIF**, **Selective**, **No Dither**, and **Colors: 8**. The area of the image covered by this slice is best optimized as a GIF because it's composed of solid colors.

The file size for this slice is now 1.7K. Your optimization results might differ from ours in the figure above because you might have drawn slices that are different sizes than ours.

Don't be confused by the fact that there are two Slice Select tool locations—one in Photoshop and one in the Save For Web dialog box. You'll use the one in the main interface to adjust the size and position of slices, as you did in the last exercise. You'll use the one in the Save For Web dialog box to select slices for optimizing, as in this exercise.

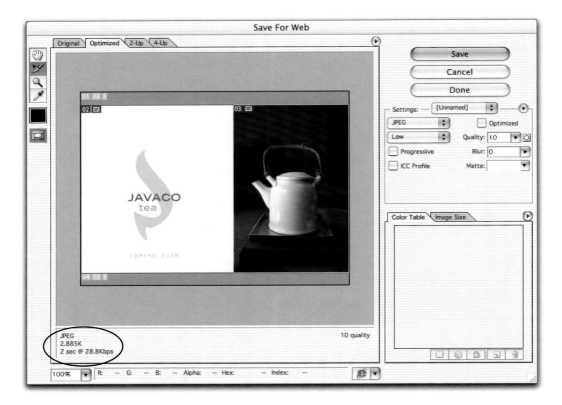

3. With the **Slice Select** tool, click the teapot image's slice. Because this image contains a photo, it will be better optimized in the JPEG format. Change its **Optimize** settings to match those shown above (**JPEG, Low**).

Note: Notice the readout at the bottom of the preview? It's showing the file size for just this particular optimized slice. Your amount may differ from ours due to the differences in the way you may have sliced the image.

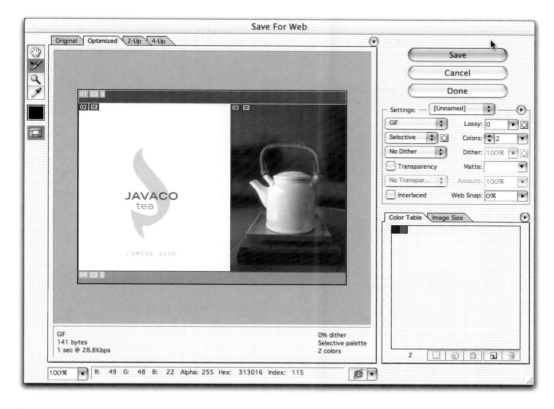

4. Using the **Slice Select** tool from the **Save For Web** dialog box, select **Slice 01**, which happens to be an auto slice (indicated by the gray slice icon). Auto slices have a special property, in that they are linked together for optimization purposes. That means that whatever setting you enter here will also affect the other auto slices in this document (Slice 04). Change the settings to match those above, (**GIF, Selective, Colors:2, No Dither**).

Notice that these settings reduce the auto slice area of the image to around 141 bytes. (Your number may be different if you drew your slices differently than ours.)

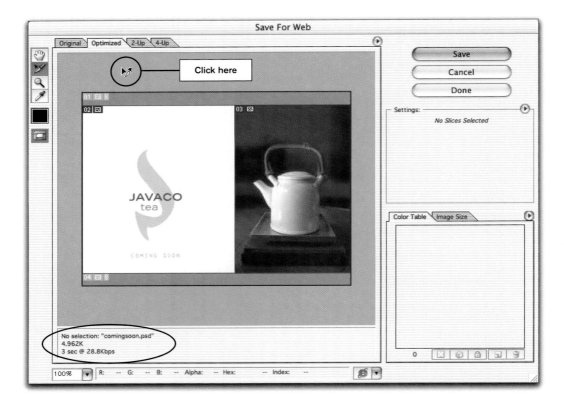

5. Click in the gray area of the **Save For Web** interface to deselect all the slices. This shows the overall file size of all the slices in the lower-left corner.

The optimized file size of the entire document is the total of the four individually optimized slices (which comes to under 5K!). If you had optimized the entire image as either a GIF or a JPEG, the overall file size and quality would not have been as good.

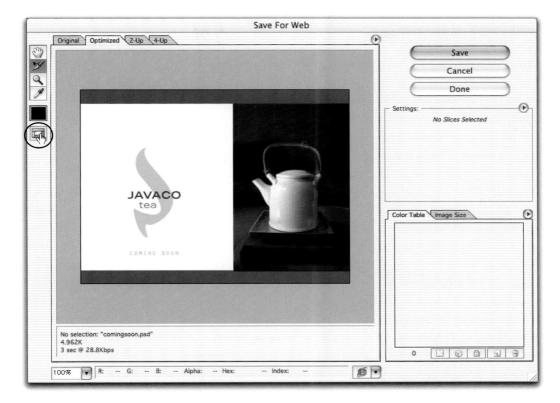

6. Toggle off the **Slice Visibility** button in the **Save For Web** dialog box to check the appearance of the image at the settings you've chosen. We toggle this button frequently so we can double-check optimization settings, because when slice visibility is on, unselected slices appear slightly discolored.

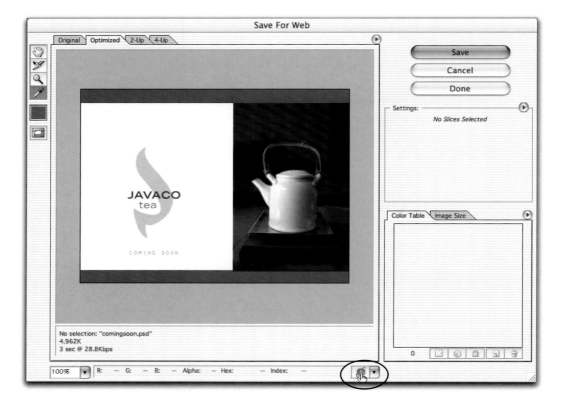

7. Press the **Preview in Browser** button at the bottom of the **Save For Web** dialog box.

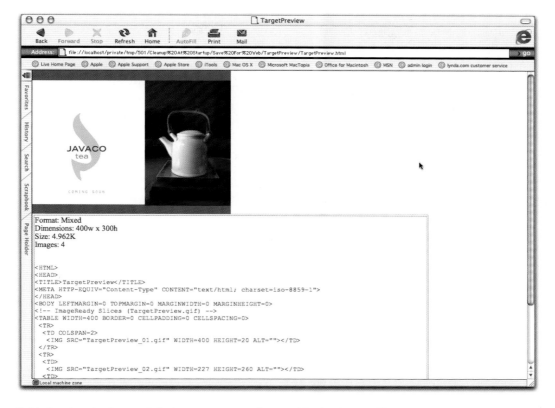

8. Notice that the image defaults to appear against a white background?

Slicing an image creates foreground images. Next you're going to learn to set a background color for this Web page that matches the green color in the auto slice regions

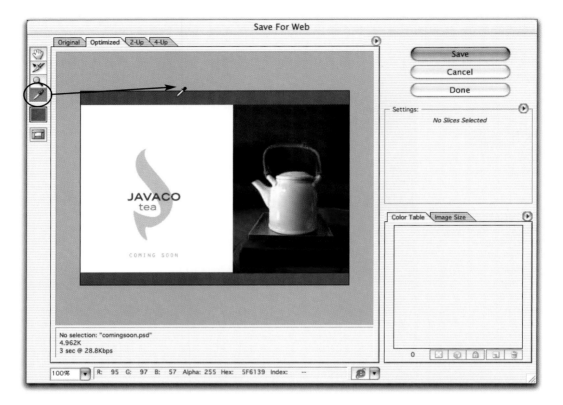

9. Return to Photoshop, where the Save For Web dialog box should still be open. Make sure slice visibility is still toggled off, so you can get a clear view of all the colors in the image from which to make your background color choice. Choose the **Eyedropper** tool and click on the olive green color on the top of your image preview. That olive green color will appear inside the Eyedropper Color swatch in the Save For Web dialog box.

10. Click the **Optimize** menu button in the **Save For Web** dialog box. From the pop-up, choose **Edit Output Settings**.

11. Change the HTML menu to **Background** in order to display options for setting the HTML background settings of a page. Click the black arrow next to the **BG Color** field, and choose **Eyedropper Color** from that pop-up menu. Click **OK**.

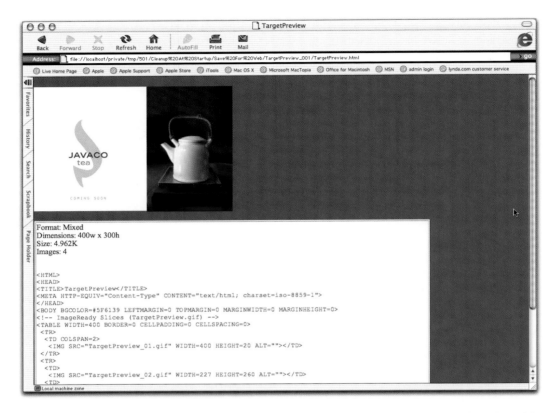

12. Preview the image again from the **Preview in Browser** button at the bottom of the **Save For Web** dialog box. Now the foreground image will appear against a green background!

There are times when it's fine to leave the background setting at its default (white) and other times when you want it to match a color in your image. You know how to do it either way at this point, so you can decide whether you need to match the background color when you work on your own projects in the future.

13. Leave this file open in the **Save For Web** dialog box for the next exercise, in which you will learn the nuances of previewing and saving a sliced document in Photoshop.

3. [PS] _____Previewing and Saving Slices

It's not enough to slice and optimize, you also have to save the slices and the resulting HTML. This next exercise will cover how to finish the project.

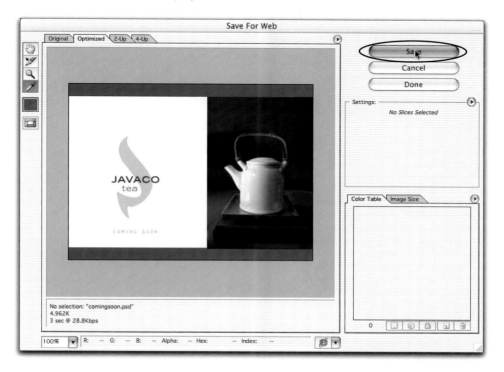

1. Now, it's time to learn how to save the actual slices and HTML. Click the **Save** button in the **Save For Web** dialog box (finally!).

2. This will open the **Save Optimized As** dialog box. Navigate to the **chap_10** folder that you saved to your hard drive. Create a new folder here, and name it **comingsoon**.

3. Make sure **HTML and Images** is selected in the **Format** field (Mac) or the **Save as type** field (Windows), and click **Save**.

4. Navigate to your hard drive to open the **comingsoon** folder you just made. You'll see the fruit of Photoshop's labor—a folder filled with four image files and one HTML file. Not bad for a few seconds' work!

Notice that three of the documents are saved as GIF and one is a JPEG. If you'll recall, you gave Slice 03 a JPEG setting in the Save For Web dialog box. The other slices were set up as GIF files. Photoshop honored those settings, as you can now see. When you're done admiring your handiwork, return to Photoshop to save a copy of the PSD document with its slices. If you want to see the final document without the preview code and optimization insert that appears when you Preview In Browser, simply double-click on the comingsoon.html *document. It will open in a browser.*

5. In Photoshop, click in the **comingsoon.psd** document window and choose **File > Save As**. In the **Save As** dialog box, name this copy **comingsoon2.psd**, and click **Save**. Leave **comingsoon2.psd** open for the next exercise.

When you choose File > Save As, you have the opportunity to make a copy of the PSD document— either by renaming the file, as you did here, or by checking the Save: As a Copy *checkbox. Now you'll have two versions of the file—the unsliced version and the sliced version. You don't always want to keep two versions of your PSD documents, but we often do when we make a significant change, in case we want to revert quickly back to the original. It's important to note that Photoshop saves all the slice information when you save a file in the PSD format.*

4. [PS] _____Using Slice Options

Slice options offer a means to manage the way slices are named when they are saved in Photoshop. In this exercise, you will learn to name and set **alt** text for the critical image files inside a document that contains slices. Alt text is what the end users will see if their images are turned off. As an added bonus in Internet Explorer, a speech balloon appears if you hover over an object that contains alt text.

1. The document **comingsoon2.psd** should be open in Photoshop from the last exercise. Choose the **Slice Select** tool from the **Toolbox**, and select **Slice 02** in the document. Click the **Slice Options** button on the **Options** bar to open the **Slice Options** dialog box.

2. In the **Slice Options** dialog box, change the **Name** of the selected slice from its default, **comingsoon2_02**, to **javaco_tea**. The **Name** field should never contain spaces or special characters because it is going to become a file name that gets addressed by HTML. Type **Javaco Tea is Coming Soon!** into the **Alt Tag** field. Notice that you can include spaces in **alt** text. Click **OK**.

Tip: *It's important not to use any spaces in the name for the file, or you might have problems with broken images once you upload this file to a live Web server. You can use an underscore if you want to simulate a space.*

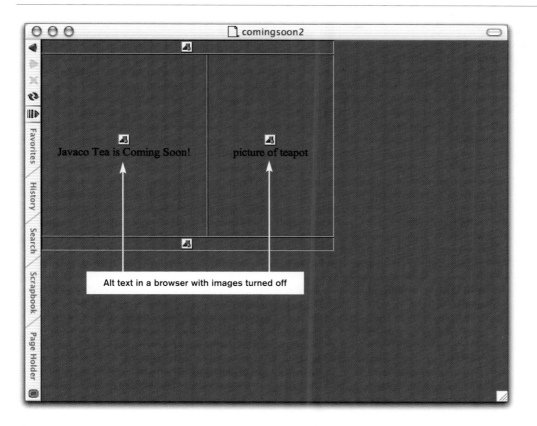

Alt text shows in a browser if the end user turns off images in the browser's Preferences or is accessing a Web page with a text-only browser. Some people turn their images off when they surf the Web to speed up downloading. Sight-impaired visitors to your site might have an automatic reader machine to "read" the alt text to them because they can't see the graphics. Alt text should not be added for every single slice, just for the critical information that would be needed if someone were viewing this page without images.

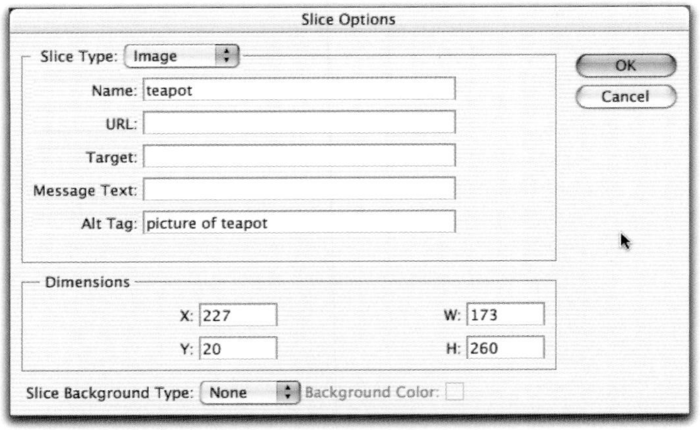

3. Using the **Slice Select** tool, click on **Slice 03**. Click on the **Slice Options** button on the **Options** bar to open the **Slice Options** dialog box. Enter **teapot** into the **Name** field. Enter **picture of teapot** into the **Alt Tag** field. Click **OK**.

If your slice numbers are different than what we've shown here, just enter the correct names into the Name *field, and your document will be just fine. Man, you are now the ultimate slicing machine!*

4. Choose **File > Save for Web**. Your optimization settings should still be there from previous exercises, so just click **Save**.

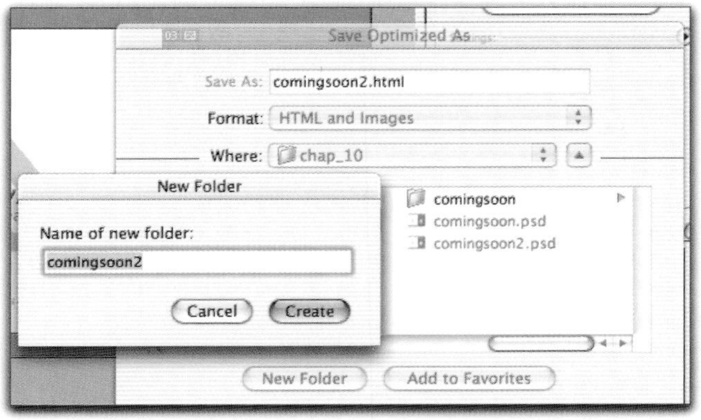

5. In the **Save Optimized As** window that opens, make sure **HTML and Images** is selected in the **Format** field (Mac) or the **Save as type** field (Windows). Navigate to the **chap_10** folder that you transferred to your hard drive. Make a new folder called **comingsoon2**. Make sure the comingsoon2 folder is selected, and click **Save**. Once again, this prevents the files from being scattered about your hard drive.

6. Return to your hard drive to look at the contents of the **comingsoon2** folder. This time, the images are named in a way that suggests what they contain, so you don't have to memorize which numbered slice relates to which image.

NOTE | What About Slicing in ImageReady?

Slicing is similar, but different in ImageReady. Fortunately, Chapter 11, "*Rollovers*" is all about this subject, so you'll get lots of practice to learn the differences.

This chapter is a wrap. Slices were used in this chapter for optimization purposes, but in future chapters you'll get to use them for rollovers and animation. Since Photoshop doesn't offer rollover or animation features, most of your future slicing practice will happen in ImageReady.

11.

Rollovers

| Rollovers Styles | Layer-Based Slicing |
| Rollover Styles For Multiple Buttons |
| Saving Rollovers | Making Manual Rollovers |
| Remote Rollovers |

chap_11

Photoshop 7/ImageReady
H•O•T CD-ROM

A rollover graphic changes appearance when an end-user's mouse interacts with it, usually by rolling over it, but sometimes by clicking on it instead. The programming behind these special types of rollover graphics is created with JavaScript. Normally, you would need to know how to program JavaScript or how to use an HTML editor such as GoLive, Dreamweaver, or FrontPage to create rollovers. What's great is that ImageReady not only lets you create the graphics for rollovers, but it then writes the code for them, so you don't have to learn a single line of code if you don't want to.

Although you can work with PSD files that originated from Photoshop, you can't program rollovers in it. ImageReady is the tool of choice for creating rollovers. For this reason, all the exercises in this chapter take place in ImageReady, not Photoshop.

In this chapter, you'll learn how to make remote rollovers, and how to trigger several events with one rollover. You will also have another chance to work with styles, layer effects, and image maps. This is where all the skills you've learned so far culminate in some pretty exciting results. This is a long, meaty chapter. Dig in, and prepare to be challenged (in a good way, of course!).

Rollover Slice Symbols

Most of the rollovers you make in this chapter and the next will be based on slices. Photoshop and ImageReady display icons, called **slice symbols**, which identify the type of slice that you've created. You first learned about slice symbols in Chapter 10, "*Slicing*." There are two new kinds of icons that you'll encounter in this chapter, because they relate to the creation and existence of rollovers.

Slice Icons for Rollovers		
	Layer-based slice symbol	A slice that is made with the layer-based slicing method, which you'll learn about in this chapter!
	Rollover symbol	Identifies a slice that contains rollover images.

I. [IR] _____Making a Simple Rollover with Rollover Styles

You were already introduced to the Styles palette in Chapter 7, "*Layer Styles*." What we didn't mention was that the Styles palette also contains some more powerful styles called **rollover styles**. This special kind of style is like the Cuisinart of Web graphics—it slices, it dices, it writes JavaScript, and it automatically creates rollover graphics in seconds. In this exercise, you will learn to identify a rollover style, as well as deconstruct what it accomplished. More significantly, later in the chapter you'll learn how to program your own rollover styles!

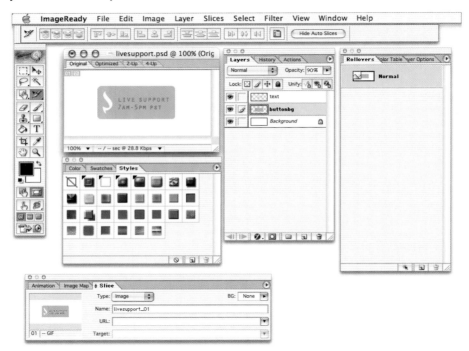

1. Make sure you are in ImageReady. As stated in the introduction to this chapter, it's not possible to program rollovers in Photoshop, which is why this exercise and all the exercises in this chapter take place inside ImageReady. Open **livesupport.psd** from the **chap_11** folder you transferred to your hard drive from the **H•O•T CD-ROM**. This document was created in Photoshop. It is easy to create artwork in Photoshop and bring it into ImageReady in order to convert it to a rollover. Simply make the artwork there and save it. Either click on the **Jump To ImageReady** button on the Photoshop Toolbar, or open the file from ImageReady as you did here.

Note that there are a variety of palettes in this shot that you should also have open: Layers, Rollovers, Slice, *and* Styles. *If you don't have any of these open, go to the* Window *menu and select the palettes that are missing from your screen.*

2. Select the **text** layer inside the **Layers** palette. Click on the third style inside the **Styles** palette (circled above).

Notice that quite a few changes happened to your screen when you simply clicked on this style. In the Original *window, notice that new slices have been added to your document. The new automatically generated slice has been given an automatic slice name which is also visible inside the Slice palette. Notice that new icons have appeared next to the* Text *layer, indicating that there is now a slice and a layer style applied to this layer. Notice that the* Rollovers *palette now contains a new layer called* livesupport 03, *which happens (not coincidentally) to be the same name as the slice that was automatically created by this single click of a rollover layer style.*

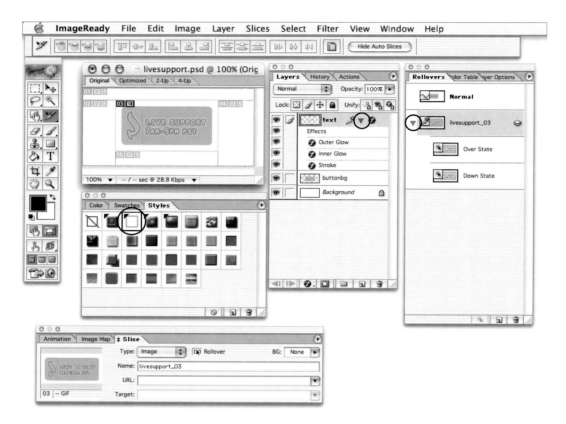

3. To better understand the significance of what just happened, notice that the style you clicked on had a black triangular tab at its upper-left corner. Any style with this telltale black tab is a rollover style. Click on the arrow in the **text** layer to see that three different layer effects were stored inside this layer style. Click the arrow in the **Rollovers** palette on the **livesupport 03** layer to see that there is an Over State and a Down State.

4. Click on the **Normal** layer inside the **Rollovers** palette. Next click on the **Over State** and the **Down State**. As you click through these different states, you will preview other changes to your screen. Notice that the layer effects change inside the Layers palette for each state: Normal, Over, and Down? You are previewing the effect that has been preprogrammed into the rollover layer style that you selected back in step 1.

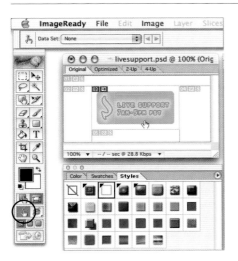

5. Click the **Preview Document** tool in the **Toolbar**. Move your mouse over the image inside the **Original** window. This is another, better way of previewing the rollover results. Try clicking as well. The Normal state represents the state before any mouse has entered the slice. The Over state represents what happens when your mouse is inside, or "over," the slice. The Down state represents what happens when you depress the mouse.

6. Click on the **Optimized** tab and set your optimization settings. You will be warned that you can't use this window if you have the Preview Document setting enabled. Click **OK**, and the Preview Document tool will become deselected. Or you can click on the tool to select and deselect it. Experiment with the best optimization settings. Unfortunately, this setting applies to all rollover states. You might want to click through them in the **Rollovers** palette to see that the settings you chose look good for all the various states.

7. Once you're happy with the optimization settings, click the **Preview in Default Browser** button (to the right of the Preview Document button). This allows you to see the file in a browser. Move your mouse over the graphic and click it. You'll see all the states at work. As well, if you scroll down, you'll see all the JavaScript that ImageReady generated. Ouch! Aren't ya glad you didn't have to write any of that by hand?

WARNING | Internet Explorer Problem

In some versions of Internet Explorer, you may find that a rollover button has an annoying black outline. This is not through any fault of ImageReady, but is a bug. There are scripts within Adobe GoLive and Macromedia Dreamweaver MX that will eliminate this issue. Unfortunately, there is nothing you can do within ImageReady to prevent the problem.

```
                    Save Optimized As
    Save As:  livesupport.html
    Format:   HTML and Images               ◆
     Where:   📁 rollover                    ◆  ▲

    📁 rollover                    ▶

                              ◀ ▶

       ( New Folder )    ( Add to Favorites )

    Settings:   Custom                      ◆
      Slices:   All Slices                  ◆

                          ( Cancel )   ( Save )
```

8. Return to ImageReady, and choose **File > Save Optimized As**. In the **Save Optimized As** dialog box, create a new folder and call it **rollover**. The filename **livesupport.html** will already be filled in, because ImageReady by default uses the filename for the HTML file. Make sure that the **Format** (Mac) or **Save as type** (Windows) field is set to **HTML and Images**. Click **Save**.

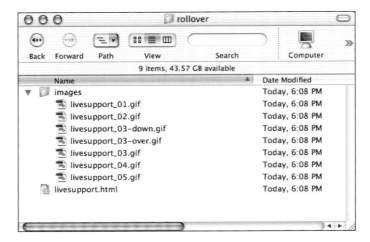

9. Locate the rollover folder on your hard drive and look at its contents. ImageReady sure generated a lot of files, didn't it? The images inside the images folder are named according to the slice names. The HTML contains the JavaScript and HTML code necessary to produce the rollover. If you double-click on the **livesupport.html** file, you'll see a page appear inside your browser that contains the image and a working rollover. The source is no longer visible as it was in step 7, because this is the final document, not the preview document.

10. Return to ImageReady and save the document as **livesupport_finished.psd** and close it. The PSD format will actually save all the rollover settings if you ever want to reopen this document to rework it! In fact, try saving and closing it, then reopening it to select the **text** layer again. This time choose a different rollover style from the **Styles** palette. This document remains very flexible, true to Photoshop's usual form!

This exercise covered a lot of different concepts, from rollover styles, to rollover states, to previewing techniques, to the results of saving a rollover. These concepts will be the foundation of your rollover building skills. Much of what happened in this exercise will become much more clear as you work through upcoming exercises in this chapter.

What JavaScript States Are Allowed in ImageReady?

When you are specifying a rollover state in ImageReady, you are invoking a JavaScript call. Here's a handy chart to describe what the possible states are.

JavaScript Rollover States in ImageReady	
Rollover State	**Definition**
Normal	When the page loads into the browser.
Over	When the mouse enters the slice or image map region.
Down	When the mouse is depressed inside the slice or image map region.
Click	When the mouse is depressed and released inside the slice or image map region. Older versions of Netscape don't support the Down state, so some developers prefer to use Click, which is supported.
Out	When the mouse leaves the slice or image map region. If there is no defined Out state, the document will automatically return to the Normal state.
Up	When the mouse is released inside the slice or image map region. If there is no defined Up state, the slice will return to the Over state when the mouse is released.
Custom	When a custom-programmed event occurs. Available to hand coders who want to write their own JavaScript event to add to the HTML.
Selected	When the end-user clicks on a slice or image map area, the Selected state appears until another rollover state is chosen. Other rollover effects can occur while the Selected state is active. For example, a Selected state for one button and an Over state for another button can occur simultaneously. However, if a layer is used by both states, the layer attributes of the Selected state override those of the Over state. Use Default Selected State to activate the state initially when the document is previewed in ImageReady or loaded into a Web browser.
None	This is a placeholder for when you want to experiment with different states but don't want to assign a real one yet. It's not supported by browsers.

2. [IR] _____Layer-Based Slicing

The last exercise yielded impressive results with little effort. Now comes the more laborious (but ultimately more customizable) process to understand how to set up rollovers from scratch on your own.
To begin, you'll learn a new way of slicing that is more flexible when it comes to programming and
designing rollovers.

1. Open **livesupport.psd** again. This should not contain any rollover content yet. If you need
to retransfer it from the **H•O•T CD-ROM**, go ahead. Alternately, you could remove the slices
from the last exercise by choosing **Slices > Delete All**.

2. Select the **buttonbg** layer in the **Layers** palette. Choose **Layer > New Layer Based Slice**.
Notice that a new slice appears that matches the exact shape of the pixel content within the
buttonbg layer.

NOTE | What Is a Layer-Based Slice?

A layer-based slice is different than a user slice or an auto slice, both of which you learned about in Chapter 10, "*Slices*." A layer-based slice is always created by choosing **Layer > New Layer Based Slice**. It always cinches in exactly to the size of whatever layer was selected when this command was chosen. As well, if you move the layer around with your mouse, the slice moves with it! If you apply a layer effect and change the settings for a large drop shadow, the shape of the slice will expand! The other, less-known reason why layer-based slices are useful is that you *must* use a layer-based slice in order to create your own rollover layer style. Why not always use layer-based slices? The only disadvantage to using a layer-based slice is that there are no resizing handles, and no obvious way to change the size of the slice if you wanted to. You can actually get the resizing handles to appear if you convert the slice from layer-based to user-based. This defeats the benefits you gain when creating rollover graphics. For this reason, most Photoshop/ImageReady professionals use layer-based slices for rollovers and user-based slices (the kind you learned to make in Chapter 10, "*Slices*") for static graphics. Another reason to use user-based slices is when you create remote rollovers, which you'll learn to do later in this chapter.

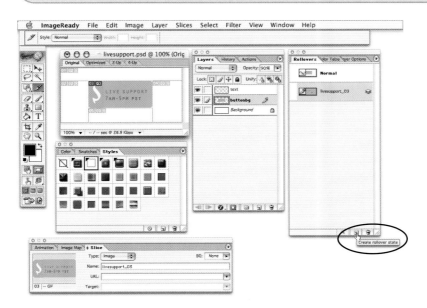

3. Make sure that the slice you created in the last step is still selected, which is indicated by an orange slice border around the graphic. Make sure that **buttonbg** is still selected in the **Layers** palette. With the **livesupport 03** layer in the **Rollovers** palette selected, click the **Create rollover state** button to generate an **Over** state. For the moment, this process will simply duplicate what appears in the Normal state. You'll change that soon!

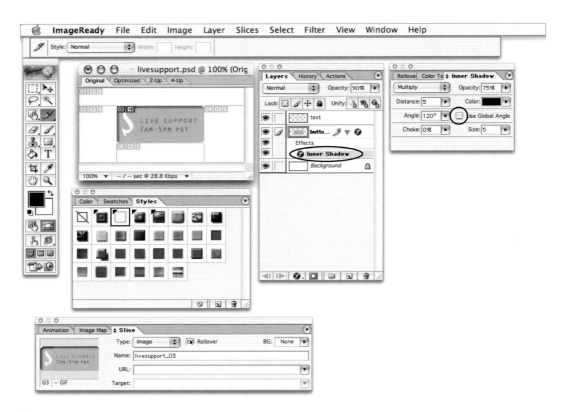

4. Make sure the **Over State** for the **livesupport 03** layer is selected in the **Rollovers** palette. In the **Layers** palette, select the **buttonbg** layer, click the *f* icon at the bottom of the palette, and choose **Inner Shadow** from the pop-up menu of layer effects. Be sure to uncheck **Use Global Angle**, because you will be changing the angle of the Inner Shadow layer effect in a later step. You'll see the Inner Shadow layer effect appear inside the Layers palette, underneath the Effects setting of the **buttonbg** layer.

5. Click the **Rollovers** tab to make it visible again. Click the **Create rollover state** button again. This duplicates what was on the **Over State** and creates a new state called the **Down State**. You'll change the Down State appearance next.

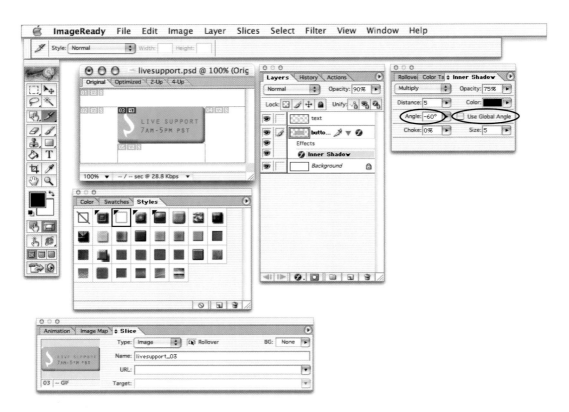

6. With the **Down State** still selected inside the **Rollovers** palette, click on the **Inner Shadow** tab to make it active again. Change the **Angle** to **−60** degrees. Be sure to uncheck **Use Global Angle**. The image will now appear differently in the document, because the angle of the Inner Shadow has been altered. This change has been recorded only for the Down State of the rollover!

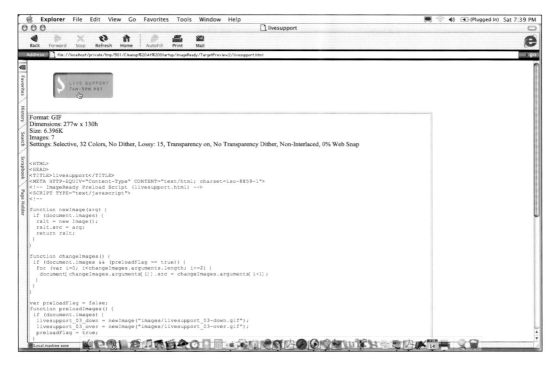

7. Click the **Preview in Default Browser** button in the ImageReady Toolbox, and move your mouse over the graphic in the browser. Click the graphic. You've just created a rollover from scratch with a Normal and an Over state!

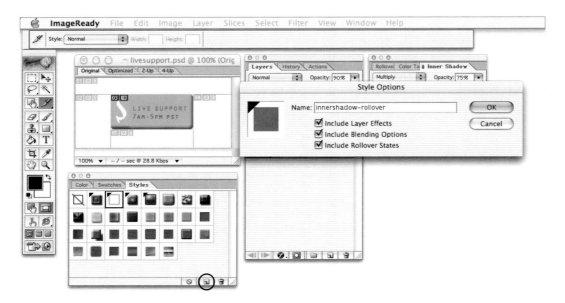

8. Return to ImageReady, and click on the **New Style** button at the bottom of the **Styles** palette. The **Style Options** dialog box will open. Type **innershadow-rollover** as the **Name**, and make sure that all the check boxes are checked. Click **OK**. The new style will appear in the Styles palette with its own black tab in the corner, indicating that it contains rollover information. ImageReady is smart—it knows you want to save this as a rollover style instead of a layer style! You'll get to try out this style in the following exercise.

9. Save this file as **rollover2.psd** and close it. You won't be using it again in this chapter. If you wanted to create the final rollover graphics and HTML, you would want to repeat the instructions that you followed in the last exercise.

3. [IR] _____Rollover Styles for Multiple Buttons

The great thing about creating a rollover style is that you can reuse it! Reusing the rollover style is the easy part—creating the style was a lot harder! This exercise will demonstrate what a powerful new workflow you're learning in this chapter. Working with rollover styles is a great way to create consistent buttons when working on complex documents.

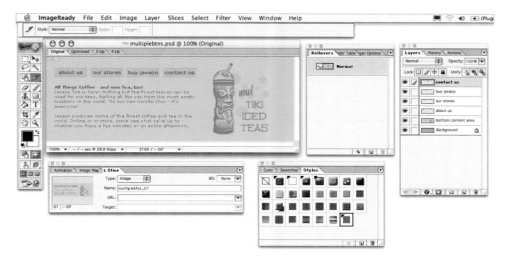

1. Set up your screen as you see ours in this picture, with the **Layers**, **Rollovers**, **Styles**, and **Slice** palettes open. Open **multiplebtns.psd** from the **chap_11** folder. Select the **contact us** layer from the **Layers** palette.

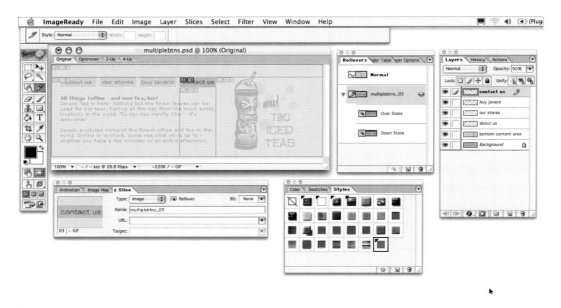

2. Click on the style that you made in the last exercise. Notice that the **contact us** button now contains a slice that is selected, and it appears in the **Slice** palette? In the **Rollovers** palette, click on the arrow next to the **multiplebtn 03** layer and notice that there is an Over and Down state. Click on the different states—notice that they look familiar from the last exercise? You're going to apply this style to the other three buttons next.

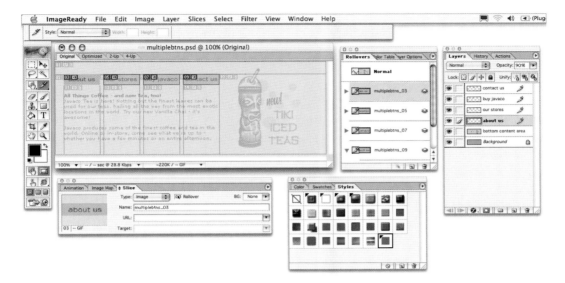

3. Click the **buy javaco** layer in the **Layers** palette, and click the style that you made in the last exercise again. A new layer-based slice will appear! Why? Because you saved this as part of the rollover style in the last exercise. Click the **our stores** layer in the **Layers** palette and click the style again in the **Styles** palette. Do the same process for the **about us** layer in the **Layers** palette. Voila! You should now have four sliced images with the same rollover applied consistently to each one! That was rather amazing, huh? In the Rollovers palette, you'll now see one Normal layer, with four other layers that contain the Over and Down state for each slice.

4. Click the **Preview in Default Browser** button again and test the rollovers. Move your mouse over each button, and don't forget to click in order to see the Down state. Pretty awesome, huh?

5. Save this file as **multiplebtns-final.psd** and leave it open for the next exercise.

MOVIE | multiple-roll.mov

To learn more about making multiple rollovers, watch the **multiple-roll.mov** located in the **movies** folder on the **H•O•T CD-ROM**.

4. [IR] _____Saving the Final Rollover Graphics and HTML

You learned how to save the images and HTML for a simple rollover in Exercise 1 of this chapter. The big difference with saving rollover graphics is that when you save a rollover, you must save not only its images, but its HTML code, too. A rollover is nothing more than multiple static images unless it retains the HTML code that contains the JavaScript that makes the rollover work. This exercise will dig deeper into the details and some of the nuances of saving rollovers in the Optimize interface. So far, all the slice names were created for you automatically. This will create a folder of images that are named cryptically, by the slice number instead of names you've assigned.

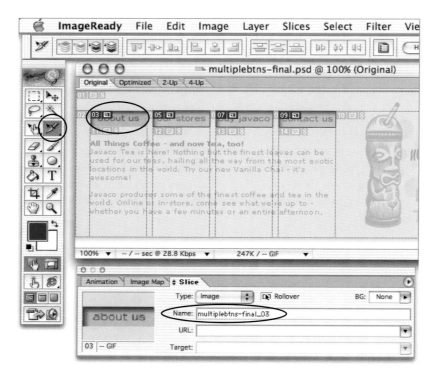

1. The document **multiplebtns-final.psd** should be open from the last exercise. Use the **Slice Select** tool to select the **about us** slice on the screen. If you look in the **Slice** palette, you'll see that the slice is currently named **multiplebtns-final_03**. You're going to change this slice name to something more logical to your project.

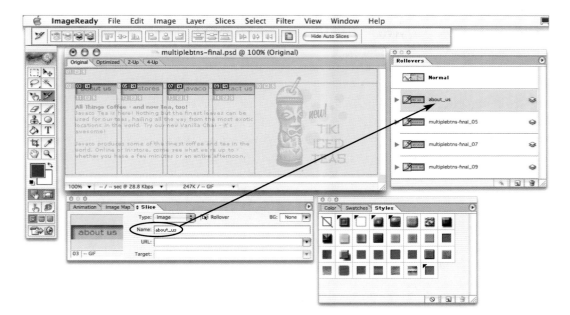

2. In the **Slice** palette, rename this slice **about_us**. Note that this name will be part of the filename, and it needs to be written properly for HTML—no spaces, special characters, or slashes. Notice that the name of this slice is reflected in the Rollovers palette? This means that the slice name is going to become the filename when the rollover images are created. Nice!

3. Select the other three slices in this document and rename them in the **Slice** palette: **our_stores**, **buy_javaco**, and **contact_us**, respectively.

4. Close the **Styles** palette to make room on your screen (if you need to!). Bring the **Optimize** palette forward by choosing **Window > Optimize**. Bring the **Color Table** palette forward by choosing **Window > Color Table**.

5. Click on the **Optimized** tab in the document window. With the **Slice Select** tool, select the **about us** button. You'll see the optimization settings for this button appear within both the Optimize and the Color Table palettes. Go through each one of the slices that you created for the rollovers and set their optimization settings to what pleases you.

Earlier in this chapter, you learned that the optimization settings you apply to a rollover slice also apply to the graphics in all states of the rollover. Click back and forth between the Normal, Over, *and* Down *states in the* Rollovers *palette to make sure the optimization settings you've chosen look okay in all states of this rollover.*

Tip: You'll have a better view of the artwork you're optimizing if you temporarily turn off slice visibility. Click the Toggle Slices Visibility *button (or just press the letter* Q *on your keyboard), which lets you toggle between hiding and showing slices.*

6. Select the auto slices in the document with the **Slice Select** tool. They are automatically linked to each other, so whatever setting one contains applies to all. If you want to break any of the links to further customize the optimization, you can do so by first selecting an auto slice, and then choosing **Slices > Unlink Slice**. The optimization settings are up to you—practice your skills!

7. Choose **File > Save**.

Saving the modified file as a PSD ensures that you can access the layers and styles settings. You haven't saved this file for the Web yet, but you've saved it as a PSD file, which you'll be happy to have in the event a client asks you to change something or you ever want to edit parts of it again. Files saved in GIF or JPEG format don't store the slices, rollover states, layer and styles information, and other editable items that are stored in the PSD format. It's important to save a master PSD file and the necessary GIFs and JPEGs, in addition to HTML, when you're working on projects so all your bases are covered.

8. Choose **File > Save Optimized As** and leave the suggested name, **mutliplebtns-final.html**, in the **Name** field. ImageReady will offer to name it for you that way, because by default the application bases the name of the HTML document it generates on the name of the corresponding PSD file. In the **Save Optimized As** window, make sure that **HTML and Images** is selected in the **Format** (Mac) or **Save as type** (Windows) field. This tells ImageReady to create and save not only the rollover images, but also an HTML file that contains the JavaScript that makes the rollovers function.

There's great information about getting rollovers into an HTML editor in Chapter 16, "Integrating with Other Programs." Don't skip ahead just yet though. There are important and challenging tasks to complete first. ;-)

9. Create a new folder and name it **rollover2** before you click **Save**. This ensures that all the files will be stored neatly inside one folder. Click **Save** in the **Save Optimized As** window.

You may have to wait a second while ImageReady does the following work for you: creates an individual image for each of the rollover states in the button slice, makes a small transparent spacer.gif *for the No Image slices, writes an HTML file that contains JavaScript to make the rollover work, and generates a table to hold the images in place.*

10. To see what ImageReady made for you, locate the **rollover2** folder that you just created on your hard drive. You should see a working HTML document (**mutliplebtns-final.html**) and an **images** folder with images in Web-ready). Notice that the rollover images carry the name of the slice from which they were made?

The HTML file and associated images could be brought into any HTML editor to be integrated into a Web site, or opened directly in a browser. If you own GoLive or Dreamweaver, you'll get a chance to try this in Chapter 17, "Integration with Other Programs."

11. Double-click on **multiplebtns-final.html** to open the file in a Web browser. Move your mouse over the graphic to see the rollover work. Congratulations! You've finished making and saving a complex series of rollover buttons.

12. Close the file; you won't need it again for this chapter.

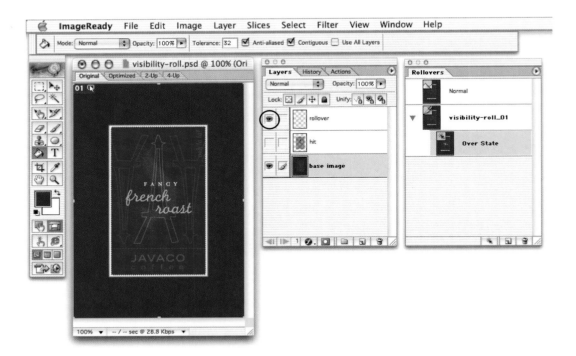

3. Select the **Over State** in the **Rollovers** palette. Turn the **visibility** icon on for the **rollover** layer in the **Layers** palette.

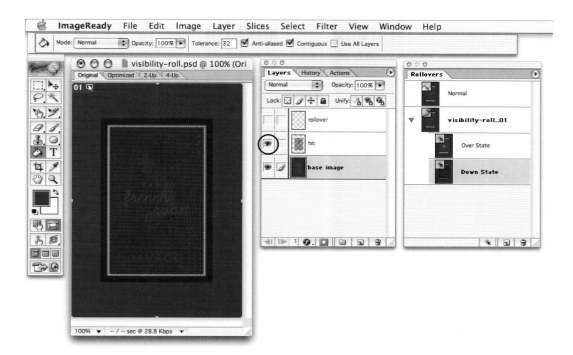

4. Click the **Create rollover state** button in the **Rollovers** palette, and the **Down State** will appear. Make sure it is selected, and turn the **visibility** icon off for the **rollover** layer and on for the **hit** layer inside the **Layers** palette.

5. Click the **Preview in Default Browser** button in the Toolbox to see the result in your Web browser. Notice that the rollover works perfectly! ImageReady memorized which layers were turned on and off for each state. Depending on how you set up your artwork, this is another equally awesome way to create rollovers.

The only problem with this rollover is that it's triggered when the mouse rolls over its farthest edge. To make the rollover happen in a more targeted area, you'll have to change the size of the slice. You'll do this next!

6. Return to ImageReady. With the **Slice Select** tool, click on one of the edges of the center slice (the **user** slice) to drag it inward. Reshape the slice so it better fits where you want the rollover to be triggered. By reshaping the slice, rather than reslicing, you keep all the rollover information you've already programmed.

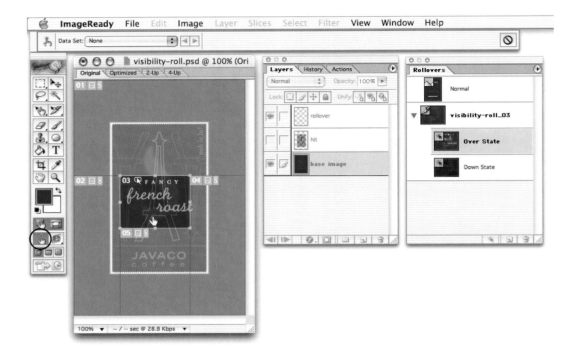

7. Once you get the shape of the rollover resized, you could also use the **Preview Document** button from the Toolbox to preview the result without going to the browser. **Tip:** Press the letter **Q** to temporarily turn off the visibility of the slices. Be sure to press **Q** again and click the **Preview Document** button (or press the letter **Y**) again before you finish this exercise.

8. Save this file as **visibility-roll-final.psd**. If you wanted to export the final file, you could do so by choosing **Save Optimized As**. Close this file; you won't be needing it again.

Warning: You must use a user-based slice to create rollovers with visibility icon changes. That's why the layer-based slice won't work using the technique you learned in this exercise.

6. [IR] _____Remote Rollovers

All the ways you've made rollovers so far in this chapter have resulted in one type of rollover, in which an image swaps itself for another image. The next type you'll learn to make is a **remote rollover**, in which multiple pieces of artwork change when the mouse enters a specified region. This exercise is going to combine what you learned in Chapter 10, "*Slicing*," with the layer visibility-based rollovers and style-based rollovers you've learned about in this chapter. Whew—that's a mouthful. You'll soon see, however, that you can put all these strange new terms to use in the process of making a useful and complex remote rollover.

1. Before you get going, it might be nice to visualize what you are about to build. In ImageReady, open **remote-final.psd**, which we've sliced up for you and filled with preprogrammed rollovers. Preview this file in a browser of your choice. Roll your mouse over the words **STORY**, **TEA**, and **TO GO**.

See how each button changes appearance and that additional information appears to the right? This is what we meant when we said that multiple pieces of artwork change at once in a remote rollover. A rollover, in this case, is triggering a change in other slices

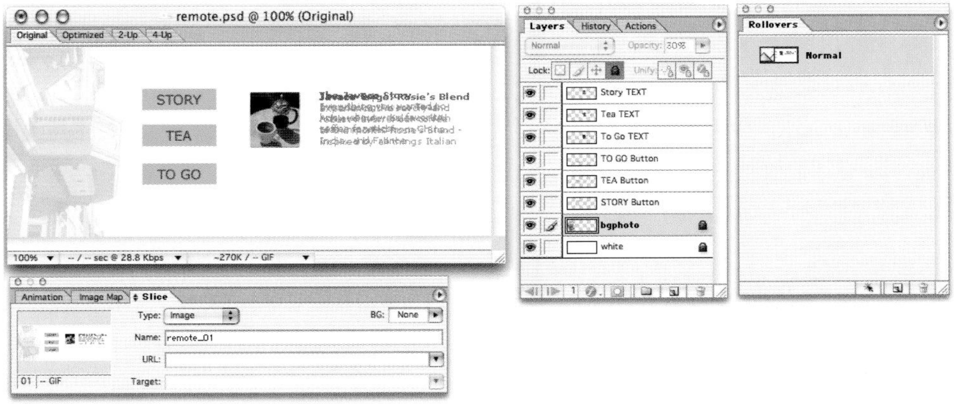

2. Return to ImageReady, close this file, and open **remote.psd** from the **chap_11** folder you copied to your hard drive. Turn all the **layers** on in the document so you can see what's on all of them at one time. It doesn't matter that all the text looks jumbled and pictures are on top of one another. We usually do this so we can see how to slice the artwork properly. **Tip:** You can click one eye icon on, leave your mouse depressed, and drag over the rest to turn them all on, which is much easier than clicking them individually.

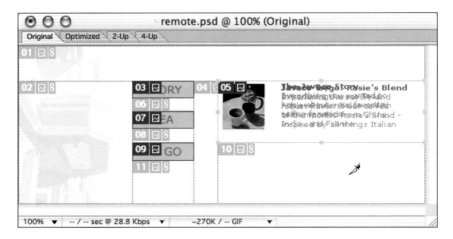

3. Using the **Slice** tool, drag a slice around each button called **STORY**, **TEA**, and **TO GO**, and the area that encompasses all the photos and description text. Try to match the same slice regions that you see in the screen shot above. If you make a mistake or want to adjust the boundaries of the slice, use the **Slice Select** tool, as you learned how to do in Chapter 10, "*Slicing.*"

Tip: When working with multiple slices and rollovers, it's very important that you make all your slices before you begin creating the rollovers. That's because it's much harder to change your mind and add a slice later after you've set up rollovers.

NOTE | Slices and Layers

You might wonder which layer should be selected while you are slicing. It actually does not matter. Slices "drill" through each layer that's turned on in the document. The only time it matters which layer is selected is when you're adding a layer effect or editing a specific layer. You do not need to select a layer to turn its visibility on or to slice through it.

4. Bring the **Slice** palette to the foreground by clicking on the **Slice** tab. With the **Slice Select** tool, click the slice you just created around the word **STORY**, and enter **story** in the **Name** field of the **Slice** palette.

5. Repeat step 4 for each of the slices you created, naming them respectively: **tea**, **to_go**, and **descriptions**. As you've learned, naming each region is important so that the resulting files will be named in a recognizable way.

Notice that the new names all appear within the Rollovers palettes. Only user-based slices, layer-based slices, and image maps appear within the Rollovers palette. Auto slices do not appear there.

Now that you've named the slices, you're ready to set up the rollovers. The first thing to do is to imagine how this series of images should look in the Normal *state, before a site visitor has moved his or her mouse over the words. The object of this exercise is to make the buttons (STORY, TEA, and TO GO) visible first.*

6. In the **Rollovers** palette, select **Normal**. In the **Layers** palette, turn off the layers named **Story TEXT**, **Tea TEXT**, and **To Go TEXT**, so that only the buttons and background are visible for the Normal state.

7. With the **Slice Select** tool, select the **story** slice in the **Original** window. In the **Rollovers** palette, this automatically selects the **story** layer. Then click on the **Create rollover state** button. This will create an **Over State** for the **story** layer.

8. In the **Layers** palette, select the **STORY Button** layer. Click the **Add a layer style** button at the bottom of the **Layers** palette, and select **Inner Shadow** from the drop-down menu. This will apply the Inner Shadow filter effect to the **STORY** button artwork on the **Over State**.

9. Next, turn the **visibility** icon on for the **Story TEXT** layer. You are telling ImageReady what to change when the **Over State** of the **STORY button** is triggered. It is going to change the appearance of the button to show the Inner Shadow effect, as well as show the descriptive text and picture. Try it out, and preview it right now.

Next, you will repeat this same set of steps for the next two buttons. We've intentionally created some abbreviated instructions—see if you can follow them. If not, refer back to the beginning of this exercise.

10. Select the slice that contains the **TEA** button in the **Original** window. Select the **tea** layer in the **Rollovers** palette. Create an **Over State** for the **tea** layer. The **TEA Button** in the **Layers** palette is automatically selected. With the **TEA Button** layer selected, add the layer effect called **Inner Shadow** to it. Turn on the **visibility** icon for **Tea TEXT**.

11. Select the slice that contains the **TO GO** button in the **Original** window. Select the **to_go** layer in the **Rollovers** palette. Create an **Over State** for the **to_go** layer. Select **TO GO Button** in the **Layers** palette. Add the layer effect called **Inner Shadow** to it. Turn on the **visibility** icon for **To Go TEXT**.

12. Preview all this work in a browser. Your remote rollover file should function identically to what you previewed at the beginning of this exercise.

MOVIE | remote_roll.mov

To learn more about making a remote rollover, as shown in this exercise, check out **remote_roll.mov** from the **movies** folder on the **H•O•T CD-ROM**.

---

13. You're finished. If you want to add more challenge, go ahead and create all the HTML and images for this complex rollover. Save this file as **remote-finished.psd** and close the file. You won't be needing it again!

Not only did you program a remote rollover, but you combined techniques from other chapters and exercises as well, including layer visibility and layer effects. The slices were key to creating multiple rollovers inside a single document. We're sure these new skills will be put to use again and again in your Web design career. Move on to the next chapter, if you're ready and able. :-)

12.

Image Maps

| Server-Side or Client-Side | What Is an Image Map? |
| Making a Tool-Based Image Map |
| Making a Layer-Based Image Map |
| Making an Image Map on Text | Image Map-Based Rollovers |
| Image Maps in Photoshop |

chap_12

Photoshop 7/ImageReady
H•O•T CD-ROM

Most buttons and navigation bars on the Web are composed of individual images that link to individual URLs. An image map is called for when you want a single image to link to multiple URLs, such as a map of the United States in which each state is linked to a different URL.

In the past, image maps were not made in image editors but in HTML editors or stand-alone image map editing software. ImageReady makes it easy to create image maps without the need for other applications. Although it isn't possible to make an image map in Photoshop, if you make and save an image map in ImageReady, and later open that document in Photoshop, it will retain the image map information until you return to ImageReady.

Server-Side or Client-Side Image Maps?

There are two types of image maps—server-side and client-side. In the early days of the Web, it was only possible to create server-side image maps. When Netscape 2.0 was released, the capability to work with client-side image maps was introduced.

What do those terms mean? Anything that is server-side resides on the Web server and is accessed through a CGI (**C**ommon **G**ateway **I**nterchange). A CGI is a type of script that can be written in Perl, ASP, AppleScript, or other programming languages. CGI scripts reside on the Web server. Typically, most Internet service providers supply their subscribers with a CGI script that can activate server-side image maps. It's then a matter of linking to the script and uploading a map definition file that should also be stored on the Web server. To further muddle the issue, there are two types of Web servers—those that follow the conventions of CERN (**C**onseil **E**uropéen pour la **R**echerche **N**ucléaire—where Tim Berners-Lee conducted research at the time the Web was being developed) and those that follow the NCSA (**N**ational **C**enter for **S**upercomputing **A**pplications) conventions. If you decide to create a server-side image map, you will need to check with your Web-hosting company to see if they are CERN- or NCSA-compliant.

Sound complicated? It is, in fact, much more complicated to create a server-side image map than a client-side image map. Calling something "client-side" means that it is performed on the client. What is a client? Why, it's a Web browser, silly. You mean you weren't born knowing that? Don't fret, neither was anyone else. The Web browser that you use on your hard drive is your very own Web client. Bet you never thought of it that way, but now you can have two kinds of clients in your life—those who pay the bills, and those that display your Web pages!

The deal is that a client-side image map is performed by the browser and doesn't involve the server at all. Client-side image maps are always easier to work with because you don't have to fuss with CGI scripts, map definition files, and knowing what kind of Web server your hosting company uses.

Most Web sites today use only client-side image maps, and that's what this chapter will cover. If you want to create a server-side image map in place of or in addition to a client-side image map, here's how: With your artwork open in ImageReady, choose **File > Output Settings > Image Maps**. This will open the Image Maps options panel of the **Output Settings** dialog box, where you can change the **Image Maps Type** setting to reflect your choice. The default is **Client-Side**, so if that's what you plan to create, you won't need to change this setting. If your choice includes a server-side image map, ImageReady will create a separate map definition file for you, in addition to an HTML file and an image file.

What Does an Image Map Look Like?

The HTML for a client-side image map contains **MAP** and **USEMAP** tags, as well as all the coordinates for the image map regions. The coordinates plot the dimensions and location of the "hot spots" in an image map.

What's a **hot spot**? It's an area on a Web page that triggers a link. Clicking inside a hot spot will activate a link to another page. Moving a cursor over a hot spot will change the cursor to a hand, which may be the only indication a viewer has that a particular spot is hot.

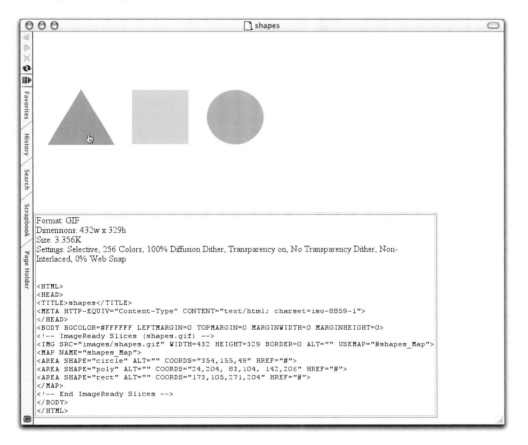

*This is an example of an image map (on a single graphic that contains all three shapes—the triangle, square, and circle), and of the HTML code for an image map that ImageReady will write. Notice that in the code there are three types of **AREA SHAPE** elements—**POLY** (polygon), **RECT** (rectangle), and **CIRCLE**. After those, you'll see a listing for **COORDS** (coordinates), followed by a lot of comma-separated numbers. Those numbers describe the coordinates of the hot regions around each shape.*

5. [IR] _____ Making Manual Rollovers

So far, you've learned how to make rollovers using a technique that combines layer-based slices and rollover styles. Depending on what kind of rollover effect you want, this isn't always the best workflow. This next exercise will show you how to build a rollover in a manual manner so you can work with turning layer visibility on and off as part of your rollover technique. A rollover style cannot save layer visibility information, so that workflow won't work in this situation.

1. Within ImageReady, open **visibility-roll.psd** from the **chap_11** folder that you transferred from the **H•O•T CD-ROM**. Make sure that the **Layers** and **Rollovers** palettes are visible.

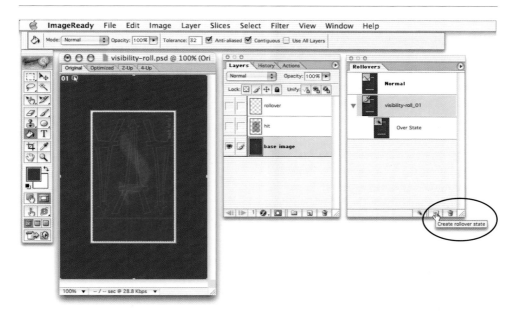

2. Click the **Create rollover state** button in the **Rollovers** palette. This will create a layer called **visibility_roll_01**, and an **Over State** for that layer in the **Rollovers** palette.

I. [IR] _____ Making an Image Map with Drawing Tools

Making image maps is a snap in ImageReady. There are two ways to create image maps in the latest release of the program—by hand with the new image map drawing tools, and automatically with the layer-based image map features.

In this exercise, you'll learn how easy it is to create and modify an image map with the image map drawing tools. This is the method to use when you want to create multiple links from artwork that is on a single Photoshop layer. The image map drawing tools are also useful when you want to create an image map hot spot that's complex in shape, because this method gives you lots of control over the form and location of a hot spot.

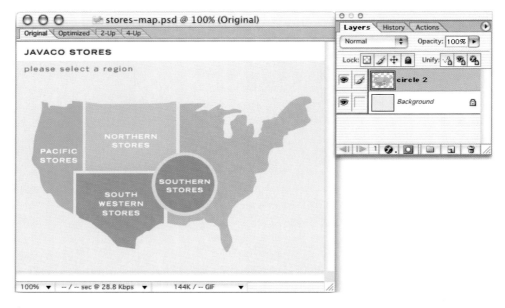

1. In ImageReady, open **stores-map.psd** from the **chap_12** folder you copied to your hard disk from the **H•O•T CD-ROM**.

Notice that all of the artwork in this image is on a single layer. When this is the case, the image map drawing tools are the ideal method for creating an image map and its hot spots. If the artwork were separated onto individual layers, you'd have the option of using either this method or the layer-based method of creating an image map (which you'll learn in the next exercise).

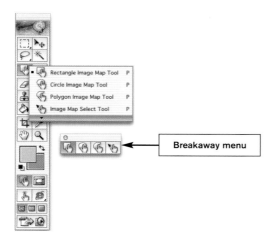

Breakaway menu

2. In the ImageReady Toolbox, click on the **Image Map Select** tool (or whichever image map drawing tool is in the foreground in your Toolbox), and move your mouse to the small **arrow** at the bottom of the tools pop-up menu. When you release the mouse, you'll see a breakaway menu that contains all of the image map drawing tools. Move the breakaway menu to a convenient place on your screen, so you'll have easy access to all of the drawing tools.

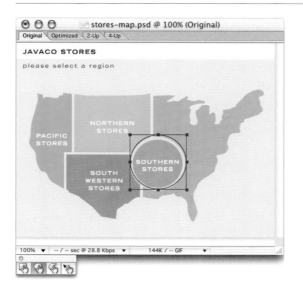

3. In the breakaway menu, click on the **Circle Image Map** tool. Then click and drag over the **Southern Stores** graphic in the document to create a circular image map hot spot. **Tip:** To draw a circular hot spot from the center out, hold down the Option (Mac) or Alt (Windows) key while dragging out the shape.

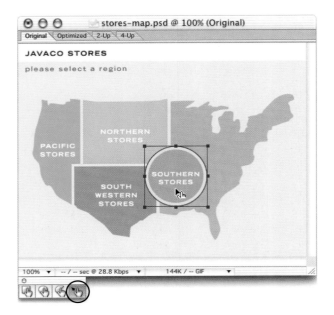

4. Click on the **Image Map Select** tool in the breakaway menu. Click inside of the hot spot you just drew, and move it into position on top of the **stores-map.psd** graphic. **Tip:** You can use the arrow keys on your keyboard to nudge the hot spot into place.

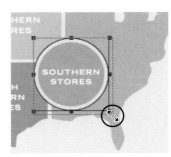

5. You can modify the shape of the hot spot you've drawn if it doesn't quite match the shape of the artwork. With the **Image Map Select** tool still selected, move your cursor over one of the corners or outside borders of the hot spot until the cursor changes to a double-pointed arrow. Drag to modify the shape of the hot spot to fit the underlying artwork.

6. Click the **Image Map Palette** button on the **Options** bar to access the **Image Map** palette.

The Image Map Palette button is a handy way to make the Image Map palette visible. An alternate way is to choose Window > Image Map. *The Options bar is context-sensitive, so it will display the Image Map Palette button only when you've chosen the Image Map Select tool.*

7. In the **URL** field of the **Image Map** palette, enter a URL of your choice. It can be an external URL to a page in another site (like **http://www.southernstores.com**) or an internal URL to a page that will be in the same site as your image map (**southern.html**, for example). ***Note:*** *These are fictitious URLs, so they will not actually work. If you want to enter a real URL and have a live Web connection, go ahead!*

NOTE | External Versus Internal URLs

If you are linking to a Web site other than the one where this document will be uploaded, you must include the entire **http://www** header information. If, however, you were uploading this image map to **lynda.com** and wanted to link to **classes.html**, you wouldn't need the **http://www** header information. The link to an outside URL is called an external link, and the link to the interior URL is called an internal link. If you are going to use internal links, it's really important to know the exact directory structure of your site. Here are some examples:

- If you stored the HTML file for this image map inside the same folder as the HTML pages to which it linked, you could specify the URL like this: **classes.html**.

- If you stored this image map inside an images folder and the HTML to which it linked inside an independent folder named html, you would specify the URL like this: **../html/classes.html**.

- If you stored this image map inside an images folder and the HTML to which it linked inside a folder named html that was inside the images folder, you would specify the URL like this: **html/classes.html**.

Many HTML editors, including GoLive and Dreamweaver, have site-management features that help you manage these links. It's easiest to link to an external URL because you don't have to know the location of the file and how it relates to the location of the image map. If you plan to link to internal pages, it might be best to set the actual links inside your HTML editor.

8. In the **Name** field of the **Image Map** palette, type **southernstores_map** instead of the default map name that appears there. **Tip:** Avoid using spaces when you name an image map. A good substitute is an underscore or a hyphen.

Custom naming an image map is optional, since ImageReady creates a name that functions just fine, but you'll find that giving your file a meaningful name will make it easier to find a particular image map in the code if you ever need to.

9. Choose **_blank** from the **Target** menu in the **Image Map** palette.

Choosing _blank as the target instructs a Web browser to open the page to which you've linked in a separate browser window. You don't have to specify a target if you don't want to. If you don't choose a target, by default the page you linked to in the Image Map palette will show up in the same Web browser window as the page that contains the image map.

10. Enter **southern stores** in the **Alt** field of the **Image Map** palette.

Entering alt text in the Image Map palette is also optional. Alt text is a way to give information about your graphics to viewers who can't see the graphics (either because they've turned image-viewing off in the browser or because they are visually disabled). It's okay to use spaces and special characters in alt tags, because they do not follow the strict naming conventions required in HTML filenames.

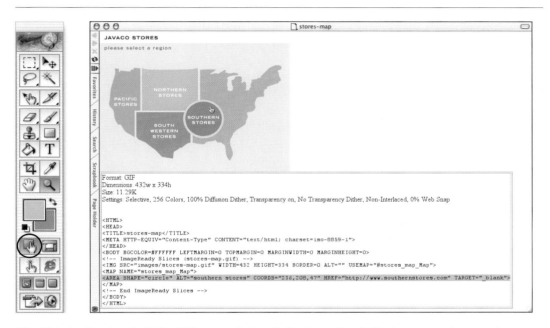

11. Click the **Preview in Default Browser** button in the ImageReady Toolbox to preview your image map in a Web browser. Move your cursor over the **Southern Stores** graphic in the browser, and notice that the cursor changes to a hand, indicating that this is a hot spot.

In the code, notice that there is a line that reads: **<AREA SHAPE="circle" ALT="southern stores" COORDS="236,208,47" HREF="http://www.southernstores.com" TARGET="_blank">.** *This is telling the browser to recognize an image map hot spot in the shape of a circle, with the coordinates of 236, 208, 47, to link it to the index page of the* southernstores.com *Web site (or whatever URL you entered), and to display that page in a separate browser window.*

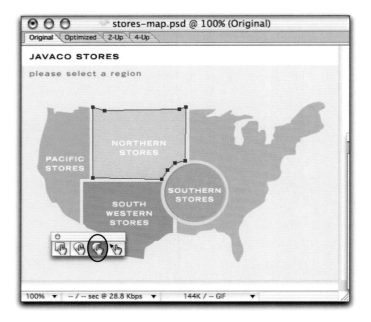

12. Back in ImageReady, select the **Polygon Image Map** tool from the breakaway menu. Click on one corner of the **Northern Stores** graphic, and move your cursor around the border of it, clicking whenever you need to create a contour. This will make a hot spot that matches the irregular shape of the Northern Stores shape. When you've gone all the way around the shape, move the cursor over the spot where you first clicked. When the cursor changes to a small circle, click to close the path.

13. In the **Image Map** palette (**Window > Image Map**), enter an external or internal URL of your choice, enter **northernstores_map** in the **Name** field, and, if you like, choose **_blank** in the **Target** field and enter **northern stores** in the **Alt** field.

14. Click the **Preview in Default Browser** button. In the browser, move your cursor around the artwork, noticing that there are now two hot regions–Southern Stores and Northern Stores–over which the cursor changes to a hand.

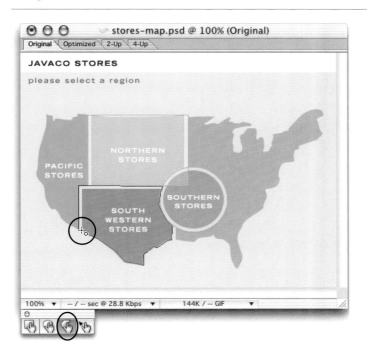

15. Return to ImageReady and use the **Polygon Image Map** tool from the breakaway menu. Click on one corner of the **South Western Stores** graphic, and move your cursor around the border of it, clicking whenever you need to create a contour. This will make a hot spot that matches the irregular shape. When you've gone all the way around the South Western Stores shape, move the cursor over the spot where you first clicked. When the cursor changes to a small circle, click to close the path.

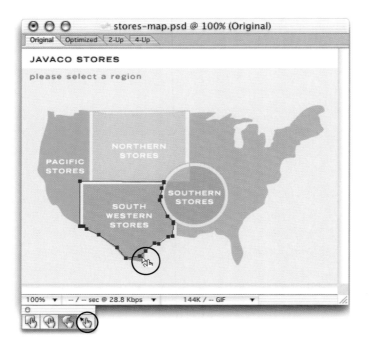

16. To adjust a section of the polygon you drew, click on the **Image Map Select** tool in the breakaway menu. Then click on one of the square points of the polygon and drag the section into position.

Tip: When you want to move a section of the image map, be sure the arrow on the Image Map Select *tool is pointing directly at the square point. If the arrow is not pointing right at a square point, the entire image map will move.*

17. In the **Image Map** palette, enter **southwesternstores_map** into the **Name** field. In the **URL** field, enter **http://www.southwesternstores.com**. Set **Target** to **_blank**, and enter **south western stores** in the **Alt** field. Click the **Preview in Default Browser** button again to test this hot spot. When you move the cursor over **South Western Stores** in the browser, the hand symbol should appear.

NOTE | URL Menu

Animation | **Image Map** | Slice

Dimensions
Name: southwesternstores_map

URL: http://www.southwesternstores.com

http://www.southwesternstores.com
http://northernstores.com
http://www.southernstores.com

Target:

Alt:

As you work with the Image Map palette, a list of URLs will appear inside a menu located at the far right side of the URL field. Click the arrow to see the list of names. This is very convenient when you work with the same link locations over and over. Instead of typing in the field, click the menu arrow and select a URL that you've already entered.

18. In ImageReady, click on the **Optimize** tab and choose optimization settings (**GIF, Selective, Colors: 8, No Dither**) in the **Optimize** palette. If you need help with this, refer to Chapter 4, "*Optimization.*" **Tip:** Although GIF is the preferred format in this case due to the flat, graphic nature of the image, you can also make an image map on a JPEG.

19. Choose **File > Save Optimized As**. In the **Save Optimized As** dialog box, make sure that the **Format** field (Mac) or the **Save as type** field (Windows) is set to **HTML and Images**. Navigate to your desktop, click the **New Folder** button, and name the new folder **image map**. Click **Save**. Go out to the desktop and open the **image map** folder to see the two files that ImageReady created—an HTML file called **stores-map.html**, and inside the **images** folder a GIF file called **stores-map.gif**.

It's important to tell ImageReady to create an HTML file along with the image file, because the image map instructions are not part of the image; they are stored separately in the accompanying HTML file. In this case, stores-map.gif *is just like any other GIF file. The only thing that makes it an image map is the code that is stored in* stores-map.html, *which tells Web browsers the coordinates of the linked regions.*

20. Save and close **stores-map.psd**. The image map content will be stored with the Photoshop document, even though it will not be visible unless viewed from within ImageReady.

2. [IR] _____Making an Image Map from Layers

There's another way to make image maps in ImageReady that is even easier than using the drawing tools. You can have ImageReady automatically create hot spots for you based on the shape of your layered artwork. In the past, creating an image map involved manually tracing around the regions of the image to which you wanted to assign a URL. What's revolutionary about the layer-based approach is that you don't have to do any drawing or positioning of the image map. The program does it for you! The key to making layer-based image maps is having the individual pieces of your artwork separated onto different transparent layers. If you've done that, ImageReady is smart enough to know where the regions of each layer are. Creating an image map this way is as simple as clicking on a layer and making a menu choice.

One of the neat things about a layer-based image map is that it will move with the layer of artwork on which it was created. This is the method to use when you want the flexibility to move artwork around after making an image map, without having to redraw the hot spots after every move. You'll see what we mean as you work through this exercise.

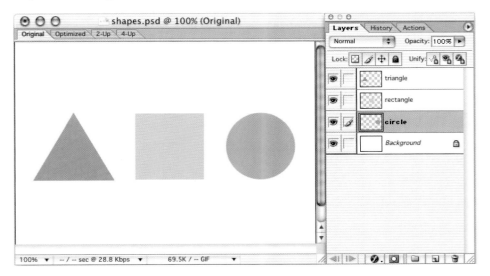

1. Open **shapes.psd** in the **chap_12** folder you transferred to your hard disk from the **H•O•T CD-ROM**.

Notice that each piece of artwork in this image—the triangle, the rectangle, and the circle—is on a separate layer, and that each of those layers has a checkerboard pattern (which, as you learned in Chapter 9, means that there are transparent pixels on those layers). This is important, because ImageReady can make an image map from a layer only if there is transparency on that layer.

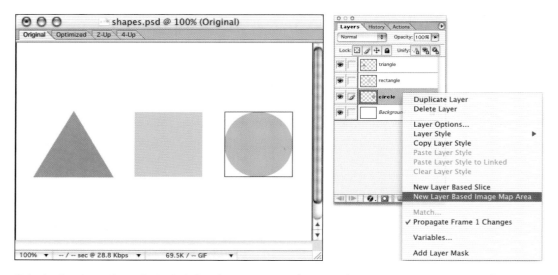

2. In the **Layers** palette, **Ctrl+click** (Mac) or **right-click** (Windows) on the layer named **circle**. (If the Layers palette isn't visible, choose **Window > Layers**.) Choose **New Layer Based Image Map Area** from the pop-up menu that appears. Or, you can choose **Layer > New Layer Based Image Map Area** from the top menu bar.

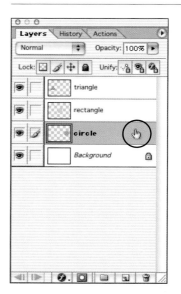

Notice that a hand symbol now shows up on the right side of the circle layer. The hand symbol indicates that this layer has an image map associated with it.

3. Click the **Image Map** tab. (If you don't see it, choose **Window > Image Map**.) With the **circle** layer still selected in the **Layers** palette, click on the **Shape** field and choose **Circle** from the pop-up menu.

By default, layer-based image maps are rectangular. Choosing circle or polygon in the Shape field may result in a closer fit between the shape of an image map hot spot and the shape of certain artwork. The better the fit, the easier it is for a viewer to locate the hot spot in a Web browser, using the artwork as a clue.

4. In the **Name** field of the **Image Map** palette, enter **circle_map** instead of the default image map name that appears there.

5. In the **URL** field of the **Image Map** palette, enter **http://www.circleville.com**, or the URL of your choice. **Note:** If you are not online when you test the preview or final file, the link to the URL you specified will not work. In this example, **http://www.circleville.com** is a fictitious URL, so it probably won't work even if you are online (unless someone has registered that domain name since this book was published).

You can add a target window or alt text in the Image Map palette, if you choose.

6. Click the **Preview in Default Browser** button in the ImageReady Toolbox. When you place your cursor over the circle shape previewed in the browser, the telltale hand will appear, indicating that this is a link.

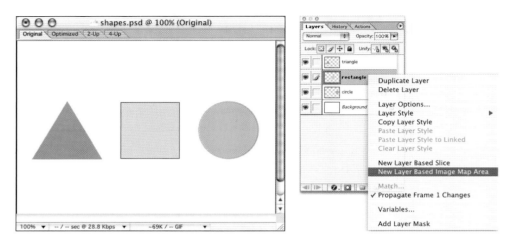

7. Return to ImageReady. **Ctrl+click** (Mac) or **right-click** (Windows) the layer named **rectangle** in the **Layers** palette. Choose **New Layer Based Image Map Area** from the pop-up menu that appears.

Notice that the image map defaults to a rectangle shape, so you don't need to change it in the Image Map palette to match the shape of the rectangle artwork on this layer.

8. In the **Image Map** palette, enter **rectangle_map** in the **Name** field, and **http://www.rectangleville.com** in the **URL** field. Add a target and alt text if you'd like.

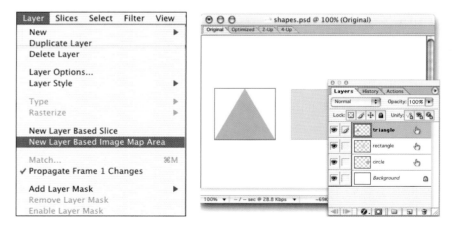

9. Select the layer named **triangle** in the **Layers** palette. From the **Layer** menu at the top of the screen, choose **Layer > New Layer Based Image Map Area**.

This is another way to create a layer-based image map. It's an alternative to using the pop-up menu from the Layers palette, as you did in steps 2 and 8 of this exercise.

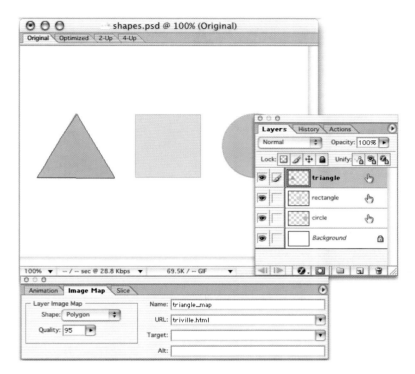

10. In the **Image Map** palette, change the **Shape** to **Polygon** and the **Quality** to **95**. Enter **triangle_map** as the map **Name**, and type in a different URL.

The quality setting affects how tightly the polygon-shaped image map will hug the underlying artwork. The higher the tolerance, the closer the match between those shapes. ***Tip:*** *You won't always want the quality to be at its highest setting, because in some cases (like complex shapes or text) that will produce hot regions that are too narrow for practical use.*

NOTE | Changing the Image Map Settings

After you've entered information into the **Image Map** palette, you might need to change your settings. If you click on the different layers, you'll notice that the information inside the palette doesn't seem to change. The only way to access the settings information again is to use the **Image Map Select** tool, and select the image map path for each shape. You'll see the settings change inside the Image Map palette for each shape, allowing you to make changes to whichever image map you want. If you save the file as a PSD, the image map settings will be stored with the file and can be changed in the future.

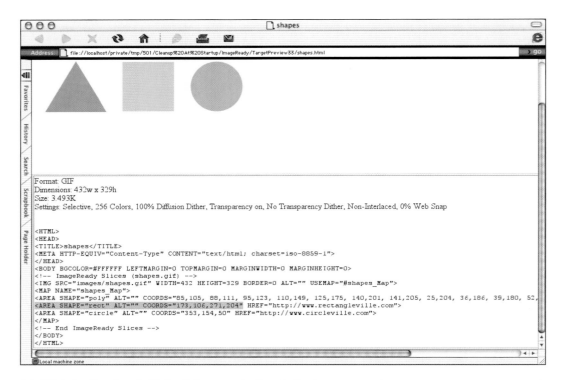

11. Click the **Preview in Default Browser** button. In the browser preview, move your cursor over each of the three graphics to see the cursor change to a hand. If you are online, you can even test the links. They should work, assuming that you entered real URLs. Notice the coordinates of the rectangular hot spot—173, 106, 271, 204. You'll want to compare them to another set of image map coordinates when you get to step 13 in a moment.

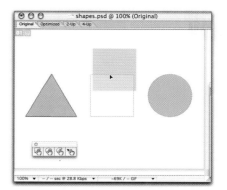

12. Return to ImageReady, and select the **rectangle** layer in the **Layers** palette. With the **Move** tool from the Toolbox, click in the document window and drag to move the artwork on the rectangle layer. Notice that when you release the **Move** tool the thin blue outline of the rectangular image map moves with the underlying artwork.

13. Click the **Preview in Default Browser** button again, and notice that the coordinates of the rectangular-shaped hot spot have changed to reflect the move (in the case of our illustration, the new coordinates are 174, 58, 272, 156, but yours may be different depending on where you moved the rectangle), proving that this layer-based image map really did move with the underlying artwork.

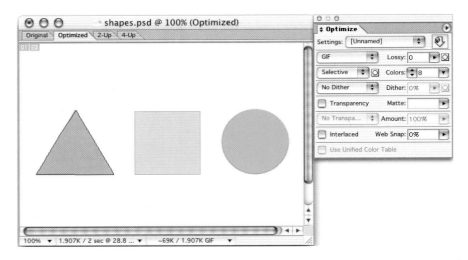

14. So far, you have only previewed the image map. Return to ImageReady to save a final version. Select the **rectangle** layer in the **Layers** palette, and with the **Move** tool, drag the rectangle artwork (with its hot spot) back into line with the other graphics. Select the **Slice Select** tool from the Toolbox, and click anywhere in the image. Click the **Optimized** tab, and create appropriate settings for the whole image inside the **Optimize** palette. (We chose **GIF**, **Selective**, **No Dither**, **Colors: 8**.) If the Optimize palette is not visible, choose **Window > Optimize** to display it.

15. Choose **File > Save Optimized As**, make sure you choose **HTML and Images** as the **Format** (Mac) or **Save as type** (Windows) setting, and click **Save**. ImageReady will save a GIF file called **shapes.gif** in the **images** folder and an HTML file called **shapes.html** that contains the image map code.

16. Choose **File > Save**, and leave **shapes.psd** open for the next exercise.

3. [IR] _____Making an Image Map to Fit Text

Making an image map to fit text or other complex shapes can be tricky. In this exercise, you'll learn how to create practical image maps for text with the image map drawing tools. You'll also see that you can use both of the image map creation methods you've learned—the tool-based method and the layer-based method—together on a single image. This is often the best solution when you're working with hybrid images that contain images with graphics and text.

1. The file **shapes.psd** should be open in ImageReady from the last exercise, in which you created layer-based image maps for the graphics in this document.

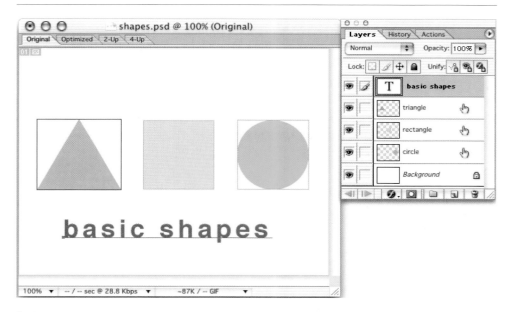

2. Select the **Type** tool from the Toolbox. In the **Options** bar, choose **Helvetica** or **Arial** as the font and **36 px** as the font size. Make sure you are on the **Original** tab, and click in the document and type the words **basic shapes**. This will add a separate type layer to the document.

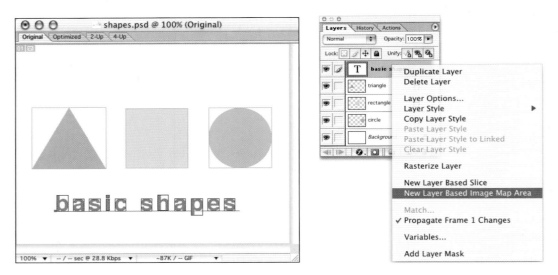

3. **Ctrl+click** (Mac) or **right-click** (Windows) on the **basic shapes** type layer in the **Layers** palette. From the drop-down menu that appears, choose **New Layer Based Image Map Area**. This will apply a layer-based image map with rectangular hot spots to the type.

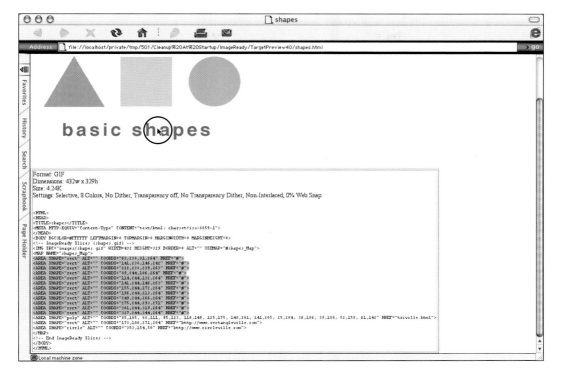

4. Click the **Preview in Default Browser** button in the ImageReady Toolbox. In the browser, move your cursor over the type. Notice that there are some areas of type over which the cursor does not change to a hand, making it difficult to discover just where to click to activate a link.

Notice the many lines of code and image map coordinates that were generated by the layer-based image map. Programmers usually try to avoid creating unnecessarily complex code, which is difficult to read and can contribute to the file size of a Web page.

5. Back in ImageReady, with the **basic shapes** type layer still selected in the **Layers** palette, go to the **Image Map** palette, and change the **Shape** field from Rectangle to **Polygon**. Leave the **Quality** setting at its default level for now.

Changing to the Polygon shape will cause the hot spots around the letters to cinch in even tighter to the text. This is not the result you want, as you'll see when you preview in a browser in the next step.

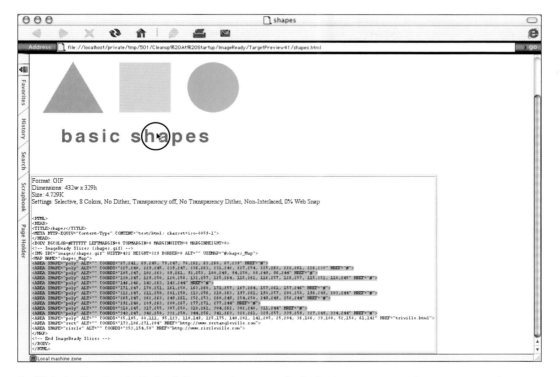

6. Click the **Preview in Default Browser** button again. In the browser, move the mouse over the type. Notice that the hot region for the type is even more difficult to find, and there are even more image map coordinates in the code than when you used rectangular layer-based hot spots (as in steps 3 and 4 of this exercise).

As the last few steps show, a layer-based image map is not ideal when the underlying artwork consists of complex shapes, like multiple letters on a type layer. The tighter the hot spots fit the letters, the more difficult it can be for a viewer to find the link regions.

7. In ImageReady, delete the layer-based image map you created by clicking the **arrow** on the right of the **Image Map** palette and choosing **Delete Image Map Area** from the drop-down menu that appears.

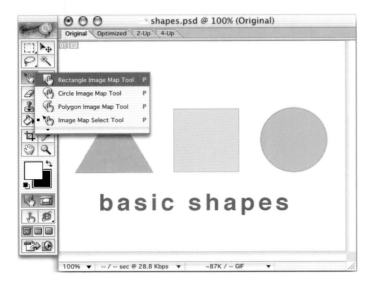

8. Click on the **Image Map Drawing** tool that is displayed in your ImageReady Toolbox, and select the **Rectangle Image Map** tool from the drop-down tools menu. **Note:** If the **breakaway tools** menu is still on your desktop from a previous exercise in this chapter, go ahead and select the **Rectangle Image Map** tool from that menu.

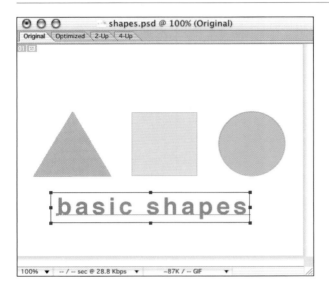

9. Click and drag to draw a rectangular hot spot around the text in the document.

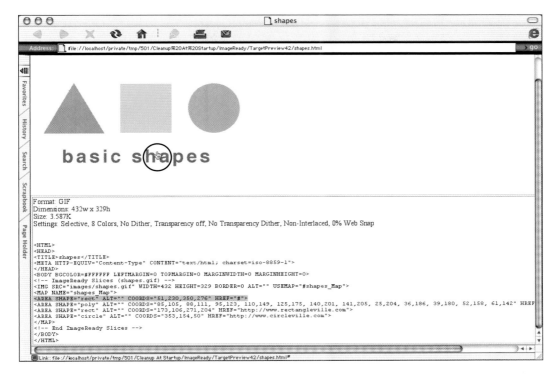

10. Click the **Preview in Default Browser** button to test this image map. Notice that when you move your cursor over the text in the browser window, it is easy to find the hot spot, which is now one contiguous area. Also notice that the code for this tools-based image map is much simpler than the code for the layer-based image maps that you made and previewed earlier in this exercise.

11. Return to ImageReady, select **File > Save**, and leave **shapes.psd** open for the next exercise.

4. [IR/PS] _____ Jumping to Photoshop with an Image Map

In the introduction to this chapter, we mentioned that Photoshop honors image map information from ImageReady even though it cannot display it. In this exercise, you'll see this for yourself.

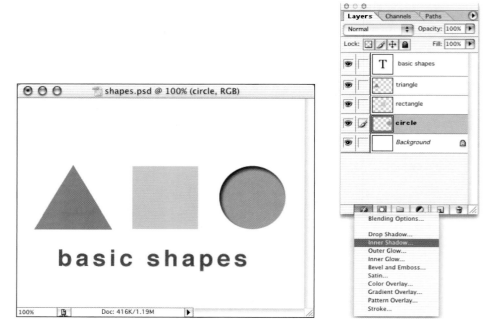

1. With **shapes.psd** open from the last exercise, click the **Jump To** button at the bottom of the ImageReady Toolbox. This will open the same document in Photoshop. In Photoshop, select the **circle** layer in the **Layers** palette, and click the **layer effect** icon (the _f_ symbol) at the bottom of the palette. Choose the **Inner Shadow** layer effect from the drop-down menu that appears. In the **Layer Styles** dialog box that opens, click **OK**.

An inner shadow will appear on the circle graphic, and an f-shaped layer effect icon will appear on the circle layer in the Layers palette. But you won't see any of the image map information while the document is open in Photoshop.

2. Click the **Jump To** button at the bottom of the Photoshop Toolbox to reopen the modified document in ImageReady.

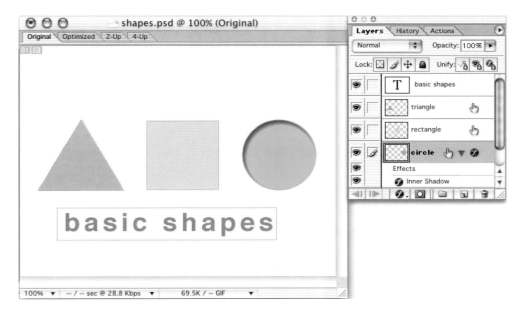

You should now be back in ImageReady, and the changes you made to the document in Photoshop should appear. Notice that the image map information that was not visible in Photoshop is still intact inside ImageReady. Told you so! You can edit freely between these two programs, and even though Photoshop does not directly support image maps, they will still be honored.

You can Preview, Save Optimized, and/or Save now by practicing what you've learned in the other exercises in this chapter.

3. Close the file when you're finished, and remain in ImageReady for the next exercise.

5. [IR] _____ Image Map–Based Rollovers

You have learned how to create rollovers based on slices in the last chapter, but many people don't realize that you can also create rollovers that are based on image maps. This technique is used when the shape that triggers the rollover is shaped differently than a rectangle or square, which is the only shape that can be generated using the slicing techniques you've worked with so far. This exercise shows you how easy it is to use this technique if you need it in the future.

1. Open **imagemap.psd**. This file is similar to a file that you worked with in Chapter 11, "*Rollovers*."

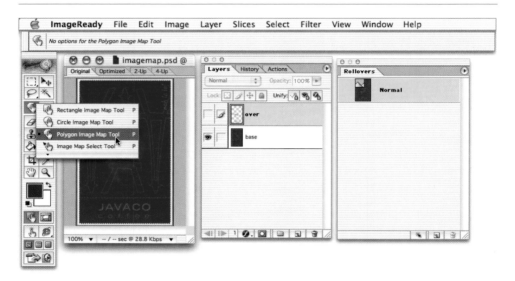

2. Choose the **Polygon Image Map** tool from the Toolbox. Any of the image map tools would work, but for the purposes of this example the Polygon Image Map tool is best.

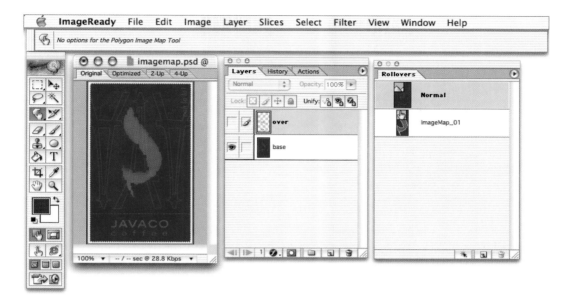

3. With this tool, draw around the shape of the **smoke logo** in the image. It doesn't matter which layer is selected in the Layers palette, because the Image Map shape will function regardless of the layer on which it is applied. You do not have to match the shape perfectly, just come close! To close the end of the path make sure that you end at the same point that you begin. After you complete the shape, notice that a new layer has been created inside the Rollovers palette called **ImageMap_01**. This name is created by default.

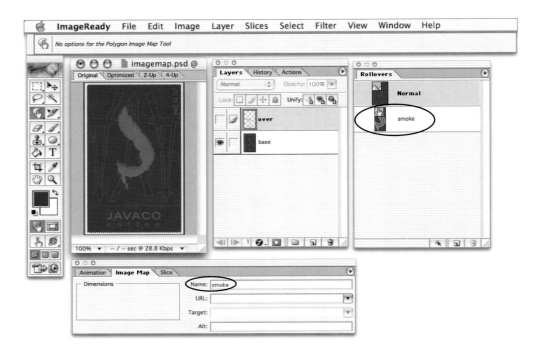

4. Open the **Image Maps** palette by choosing **Window > Image Map**. Name the image map **smoke**. Notice that the name **smoke** now appears inside the Rollovers palette? As you've already learned, this name change will affect the way the rollover images get named inside the final HTML and image documents.

5. Select the **smoke** layer in the **Rollovers** palette, and click the **Create rollover state** icon to create an **Over** state.

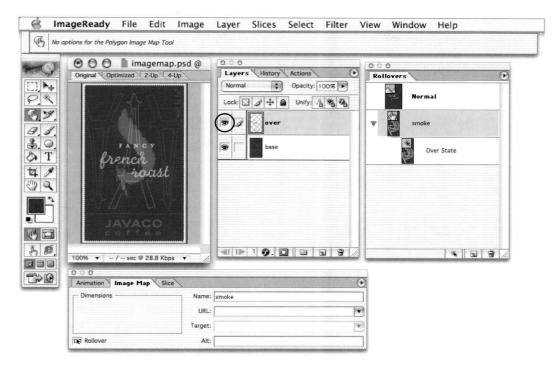

6. In the **Layers** palette, turn the **visibility** icon on for the **rollover** layer.

---

7. Test your result by clicking the **Preview in Default Browser** button. The rollover doesn't work until your mouse moves over the smoke shape. **Tip:** You might have to refresh the browser so the old rollover from Chapter 11, "*Rollovers*," isn't cached. Do this by clicking **Option** (Mac) or **Alt** (Windows) and the **Refresh** button in the browser software.

Use this technique when you have an irregular shape from which you want to trigger the rollover.

---

8. Save this file as **imagemap-final.psd**. If you want to practice optimizing and saving the final rollover, go ahead! You've already learned how in past exercises. Close the file, you won't be using it again in this chapter.

Creating image maps is a fairly easy practice, once you get the hang of it. Move on to the next chapter if you've still got juice. If not, it will still be there another day!

13.

Animated GIFs

Frame-by-Frame	Setting Speed and Looping
Optimizing and Saving	Transparent Animated GIFs
Tweening	Reversing and Looping Frames
Animated GIF Rollovers	Designing Entire Interfaces

chap_13

Photoshop 7/ImageReady
H·O·T CD-ROM

One of the coolest things about authoring for the Web is that you can include animation, which is something that print publishing obviously can't offer. If you have a background in printing, It's likely that this is the first design medium you've ever worked in that supports animation. If that's the case, you're very lucky that you get to learn with such great tools as Photoshop and ImageReady. If you've done animation before, you'll still be grateful for these tools, because you probably had to learn on systems that were much more difficult.

Although animation appears to move when seen on a computer screen, the movement is actually created from a series of still images. The GIF format is popular for Web animation because it can contain a series of static images and display them one after the other in sequence, much like a slide show. It's also popular because it is backwards-compatible with older browsers.

Although you can prepare images for animation in Photoshop, the only place that you can write animated GIFs is inside ImageReady. For this reason, all the exercises in this chapter take place in ImageReady.

Animation Terms

If you are new to creating animation in ImageReady, here are some illustrations to help familiarize you with several new terms and interface elements.

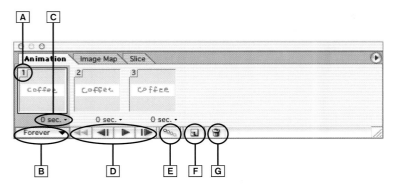

Animation palette: You'll create animations in ImageReady by using the Animation palette. **A:** This displays the frame number. **B:** Here is where you set how many times the animation plays. **C:** Here is where you set the delay of each frame. **D:** These are the playback controls. **E:** The Tween button tells ImageReady to automatically generate intermediate frames between keyframes you create. **F:** The New Frame icon creates a new frame by duplicating the selected frame. **G:** Use the Delete Frame icon to delete a frame.

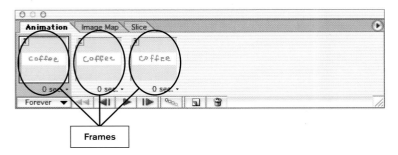

Frames

Frames: ImageReady's Animation palette numbers frames sequentially. A single frame indicates that the image is static, but two or more different frames displayed in sequence will create the illusion of movement.

Frame-by-frame animation: You create this kind of animation by turning on and off different layers over a series of frames.

Position tween: You create a tween in ImageReady by taking two different frames (called keyframes) and applying the Tween command, which automatically creates additional frames between the keyframes. When you apply a position tween, one layer of artwork changes position over a number of frames.

Opacity tween: You can apply an opacity tween to a layer of artwork to change its opacity over a number of frames.

Layer effect tween: You can apply a layer effect to a layer of artwork and then tween that effect so that it changes over a number of frames.

Animated GIF Format

The GIF file format supports animation, but the JPEG format does not. A Web browser treats an animated GIF file no differently than a static GIF file, except that an animated GIF displays multiple images in a sequence, much like a slide show, instead of a single image. Additionally, different frames can contain different timings, allowing you to design your animations so that one frame pauses for a few seconds while other frames display in a quicker sequence.

Animated GIF files do not require browser plug-ins, which means they are accessible to all Web browsers (with the exception of text-only or 1.0 browsers). The HTML code for inserting an animated GIF is no different than that for a static GIF, so working with these animation files requires no extra programming expertise. Animated GIF files can be instructed to loop (or repeat endlessly), to play only once, or to play a specific number of times. The number of repetitions is stored in the file itself, not in the HTML code.

Compression Challenges

The animated GIF format uses the same principles of compression that apply to static GIF images. Large areas of solid color compress better than areas with a lot of noise or detail. If you do use photographic-style images in an animated GIF, be sure to add **lossy** compression. It will make a substantial difference in file savings.

Animated GIFs will always be larger than static GIFs. ImageReady has two animation compression features—**Bounding Box** and **Redundant Pixel Removal** that are turned on by default. What this means is that ImageReady will add file size only for the areas that have changed in your animation. If you have a photographic background, and the only thing that changes is some lettering that fades up over it, the photographic area will be written only once to the file, limiting the total file size. If you change every pixel of an animation, as in the animated slide show example in Exercise 10 in this chapter, the Bounding Box and Redundant Pixel Removal features won't be able to help keep the file size down.

When you compress an animated GIF, keep in mind that the file will stream in, meaning that frames will appear before the entire file has finished loading. For this reason, we usually divide the file size by the number of frames, and that makes us feel a lot better about big file sizes. For example, if we have a 100K animated GIF file that is 10 frames long, in reality each frame is only 10K, which makes us feel more at ease about publishing such a big file to the Web.

Controlling the Timing of Animated GIFs

Animation is time-based, meaning that it depends on time passing as well as its artwork changing. If you alter artwork very slowly in an animation, it doesn't appear to move, but to sit for a long time and then change. If you change artwork very quickly, it appears to have more fluid movement.

Sometimes slide-show style animation is what you'll want, and other times you'll want to make movement happen more quickly. The GIF format supports delays between frames, which allows for the timing to change within a single animation file.

Video and film animation are also time-based mediums, with one key difference from animated GIFs: Video and film play back at specific frame rates (30 frames per second for video, 24 frames per second for film). Unfortunately, animated GIF files may play back at different speeds depending on the computer upon which they are viewed. A slow Mac or PC (386, 486, 030, 040, or Power PC) will play an animation much more slowly than a new G4 or Pentium IV. There's no controlling that the animation you author will play back at different speeds on different processors. The only suggestion we can make is that you view your work on an older machine if you can, before you publish it to the Web. This isn't always possible or practical, and the truth is that most people don't have a lot of old computers lying around to test with. It doesn't stop anyone from publishing animation, but it does mean that you might be surprised when you view your work on older machines.

Animation Aesthetics

Animation draws your end-user's eye much more than a static image. Make sure that the subject matter you pick for animation is worthy of more attention than other images on your screen. We've seen Web pages containing so much animation that it distracts from the important content rather than enhancing it. Good uses for animation might include ad banners, making certain words move so they stand out, diagrams brought to life, slide shows of photographs, or cartoon characters. You'll learn how to do some of these different kinds of animation in this chapter.

I. [IR] Frame-by-Frame Animation with Layers

This exercise walks you through the process of establishing frame-by-frame animation by turning layers on and off.

ImageReady can work with existing files made in Photoshop, or with artwork you create in ImageReady. It is important to note, however, that Photoshop 7 cannot write animated GIF files, which is why this entire chapter takes place in ImageReady.

1. In ImageReady, open **animation_finished.psd** from the **chap_13** folder that you transferred to your hard drive from the **H•O•T CD-ROM**.

2. Make sure the **Animation** and **Layers** palettes are open (**Window > Animation** and **Window > Layers**). Click the **Play** button at the bottom of the **Animation** palette to watch the animation play inside the document window. You'll see the letters in the word **coffee** jitter on the screen. (If the image doesn't look any different, either make sure you clicked the Play button, or cut back on the caffeine!)

When you clicked the Play button, it immediately became the Stop button. Click the Stop *button now that you've watched the animation.*

3. Select each frame in the **Animation** palette, and notice that as you do, the **Visibility** icons (the **Eye** icons) on different layers in the **Layers** palette turn on and off.

This animation was created by writing the word coffee three times, on three different layers. The layers were then selectively turned on and off in each frame of the animation. You will learn how to build this file in the following steps.

---

4. Close **animation_finished.psd**, and do not save if prompted.

---

5. Open **animation.psd** from the **chap_13** folder. It contains only a single frame in the Animation palette.

To make this document into an animation, the Animation palette must contain at least two frames with different content in each one. One way to achieve this is to turn the visibility of different layers on and off between frames, as you just witnessed. The layers in this exercise have already been created for you. You will learn to create new frames and turn layers on and off in the following steps.

---

6. On the first frame, make sure that there is an **Eye** icon next to the **animation 1** and **white background** layers, so that those layers are visible.

7. Click the **New Frame** icon at the bottom of the **Animation** palette to create **frame 2**, which will be a duplicate of **frame 1**. Make sure **frame 2** is selected in the **Animation** palette (it should be selected by default). In the **Layers** palette, turn off the visibility of the layer **animation 1** by clicking its **Eye** icon off, and turn on the visibility of the layer **animation 2** by clicking its **Eye** icon on. Leave the layer **white background** turned on.

It does not matter which layer is selected in the Layers palette when you are turning layer visibility on or off with the Eye icons. ImageReady and Photoshop allow you to turn layers on and off without selecting a particular layer.

8. With **frame 2** selected, click the **New Frame** icon on the **Animation** palette again to create a third frame. Frame 3 is a duplicate of frame 2. With **frame 3** selected, turn off **animation 2** and turn on **animation 3** in the **Layers** palette. Leave the layer **white background** turned on.

9. Click the **Play** button on the **Animation** palette to watch your work. Click **Stop** when you're through admiring it.

10. Choose **File > Save** and leave the file open for the next exercise.

You might be surprised at how easy it was to set up your first animation in ImageReady. Animated GIFs have never been easier to make as far as we're concerned!

2. [IR] _____Setting the Speed and Looping

This exercise focuses on how to slow down the speed and change the looping from a **Forever** setting, like the one you just played and stopped, to a specific number of repeats.

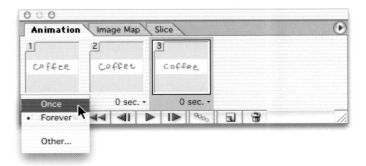

1. With **animation.psd** open from the last exercise, play the animation again by clicking the **Play** button on the **Animation** palette. Notice that it loops indefinitely? Click and hold down on the **Forever** pop-up menu at the bottom left of the **Animation** palette. Change it to **Once**, and click **Play** again. The animation should play only once. Return the setting to **Forever** once you've explored this setting.

Tip: If you want the animation to play more than once but less than forever, choose the Other *setting and enter the number of repeats you prefer. This particular animation will look best if it loops forever, but now you know how to change the looping if you want to for future animation projects.*

```
coffee
```

```
Format: GIF
Dimensions: 229w x 68h
Size: 8.308K
Settings: Selective, 0 Colors, 100% Diffusion Dither, 3 frames, Transparency on, No Transparency Dither, Non-Interlaced,
0% Web Snap


<HTML>
<HEAD>
<TITLE>animation</TITLE>
<META HTTP-EQUIV="Content-Type" CONTENT="text/html; charset=iso-8859-1">
</HEAD>
<BODY BGCOLOR=#FFFFFF BACKGROUND="" LEFTMARGIN="0" MARGINHEIGHT="0" MARGINWIDTH="0" TOPMARGIN="0">
<!-- ImageReady Slices (animation.gif) -->
<IMG SRC="images/animation.gif" WIDTH=229 HEIGHT=68 ALT="">
<!-- End ImageReady Slices -->
</BODY>
</HTML>
```

2. Preview this file in a browser by clicking the **Preview in Default Browser** button in the ImageReady Toolbox. Notice that the animation plays much faster than it did when you previewed it by clicking Play. That's because ImageReady builds the animation as it plays back, while the browser plays the animated GIF that is already built. You'll notice that the animation plays too fast in the browser. Return to ImageReady to slow down the pacing.

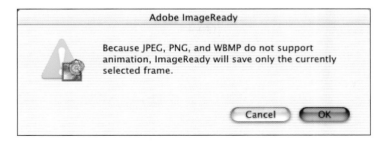

Note: If you see the message above when clicking on the Preview in Default Browser *button, make sure that you have* GIF *selected in ImageReady's* Optimize *palette. Only GIFs can be animated.*

It's impossible to estimate the speed of the animation unless you preview it in a browser. In most cases, this one included, the animation plays much faster in the browser than it does in ImageReady. For this reason, it's always important to view the animation in a browser before you finalize your speed settings. However, even in your browser you can't tell the true speed of the animation, because that depends in part on the speed of the processor in each viewer's computer.

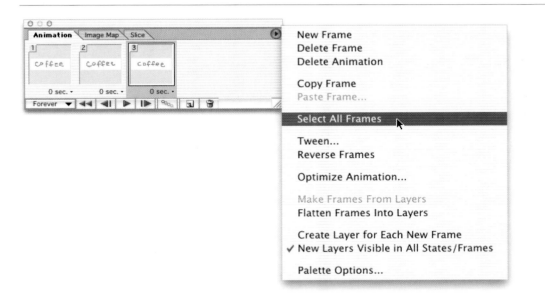

3. Click the arrow in the upper-right corner of the **Animation** palette and choose **Select All Frames**.

Don't be confused by the fact that all the frames don't have a black border. The highlighting that's now around all the frames indicates that they are all selected.

4. Click and hold down on any of the frame delay settings that currently read **0 sec**. From the pop-up menu choose **0.1 seconds**. All the frames should change at once.

5. All of the frames should now appear with the **0.1 sec**. timing in the pop-up menu. Preview in the browser (**Preview in Default Browser** button) to see how the timing of the animation slowed down a little. **Tip:** You can change the rate of individual frames if you want, or change all of them at once by selecting all the frames first, as you did here.

6. Leave the document open for the next exercise. Don't save yet. You'll focus on saving an animated GIF in the following exercise.

3. [IR] ——————Optimizing and Saving an Animated GIF

Has all of this seemed too simple so far? Perhaps you're thinking that there must be something more to creating animations in ImageReady? Nope. The only thing left to do is to optimize this animation and save it as a GIF. You'll see that there is little difference between saving an animated GIF and saving just a plain old static GIF.

1. Make sure that the **Optimize** and **Color Table** palettes are open (**Window > Optimize**). Note that there may be nothing in the Color Table, and the warning symbol may appear at the lower-left corner of this palette, which is there to alert you that this document has never been optimized. Switch to the **Optimized** tab in the document window, and the warning symbol will disappear.

NOTE | Animation Must Be Saved As GIF

When creating animation, it's essential that you use the GIF setting instead of JPEG. There is no such thing as an animated JPEG. If you do use JPEG or PNG, you'll see only the first frame of the document in the browser, and the animation won't play.

Remember to click the
Optimized tab so you can see
the results of the selections you
make in the Optimize palette

animation.psd @ 100% (Optimized)

Original Optimized 2-Up 4-Up

Coffee

100% ▼ 3.008K / 2 sec @ 28.8 ... ▼   ~38K / 3.008K GIF   ▼

Animation Image Map Slice

1	2	3
coffee	Coffee	coffee
0.1 sec. ▾	0.1 sec. ▾	0.1 sec. ▾

Forever ▼ ◄◄ ◄▐ ► ▐►

Optimize Info

Settings: [Unnamed]

GIF   Lossy: 38

Selective   Colors: 8

Diffusion   Dither: 100%

Rollover **Color Table** Layer Options

8

2. Go ahead and experiment with changing the settings in the **Optimize** palette.

The optimization settings that you apply to an individual frame will automatically apply to all the frames in your animation. So if you've used very different artwork on different frames, it's a good idea to click through the frames in the Animation palette to check that the optimization settings you've chosen look good on all frames. This isn't an issue with this particular file, because the artwork on each frame is so similar.

Notice that we have set Lossy *to* 38. *Lossy compression will often help animated GIFs (as well as static GIFs) get much smaller. This compression feature was introduced back in ImageReady 2.*

4. [IR] _____ Making a Transparent Animated GIF

What if you want to make a transparent animated GIF? The process is almost identical to making a transparent static GIF, with a few other issues thrown into the mix, like how to effect a change throughout an entire animation by using the **Match Layers Across Frames** setting. This exercise lets you practice this technique.

1. With **animation.psd** still open from the last exercise, make sure you have **frame 3** selected. Turn off the **Eye** icon for **white background** in the **Layers** palette. Click on the **Original** tab, and you should see a checkerboard background inside the document window. This indicates a transparent GIF.

If you look carefully at the Animation palette, you will see that this change was made only for the frame that was selected, which means that ImageReady doesn't yet know that you want this change to occur throughout the entire animation. You'll remedy that next.

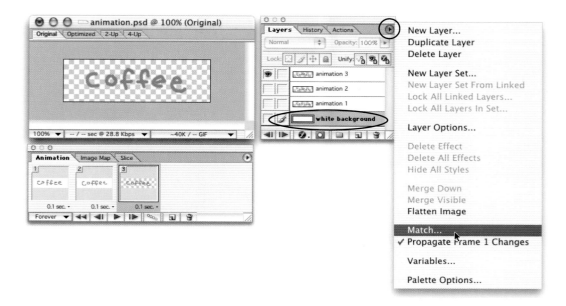

2. Select the **white background** layer inside the **Layers** palette. If the **Eye** icon appears, click it to turn it off again. Click on the arrow in the upper-right corner of the **Layers** palette, and choose **Match** from the pop-up menu.

3. In the **Match Layer** dialog box, click **Current Animation** in **Frames to Match**, and make sure all three check boxes are selected under the **What to Match** section. Click **OK**. You'll see that all the frames now have a transparent background.

When using the Match Layer Across Frames feature, it's essential that the layer you are matching is selected inside the Layers palette.

Output Settings

Settings: Custom

Background

View Document As
○ Image   ○ Background

Background Image
Path: Macintosh HD:chap_13:fine_bg2.gif   Choose...

BG Color: Matte

OK
Cancel
Prev
Next
Load...
Save...

4. Choose **File > Output Settings > Background**, and click on **Choose** to select **fine_bg2.gif** from the **chap_13** folder. Click **Open** and then **OK**.

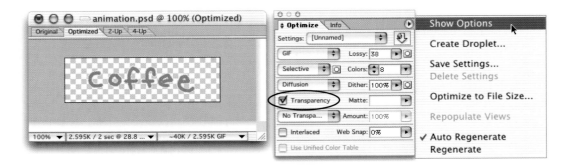

5. Click on the **Optimized** tab of the document window to check the optimization settings. Make sure the **Optimize** and **Color Table** palettes are open. Make sure that **Transparency** is checked in the **Optimize** palette. If you cannot see the Transparency check box, click on the arrow in the upper-right corner of the palette and choose **Show Options**.

6. Preview this in a browser by clicking the **Preview in Default Browser** button in the Toolbox. The animation appears over the background image.

There's that unattractive white edge again, which you might remember from making transparent GIFs in Chapter 9, "Transparent GIFs." The next step will show you how to fix the problem.

7. Return to ImageReady, choose **File > Open**, and navigate to **fine_bg2.gif** in the **chap_13** folder. Use the **Eyedropper** tool from the Toolbox to capture the color from this image. Go back to **animation.psd**. (You can either click on it to make it active, or choose **Window > Documents > animation.psd**.)

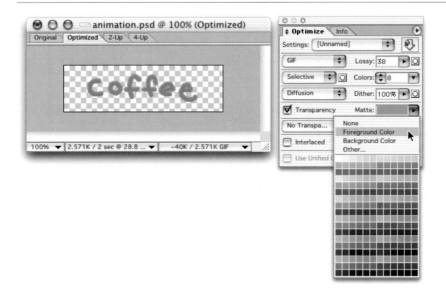

8. In the **Optimize** palette, click on the arrow to the right of the **Matte** field and choose **Foreground Color** from the pop-up menu. Changes in the Optimize palette apply to all the frames in the animation.

9. Preview in the browser again and you should see a perfect transparent animated GIF.

If you need help running through this process, revisit Chapter 9, "Transparent GIFs," to jog your memory. Making an animated transparent GIF has the same challenges as making a static transparent GIF. It's our hope that you can now transfer the skills you built in Chapter 9 to this new application of the same principles.

10. Return to ImageReady and save **animation.psd** and close it. Close **fine_bg2.gif**.

5. [IR] _____Tweening with Opacity

So far, you've been making animations by turning on and off layer visibility. This is one way to do it, but ImageReady has a few other tricks up its sleeve. This next exercise will introduce you to the **Tween** feature.

1. Open **green_tea.psd** from the **chap_13** folder.

2. Make sure the **Green Tea** layer is selected in the **Layers** palette; then enter **Opacity: 1%**. The words **Green Tea** should disappear.

3. Click the **New Frame** icon at the bottom of the **Animation** palette.

This will create a second frame with the exact settings that were in frame 1. To create another Opacity setting, which you need for the tween, you'll change frame 2 in the next step.

Frame 1 and frame 2 are the keyframes for this animation. When you tween later in this exercise, ImageReady will generate intermediate frames between these keyframes.

4. The new **frame 2** you just created is highlighted, so any changes you make will apply to it. Select the **Green Tea** layer in the **Layers** palette and enter **Opacity: 100%**. This makes the words **Green Tea** visible in **frame 2**.

Now that you've established the two keyframes, you'll have ImageReady tween the animation between the two frames.

5. Click the **Tween** button on the **Animation** palette.

Note: *Another way to tween is to click the arrow on the upper-right corner of the* Animation *palette and choose* Tween *from the pop-up menu.*

Tween

Tween With: Previous Frame ◆   OK

Frames to Add: ◆ 10   Cancel

┌ Layers ─────────────
◉ All Layers
○ Selected Layer

┌ Parameters ─────────
☑ Position
☑ Opacity
☑ Effects

6. When the **Tween** dialog box appears, enter **Frames to Add: 10**. Make sure there is a checkmark next to the **Opacity** parameter, because opacity is the quality you want to tween. Click **OK**.

The default is for all three of the parameters—Position, Opacity, and Effects—to be checked in the Tween dialog box. We usually leave it that way, so we don't have to think about which box to check each time.

7. You now have 12 frames in the **Animation** palette. Click **Play** to test the animation. You should see the word **Green Tea** fade up over the photographic background. Click **Stop**.

This particular animation might look best if it only plays once. Do you remember how to change the Forever setting? If not, revisit Exercise 2 in this chapter.

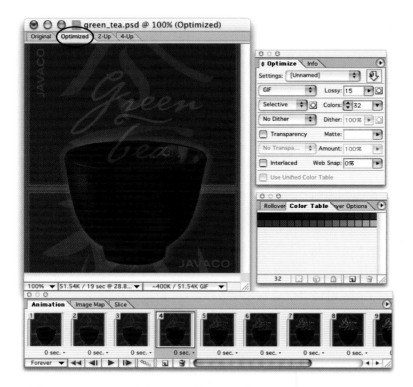

8. Click on any frame, click on the **Optimized** tab in the document window, and change the settings in the **Optimize** palette to match those in this figure. Click the **Preview in Default Browser** button to preview the animation in a browser.

Although it's convenient to preview your animation in ImageReady, don't forget to test this file in a browser as well, because you'll always get the best indication of speed in the browser, not in ImageReady.

We asked you to optimize because otherwise ImageReady will use the optimization settings from the last image that you worked on, which will make it difficult to see this animation in a browser. But don't get too worried about how you optimize this image. This exercise was created to familiarize you with tweening; other exercises in this chapter cover optimization techniques for animated GIF files.

9. Save and leave the file open for the next exercise.

MOVIE | tweening_opacity.mov

To learn more about Exercise 5, "Tweening with Opacity," check out **tweening_opacity.mov** from the **movies** folder on the **H•O•T CD-ROM**.

6. [IR] _____Selecting, Duplicating, and Reversing Frames

What if you wanted to make the words fade up, then hold, then fade out? This type of change is not only possible to do in ImageReady, it's easy once you know the steps.

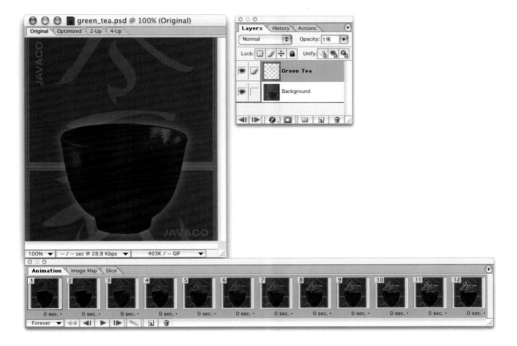

1. With **green_tea.psd** still open from the previous exercise, click on **frame 1** in the **Animation** palette. Hold down your **Shift** key and click the last frame. All the frames should be selected.

---

2. With all the frames selected, click on the **New Frame** icon at the bottom of the **Animation** palette. This duplicates all the selected frames and appends them to the end of the frames that were already there.

Tip: This technique offers a fast way to copy and paste. There's another way to do this in ImageReady. With all the frames selected, you can click the arrow at the upper-right corner of the Animation *palette, and choose* Copy Frames *from the pop-up menu. Then click on the last frame (*frame 12*), click the same arrow again, and choose* Paste Frames. *In the* Paste Frames *dialog box that appears, choose* Paste After Selection, *and click* OK.

---

3. Use the **scroll bar** at the bottom of the **Animation** palette, and you'll see that the 12 frames you copied were just pasted at the end of the animation sequence (as frames 13–24). They should already be selected.

Note: *If you accidentally click off of these frames and deselect them, you can use the* Shift+click *method to reselect them. Click frame 13, hold down your* Shift *key, and click frame 24. This selects all the frames that you just duplicated.*

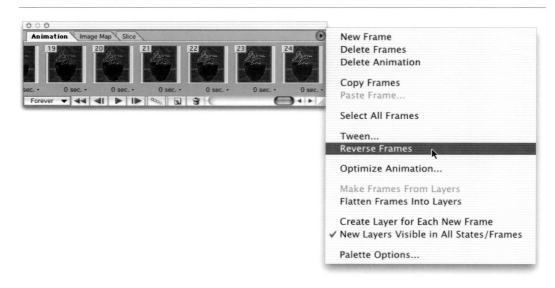

4. Click the arrow in the upper-right corner again and choose **Reverse Frames**. This puts all the selected frames in the reverse order.

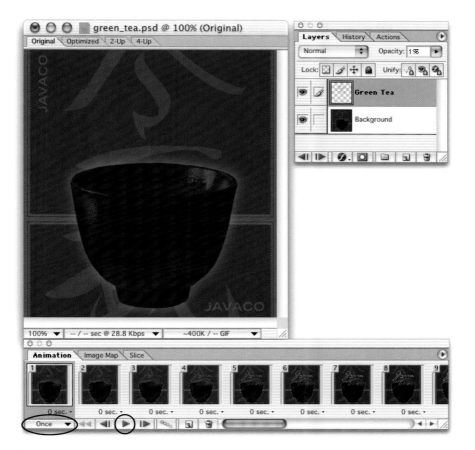

5. Change the **Looping options** setting to **Forever** and click **Play**. The animation fades up and down. Click **Stop** when you're through admiring your handiwork.

6. Click on **frame 12** and change the timing of that frame to **1.0** second, as shown above. Rewind the animation by clicking on the **Rewind** button at the bottom of the **Animation** palette. Click **Play** to watch the result of this change. The animation should now stop and hold in the middle and then continue to play. When you're finished watching, click the **Stop** button.

You can change the timing of all the frames, like you did in Exercise 2, or you can change the timing of individual frames.

7. Save and leave the file open for the next exercise.

This exercise taught you how to set the number of repeats with which an animation will play. You learned to create a loop by selecting, duplicating, and reversing frames, and how to set delays on individual frames.

MOVIE | reversing.mov

To learn more about Exercise 6, "Selecting, Duplicating, and Reversing Frames," check out **reversing.mov** from the **movies** folder on the **H•O•T CD-ROM**.

Different Ways to Duplicate Frames

In Exercise 6, you learned to duplicate a series of frames that were selected by clicking on the **New Frame** icon. Before you duplicate frames, you must first select them. You can select frames by holding down the **Shift** key, or you can use the arrow in upper-right corner of the **Animation** palette to choose **Select All Frames** from the pop-up menu. There are a few different ways to duplicate frames, and this chart outlines them.

Methods for Duplicating Frames	
Method	**Results**
From the **Animation** palette, select frames and click on the **New Frame** icon.	Duplicates the frames and appends them to the end of your animation.
Click on the arrow in the upper-right corner of the **Animation** palette to access the **Copy Frames** and **Paste Frames** features.	This is the method to use for copying animation from one document to another—ImageReady copies all the appropriate artwork to the target document. You'll also use this method when you want to append the copied frames someplace other than at the end of your animation. The **Paste Frames** dialog box gives you the choice of pasting before or after frames you've selected, or of replacing selected frames, all without creating additional layers. Replacing frames might be good if you had, let's say, an animation of a logo in one PSD file that you wanted to transfer to an ad banner that was being built inside a different PSD file. Another option in the **Paste Frames** dialog box is **Paste Over Selection**, which not only replaces the selected frame, but also creates additional layers in the **Layers** palette.

3. Choose **File > Save Optimized As**, and you'll be prompted to save this as **animation.gif**. You do not need to save HTML in this instance, just choose **Images Only** in the **Format** (Mac) or **Save as type** (Windows) field. Navigate to the **chap_13** folder that you copied to your hard drive and click **Save**. That's all there is to it.

You might wonder why we suggested that you save the images (but not the HTML) in this instance. An animated GIF file knows to function properly with or without the accompanying HTML. You can insert this animated GIF into an HTML editor just as you would insert any static GIF. You can even load an animated GIF directly into a browser without having any HTML. Try it, if you'd like. In Netscape Navigator, choose File > Open > Page, *or in Internet Explorer, choose* File > Open File, *and navigate to* animation.gif, *or simply drag and drop* animation.gif *into an open browser window. How does the browser know to display this file as an animation? The browser recognizes an animated GIF if more than one frame has been saved in the file.*

4. Choose **File > Save** to save **animation.psd**, and keep it open for the next exercise.

7. [IR] _____ Tweening a Tweened Sequence

You can also tween an animation more than once. This is useful in the event that you change your mind about a tween setting, such as the number of frames between keyframes.

1. In **green_tea.psd**, be sure that the **Green Tea** layer is selected in the **Layers** palette. Next, click on **frame 3** in the **Animation** palette to select it. In the **Layers** palette on the **Green Tea** layer, enter **Opacity: 100%**.

MOVIE | tweening_a_tween.mov

To learn more about Exercise 7, "Tweening a Tweened Sequence," check out **tweening_a_tween.mov** from the **movies** folder on the **H•O•T CD-ROM**.

2. With **frame 3** selected, hold your **Shift** key and click on **frame 1** to select **frames 1–3**. Click the arrow in the upper-right corner of the **Animation** palette to choose **Tween**. Click **OK**. Notice that you are not given the option to choose the number of frames, but that the **Tween With** setting is on **Selection**. That's because you selected multiple frames before you selected the **Tween** option.

Tip: The Tween button doesn't work when you're trying to tween a selection of frames. You have to use the method described in this step.

3. Play the animation or preview it in a browser. You'll see a short fade up at the beginning and an abrupt change in opacity as a result of the changes you made.

If you don't see the animation when you preview in a browser, it's because you didn't optimize the file in the last exercise. Try increasing the number of colors in the Optimize *palette to fix the problem.*

ImageReady allows you to tween either by defining a selection or defining a number of frames to insert between two keyframes.

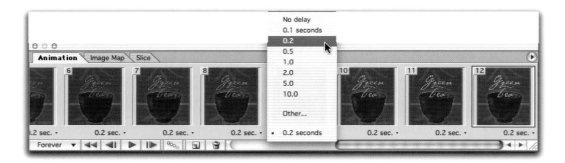

4. If it seems too fast for you, can change the speed. Select all the frames by **Shift-clicking** on the first and last frame, or by clicking the arrow in the upper-right corner of the **Animation** palette and choosing **Select All Frames**. Click the **Selects frame time** button on any frame and pick a new delay duration. The change will affect all the selected frames.

5. You've completed this exercise and don't need to save this document. In fact, the next exercise will require this same file without any animation. Delete the animation in **green_tea.psd** by clicking the arrow in the upper-right corner of the **Animation** palette and selecting **Delete Animation**. When prompted, click **Delete** (Mac) or **Yes** (Windows). This will leave the layers intact in the Layers palette but delete all the frames in the Animation palette.

6. Leave this file open for the next exercise.

8. [IR] _____Tweening with Position

So far, you've learned to create animations two different ways. Exercise 1 showed you how to create animation by turning on and off layers on different frames. Exercise 5 introduced you to creating animation by using the Tween setting and adjusting opacity between frames. There are two other types of tween parameters you can work with—**Position** and **Effects**. This exercise will show you how to tween with position. ImageReady will memorize the position of a layer between two frames, and those two stored positions can be tweened. You'll see how in this exercise.

1. With **green_tea.psd** still open from the last exercise, make sure the **Green Tea** layer is selected in the **Layers** palette and that **Opacity** is **100%**. Make sure that you are on the **Original** tab.

2. Using the **Move** tool from the Toolbox, click and drag inside the document window to move the lettering to the top. **Note:** If you are not on the **Original** tab, you will not be able to move the lettering.

3. Click on the **New Frame** icon at the bottom of the **Animation** palette. With the second frame selected, move the lettering to the bottom of the document window by using the **Move** tool. It's even okay to position the artwork so that it goes off the edge. **Tip:** If you're having trouble moving the artwork off the edge, try using the arrow keys to move the artwork instead of clicking and dragging. To do this, you must have the **Move** tool selected.

```
                    Tween
    Tween With:  [ Previous Frame  ▼]      ( OK )
    Frames to Add: [▲▼] 5                  ( Cancel )
    ┌─ Layers ──────────────────────┐
    │  ● All Layers                  │
    │  ○ Selected Layer              │
    └────────────────────────────────┘
    ┌─ Parameters ──────────────────┐
    │  ☑ Position                    │
    │  ☑ Opacity                     │
    │  ☑ Effects                     │
    └────────────────────────────────┘
```

4. Click the **Tween** button at the bottom of the **Animation** palette. Enter **Frames to Add: 5**. Make sure there's a checkmark next to **Position**. Click **OK**.

---

5. Preview the results. You've just learned to create an animation by letting ImageReady tween between two different positions on the screen.

| New Frame |
| Delete Frame |
| Delete Animation |
| Copy Frame |
| Paste Frames... |
| Select All Frames |
| Tween... |
| Reverse Frames |
| Optimize Animation... |
| Make Frames From Layers |
| Flatten Frames Into Layers |
| Create Layer for Each New Frame |
| ✓ New Layers Visible in All States/Frames |
| Palette Options... |

If you aren't pleased by what you see, you can go back and select any frame and make adjustments with the Move *tool; but the main point is that you have now learned how to tween with position changes.*

---

6. You won't need this animation for the next exercise, so go ahead and delete it by clicking the arrow in the upper-right corner of the **Animation** palette and choosing **Delete Animation**. When prompted, click **Delete** (Mac) or **Yes** (Windows). Leave the document open for the next exercise.

---

9. [IR] _____ Tweening with Effects

ImageReady can also tween effects using **styles** or **layer effects**. This next exercise will walk you through the process.

> **1.** In **green_tea.psd**, which should still be open from the last exercise, select the **Green Tea** layer in the **Layers** palette. Use the **Move** tool to move the words **Green Tea** back to the center of the document window.

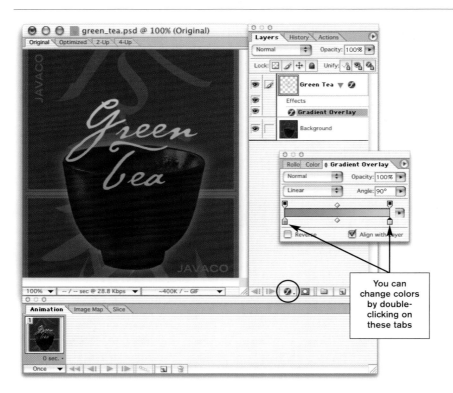

> **2.** In the **Layers** palette, click the **Add a layer style** icon at the bottom of that palette, and choose **Gradient Overlay** from the pop-up menu. In the **Gradient Overlay** palette, enter **90** in the **Angle** field. (If you don't see the **Gradient Overlay** palette, choose **Window > Show Layer Options/Style**).
>
> *Notice how the Gradient Overlay layer effect pulls colors from the foreground and background colors in the ImageReady Toolbox? That's why the colors of your gradient might not be the same as those in the figure above. If you want to change the colors, you can double-click on the tabs at the bottom of the* Gradient Overlay *palette.*

3. Click on the **New Frame** icon at the bottom of the **Animation** palette to add a new frame.

4. Change the gradient settings in the **Gradient Overlay** palette. We simply reversed the gradient by checking **Reverse**.

5. In the **Animation** palette, click on the **Tween** button. Choose **Tween With: Previous Frame**. Enter **Frames to Add: 15**. Make sure there's a checkmark next to **Effects**. Click **OK**.

6. Preview the results in a browser. You could also click the **Play** button on the **Animation** palette, but you would get less accurate feedback of the timing.

You should know how to make any adjustments that you want if you aren't pleased, but the main point is that you've now learned to tween effects. What you might not realize is that you can combine animating opacity, position, and effects in a single tween. Try your own experiments with this and you'll see.

7. Save and, finally, close the file.

NOTE | How Many Frames?

You might be wondering why we chose different numbers of frames to add in the **Tween** dialog box in different exercises. Some types of animations look better if they happen over a longer or shorter amount of time. Most animations will play more smoothly if they have more frames; but the more frames an animation has, the larger its file size and the longer its download time will be. How did we know how many frames to instruct you to add, or, more importantly, how will you know how many frames to add when you make your own animated GIFs? Experience has given us a good instinct about timing. We can imagine how something will look if it happens quickly versus if it happens slowly. You will be able to build this same skill if you make a lot of animated GIFs yourself. In the interim, don't be afraid to experiment! You can always delete the animation and try again, right?

10. [IR] _____Animated Slide Show

Let's say that you have a number of photographs from which you want to create a slide show. There are two types of slide shows you can make. You can simply turn each image on and off and set a delay to last for a few seconds, which would be no different from what you did in Exercise 1. You can also create a slide show that fades up on one image and fades down on another (called a cross-fade in filmmaking). This is something that ImageReady does naturally without requiring that you set the opacity. You'll see how simple it is—just try it!

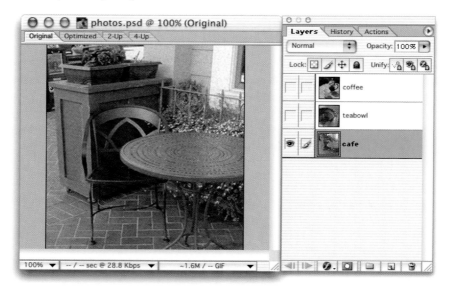

1. Open **photos.psd** from the **chap_13** folder.

This is a simple file that you could easily make. It contains three layers, each with a different image. The images could be photographic or graphic.

MOVIE | slideshow.mov

To learn more about Exercise 10, "Animated Slide Show," check out **slideshow.mov** from the **movies** folder on the **H•O•T CD-ROM**.

2. Make three frames and set three images so that only one appears on each frame. Do this by turning the layer for **cafe** on, and the layers for **teabowl** and **coffee** off. Click on the **New Frame** icon to add a second frame, which is a duplicate of the first frame. Turn off the layer for **cafe**, turn on the layer for **teabowl**, and turn off the layer for **coffee**. Click on the **New Frame** icon to add another frame. Turn off the layers for **cafe** and **teabowl**, and turn on the layer for **coffee**. The result should look similar to what you see here.

3. In the **Animation** palette, select the first frame, and click the **Tween** button.

4. Notice that the **Tween** dialog box is already set to **Tween With: Next Frame**. Use the settings above (**Frames to Add: 5**), and click **OK**.

If you click on the first frame in the Animation *palette, ImageReady defaults to* Tween With: Next Frame *but gives you the option of changing to* Tween With: Last Frame.

5. Select the **last frame** in the **Animation** palette (**frame 8**) and click the **Tween** button.

This time, ImageReady defaults to Tween With: Previous Frame *because you selected the last frame in the sequence. Click* OK.

6. Click on the **Play** button or preview the animation in a browser.

It would be nice if it made a complete loop, wouldn't it?

7. Select the **last frame** in the **Animation** palette (**frame 13**).

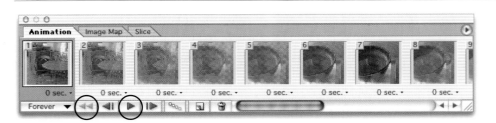

8. Click the **Tween** button. Notice that **Tween With** is set to **Previous Frame**. Click on **Previous Frame** and change this setting to **First Frame**. **Frames to Add** is still set to add **5** frames, which is perfect because all the other tweens were set to **5** frames, and this will be consistent. Click **OK**.

9. Click the **Rewind** button on the **Animation** palette. Then click the **Play** button. Notice that there is now a smooth fade between all the images.

Now your animation is complete. The challenge will be to compress this to a small file size. Remember that your content is photographic, so lossy compression will really cut down on the file size. If you'd like a refresher about optimizing animation, revisit Exercise 3 in this chapter.

---

10. To save the final animated GIF, choose **File > Save Optimized As**, and set the format field to **Images Only**. To save the Photoshop document, choose **File > Save**. Once you're finished saving your work, close the file.

II. [IR] _____Animated GIF Rollovers

It might not be immediately obvious to you, but it is also possible to combine animation and rollover techniques in a single ImageReady document. This is the only image editor we know of on the market that can easily do this. If you've never made animated rollovers in ImageReady before, it is likely that you might find the steps in this exercise a bit strange. The steps make sense once you've gone through them and have seen the results, but we find that many students in our lab have trouble understanding this exercise until they've tried it a few times.

1. Open **bean.psd** from the **chap_13** folder. Choose **Window > Rollovers** to view the **Rollovers** palette.

MOVIE | animated_roll.mov

You might like to look at the movie **animated_roll.mov** from the **movies** folder on the **H•O•T CD-ROM** before you embark on these steps.

2. Click on the **New Rollover State** icon at the bottom of the **Rollovers** palette. This will create a slice called **bean_01** and will add a new frame (**Over State**) to the **Rollovers** palette, but won't affect the **Animation** palette.

Notice that the first frames in the Animation and the Rollovers palettes are identical? This means that the Normal state will look just like what's on the screen. In other words, in the Normal state there will be no animation.

NOTE | Preload Issues

When designing animated rollovers, you need to set the animation to play at least two cycles (the **Forever** setting that generates an endless loop is our favorite). This is because ImageReady automatically writes a script that "preloads" the images. If the animation is set to play one time only, it will play in the preloading process and will not play when you finally see the image in the browser.

You'll now create the animation that will play when the end users rolls the mouse over the coffee bean.

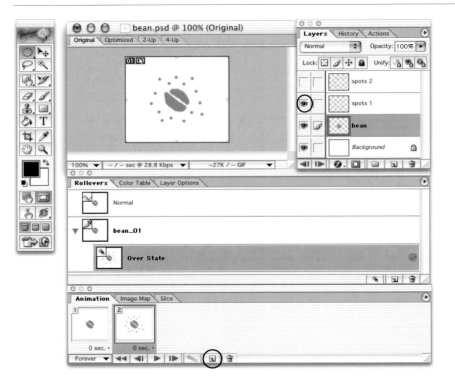

3. In the **Rollovers** palette, make sure the **Over State** is selected. Click on the **New Frame** icon at the bottom of the **Animation** palette. In the **Layers** palette, turn the **Eye** icon on for the layer called **spots 1** (leaving the **Eye** icons on for the **Background** and **bean** layers).

This should result in two rollover states and two animation frames. If you click on the Normal *state in the* Rollovers *palette, you'll see spots from the* spots 1 *layer disappear, and if you click on the* Over State, *the spots will reappear. That's because the animation is going to be triggered by the* Over State. *Be sure that the* Over State *is selected before you go to the next step.*

WARNING | Netscape Animation Bug

Unfortunately, if you click on an animated rollover in Netscape, the animation will not resume if you move your mouse over the artwork again. This is not true in Internet Explorer. The problem is not with the code that ImageReady generates but in the way that Netscape renders animated GIF files. At this point, there is nothing we can suggest to get around this.

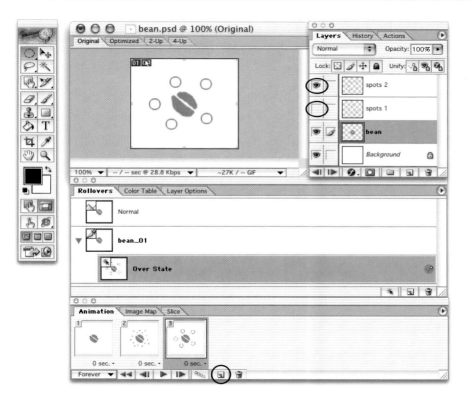

4. Click on the **New Frame** icon at the bottom of the **Animation** palette. This will create a third frame in the palette. In the **Layers** palette, turn on the layer **spots 2** and turn off the layer **spots 1**.

In the last step, we suggested that you click on the Normal and the Over States to watch the animation frames disappear. Now we're going to suggest that you click on frame 2 *in the* Animation *palette. Notice that frame 2, like frame 1, appears in the Over State of the Rollovers palette? That's because all of the frames of the animation will be triggered by the Over State of the rollover. This can be very confusing, but ImageReady is simply previewing whatever frame or state is selected. Be sure to select* frame 3 *in the* Animation *palette again before progressing to the next step.*

5. Click on the **New Frame** icon again at the bottom of the **Animation** palette, and turn off the **spots 2** layer in the **Layers** palette.

You should see four frames of animation and two rollover states. This won't necessarily make sense until you preview the results of your work.

6. Click the **Preview in Default Browser** button and move your mouse over the artwork. Notice that the animation happens when the mouse is on the rollover artwork.

Assuming all went well, you just learned how to create an animated rollover. What's interesting about ImageReady is that any rollover can be made to have an animated state.

7. Return to ImageReady to save and close the file.

12. [IR] _____Designing Entire Interfaces

In the past three chapters you've learned about slicing, rollovers, and animation. It might not seem obvious that all these techniques can be combined to design an entire Web interface. This next exercise should bring into practice a lot of skills you've just learned and open your eyes to further possibilities. We'll be truthful with you, however—this is a complex exercise. Don't be surprised if you have to try it a few times or watch the movies over and over. You won't be alone; when we teach this at our training center, most of our students suffer along until the big "aha!" moment comes and it finally makes sense. ImageReady is a powerful and complex tool, and this exercise really shows off its strengths and challenges.

1. Open **finished_layout.psd** from the **chap_13** folder.

2. Preview it in a browser and notice that the coffee cup at the bottom animates all the time. Move your mouse over the three images at the center of the page. Notice that remote rollover words appear in the area below the center image.

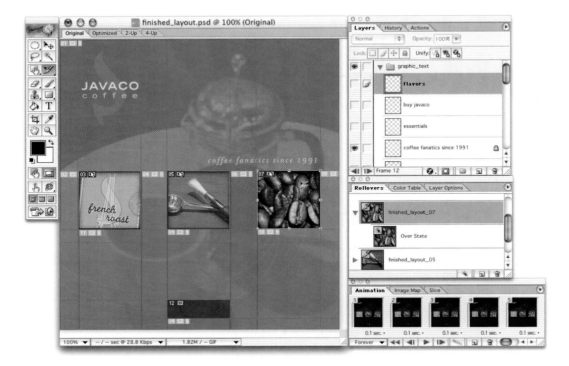

3. Return to ImageReady and make sure that the slices are visible (the shortcut is the letter **Q**). Use the **Slice Select** tool to click each of the three photographs in the middle of the image. You'll see that each has rollovers associated with it.

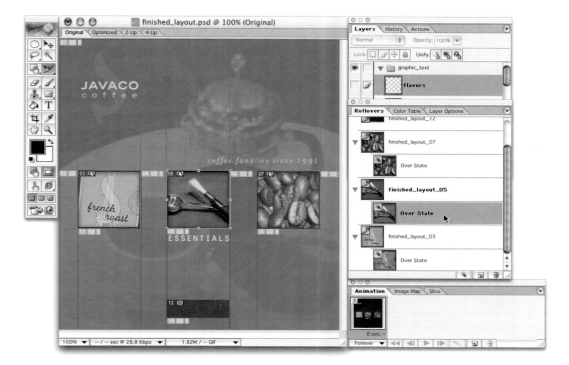

4. In the **Rollovers** palette, click the **Over State** for **finished_layout_07**, **finished_layout_05**, and **finished_layout_03**. You'll see the screen change and text appear in the area below the center photo.

Deconstructing a finished piece can teach how to construct a complicated document like this.

MOVIE | deconstructing.mov

To learn about deconstructing this piece, check out **deconstructing.mov** from the **movies** folder on the **H•O•T CD-ROM**.

---

5. Now that you have observed some of the techniques used in this exercise, **close** this file, and choose **File > Open > unfinished_layout.psd** from the **chap_13** folder.

The first thing to set up is the coffee cup animation. Why? Because you want this animation to take place on the Normal *state of every single slice in this document. Whenever you want animation to play at the onset of a page, you must set it up in the* Normal *state.*

6. Do not select any slice just yet, because the goal here is to create an animation that is in the **Normal** state of the entire document. Add a second frame to the **Animation** palette. With the new frame selected (**frame 2**), turn on the layer **cup_roll**.

Next, you'll tween between the frames to create smooth animation of the coffee cup fading in and out.

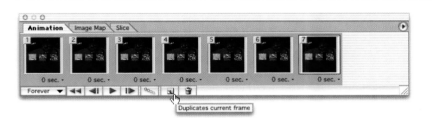

7. With **frame 2** selected, click the **Tween** button. In the **Tween** dialog box, set **Tween With** to **Previous Frame** and add **5** frames. Click **OK**.

Next, you'll copy and reverse the frames just like you did in Exercise 6.

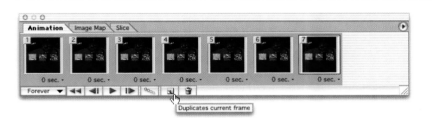

8. Frame 7 should already be selected. Hold **Shift** and click **frame 1** to select all the frames. Click the **New Frame** button. Your new frames will be created. With the new frames selected, click the arrow in upper-right corner of the **Animation** palette and choose **Reverse Frames**. You now have a smooth tweened animation of the coffee cup fading in and out.

If you want to preview your animation, go ahead and look at it in the your browser. The coffee cup will be animated, but no rollovers will work because you haven't specified any yet. Whenever we are building a document of this complexity, we preview often and after each step. We usually preview in the browser because you can't preview the rollovers in ImageReady itself.

By the way, this is no different than what you learned in the last exercise, except that this is on a more complicated, sliced-up document. If you want to watch us set this up, check out deconstructing.mov *from the* movies *folder.*

Now you'll create the rollover effects for each of the three images in the center of the document. This may seem involved at first, but after you've create a few rollovers, you'll start to see that it's not all that complicated.

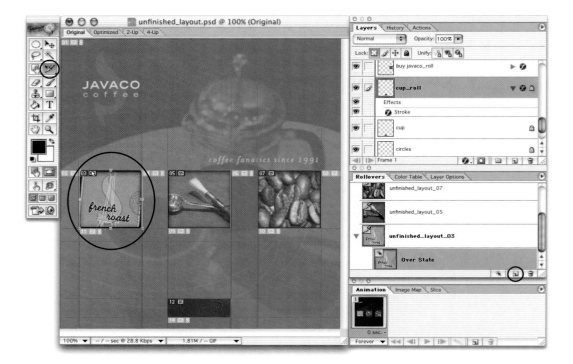

9. Using the **Slice Select** tool, select **slice 03** inside the document window. Add an **Over State** in the **Rollovers** palette by clicking on the **Create Rollover State** icon.

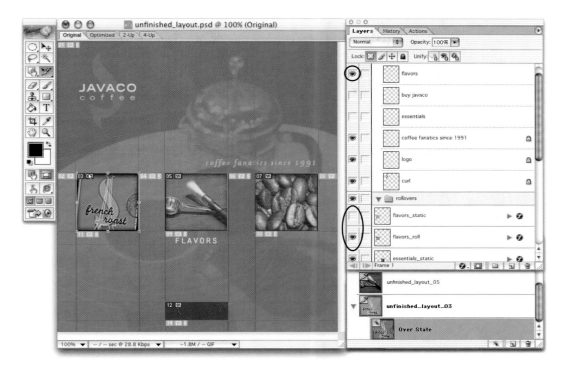

10. The **Over State** should now be selected in the **Rollovers** palette. Now you'll turn on the proper layers to display the images you want the end user to see when he or she rolls the mouse over **slice 03**. From the **Layers** palette, turn off the **flavors_static** layer and turn on the **flavors_roll**. Next, turn on the **flavors** layer.

You just specified that when your end-user's mouse rolls over the picture in slice 03, it will change color, and the word FLAVORS *will appear. Next you'll get to do the same for the rest of the pictures.*

Note: This document was complicated to create, and it made good use of layer folders. This feature was introduced back in Photoshop 6, and helps you organize layers. All of the text rollover callouts are located inside a layer folder called graphic_text, *and all the rollover layers are located inside a rollover folder called* rollovers. *Layer folders look like folder icons and can be collapsed or opened easily to organize files with lots of layers.*

11. Using the **Slice Select** tool, select the **center** slice (**slice 05**). Add an **Over State** in the **Rollovers** palette.

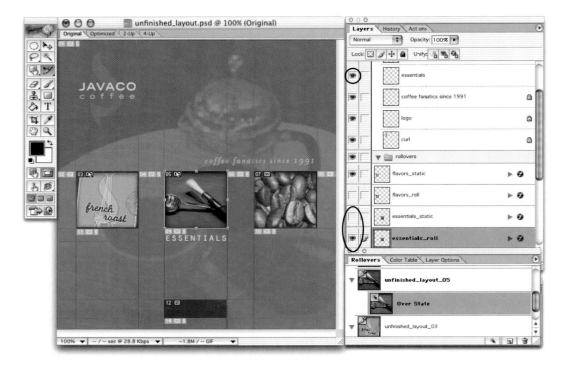

12. From the **Layers** palette, turn on the **essentials** and **essentials_roll** layers. Turn off the **essentials_static** layer.

You just specified that when your end-user's mouse rolls over the center image, it will change color, and the word ESSENTIALS *will appear. Again, preview. If it doesn't work, retrace your steps to see if you can figure out what went astray. You might want to watch the movie* deconstructing.mov *to see us do it.*

---

13. Using the **Slice Select** tool, select the final image slice (**slice 07**). Add an **Over State** in the **Rollovers** palette.

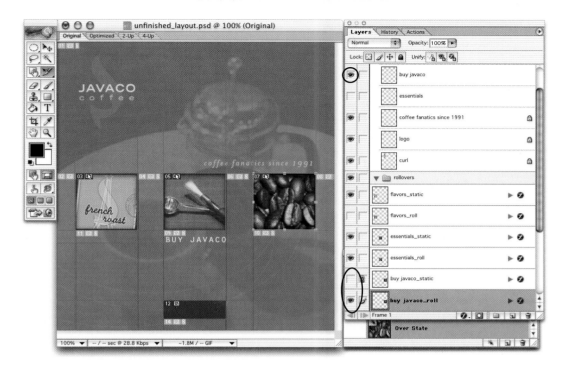

14. From the **Layers** palette, turn on the **buy javaco** and **buy_javaco_roll** layers. Turn off the **buy_javaco_static** layer.

You just specified that when your end-user's mouse rolls over the picture of the coffee beans, it will change color, and the words BUY JAVACO will appear.

15. You're done! Preview in a browser to check to see if everything works. When you're finished, close and save the file. Remember that **Save Optimized As** will save all the parts–the HTML, the JavaScript to make the rollovers function, and the images. **File > Save** will save the PSD file.

We know this might have been a challenging chapter, but these skills afford wonderful bragging rights once you've mastered them!

14.
Automation

Web Photo Gallery	Customizing Web Photo Gallery
Actions in Photoshop	Batch Processing with Actions
Actions in ImageReady	Batch Processing with Droplets

As we're sure you've realized by this chapter, there are tons of practical and creative things that you can do with Photoshop and ImageReady. This chapter addresses features you can use when you want to do something useful and creative, but to an entire folder of images at once. This can be a huge timesaver—who wants to repeat the same operation over and over when the computer can do it for you?

Photoshop and ImageReady both offer Actions, which allow you to store a series of operations as a recording that can be played back over a single image or multiple images that are in the same folder. Although it's possible to create actions in both Photoshop and ImageReady, they cannot be created in one program and played in the other.

ImageReady has another feature called droplets, which store optimization settings that can be applied to a folder of images by drag-and-drop methods. Photoshop has a droplets feature too, but Photoshop droplets do not store optimization settings; they are just another way of storing and applying actions. Photoshop has other automation features, like the popular Web Photo Gallery. This chapter offers hands-on training in all these features: actions, droplets, and the Web Photo Gallery. This is the sort of stuff computers were made for. Enjoy!

What Is the Web Photo Gallery?

The Web Photo Gallery is a convenient feature that automatically and quickly creates a Web site that displays a series of images in thumbnails and larger formats. This process automatically optimizes the images and writes HTML to produce a Web site suitable for publishing online. The Web Photo Gallery is a great tool for artists to display their work, for architects to show renderings to clients, for photographers to show proofs, for families to share personal photos on the Web, and for many other purposes too numerous to list here. In Photoshop 7, the Web Photo Gallery has been enhanced with more options and more opportunity for you to control the look of the Web sites Photoshop builds for you.

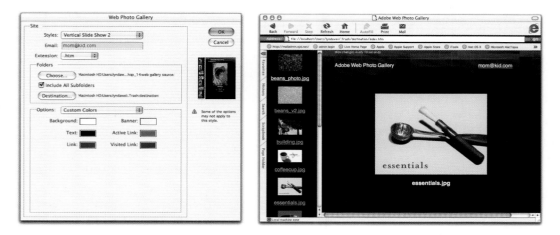

The Web Photo Gallery can be customized with many different appearances. In this example, the Vertical Slide Show style was chosen. You'll have a chance to learn how simple it is to create a Web Photo Gallery in this chapter.

When you make a Web Photo Gallery, Photoshop starts with a folder of images you provide and does all of the following for you:

- The program copies, resizes, and optimizes the images, and then creates a thumbnail and a larger JPEG of each image in the folder.

- Photoshop also writes all the HTML code for a Web site that includes a page of thumbnails and a separate page for the larger version of each image.

- Photoshop even generates arrow keys for **next**, **previous**, and **home** buttons!

Photoshop gives you lots of options for customizing your Web Photo Gallery, but you can modify it even further by bringing it into an HTML editor such as Adobe GoLive, a text editor, or a word processing application. To do so, you simply launch that other application and choose **File > Open** to open any of the **HTM** files that Photoshop generated. (At the end of each HTML file, Photoshop puts the file extension .htm, which works just the same as .html in any Web browser.)

It should be noted that in order to publish a Web Photo Gallery to the Web, you must first obtain an account for server space, plus know how to upload using a stand-alone FTP application such as Fetch (Mac) or WS-FTP (Windows), or the uploading features in an HTML editor such as Adobe GoLive. If you want to add a Web Photo Gallery to an existing Web site, you'll also need to know how to link to the Gallery from other pages in your site.

I. [PS]_____Creating a Web Photo Gallery

This exercise walks you through the steps for creating a Web Photo Gallery in Photoshop. Once you learn how to do this to the folder of images supplied on the **H•O•T CD-ROM**, try it on a folder of your own images. We predict you'll be amazed at how simple it is to generate an entire Web site without needing any HTML coding knowledge whatsoever.

1. For this exercise, you do not need to open a document right away, simply open Photoshop. From Photoshop, choose **File > Automate > Web Photo Gallery**. The **Web Photo Gallery** dialog box will appear. From the **Styles** menu, choose **Vertical Slide Show 2**. (A chart that shows all the Styles options is at the end of this exercise). Enter your email address in the **Email** field.

2. In the **Folders** area, click the **Choose** button to locate the folder of images that you want to use. Navigate to the **chap_14** folder that you copied to your hard drive and select the **web gallery source** folder. Click the **Destination** button, and navigate to the **chap_14** folder. Create a new empty folder here, and name it **destination**. When you're finished, the screen should look as ours does above.

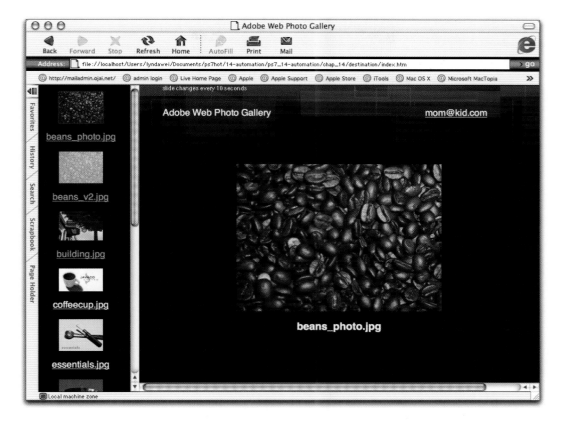

3. You can now click **OK** in the **Web Photo Gallery** dialog box. Photoshop will create the site, open a browser, and show you the Web site it just built! This will take minutes, or seconds, depending on the speed of your computer and the number of images in your source folder. Test it out by clicking on the thumbnails or watching the automatic slide show in the middle of the screen.

4. Go to your hard drive to look inside the **chap_14** folder; then open the **destination** folder to see that Photoshop created folders for HTML pages, images, and thumbnails for you.

Note: If you want to change the appearance of the site, you will need to return to Photoshop and change settings in the Web Photo Gallery dialog box, which you'll get to do in the next exercise.

5. Return to Photoshop for the next exercise.

2. [PS] Customizing a Web Photo Gallery

The only way to modify an existing Web Photo Gallery is in an HTML editor or by editing the HTML yourself. If you want to change the way a Web Photo Gallery looks, the easiest way is to remake it, and use the customization features built into Photoshop. You'll learn how to customize the settings in this exercise.

1. Choose **File > Automate > Web Photo Gallery**. The settings from the last exercise are still sticky, so **Vertical Slide Show 2** is still selected. Notice the warning **Some of the options may not apply to this style**. This means that this particular style cannot be fully customized. You'll change the style in the next step.

2. Choose **Styles: Simple**. Notice that the warning on the right disappears, and that the thumbnail preview changes. You've chosen a style that can be customized, which is what you'll learn to do next.

3. Select **Banner** from the **Options** menu. All of the setting fields will change. Feel free to use the text we've entered, or enter anything you want. You'll see the results when the site is created. Don't click OK yet!

4. Select **Large Images** from the **Options** menu. This is where you would change how images are sized in the Web Gallery interface. A chart that details all the options in this section is at the end of this section. We didn't change anything here—but feel free to change a setting if you want to. Don't click OK yet!

5. Choose **Thumbnails** from the **Options** menu. This is where you would change the settings for the size of the thumbnail images that will link to larger images in your final Web Gallery pages. We didn't make any changes here either. A chart describing all the settings for this option is at the end of this exercise.

6. Choose **Custom Colors** from the **Options** menu. We changed the colors by clicking inside each color swatch and choosing a different color in the **Color Picker** that appears.

7. Choose **Security** from the **Options** menu. A submenu called **Content** appears as well, with additional settings. These setting relate to the metadata in the file. Huh? What's that? Read the note that follows this step to learn about metadata. We didn't make any changes to this setting either.

NOTE | Metadata and Security Settings

Photoshop can store special information, called metadata, about a file that is invisible to the end user. Metadata can include the name of the file (filename), copyright information, a caption that describes the image, credits for who created the image, and a title for the image. You can set the metadata of a file by choosing **File > File Info**.

File Info
Section: General
Title:
Author:
Author's Position:
Caption:
Caption Writer:
Job Name:
Copyright Status: Unmarked
Copyright Notice:
Owner URL:
Go To URL

OK Cancel Load... Save... Append...

The **File Info** dialog box is where you enter metadata. Once you enter the information here for each file in your Web Gallery, then you can format the pictures to include some of the metadata in the Security settings.

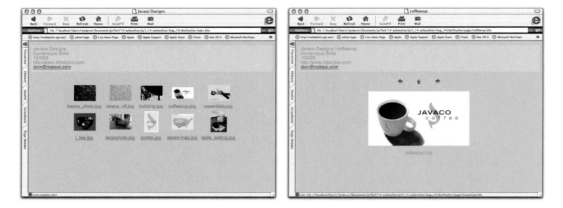

8. Click **OK**. Finally! The results will appear inside the Web browser. You should see a custom interface to your Web Photo Gallery.

9. Return to Photoshop for the next exercise.

NOTE | Tokens

Adobe has created its own code, called tokens, that allow you to customize the HTML for an automatically generated Web Photo Gallery. This is an advanced feature that programmers will likely be comfortable with, but designers who have never written custom code will not. To see a list of tokens and what aspects of the Web Photo Gallery can be altered, look up **Using tokens in Web photo gallery styles** in the Help Web pages that are found by choosing **Help > Photoshop Help**.

What Do All the Web Photo Gallery Settings Do?

The Photoshop Web Photo Gallery contains many settings, most of which were left at their defaults in this exercise.

	Web Photo Gallery Settings
Setting	**Description**
Choose	This button lets you select the folder of images from which Photoshop will build the Web Photo Gallery.
Destination	This button lets you select the destination folder to which Photoshop will write the images and HTML once it's finished creating the Web Photo Gallery.
Styles	Use this button to choose from the available site layouts.
Banner Options	
Site Name	The name you put in this field will appear in the banner on each page in the site and in the title bar of a Web browser displaying the first page of the site.
Photographer	Enter the name of the person who gets credit for creating the images here. Sadly, Photoshop uses the word *Photographer* for this field. The Web Photo Gallery is used for many types of artwork—and authors are not always photographers. The good news is that the word *Photographer* does not appear in the actual Gallery site.
Date	Photoshop automatically inserts the date on which the Web Photo Gallery is created. You can change this manually if you want.
Font	Choose **Arial**, **Helvetica**, **Courier**, or **Times New Roman** as the font of the HTML text in the banners.
Font Size	This setting determines the relative size of the HTML text in the banners on each page in the site. The higher the number, the larger the text will be. Unfortunately, you can't determine the actual size at which text will be displayed in a Web browser. Text size is relative to a default base text size, which a viewer can modify in his or her browser.

continues on next page

Web Photo Gallery Settings *continued*	
Gallery Thumbnails Options	
Captions	Here you choose the captions that will appear beneath each thumbnail image on the first page of the site. Leave both boxes unchecked if you want no captions. Check **Use File Name** to create captions from the file names of each image in the source folder. Check **Use File Info Caption** to use custom captions you previously embedded in each image in the source folder. (To embed a caption in a source image, open that image in Photoshop, choose **File > File Info**, choose **Caption** from the drop-down **Section** menu, and type a name into the **Caption** field. Click **OK**, and choose **File > Save.**)
Font and Font Size	This setting dictates the font (**Arial**, **Helvetica**, **Courier**, or **Times New Roman**) and relative size of the text in the thumbnail captions.
Size	This setting determines the width in pixels of all of the thumbnail images on the first page of the site. If you start with images of unequal width, Photoshop will make all the thumbnails the same width, but different heights that are proportional to the originals.
Columns and Rows	This setting dictates the number of columns and rows in the arrangement of the thumbnail images on the first page of the site.
Border Size	This sets the size in pixels of the border around each of the thumbnail images on the first page of the site.
Gallery Image Options	
Border Size	This sets the size in pixels of the border around each of the larger images to which the thumbnails are linked (the Gallery images).
Resize Images	This setting dictates the width in pixels of all of the Gallery images Photoshop will generate. Check the **Resize Image** box and choose from the presets, or type in a custom number of pixels. If you leave the **Resize Image** box unchecked, the Gallery images will be the same size as the original images in the source folder.
JPEG Quality	The Web Photo Gallery optimizes images as JPEGs only. You can choose a compression setting from **0** to **12** (**0** applies the maximum amount of compression; **12** applies the minimum). Use the slider or the presets, or type in a compression setting.

continues on next page

Web Photo Gallery Settings *continued*	
Custom Colors Options	
Background	The background color you choose will fill the background of each page in the site.
Banner	The banner color you choose will fill the horizontal banner at the top of each page.
Text	The Text color will affect the text in each banner.
Link, Active Link, Visited Link	Each thumbnail caption on the first page of the site will be the **Link** color initially, the **Active Link** color when clicked, and the **Visited Link** color after being clicked.
Security	These settings affect the formatting of **File Information** (also known as metadata) that can be set for each image by choosing **File > File Info.** You would enter this data for each image *before* you created a Web Photo Gallery.

Actions That Ship with Photoshop and ImageReady

This chapter will show you how to create your own custom actions. Once you get acquainted with the Actions feature in both Photoshop and ImageReady, you'll notice that there are already actions inside the **Actions** palette. If you'd like to try some of these, you can simply click on the **Play** button at the bottom of the Actions palette to see what happens. On playback, certain actions contain prompts that explain how the action is supposed to work.

If you click on the arrow to the left of the **Default Actions.atn** folder in the **Actions** palette, you'll see the contents of that folder. Some of the actions have qualifying words in parentheses, such as **Vignette (selection)**, **Cast Shadow (type)**, and **Sepia Toning (layer)**. Those are hints that these actions work only under certain conditions, such as when there is a selection active, when there is editable or rendered type, or when there is an independent layer in a document. Note that the actions that have been described so far are from Photoshop. ImageReady ships with different actions.

It's very easy to try out these default actions. Simply open any image and click on the action you want (exactly the same as you would select a layer in the **Layers** palette) and then click on the **Play** button at the bottom of the palette. If you don't have the proper condition set up for the action to play, it will either warn you or it will not work. That's the worst that can happen, so feel free to explore how these prebuilt actions work.

3. [PS] _____Creating an Action

Photoshop's Actions feature lets you streamline your workflow by recording a series of commands and automatically applying those commands to a single file or to many files at once. Actions are a great way to automate repetitive tasks, like creating Web-ready thumbnails of images, which you'll get to do in this exercise. Actions are good for zillions of other things, but we've chosen this example to teach you the basics of recording your own actions. You'll create an action that resizes a copy of an image to thumbnail size and saves it as an optimized GIF. In the following exercise, you'll apply that action to a whole folder of image files in just a single step with Photoshop's **Batch** command. You can also create actions in ImageReady in an identical fashion, which you'll get to do later in this chapter.

1. Open **beans_photo.psd** from the **web gallery source** folder from the **chap_14** folder.

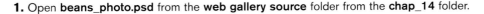

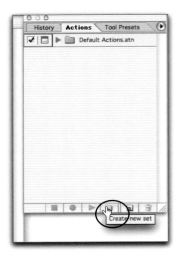

2. Choose **Window > Show Actions**, or click on the **Actions** tab to bring the **Actions** palette to the foreground. You'll notice that there is a folder called **Default Actions.atn**. These are actions that ship with Photoshop. Click on the **Create new set** icon at the bottom of the **Actions** palette to create a folder to contain the actions you make yourself.

3. In the **New Set** window that opens, enter **Name: HOT book** and click **OK**.

4. Click on the **Create new action** icon at the bottom of the **Actions** palette.

5. In the **New Action** window that opens, enter **Name: thumbnail** to name the action that you are creating. Make sure **HOT book** is selected in the **Set** field. Leave the **Function Key** and **Color** fields at their defaults. **Note:** You can trigger the action by clicking **Play** or assigning a function key to it. Click on the **Record** button in the **New Action** window to begin recording the **thumbnail** action. Everything you do in Photoshop from now until you stop recording will be part of the action. The red dot at the bottom of the **Actions** palette indicates that you are now in recording mode.

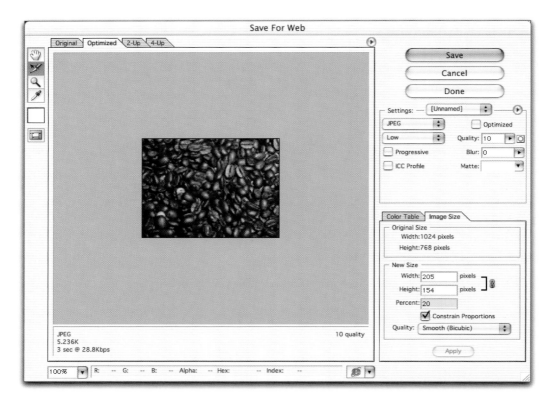

6. Choose **File > Save for Web**. This is the first step of the action. In the **Save For Web** dialog box that opens, click on the **Image Size** tab to bring the **Image Size** palette to the foreground. In the **Image Size** palette of the **Save For Web** dialog box, enter **Percent: 20** to reduce the graphic to a thumbnail. Make sure there is a check in the **Constrain Proportions** check box so that your image does not distort when resized. Click **Apply** to resize the image. Choose image optimization settings—try **JPEG**, **Low**. Click **Save**. We suggest these settings because they seem to create the best-looking thumbnail.

---

7. Next, you'll save the result inside a new folder that you'll create. Navigate to the **chap_14** folder and create a new empty folder called **Actions_Destination**. Once you've created this folder, click **Save**.

---

8. Back in Photoshop, close the original image without saving. This will preserve the PSD file without any changes.

This is the last step of the action, and you'll program it as such in the next step.

---

9. Click on the gray square **Stop Recording** button (it will turn blue when you mouse over it) at the bottom of the **Actions** palette.

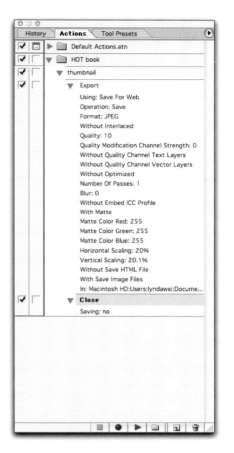

10. The arrow next to the **thumbnail** action in the **Actions** palette will be pointing down, revealing all of the commands included in this action. Click on the arrows next to **Export** and **Close** (the action's two commands) to see the settings and steps included in each command.

You just successfully programmed an action. Photoshop recorded everything you did, and now you can play back the recording on any images you like. The following exercise will show you how to take this action and play it over a series of images contained in a folder.

4. [PS]_____Batch Processing with an Action

In this exercise, you'll use Photoshop's **Batch** feature to apply the thumbnail action you created in the last exercise to a folder full of images. You can sit back and watch Photoshop automatically create thumbnails from each of the images in the folder. It's rather wondrous when you think how long it would take to do this process manually.

1. In Photoshop, no files should be open. Choose **File > Automate > Batch**.

2. In the **Batch** dialog box that opens, many of the choices may already be filled in. If not, choose **Set: HOT book**. This is the set of actions in which your **thumbnail** action is located. Choose **Action: thumbnail** (the action you created in the last exercise). Chose **Source: Folder** and click **Choose**. Navigate to the **chap_14** folder and select the **web gallery source** folder and click **Choose**. In the **Destination: Folder** area, click the **Choose** button. Navigate to the **chap_14** folder and select the **Actions_Destination** folder and click **Choose**.

> **WARNING | A Problem with Batch**
>
> The Batch dialog box is supposed to enable you to select a destination folder by clicking on the **Destination: Choose** button. Unfortunately, this doesn't work when Save For Web is part of your action. If you record an action that involves Save For Web, as the **thumbnail** action did, the destination folder you select while recording will become the destination folder regardless of whether or not you select a different folder in the Batch dialog box.
>
> The action you just recorded and batch processed will work correctly because you will have selected the same Destination folder in the action recording and the Batch dialog box. If you choose a different destination in the Batch dialog box, your thumbnails will still be saved in the destination you chose when you recorded the action.

3. Click **OK** to begin playing the thumbnail action on all the images in the **Photo Gallery Source** folder.

4. A **Replace Files** warning dialog box will appear. That's because Photoshop already made a JPG thumbnail for the **beans_photo.psd** image when you recorded the action. Click **Replace**. Since this is the only file that Photoshop will have to repeat the action on, it's the only time you'll see this warning.

Kick back and watch Photoshop automatically resize, optimize, and save a thumbnail copy of each image. This is the good life, isn't it?

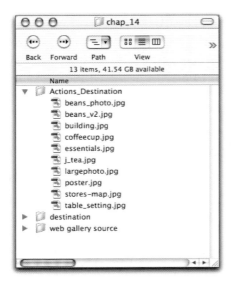

5. Open the **Actions_Destination** folder in the **chap_14** folder to see all of the thumbnails that Photoshop just created for you.

TIP | Applying an Action to a Single File

Batch processing is awesome, as you can already tell from Exercise 4. But what about those times when you want to work with only one file? As an alternative to batch processing, you can apply your thumbnail action to just a single file.

Here's what to do: Simply open the file on which you want to apply the action and click on the **Play** button at the bottom of the **Actions** palette. The action will perform its task on the one file and will still be a great timesaver.

NOTE | Actions in ImageReady

Now that you've learned to create an action in Photoshop, you might wonder if you can do the same thing in ImageReady. Yes, you can. ImageReady also contains an **Actions** palette, and recording actions is done identically there. The difference is that there is no **Automate** menu item in ImageReady. If you want to apply an action you make in ImageReady to a folder of images, you will need to make a **droplet** instead. You'll learn how to make droplets later in this chapter.

Adding, Changing, Deleting, or Pausing an Action

Once you've created an action, you can always change it later. You can easily initiate a pause, and add or delete steps. Just click the arrow in the **Actions** palette to reveal the steps you want to change and delete a section (select it and click the **trash** icon (Mac) or press **Delete** [Windows]) or insert your cursor where you want to add some steps. Here's a chart to reference if you want to do any operations with actions beyond what the preceding exercises have taught.

Working with Actions	
Operations	**Methods**
To add an Item	To add another item into an action, click on the arrow in the upper-right corner of the **Actions** palette, and choose **Start Recording** from the pop-up menu. Whatever you do at this point will be inserted at the end of the existing action. When you're finished, click the **Stop Recording** button at the bottom of the **Actions** palette. If you want to add another item somewhere in the middle of the recording, simply select whichever line item it should come after and then record your change.
To delete an Item	To delete a portion of an action, simply select that portion in the **Actions** palette and click on the **trash can** icon at the bottom of the palette or click on the arrow in the upper-right corner and choose **Delete.** Either way, you will be asked if you want to delete that section and you should click **OK**.
To set a pause	Setting a pause enables the action to stop in the middle of play-back. Let's say you want to create a new document with an action. If you inserted a pause, you could enter the dimensions of the new document instead of having the new document always open at the same dimensions. To set a pause, wait until after you have completed recording the action. Click in the column to the left of the command in which you want to initiate a pause. The icon that will appear in that column indicates that a pause has been set at that point in the action.

5. [IR] _____Creating an Action in ImageReady

Optimizing images can be a time-consuming, repetitive process. ImageReady's **droplet** feature makes optimization of multiple images efficient and easy. A droplet is a tiny application that runs an ImageReady action on images you identify by dragging and dropping. In this exercise, you will learn to create a droplet that stores the optimization settings of one image. You'll then automatically apply those settings to a folder full of images by simply dragging the folder onto the droplet.

1. Make a copy of the **web gallery source** folder inside your **chap_14** folder. This is done differently in different operating systems. Generally, you can select a folder and hold down **Option** (Mac) or **Alt** (Windows) to drag a duplicate folder away from the original. Rename the duplicate folder **ImageReady source**. Open **beans_photo.psd** from the **ImageReady source** folder from within ImageReady. You can do this by choosing **File > Open** and navigating to the **ImageReady source** folder.

Unlike Photoshop actions and Photoshop batch processing, you cannot record or select a destination folder for the images when running a droplet process. That's why it's essential that you create a duplicate folder so you don't overwrite precious original files. In general, even in Photoshop, it's a good practice to work from duplicates so you don't risk ruining your originals.

2. Click the **Create new action** button at the bottom of the **Actions** palette. Notice that there are no sets in the ImageReady Actions palette, like there are in Photoshop. You can only add or delete actions here—you cannot create new sets.

3. In the **New Action** dialog box, enter **Name: thumbnail**. Click **Record**.

4. Choose **Image > Image Size**, and the **Image Size** dialog box appears. Change **Percent** to **20%**. Make sure that **Constrain Proportions** is checked. Click **OK**.

5. In the **Optimize** palette (**Window > Show Optimize**), choose compression settings that create the smallest image that is of acceptable quality. Try **JPEG**, **Low**.

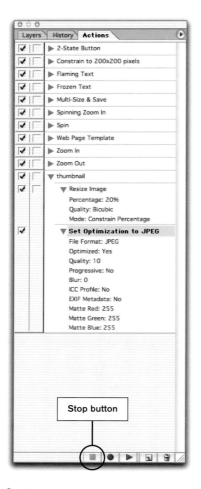

Stop button

6. Click the **Stop Recording** button. Click the arrows to the left and below the **thumbnail** action to see the steps that you saved within this action.

You've successfully recorded an action in ImageReady. To play this action on a single image, simply open an image, select thumbnail *from the* Actions *palette, and click the* Play *button at the bottom. Next you'll learn how to run this action over an entire folder of images through a new process called a droplet.*

7. Close **beans_photo.psd** and don't save. The steps are saved in the **thumbnail** action that you just created, and you'll apply it to the **beans_photo.psd** and the rest of the images in the **ImageReady source** folder next. Leave ImageReady open and proceed to the next exercise!

6. [IR] _____Batching an ImageReady Action with a Droplet

To run an action over an entire folder of images in Photoshop, you worked with the batch feature under the **Automate** menu. In ImageReady, there is no batch feature, but there is something called a droplet, which does the same thing. The only distinction is that you cannot build a destination location into the action. With droplets, you drop a folder onto the droplet icon, and ImageReady automatically runs the stored actions on every image in the folder. The new files (in this example, the **thumbnail** JPEGs) will go into the same folder that was dropped on the droplet. You'll see this in action by following this exercise.

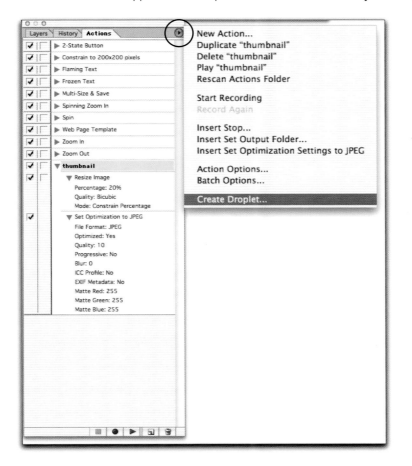

1. Select **thumbnail** in the **Actions** palette. Click on the **Options** menu (circled above) and choose **Create Droplet**. Leave the name **thumbnail**, and navigate to the **chap_14** folder and save the file there.

2. Go to your hard drive and open the **chap_14** folder. You should see the **ImageReady source** folder and the **thumbnail** droplet. The droplet is identified by a downward-pointing arrow icon. Drag the **ImageReady source** folder onto the **thumbnail** droplet icon.

---

3. Your screen will change to show the **Batch Progress** dialog box in ImageReady. Every file is being opened, resized, and optimized according to the droplet settings. This process will automatically stop when all the images are processed.

4. When the Batch Progress dialog box disappears, return to the **chap_14** folder, and open the **ImageReady source** folder. You'll see that images with the .jpg and the .psd extensions have populated the folder. By default, ImageReady stores the result of the droplet into the source folder. You can change the destination setting. To learn how, read the following note entitled "Changing the Droplet."

MOVIE | droplet.mov

To learn more about creating a droplet, check out **droplet.mov** from the **movies** folder on the **H•O•T CD-ROM.**

NOTE | Changing the Droplet

By default, droplets save the optimized images in the same folder as the original images. If you wanted to save the optimized images in a destination folder, you could use the **Batch Options** dialog box. This dialog box is reachable only by double-clicking on the droplet that you saved (in this case to the chap_14 folder).

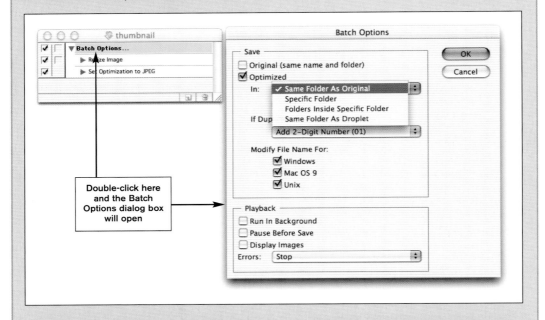

When it opens, you'll see a new window that resembles layers in the Actions palette. Double-click on **Batch Options**, and the **Batch Options** dialog box will appear. Here, you can alter the way the droplet saves the results through a number of different settings and pop-up menus. For example, you could change the **Optimized In** field to **Specific Folder**, navigate to a particular destination folder, and click **Choose**.

More About Droplets

There are a few other neat things to share about actions:

• A droplet is similar to an action in that it records and plays back over a series of images. In the last exercise, you saved the droplet to the desktop. You can put droplets inside other folders on your hard drive, and they will still function just fine.

• Photoshop 7 also offers a limited capability to make and apply droplets. In Photoshop, you can create a droplet directly from an action, but you can't make or apply a droplet that stores optimization settings.

• You can make droplets from the Actions palette in ImageReady and in Photoshop. In ImageReady, go to the **Actions** palette, select the action from which you want to make a droplet, and click on the arrow in the upper-right corner to choose **Create Droplet** from the pop-up menu. In Photoshop, choose **File > Automate > Create Droplet**, click **Choose** to select a destination for the droplet icon, select the **Set** and **Action** from which to create the droplet, and click **OK**.

• If ImageReady isn't open, you can drag a folder or image onto a droplet and it will launch that application for you to execute the optimization procedures. You can't really undo a droplet. If you want to change one, it's easiest if you just start over the process of creating it in the first place.

• Droplets are cross-platform, so you can share them between Mac and Windows users. However, for Windows machines to recognize that a droplet is an application, you need to add *.exe* to the end of the droplet name.

• ImageReady lets you drag and drop steps from the History palette into the Actions palette, which is a fast way to add steps to an action.

• For the true geeks, ImageReady actions are written in JavaScript and can be edited or generated once you look at a sample action to see how the instructions and settings are structured.

As you now know firsthand, actions and droplets hold a great deal of power to save you time and prevent human error. Another chapter down, just two more to go. If you have any files open in ImageReady, go ahead and close them without saving.

15.
Data Sets

| Viewing a Data Set |
| Creating Variables and Data Sets |
| Replacement Pixel Variables |

chap_15

Photoshop 7/ImageReady
H•O•T CD-ROM

When the Web publishing medium was young, designers and developers built everything page-by-page and graphic-by-graphic. Today, a new emphasis has emerged on data-driven content, templates, and dynamic content. What are all these buzzwords, and how do they relate to Photoshop and ImageReady? You'll learn about these terms early in this chapter.

After you learn those terms and understand the objectives of building data-ready documents, you'll move on to learning how to build an image-based template in ImageReady (called a data set). Later, in Chapter 16, "*Integration with Other Programs*," you'll learn how to manipulate a data set in Adobe's HTML editor, GoLive 6. This is the direction that the Web is moving towards, and fortunately Photoshop/ImageReady will help you get there!

Buzzwords and Definitions

Data-driven: This has to do with changing content that is fed to a template. It is assumed that the data will change from page to page, but that the page format already exists as a template, ready to accept the data. Usually, templates and data are text-based; however, images can by data-driven as well. In fact, what you will learn in this chapter will help you build the skills necessary to generate data-driven graphics with ImageReady (Photoshop doesn't directly support this feature).

Dynamic content: Dynamic content has to do with changing content. "Dynamic," in this context, means change.

Dynamic graphics: Dynamic graphics are generated on-the-fly. Learning how to work with data sets and variables, as you will in this chapter, offers "hooks" into GoLive and Adobe's Graphic Server product in order to generate dynamic images. You'll learn about GoLive integration with data sets and variables in Chapter 16, *"Integration with Other Programs."* See the "Adobe Graphics Server" sidebar on the following page.

Variables: A variable is something that you declare in ImageReady in order to flag content that can change. There are two kinds of changing, or variables, in ImageReady data sets: the ability to turn on or off a layer, and the ability to change text in a text layer. You'll get to define variables in this chapter.

Data sets: Data sets are holders for different versions of a single graphic template. You'll get to make data sets in this chapter.

NOTE | Adobe Graphics Server

```
                          Adobe Graphics Server 2.0 – Repurposing images
  Back    Forward   Stop   Refresh  Home    AutoFill   Print   Mail
  Address:  http://www.adobe.com/products/server/graphics/overview1.html                                    go
  http://mailadmin.ojai.net/   admin login   Live Home Page   Apple   Apple Support   Apple Store   iTools   Mac OS X   Microsoft MacTopia   Office for Macintosh
```

Adobe Graphics Server 2   ✓ order

◄ Products ◄ Graphics Server

Products   Support   Purchase   Company info   Search | Contact us | 🛒
Acrobat family   Digital imaging   Digital video   Print publishing   Web publishing
Downloads   Tryouts   Registration

Overview
Repurposing images
• Overview
• Changing the size of images
• Changing the file type and color mode

Photoshop file support
• Overview
• Editing images and graphic effects

Text editing
• Overview
• Replacing text

Open APIs and XML commands
• Overview

Using Photoshop and Illustrator SVG templates
• Overview
• Using templates

Data-driven graphic creation
• Overview
• Creating graphs
• Creating images

Adding pan and zoom
• Overview
• Adding pan and zoom

Repurposing images
Adobe® Graphics Server software can reduce the time it takes to repurpose your images for use in different media. It enables you to reuse existing images by automatically generating variations based on different color modes, sizes, resolutions, and file types. Scripts can be developed to automate routine tasks, making it quick and easy to apply changes to a large number of files.

• Supports import of GIF, animated GIF, JPEG, TIFF, EPS, PDF, PSD, and SVG from Adobe Illustrator® formats

• Supports export of GIF, animated GIF, TIFF, JPEG, PNG, EPS, PDF, PSD, SVG, WBMP, and I-mode wireless formats

• Supports the same range of image optimization settings available in Adobe Photoshop®, Adobe ImageReady®, and Illustrator

• Supports image resizing and cropping

• Supports color-mode conversion for print and Web

• Supports sharpening an image, changing opacity, cropping, rotating, changing canvas size, and many more

next ▶

Copyright 2002 Adobe Systems Incorporated. All rights reserved.
Terms of Use | Online Privacy Policy (updated 8/19/2002) | Adobe and accessibility | Avoid software piracy | Permissions and Trademarks

Internet zone

The Adobe Graphics Server 2 is a product (formerly called Altercast) that integrates with a database and generates dynamic graphics on-the-fly. You can learn about this product at **http://www.adobe.com/products/server/graphics/**. You would need to set your graphic templates up in ImageReady to be compatible with the Adobe Graphics Server system, so you're part way there once you complete the lessons in this chapter!

I. [IR] _____Observing Data Sets and Variables

The best way to understand what data sets and variables are is to look at a file that already contains them. With ImageReady alone, there is little compelling reason to work with data sets and variables. It offers a way to see variations of a single image, but you could do the same thing by just turning layers on and off, too. The true power of data sets and variables is when they integrate with a database or HTML Editor. You'll get a chance to try a practical use of this technique in Chapter 16, "*Integration with Other Programs*." This entire chapter takes place in ImageReady, since Photoshop does not support data sets and variables directly.

1. Make sure that you're in ImageReady. Open **dataset_CTG.psd** from the **chap_15** folder that you copied to your hard drive. Before you look at the data sets and variables, notice that there is one text layer (hence the **T** symbol in the thumbnail). All the other layers contain images or graphics. Some have layer effects.

2. Choose **Image > Variables > Data Sets**. You are looking at the **coffee** data set. Notice the column to the right called **Layer**? The **coffee picture** layer is visible, the **tea picture** layer is invisible, the **coffee** layer (which is the **text** layer) is set to the value **coffee**, and the **gifts picture** layer is invisible.

3. Click the **Next data set** button (circled). This takes you to the **tea** data set. Here you'll see that the **coffee picture** layer is invisible, the **tea picture** layer is visible, the **coffee** layer has been set to a value of **tea**, and the **gifts picture** layer is invisible. The data set is controlling which layers to turn on and off, and has changed the **text** layer to read **tea** instead of **coffee**.

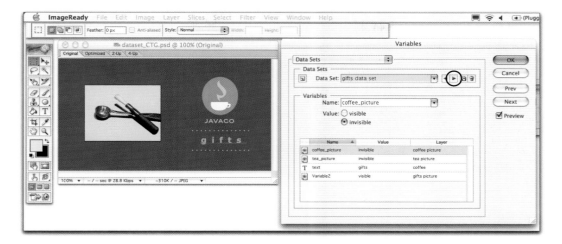

4. Click the **Next data set** button again (circled). This takes you to the **gifts** data set. Here you'll see that the **coffee picture** layer is invisible, the **tea picture** layer is invisible, the **coffee** layer has been set to a value of **gifts**, and the **gifts** picture is visible. The new data set is controlling different layers to turn on and off, and has changed the **text** layer to read **gifts** instead of **tea**.

---

5. Close **dataset_CTG.psd**. You won't need it again.

There you have it! That's all there is to viewing a data set and its variables. Setting up this document is a little more work, but we think you'll be very pleased to learn how much easier it is than you might think.

---

2. [IR] _____ Creating Data Sets and Variables

Now for the hard part—creating the data sets and variables. Just kidding! It isn't that hard—you'll see once you get to do it yourself.

1. In ImageReady, open **coffee-tea-gifts.psd** from the **chap_15** folder that you transferred to your hard drive. Choose **Image > Variables > Define**. If the **Layer** is not set to **coffee**, locate the **coffee** layer from the pop-up menu (circled). Check **Text Replacement** and enter **Name: text**. This indicates that you want to define this variable to be changing text. You've given it the name **text** instead of **coffee**, because it won't always say **coffee** (even though the layer in the ImageReady document will always be referred to as **coffee**). If this doesn't make sense, it soon will.

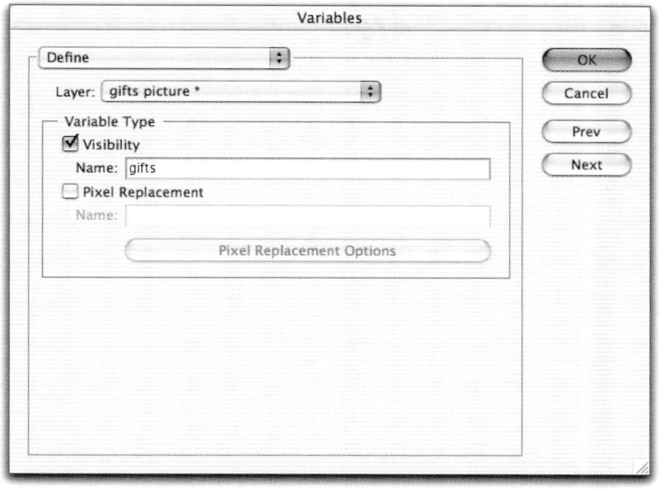

2. Change the **Layer** setting to **gifts picture**. Check **Visibility** and change it to **Name: gifts**. You are setting the ImageReady layer **gifts picture** to be able to be turned on or off. You are giving it an abbreviated name **gifts**.

Note that the variable name cannot contain spaces or special characters. ImageReady will issue a warning if you give it an illegal name, so you don't have to worry too much!

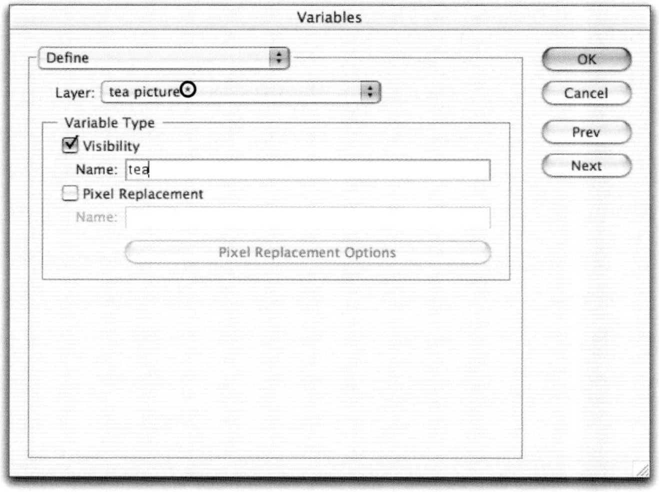

3. Change the **Layer** setting to **tea picture**. Check **Visibility** and enter **Name: tea**. Notice the asterisk that appears to the right of the words **tea picture**? This indicates that you've set a variable for that layer.

4. Change the **Layer** setting to **coffee picture**. Check **Visibility** and enter **Name: coffee**.

5. Change the top pop-up menu to read **Data Sets**. Change the name of this **Data Set** to **coffee data set**. You cannot create a data set before you set variables. That's why we had you set the variables for all the layers first! The values are set to the defaults of the document here—the **coffee picture** layer is turned on (visible), the **gifts picture** and **tea picture** layers are off (invisible), and the text's value is **coffee**.

6. Click on the **Create new data set** button (circled). This simply copies all the data from the last data set and calls it **Data Set 2**. You'll change all of this, of course!

7. Change the name of the data set to **tea data set**. Click on the **coffee picture** layer, and set the value to **invisible**. Click on the **gifts picture** layer and set the value to **invisible**. Click on the **tea picture** layer and change the value to **visible**. Click on the **coffee** layer (**text**) and enter **tea** in the **Value** field (circled.) Click down below in the **coffee** layer and the text will change to **tea** in the Value field and on your screen!

◯ MOVIE | dataset.mov

To watch a movie of the steps in this exercise, open **dataset.mov** from the movies folder on the **H•O•T CD-ROM**.

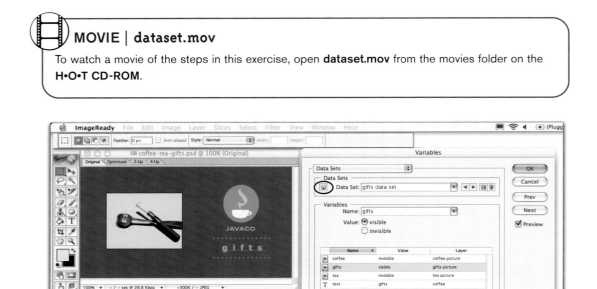

8. Click the **Create new data set** button (circled). You will be prompted to save before you continue. Change the name of the data set to **gifts data set**. Click on the **coffee picture** layer, and set the value to **invisible**. Click on the **gifts picture** layer and set the value to **visible**. Click on the **tea picture** layer and change the value to **invisible**. Click on the **coffee** layer (**text**) and enter **gifts** in the **Value** field. Click down below in the **coffee** layer and the text will change to **gifts** in the **Value** field and on your screen!

9. Click on the **Save data sets button** (circled). Now you can use the forward arrow to cycle through all the data sets. Congratulations—you did it! It really wasn't that hard, once you were guided through it, was it? The terms variables and data sets sound a lot more intimidating than they really are, once you get the hang of it. Click **OK**. Leave this file open for the next exercise.

3. [IR] _____Pixel Replacement Variables

There's just one last frontier to this chapter—learning about pixel replacement variables. This type of variable allows you to browse your hard drive and load external images into an ImageReady document. This is how you would set up templates that were going to load dynamically changing images.

1. Choose **Images > Variables > Define**. The **Variables** dialog box will open. Change **Layer** to **bgcolor**. Check **Pixel Replacement**. Enter **Name: background**. Click the **Pixel Replacement Options** button. Change the **Method** to **Fill** and click **OK**. (A chart outlining the **Method** choices is at the end of this exercise.)

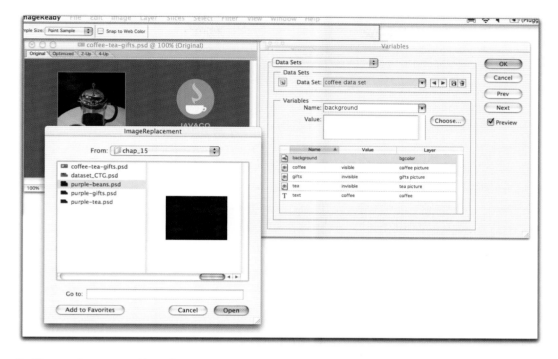

2. Change the menu to **Data Sets**. The **coffee** data set will appear. The layer **bgcolor** is now identified as a variable with the name **background**, and is set to the **Replacement Pixels** type of variable. Click the **Choose** button to browse your hard drive. Navigate to the **chap_15** folder and select **purple-beans.psd**. Click **Open**.

The external PSD file will populate the background image in your open document. Neat!

Adobe ImageReady

Save changes to data set "coffee data set"?

Cancel   Save

---

3. Click the **forward** arrow to go to the next data set. You will be prompted to save **coffee data set**. Click **Save**.

---

4. The **tea data set** will appear. Click the **Choose** button and navigate to the **chap_15** folder. Select **purple-tea.psd** and click **Open**. This image will appear in the background!

5. Click the **forward** arrow. You will be prompted to save again. Click **Save**. The **gift data set** will appear. Click the **Choose** button and navigate to the **chap_15** folder. Select **purple-gifts.psd** and click **Open**. The image will appear in the background. Click the **disk** icon to save this data set. Feel free to use the **forward** arrows to check your work. When you're satisfied (and perhaps impressed with yourself?), click **OK** to close the dialog box.

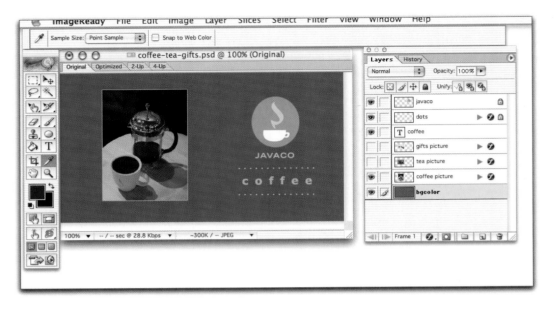

When you return to the regular interface, you might be sad to see the background images disappear. The only way to see these images is to look through the data sets by choosing Image > Variable > Data Sets.

The significance of this feature is really best realized in an editor such as GoLive or a dynamic graphics environment such as the Adobe Graphics Server 2. You know how to set up this feature, however, in the event you ever need to work with these outside programs!

Replacement Pixel Scaling Methods	
Fit To Scale	The image will scale to fit the height, which may leave the sides empty.
Fill to Scale	The image will fill the entire layer with constrained proportions, which might cause part of the image to extend beyond the dimensions of the file.
As Is	Doesn't scale the image at all.
Conform to Scale	Causes the image to scale to fit nonproportionally.
Click a handle on the alignment icon	Choose an alignment for placing the image inside the bounding box.
Clip to Bounding Box	Clips areas of the image that do not fit within the bounding box. Only available when **Fill** or **As Is** is selected.

NOTE | Setting Up the PSD Files

When you're developing a PSD file for variables and data sets, it's helpful to know a few tips:

- Make sure you center or left align your text, depending on the layout. You want to make sure that the text block is going to look consistent throughout the template data sets.

- Test the lengths of your text blocks to ensure they'll fit in the space you've allotted.

- Use filter effects liberally—they work on text layers and image layers that have visibility settings.

That's a wrap! You may not put these skills to work right away, but this is the workflow of the future. Next up, learning to integrate Photoshop and ImageReady files with other programs.

16.

Integration with Other Programs

Update HTML	ImageReady Rollovers Into GoLive 6
Smart Objects	Edit Original	Data Set
Dreamweaver MX	Illustrator 10
ImageReady to QuickTime	Photoshop to PDF

chap_16

Photoshop 7/ImageReady
H•O•T CD-ROM

This chapter addresses advanced issues of integrating with programs other than Photoshop and ImageReady. We explain how to import and export file formats (other than PSD, GIF, and JPG) to and from Photoshop and ImageReady. We don't know whether you have some of the programs described here, such as GoLive, Dreamweaver, or Illustrator, so we can't anticipate whether you'll know how to use those applications. It's obviously beyond the scope of this book for us to teach those applications as well as Photoshop and ImageReady. For that reason, keep in mind that parts of this chapter are for advanced users who know how to perform tasks in those applications (GoLive, Dreamweaver, or Illustrator) without much coaching.

This chapter will be helpful to those of you who are interested in importing and exporting HTML, Illustrator, JavaScript, and QuickTime files. Most books touch upon only a single application, but because Web development almost always involves more than one program, we had an idea that this chapter might be useful to many of you readers out there. ;-)

I. [IR] _____Update HTML in ImageReady

Update HTML is an ImageReady command that writes over existing ImageReady-generated HTML files and updates only things that have changed. Suppose that you made a remote rollover in ImageReady and had saved the images and HTML in a folder on your hard drive. Your client looks at the work and likes everything but notices a spelling error. If you had saved the PSD version of the file, too, it would be easy to correct the spelling mistake, but it would require that you re-export all the optimized images and HTML. Or would it? The Update HTML command is useful when you make a change to an existing HTML file or its images. It saves you the headache of managing multiple versions of a document because it updates the HTML and images to reflect any changes you make to the PSD file.

1. In ImageReady, open **nav.psd** from the **chap_16** folder that you transferred to your hard drive from the **H•O•T CD-ROM**.

This is a sliced document with rollovers that was made in ImageReady. Its optimization settings have already been set, and are stored with the document. Any time you set optimization and save in the PSD format, those settings are saved with the document.

2. Choose **File > Save Optimized As** and navigate to the **chap_16** folder. Create a new folder called **navigation1**. Click **Save**.

3. On your hard drive, locate the **chap_16** folder, open the **navigation1** folder you just made, and double-click on **nav.html**. This will open that HTML file in a browser. Notice the spelling error in the word **tee**. Return to ImageReady to fix this problem.

4. To fix the error, press the letter **Q** on your keyboard to turn Slice visibility off, if it isn't off already. This makes it easier to see the problem. Select the **Type** tool from the Toolbox and select the misspelled word **tee**. Type **tea** in its place.

5. Once the spelling error is fixed, choose **File > Update HTML**, and navigate to open the **navigation1** folder you just created inside the **chap_16** folder. Select **nav.html**, and click **Open**.

6. Click **Replace** when prompted. This will replace all the image files inside the **navigation1** folder that are related to **nav.html**, as well as the HTML file itself.

7. ImageReady will tell you that one table in the HTML file was updated. Click **OK**.

ImageReady just rewrote all the files that you created in step 2, and you avoided having to save a duplicate set just to make this one change to your file. Whenever we're making changes to an ImageReady-generated HTML file or images, we use Update HTML *so we don't have multiple folders lying around with different versions of artwork and HTML.*

This technique is useful for more than just spelling errors. You could change anything about the document—its styles, the type, its position, slice names, layers being turned on and off, etc.

8. Leave **nav.psd** open in ImageReady for the next exercise.

Note: *If you try to view your changes in Internet Explorer, and you do not see the changes you made when you reload the page, you may need to do a force reload or have to clear the browser cache first.*

2. [IR] _____Getting ImageReady Rollovers into GoLive

Making rollovers in ImageReady was pretty fun back in Chapter 11, "*Rollovers*," but as you followed the exercises you were probably asking yourself, "How do I get this into an HTML editor?" You can open an ImageReady HTML file inside any HTML editor and it will work properly. The harder thing to do is to integrate something you made in ImageReady (like a rollover) into an existing HTML page that you made in the HTML editor. You might want to design the rollover in ImageReady and then use it on other pages inside an existing site. This exercise will show you how to accomplish this in **GoLive 6**. The instructions are different for GoLive than for other HTML editors, probably because it's an Adobe product and the engineers were able to make ImageReady files easier to use with GoLive. The main trick to getting ImageReady rollovers to work in GoLive is to be sure to set ImageReady to write GoLive code, which you'll learn how to do here.

1. In ImageReady, you should still have **nav.psd** open from the previous exercise.

2. Choose **File > Output Settings > HTML**. In the **Output Settings** dialog box, check **Include GoLive 5 (or Earlier) code**. This works for GoLlve 6, too. ImageReady was released before GoLive 6, so Adobe couldn't mention it yet! Click **OK**.

MOVIE | golive_rollovers.mov

To learn more about getting your ImageReady-created rollovers to work in GoLive, check out **golive_rollovers.mov** from the **movies** folder on the **H•O•T CD-ROM**.

3. Choose **File > Save Optimized As**. Navigate to the **chap_16** folder. Create a new folder there and name it **navigationGL**. Click **Save**. This saves the **nav.psd** content in GoLive-formatted HTML into its own folder.

Adobe GoLive

Please choose one of the following options

New Page
Click to create a new untitled HTML page.

New Site
Click to open the wizard for creating new sites.

Open
Click to open a Web page or site project file (with the filename extension ".site").

☐ Don't show again. (You can also choose this option in the General Preferences dialog box.)

Close

4. Open **GoLive 6**. Click **Open** in the **Adobe GoLive** dialog box.

This will open a GoLive site that we made for you using GoLive 6. Note that you cannot open this site if you are using an earlier version of GoLive, because GoLive 6 files are not backwards-compatible. Sorry.

5. Navigate to the **chap_16** folder and select **IRGL-SITE > ImageReady Site.site**. Click **Open**. The **ImageReady Site.site** window in GoLive will appear with two files: **index.html** and a **GeneratedItems** folder. Next, you will learn how to bring the ImageReady HTML and images into this GoLive site.

6. From the main GoLive menu, choose **File > Import > Files to Site**. Navigate to the folder **chap_16 > navigationGL**. Click **Add**. The **navigationGL** folder should appear inside the **Add** window. Click **Done**.

7. The **Copy Files** dialog box will appear. Click **OK**.

This is GoLive's way of updating the ImageReady HTML so that it is relative to the GoLive site. It's one of the strong points of GoLive's site management capabilities, because it ensures that all the links that were generated in ImageReady translate to GoLive properly.

8. The site window will now contain a new folder called **navigationGL**. This is the folder you created in step 3. Click the arrow to see the contents. Double-click on **nav.html** to open it.

9. Select all the contents of this page. This can be done by clicking underneath the comment symbol (looks like a cartoon dialog bubble) and dragging your mouse upwards until everything is darkened, as you see above. Alternately, you could choose **Cmd+A** (Mac) or **Ctrl+A** (Windows). Copy this content, by choosing **Edit > Copy** or using the shortcut keys for this operation. It's essential that you select and copy the comment tags (indicated by the comments symbols) as well as all the artwork and table.

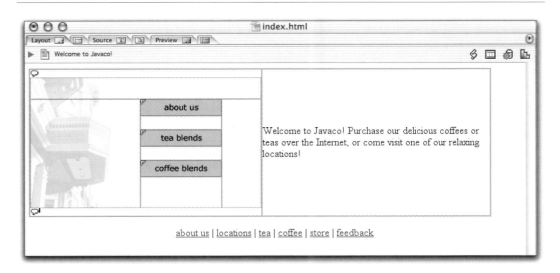

10. Return to the **Site** window by choosing **Window > ImageReady Site.site**, and open **index.html** by double-clicking on it. This file will open in its own window in GoLive. Click inside the middle table cell, as shown above.

11. Choose **Edit > Paste**. This will paste the contents of the clipboard (the rollovers you copied from **nav.html**) into the table on the **index.html** page.

12. To preview this page in a browser, press **Cmd+T** (Mac) or **Ctrl+T** (Windows). You'll see that it works just fine in the browser.

13. You're finished with this exercise and can return to GoLive. Leave this file open for the next exercise.

NOTE | Rollover Objects and GoLive

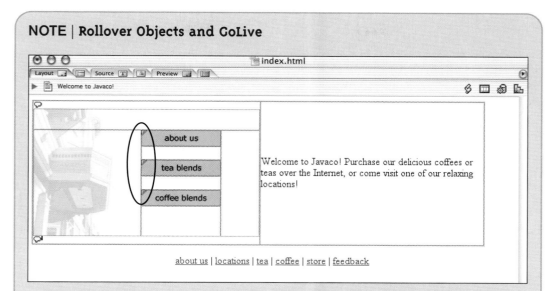

Notice the green corners on each of the rollovers? That indicates that GoLive is recognizing the ImageReady rollovers as GoLive **rollover objects**. If you are not familiar with rollover objects in GoLive, you can learn about them from the GoLive manual or from the 18-hour-long Lynda.com CD-ROM:

Learning GoLive 6
By Shane Rebenschied
18-hours long
Available as a CD-ROM ($149) or as part of our Online Movie Training Library ($25 per month).

Note: If you had not instructed ImageReady to **Include GoLive Code** in step 2, the rollovers would not appear as rollover objects in GoLive, and they would not work correctly in a browser. That's because the **Include GoLive Code** instruction in ImageReady tells ImageReady to format the JavaScript code it writes in a way that GoLive recognizes.

3. [PS/IR] _____Smart Objects in GoLive 6

Smart objects are new to GoLive. This feature allows GoLive to open a PSD document directly, eliminating the need for you to save your optimized slices and HTML from ImageReady. This is more a GoLive lesson than an ImageReady one, since you already know how to make PSD files! Still, it's a pretty neat workflow between the two applications, so we thought we'd share how to do it!

1. In GoLive, inside **index.html**, select the navigation content, including all the comments. Press **Delete** to remove them. This will leave a blinking insertion cursor inside the empty table cell.

2. In the **Objects** palette, select the **Photoshop Smart Objects** icon and drag it into the empty table cell.

3. Make sure the smart object is selected, and open the **Inspector** palette. Click the folder icon for the source, and browse to the **chap_16** folder. Locate **nav.psd** and click **Open**.

4. The **Variable Settings** dialog box will open. This isn't really applicable to the **nav.psd** file because no variables have been declared. Regardless, by default GoLive asks this information for any Photoshop smart object. Don't worry about it and click **OK**.

5. The **Save For Web** dialog box will open. Look familiar? The Save For Web dialog box is inside GoLive 6, too! Notice that the same slices show up here that were in the ImageReady document? All the optimization settings are there, too—you probably don't have to make any changes. Click **Save**.

Why did the Save For Web dialog box appear? Think about it—you opened a PSD file, not an HTML file! This workflow allows you to avoid Save Optimized from ImageReady or use Save For Web from Photoshop. You have to optimize and save the graphics somewhere, so GoLive lets you do it here. **Warning:** *You still need to create the slices and the rollovers initially in ImageReady, however, because GoLive is not a full-fledged image editor.*

On another note, you might see that the spelling error "tee" is still present in this document. When you fixed this problem earlier, it was fixed in the HTML and Web images, but not in the master PSD file. You could have fixed it earlier by not just choosing Update HTML, *but also saving the corrected PSD. You'll get a chance to fix it in the next exercise, when you learn about the* Edit Original *feature.*

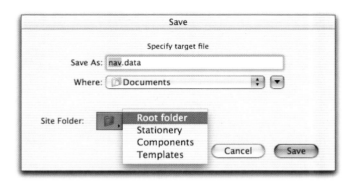

6. The **Save** dialog box will appear. It's important that you save the resulting document in the **Root folder** of the site. GoLive makes this very easy by supplying a handy button and menu. Click **Save**.

In Exercise 2, you got the ImageReady content into the GoLive site by choosing to import it. This step achieves the same result in a different way. The HTML and images will now be stored inside the GoLive site.

7. The **navbar.psd** image should appear inside the table in GoLive. Preview this in the browser by pressing **Cmd+T** (Mac) or **Ctrl+T** (Windows).

You can see that the rollovers work and the end result is identical to that of Exercise 2. Why would you use this technique over the one you learned about there? It's just a matter of convenience—why go through saving all the rollover HTML and Images in ImageReady when you can do the same thing in GoLive? Most people who use the two programs together would prefer to use the method you learned about here.

8. Leave this document open for the next exercise.

4. [PS/IR]_____Edit Original

Edit Original is a GoLive feature that allows you to edit the PSD from which a smart object is based. You can make a change to the PSD, and the change will ripple all the way through to GoLive and all the final slices and Web images. You'll get to try out this feature in this exercise by making a color change.

1. Ctrl+click (Mac) or **right-click** (Windows) on the smart object. In the contextual menu that appears, choose **Source Link > Edit Original**.

2. Select the **bgphoto** layer. Click and hold the **filter effect** button to select **Color Overlay** from the drop-down menu. For a moment, the **bgphoto** layer will look unrecognizable. You'll change the settings next.

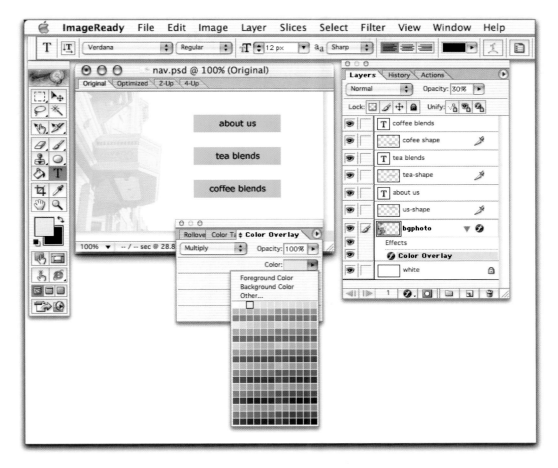

3. In the **Color Overlay** palette, change the mode to **Multiply** and select a light yellow from the **Color** menu. Now the **bgphoto** layer will look better. Choose **File > Save**.

4. Return to GoLive. It might take a few minutes, but eventually the changes will appear! What was taking so long? GoLive was generating all the graphics for the Web images, plus updating the HTML, and changing the preview on the screen. Not bad for a few minutes work, huh?

Option+click or Alt+click on the Refresh button in the browser if the changes don't show up right away. This clears the cache and shows the most current content.

5. Test the results in the browser. If you need to, you might have to **Option+click** (Mac) or **Alt+click** (Windows) on the **Refresh** button in the browser.

6. Leave this document open for the next exercise.

5. [IR] _____Working with an ImageReady Data Set in GoLive

This next exercise shows how to put an ImageReady-generated data set to work in GoLive 6. Although you have worked with data sets within ImageReady, they become much more powerful in GoLive. In this example, variables have been established for text layers for the rollover file. This enables you to change the button names within GoLive and generate rollovers with brand new labels without touching ImageReady. Hold on to your hats—this is a really amazing feature!

Before starting on this exercise, you might wonder how the file was prepared first in ImageReady. We made three text layers and defined them as variables—button_one, button_two, and button_three. The text layers are set up for text replacement variables—you learned about these in Chapter 15, "*Data Sets*."

1. In GoLive, inside **index.html**, select the navigation content, including all the comments. Press **Delete** to remove them. This will leave a blinking insertion cursor inside the empty table cell. You're removing the content so that you can import new content that contains a data set and variables.

If you have trouble selecting all of the content within the table cell, simply click on any image in the navigation content, and then at the bottom of the index.html *page window, click on the* **<td>** *tag. This will select all of the content in that table cell and then you can just press* Delete. *Easy!*

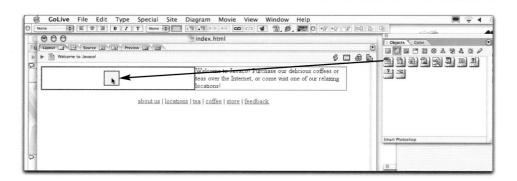

2. In the **Objects** palette, select the **Photoshop Smart Objects** icon and drag it into the empty table cell.

3. Make sure the smart object is selected, and open the **Inspector** palette. Click the folder icon for the source, and browse to the **chap_16** folder. Locate **dataset.psd** and click **Open**.

4. The **Variable Settings** dialog box opens. Check **button_one**, **button_three**, and **button_two**. These were not present in the last document because they hadn't been first set up in ImageReady. Click **OK**.

5. The **Save For Web** dialog box opens, only this time the button slices look empty. When you set the text up to be variables, it allows you to type the content in GoLive. The power of this is that you can put different text on different pages of your site, and use the ImageReady slices over and over. Click **Save**.

6. Once again, as you did in the last exercise, click the **Site Folder** button to access the menu and choose **Root folder**. Click **Save**.

7. The image appears inside the **index.html** document, only there's no text. You'll remedy that soon.

8. With the smart object selected, a **Variables** button will appear inside the **Inspector** palette. Click that button, and the **Variables Settings** dialog box will open. Select **button_one** and type the word **locations**. Click **OK**.

9. Preview the document in a browser by pressing **Cmd+T** (Mac) or **Ctrl+T** (Windows). All the rollovers work, and the text is bitmap text, not HTML! GoLive controlled the ImageReady text layer.

The power of this workflow is really amazing. You could take the same PSD file and use it as a smart object on multiple pages, changing the navigation buttons on every page. You could make a header graphic and change its name on every page—animated GIF files that change! The possibilities are unlimited. So cool, huh?

10. Quit GoLive and save the changes. You'll be moving on to other programs now.

6. [IR] _____ImageReady Rollovers in Dreamweaver MX

This next exercise shows how to put an ImageReady-generated rollover into **Dreamweaver MX**. These instructions also work for **Dreamweaver 3** and **4**. If all you want to do is use an ImageReady HTML file in its original form, you just need to open the file in Dreamweaver, and it will work just fine. This exercise shows you how to do something a little harder, which is to get the ImageReady rollover to work inside an existing HTML page that Dreamweaver generated.

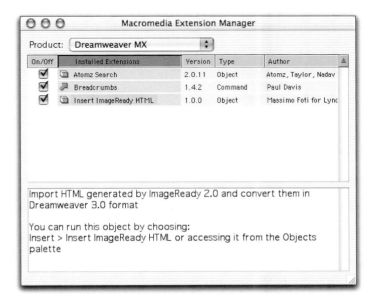

This shows how the extension will look once it's installed. Note that we had other extensions installed as well. The Macromedia Extension Manager works with single or multiple extensions.

1. Look in the software folder of the **H•O•T CD-ROM**, and double-click on the **ImageReady HTML.mxp** file. This is a Macromedia Extension Manager document written by Massimo Foti for Lynda.com. If you have Dreamweaver MX installed, it will launch the Extension Manager application and will prompt you through a series of screens to allow you to install the file.

NOTE | What Is the ImageReady HTML.mxp File?

A few years ago, Lynda.com commissioned a well-known Dreamweaver extension developer, Massimo Foti, to create an extension to Dreamweaver that would convert ImageReady rollover code into a native Dreamweaver behavior. Since Adobe wouldn't be likely to create a product for Dreamweaver users, and Macromedia wouldn't be likely to create a product for Photoshop users, we saw this as an opportunity to support our customers who might be combining these two products. We offer it for free to any visitor to the Lynda.com site. It is located at **http://www.lynda.com/files/** along with other free files we offer.

Site Definition for Unnamed Site 1

Basic | Advanced

Site Definition

Editing Files   Testing Files   Sharing Files

A site, in Dreamweaver, is a collection of files and folders that corresponds to a website on a server.

What would you like to name your site?

dreamweaver

Example: MySite

Help   < Back   Next >   Cancel

---

2. Once the extension is successfully installed, launch Macromedia Dreamweaver MX. Choose **Site > New Site** and the **Site Definition for dreamweaver** window will open. Type **DreamweaverSite** as the name and click **Next**.

---

3. A new screen will appear. Check the **No, I do not want to use a Server technology** radio button. This means that you won't be integrating this file with a server technology, such as ASP or ColdFusion. If you know how to use scripts and servers, enter another choice. This book does not attempt to go deeply into Dreamweaver. Click **Next**.

4. A new screen will appear. Check the **Edit local copies on my machine, then upload to server when ready (recommended)** radio button—this means that you will be working with files on your hard drive, not on a server. Click on the blue folder icon, browse to the **chap_16** folder, and select the **DreamweaverSite** folder. Click **Choose**. A path will appear inside the field next to the blue folder that shows Dreamweaver where the files are that you will be working with. Click **Next**.

5. A new screen will appear. Select **None** from the menu below **How do you want to connect to a remote server?** This book does not go into coaching you through uploading your final files to a server. Click **Next**.

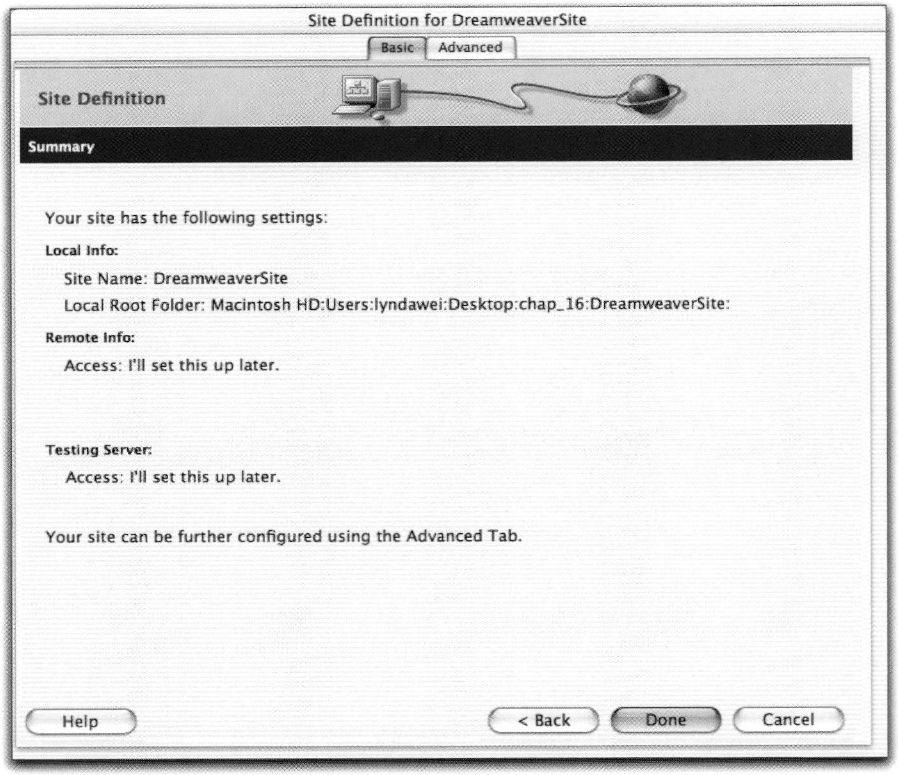

Site Definition for DreamweaverSite

Basic | Advanced

Site Definition

Summary

Your site has the following settings:

Local Info:

Site Name: DreamweaverSite

Local Root Folder: Macintosh HD:Users:lyndawei:Desktop:chap_16:DreamweaverSite:

Remote Info:

Access: I'll set this up later.

Testing Server:

Access: I'll set this up later.

Your site can be further configured using the Advanced Tab.

Help   < Back   Done   Cancel

---

6. A **Summary** screen will appear and should look like the one above. Click **Done**.

7. Dreamweaver MX will open and the **Site** window will appear. Double-click on the **index.html** file.

This was made ahead of time for you to simulate the workflow of putting an ImageReady rollover into an existing HTML page.

8. Next, you'll create a new empty file. Choose **File > New**. The **New Document** dialog box will open. Make sure **Basic Page: HTML** is selected and click **Create**. This creates a new, untitled document.

9. Choose **File > Save As** and change the name to **imageready.html**. Make sure you are in the **DreamweaverSite** folder and click **Save**. This simply saves the new, empty HTML page. It's very important to save this file before you use the **Insert ImageReady** command. Dreamweaver does not like to work with unsaved documents.

10. Make sure the **Common** tab is selected in the upper Toolbar, and click on the **Insert ImageReady** command that you installed earlier in this exercise. The **ImageReady HTML** dialog box will appear. Click the **Browse** button and navigate to the **chap_16 folder > navigation1 > nav.html**. Click **Choose**.

This last step allowed you to choose the rollover images and HTML that you created in Exercise 1 of this chapter. This rollover was saved before you changed the options to save GoLive code in Exercise 2. You do not want to set ImageReady to write GoLive code if you plan to use the rollovers in Dreamweaver.

11. In the **ImageReady HTML** dialog box, click **Insert**. You will be warned that the process might take a few minutes.

12. The familiar navigation graphic will appear! Select everything on the screen and choose **File > Copy** or use the shortcut keys to copy this information. Be sure to select the comment tags before you copy this data!

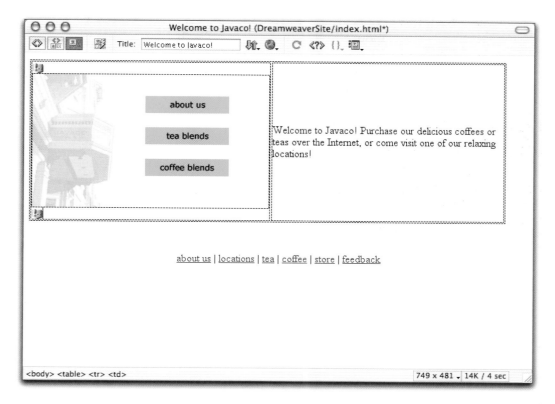

13. Make the **index.html** page active by choosing **Window > index.html**. Click inside the empty table to the left and choose **Edit > Paste**. Voila! The nav bar will appear! Press **F12** to look at this in a browser. Everything will operate as you would expect.

When ImageReady wrote the file navbar.html, *it contained references to all the images that appear in the rollover. If you move the HTML file away from those images, the links to them will break. Fortunately, the* Insert ImageReady *command not only allowed you to browse to find the files, but it also copied and moved them into the DreamweaverSite directory. That's why it's important that you define the Site settings before you begin this type of operation.*

14. Quit Dreamweaver, and save when prompted.

MOVIE | dreamweaver_rollovers.mov

To learn more about putting your ImageReady-created rollovers into Dreamweaver, check out **dreamweaver_rollovers.mov** from the **movies** folder on the **H•O•T CD-ROM**.

NOTE | Learning Dreamweaver MX Resources

These are some resources we recommend for more information on learning about site management in Dreamweaver:

Learning Dreamweaver MX (CD-ROM)
By Garo Green
http://www.lynda.com/products/books/dwmxhot

Dreamweaver MX Hands-On Training (H•O•T)
By Garo Green and Abigail Rudner, developed with Lynda Weinman
lynda.com/books and Peachpit Press
ISBN: 0321112717
$44.99

7. [PS/IR] _____Exporting Illustrator 10 Files

The best way to prepare documents in Illustrator for ImageReady or Photoshop is to first work in layers in Illustrator. This example uses an Adobe Illustrator file (**final_javaco_logo.ai**) that contains named layers. This exercise works in **Illustrator 8, 9**, and **10**.

1. Launch **Illustrator 10**, and choose **File > Open**. Navigate to the **chap_16** folder to select **final_javaco_logo.ai**. Notice that this file contains four layers. The object of this exercise is to export a file that contains the same four layers so that it can be further edited in Photoshop.

2. From Illustrator, choose **File > Export**. In the **Export** window, from the **Format** (Mac) or **Save as type** (Windows) pop-up menu, choose **PSD**. Navigate to the **chap_16** folder on your desktop and click **Export** (Mac) or **Save** (Windows).

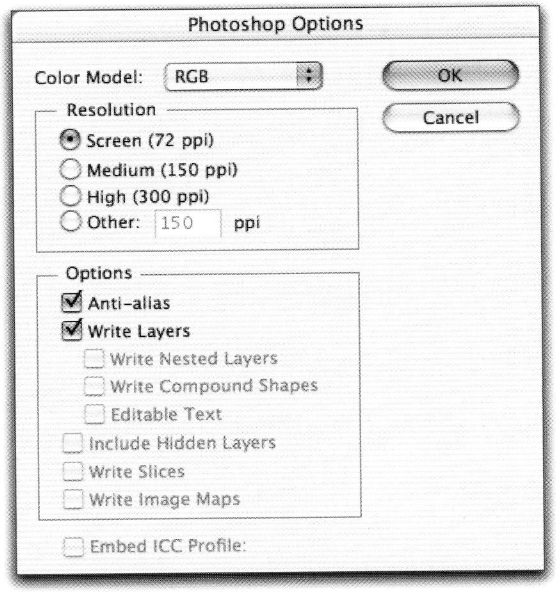

```
                    Photoshop Options

  Color Model:   [ RGB        ◆ ]    (    OK    )

  ┌─ Resolution ──────────────┐    (  Cancel  )
  │  ⦿ Screen (72 ppi)        │
  │  ○ Medium (150 ppi)       │
  │  ○ High (300 ppi)         │
  │  ○ Other: [150]  ppi      │
  └───────────────────────────┘

  ┌─ Options ──────────────────┐
  │  ☑ Anti-alias              │
  │  ☑ Write Layers            │
  │      ☐ Write Nested Layers │
  │      ☐ Write Compound Shapes│
  │      ☐ Editable Text       │
  │  ☐ Include Hidden Layers   │
  │  ☐ Write Slices            │
  │  ☐ Write Image Maps        │
  └────────────────────────────┘

  ☐ Embed ICC Profile:
```

3. In the **Photoshop Options** dialog box that appears, match your settings to those shown above and click **OK**.

It's very important that RGB and 72 dpi are chosen, since this is the only color mode and resolution that works for the Web.

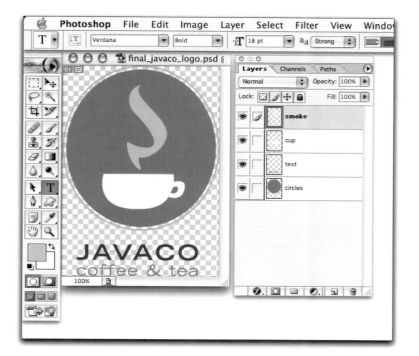

4. Launch Photoshop or ImageReady. Choose **File > Open** in that program, and navigate to the Photoshop document that you saved into the **chap_16** folder from Illustrator (**final_javaco_logo.psd**). It will open with all the layers named exactly as they were in Illustrator.

The advantage to this technique is that the Illustrator file is brought into Photoshop or ImageReady with layers that were prenamed and separated correctly. Now you're ready to create rollovers or animated GIF files from this layered document.

NOTE | Save For Web in Illustrator

Just like Photoshop, Illustrator 10 has a Save For Web feature. This allows you to save GIF, JPEG, PNG, and even Macromedia Flash files from Illustrator. Because you already know the Save For Web interface in Photoshop, you will be quite comfortable with the Save For Web feature in Illustrator. If you plan to bring Illustrator files into Photoshop or ImageReady, it's best to output to the PSD file format so you have the most flexibility. It's important to note that you can save Web files directly from Illustrator if you want to though!

8. [IR] _____ Exporting ImageReady to QuickTime

In addition to writing animated GIF files, ImageReady will also export animation files to QuickTime. You might want to do this if you are working on a multimedia project instead of an HTML project.

1. In ImageReady, open **photos_anim.psd** from the **chap_16** folder on your desktop.

2. Choose **File > Export Original**, the **Export Original** dialog box will open. Choose **QuickTime Movie** in the **Format** (Mac) or **Save as type** field (Windows). The .mov extension will automatically be added to the end of the filename. Navigate to the **chap_16** folder and click **Save**.

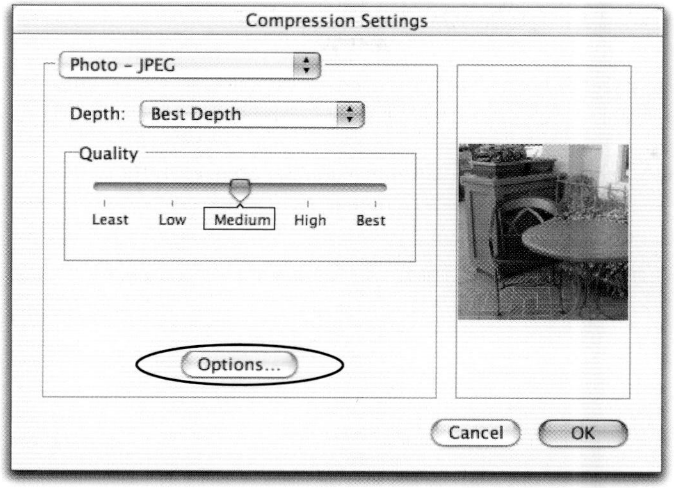

3. The **Compression Settings** dialog box will appear at its **Photo – JPEG** default. This is a good format if your animation includes continuous-tone imagery. The image you're working with is certainly a continuous-tone photograph, so leave the compression setting set to **Photo – JPEG**. Click on the **Options** button.

4. Check **Optimize for streaming** if you plan to publish this QuickTime movie to the Web. Click **OK**.

5. In the **Compression Settings** dialog box, click **OK**, and the file will be saved. To see it, go to the **chap_16** folder where you saved it, double-click on the file **photos_anim.mov**, and it should open up in the **QuickTime Player** that ships with QuickTime.

6. Close **photos_anim.mov** and **photos_anim.psd**.

9. [IR] Converting from QuickTime to ImageReady

You can also convert from QuickTime to an animated GIF in ImageReady. You might want to do this if someone gives you a QuickTime movie that was created for some other purpose (such as one that contained live action and was shot with a movie camera), but that you'd prefer to convert to an animated GIF.

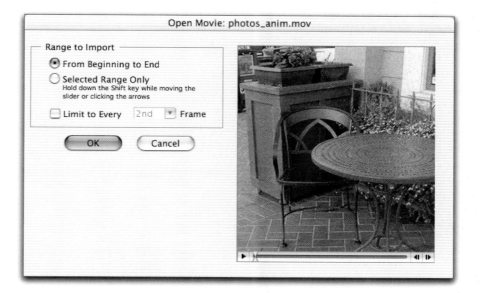

1. In ImageReady, choose **File > Open**. Locate the **photos_anim.mov** file that you just created and click **Open**. The **Open Movie** dialog box will appear.

You can choose to import the entire movie, a select range of frames, or you can skip frames to specified increments, such as every five frames or whichever setting is appropriate.

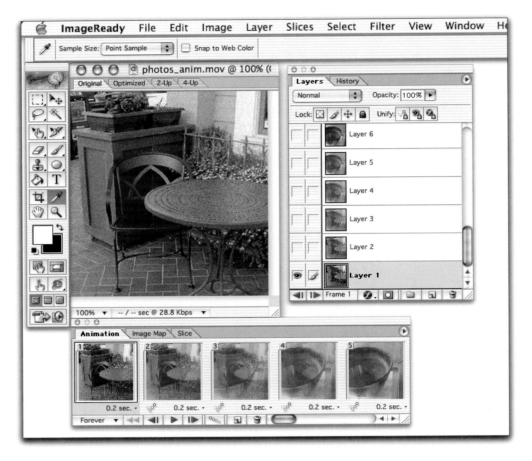

2. Click **OK** inside the **Open Movie** dialog box. These default settings will work perfectly for this example.

The file will be converted to layers, and the frames will automatically appear inside the Animation palette. It will take whatever timing was set as the frame rate from the QuickTime movie.

3. To save this as an animated GIF, make sure the optimization settings are in the **GIF** format and choose **File > Save Optimized As**. It's that easy, really!

4. Close **photos_anim.mov**. Quit ImageReady, there will be no more exercises there in this chapter. You now know how to convert a movie to a layered ImageReady document, or an animated GIF! Pretty cool—and simple, too! :-).

10. [PS]_____Converting PSD to a PDF

One of the coolest new features in Photoshop 7 is the capability to easily save a PDF from a Photoshop document. PDF (**P**ortable **D**ocument **F**ormat) is used to exchange documents when the formatting of the document is critical, but the end party might not have the application the document was created with (in this case, Photoshop or ImageReady). Sure, you could send a GIF or a JPEG and they wouldn't need Photoshop either, but PDF has a few other neat features, like the capability to set password protection, and leave all the text accessible to someone who has visual impairments! We're enthused about this new feature for these reasons, and it's great to end the book and this chapter on this wonderful new feature.

1. Open Photoshop, if it isn't already open. From Photoshop, open **coupon.psd** from the **chap_16** folder. This document contains a text layer and a graphic layer.

2. Choose **File > Save As**. For **Format**, choose **Photoshop PDF** from the drop-down menu. In the bottom **Save** settings, check **Layers**. Click **Save**.

A chart that describes the other PDF Save settings is at the end of this exercise.

3. The **PDF Options** dialog box will open. Check **JPEG**, **PDF Security**, and **Include Vector Data**. Click the **Security Settings** button.

A chart describing the PDF Options is at the end of this exercise.

PDF Security

Password Required to Open Document

User Password: **** ← Type **user** here

Password Required to Change Permission and Passwords

Master Password: ****** ← Type **master** here

Encryption Level: 40–bit RC4 (Acrobat 3.x, 4.x)

☑ No Printing
☑ No Changing the Document
☑ No Content Copying or Extraction, Disable Accessibility
☐ No Adding or Changing Comments and Form Fields

⚠ If set, the Master Password is required each time the file is opened in Photoshop. Other security restrictions (such as printing) are applied to the file only when it is opened in Adobe® Acrobat®.

OK

Cancel

4. The **PDF Security** dialog box will open. Check the same settings that you see here. In the **User Password** field, type **user**. In the **Master Password** field, type **master**. Click **OK**.

A chart describing the other PDF Security options is at the end of this exercise. The User Password is what someone else will type in to view this document in Acrobat Reader. The Master Password is so that you can override the User Password in the event that you want to change the security for this document. We have picked the passwords user *and* master *as simple examples. You might want to create more original passwords when you work with this feature in the future!*

Confirm Password

Confirm Password: ****

⚠ Please confirm the user password.

OK

Cancel

5. The **Confirm Password** dialog box will appear. This is for the user password, so retype **user**. Click **OK**.

6. The **Confirm Password** dialog box will appear again. This second one is for the master password, so retype **master**. Click **OK** in the **PDF Security** window, and then click **OK** once more on the **PDF Options** window. This is the final step, and Photoshop will now write the PDF.

7. Look at the **chap_16** folder on your hard drive to locate the resulting file (**coupon.pdf**).

8. If you double-click on this file and own Photoshop, it will open in Photoshop. All the layers will be intact, and it will function as a normal PSD file, even though it is stored in the PDF format.

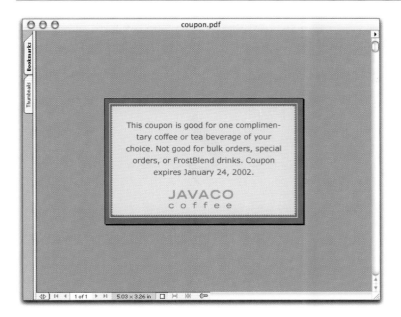

9. In order to see how this would look in Acrobat Reader, you have to first open that program. From Acrobat Reader, choose **File > Open**. Navigate to the **chap_16** folder, and locate **coupon.pdf** to open it. A **Password** warning dialog box will open. Type **user** in the **Password** field and click **OK**.

10. The file opens! You won't be able to print, because you disabled that feature in the Security Settings. For more detailed information on the security settings, read the upcoming charts.

PDF Save Settings	
Category	**Description**
Save:	
As a Copy	Saves a flattened copy of the PSD document
Alpha Channels	Includes alpha channels in the PDF document
Annotations	Includes annotations in the PDF document
Spot Colors	Includes spot colors in the PDF document
Layers	Includes Photoshop layers in the PDF document
Color:	
Use Proof Setup: Working CMYK	Retains CMYK settings
Embed Color Profile	Embeds a color profile in the PDF document

PDF Options	
Category	**Description**
ZIP	Compression method that is good for images with large areas of solid colors.
JPEG	Good for photographic or continuous tone content.
Quality	Applies to the JPEG format only.
Save Transparency	Includes transparent layer information.
Image Interpolation	Anti-aliases the printed appearance of a low-resolution image.
Downgrade Color Profile	If Embed Color Profile was chosen, this will enable programs that don't support profiles to view the image.
PDF Security	See the following chart, called "PDF Security."
Include Vector Data	Preserves any vector graphics as resolution-independent objects.
Embed Fonts	Ensures that all fonts in the file will display and print properly. Increases the PDF file size.
Use Outlines for Text	Saves text as paths. Use when embedded fonts don't display properly.

PDF Security	
Category	**Description**
Password Required to Open Document	This is what the end-user would type to see the file in Acrobat Reader.
Password Required to Change Permissions and Passwords	This is what you would type in order to change the user password or other security settings.
Encryption Level	Choose 40-bit or 128-bit encryption for a low or high level of security (relates to password protection).
No Printing	Prevents users from printing the PDF. The document can only be viewed onscreen.
No Changing the Document	Disables the Editing tools. Prevents the user from adding form fields, links, bookmarks, articles, and movies. Also prevents the user from changing text with the TouchUp Text tool or moving objects with the TouchUp Object tool. Comments can still be added to the PDF.
No Content Copying	Disables **Edit > Copy**, preventing users from copying text or images from the document. Disables **File > Export > Extract Images As**, preventing users from extracting images from the PDF. Also disables the Accessibility interface.
No Adding or Changing Comments and Form Fields	Prevents users from using the Comment tools and the Form tool. Users will not be able to fill in existing form fields.

That's all there is to saving a PDF from Photoshop! It's a great new feature, and makes it much easier to communicate with clients, copy editors, team members, etc.

You're finished with the last chapter, and now it's time to go out into the world on your own and make great Web art and movies. Rock on!

17.

Troubleshooting FAQ

| H•O•T |

| Hands-On Training |

Photoshop 7/ImageReady

For the Web

If you've run into any problems while following the exercises in this book, this Troubleshooting FAQ (Frequently Asked Questions) should help. This document will be maintained and expanded upon at this book's companion Web site: **http://www.lynda.com/ books/ps7irhot**.

If you don't find what you're looking for here or in the companion Web site, please send an email to **ps7irhot@lynda.com**.

If you have a question related to Photoshop 7 or ImageReady that is not related to a specific exercise in this book, visit the Adobe site (**http://www.adobe.com**) or call their tech support hotline at: 206-675-6203 (Mac) or 206-675-6303 (Windows).

Q: I'm on a Windows system, and all the files on the **H•O•T CD-ROM** are locked, even though I transferred them to my hard drive. What should I do?

A: Unfortunately, some versions of the Windows operating system treat files copied from a CD-ROM to be "read only" files. That means that you can't make changes to any of the files you've transferred to your Windows hard drive from the CD-ROM until you unlock them. Read the Intro chapter to find specific information to your operating system for a solution to this problem.

Q: I'm on a Mac using OS 9 or below, and I get weird refresh problems with my desktop flashing and everything running really slow. Do you have any ideas why this always happens to me?

A: You are probably running low on RAM. Close one or more applications, and it should improve. You might have to quit ImageReady, Photoshop, or the browser during exercises so that you keep only one program open at a time. Consider getting more RAM if you plan to do this sort of work often.

Q: My Optimize palette in ImageReady doesn't show all of the options that yours does. For example, I can't see the Transparency check box or the Matte setting. What's wrong?

A: There's nothing really wrong. All you need to do is click the small double-pointed arrow on the **Optimize** palette tab to cycle through a few expansions of that palette.

Q: What if I use color profiles in my print work? It's kind of disconcerting to turn them off, as you suggested in Chapter 2, "*Interface.*"

A: You can always program an **action** that will turn them off and/or back on. You learned how to make actions in Chapter 14, "*Automation,*" but here's a brief refresher. Simply start recording an action before you turn profiles on or off, and the action will remember your steps. Once you've finished recording, click the **Stop** button. Bingo, you have an action for that task!

Q: What should I do about CMYK images that I created for print? Can I use them on the Web?

A: You won't be able to use CMYK images on the Web. You'll have to convert those images to RGB first. Do this in Photoshop by choosing **Image > Mode > RGB Color.** There might be some color shifting during this process because CMYK and RGB are two different color spaces that cannot achieve an exact translation.

Q: In Chapter 4, "*Optimization*," you suggest that I leave the Save For Web dialog box open for many exercises in a row. What happens if I have to quit and come back to the exercise another time?

A: You're in luck. The **Save For Web** dialog box will remember the last settings you used, even if you quit Photoshop. So you can quit, and you won't have to redo the exercises again from scratch.

Q: What should I do when I'm in the Save For Web dialog box and see an orange warning triangle?

A: Click the menu arrow to the right of **Settings** in the **Save For Web** dialog box and choose **Repopulate Views.** This should cause all the views to refresh and the warning icon to disappear.

Q: My Layers palette doesn't look like yours! What's up with that?

A: To access any palette in its entirety, not just the Layers palette, just drag its bottom-right corner.

Q: Anytime I go to any file in ImageReady and click the Optimized tab, instead of seeing the image in the background, I get a checkerboard pattern.

A: If you're having trouble seeing an image in the **Optimized** tab, click on the menu arrow in the top-right corner of the **Optimize** palette and make sure that **Auto Regenerate** is checked in the pull-down menu. Remember, that checkerboard pattern indicates that this is a transparent GIF.

Q: Sometimes I don't see any color chips in the Color Table in ImageReady when I'm optimizing a GIF. Why not?

A: You may have to give the program a jump start by clicking the **yellow triangle** at the lower left of the **Color Table** palette. This will regenerate the Color Table.

Q: Please remind me what each of the optimization tabs in the ImageReady Document window means.

A: Glad to. The first is **Original** and that's self-explanatory. It's the original, non-optimized image. **Optimized** is self-explanatory, too. It shows you the optimized version of an image. We prefer to do all our work in Original, because Optimized constantly updates the image, which can really slow things down. The last two, **2-Up** and **4-Up**, offer two and four versions of the image, respectively. They're useful for comparing an image at different optimization settings.

Q: Every time I save a file I get this annoying box asking me where I want to update it.

A: We know what you mean when you say it's annoying. There's a simple way to fix this, and it involves changing your Preferences. In both applications, choose **Edit > Preferences > General.** In Photoshop, put a check next to **Auto-update open documents**; in ImageReady, put a check next to **Auto-Update Files**. Click **OK**, and you'll never have to see that pesky box again.

Q: When I type, the type shows up behind the button, not over it. Why does this happen?

A: The stacking order of layers in the **Layers** palette is from bottom to top. If your type is under another layer, it might be hidden. Drag the **type** layer above all the others and you will see it. Another problem is that you might be typing in the same color as your button. Hey, it happens even to the pros—we swear it does!

Q: I keep going to the Photoshop Toolbox to get to the Magic Eraser, but it's nowhere to be found, though I do see the Eraser. How do I access it?

A: See the tiny triangle at the bottom right of the **Eraser** tool icon? Click there, leave your mouse depressed, and you'll see the other Eraser options, including the **Magic Eraser.** You can drag out to select any of the erasers in this fly-out menu. All the tools that have the same tiny arrow have more than one tool option, just like this one.

Q: Not to complain, but I get sick of zooming in and out of my files. Is there a quick way to get a big view?

A: If you double-click on the **Hand** tool inside the Toolbox, the image will expand to fill your screen. If you double-click on the **Zoom** tool in the Toolbox, it will change to **100%.** The trick is to double-click right in the Toolbox, not on your image.

Q: I am working away on an image in ImageReady, and it's taking forever for the program to accept my edits. I am slowly going crazy.

A: Our guess is you're working in the **Optimized** tab, which tells ImageReady to constantly optimize your graphic while you're editing it. Switch over to the **Original** tab. It will go faster—we promise.

Q: Is there a quick one-step way to hide all those palettes that are cluttering up my desktop?

A: Press the **Tab** key to toggle on and off all the palettes in either Photoshop or ImageReady. It's a beautiful thing!

Q: I keep trying to select a slice but for some reason I can't. Help!

A: Are you using the **Slice Select** tool? It's in a fly-out menu under the **Slice** tool in the ImageReady and Photoshop Toolboxes. Use the **Slice** tool to cut up an image into slices and then use the **Slice Select** tool to adjust those slices. The Slice Select tool lets you drag, reposition, delete, and select a single slice or more at one time. To select multiple slices, hold down the **Shift** key. The shortcut key for the Slice Select and Slice tools is the letter **K** on your keyboard.

Q: I want to create a rollover, but nothing is showing up in the Rollover palette. What am I doing wrong?

A: You must first select a slice (with the **Slice Select** tool) before the Rollover palette is operational. That's because you define rollovers according to a trigger slice. If you don't have a slice defined, ImageReady has no way of knowing which slice is going to trigger the rollover.

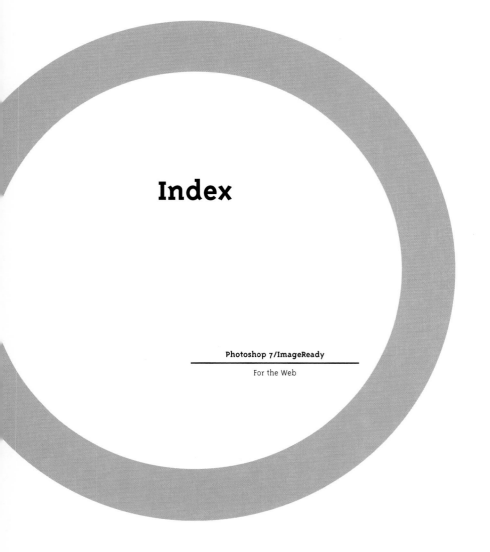

Index

Photoshop 7/ImageReady

For the Web

S

...NS:

... consideration of payment of the License Fee, which was a part of ti... ...s product, LICENSOR grants to you (the "Licensee") a non-exclusive righ... ...play this copy of a Software program, along with any updates or upgrade re... ...e Software for which you have paid (all parts and elements of the Software as we... ...the Software as a whole are hereinafter referred to as the "Software") on a single computer only (i.e., with a single CPU) at a single location, all as more particularly set forth and limited below. LICENSOR reserves all rights not expressly granted to you as Licensee in this License Agreement.

2. OWNERSHIP OF SOFTWARE. The license granted herein is not a sale of the original Software or of any copy of the Software. As Licensee, you own only the rights to use the Software as described herein and the magnetic or other physical media on which the Software is originally or subsequently recorded or fixed. LICENSOR retains title and ownership of the Software recorded on the original disk(s), as well as title and ownership of any subsequent copies of the Software irrespective of the form of media on or in which the Software is recorded or fixed. This license does not grant you any intellectual or other proprietary or other rights of any nature what-soever in the Software.

3. USE RESTRICTIONS. As Licensee, you may use the Software only as expressly authorized in this License Agreement under the terms of paragraph 4. You may phy-sically transfer the Software from one computer to another provided that the Software is used on only a single computer at any one time. You may not: (i) electronically transfer the Software from one computer to another over a network; (ii) make the Software available through a time-sharing service, network of computers, or other multiple user arrangement; (iii) distribute copies of the Software or related written materials to any third party, whether for sale or otherwise; (iv) modify, adapt, translate, reverse engineer, decompile, disassemble, or prepare any derivative work based on the Software or any element thereof; (v) make or distribute, whether for sale or otherwise, any hard copy or printed version of any of the Software nor any portion thereof nor any work of yours containing the Software or any component thereof; (vi) use any of the Software nor any of its components in any other work.

8. THIS IS WHAT YOU CAN AND CANNOT DO WITH THE SOFTWARE. Even though in the preceding paragraph and elsewhere LICENSOR has restricted your use of the Software, the following is the only thing you can do with the Software and the various elements of the Software:DUCKS IN A ROW ARTWORK: THE ARTWORK CONTAINED ON THIS CD-ROM MAY NOT BE USED IN ANY MANNER WHATSOEVER OTHER THAN TO VIEW THE SAME ON YOUR COMPUTER, OR POST TO YOUR PERSONAL, NON-COMMERCIAL WEB SITE FOR EDUCATIONAL PURPOSES ONLY. THIS MATERIAL IS SUBJECT TO ALL OF THE RESTRICTION PROVISIONS OF THIS SOFTWARE LICENSE. SPECIFICALLY BUT NOT IN LIMITATION OF THESE RESTRICTIONS, YOU MAY NOT DISTRIBUTE, RESELL OR TRANSFER THIS PART OF THE SOFTWARE DESIGNATED AS "CLUTS" NOR ANY OF YOUR DESIGN OR OTHER WORK CONTAINING ANY OF THE SOFTWARE DESIGNATED AS "DUCKS IN A ROW ARTWORK" NOR ANY OF YOUR DESIGN OR OTHER WORK CONTAINING ANY SUCH "DUCKS IN A ROW ARTWORK," ALL AS MORE PARTICULARLY RESTRICTED IN THE WITHIN SOFTWARE LICENSE.

5. COPY RESTRICTIONS. The Software and accompanying written materials are protected under United States copyright laws. Unauthorized copying and/or distribution of the Software and/or the related written materials is expressly forbidden. You may be held legally responsible for any copyright infringement that is caused, directly or indirectly, by your failure to abide by the terms of this License Agreement. Subject to the terms of this License Agreement and if the software is not otherwise copy protected, you may make one copy of the Software for backup purposes only. The copyright notice and any other proprietary notices which were included in the original Software must be reproduced and included on any such backup copy.

6. TRANSFER RESTRICTIONS. The license herein granted is personal to you, the Licensee. You may not transfer the Software nor any of its components or elements to anyone else, nor may you sell, lease, loan, sublicense, assign, or otherwise dispose of the Software nor any of its components or elements without the express written consent of LICENSOR, which consent may be granted or withheld at LICENSOR's sole discretion.

7. TERMINATION. The license herein granted hereby will remain in effect until terminated. This license will terminate automatically without further notice from LICENSOR in the event of the violation of any of the provisions hereof. As Licensee, you agree that upon such termination you will promptly destroy any and all copies of the Software which remain in your possession and, upon request, will certify to such destruction in writing to LICENSOR.

8. LIMITATION AND DISCLAIMER OF WARRANTIES. a) THE SOFTWARE AND RELATED WRITTEN MATERIALS, INCLUDING ANY INSTRUCTIONS FOR USE, ARE PROVIDED ON AN "AS IS" BASIS, WITHOUT WARRANTY OF ANY KIND, EXPRESS OR IMPLIED. THIS DISCLAIMER OF WARRANTY EXPRESSLY IN-CLUDES, BUT IS NOT LIMITED TO, ANY IMPLIED WARRANTIES OF MERCHANTABILITY AND/OR OF FITNESS FOR A PARTICULAR PURPOSE. NO WARRANTY OF ANY KIND IS MADE AS TO WHETHER OR NOT THIS SOFT-WARE INFRINGES UPON ANY RIGHTS OF ANY OTHER THIRD PARTIES. NO ORAL OR WRITTEN INFORMATION GIVEN BY LICEN-SOR, ITS SUPPLIERS, DISTRIBUTORS, DEALERS, EMPLOYEES, OR AGENTS, SHALL CREATE OR OTHERWISE ENLARGE THE SCOPE OF ANY WARRANTY HEREUNDER. LICENSEE ASSUMES THE ENTIRE RISK AS TO THE QUALITY AND THE PERFOR-

MANCE OF SUCH SOFTWARE. SHOULD THE SOFTWARE PROVE DEFECTIVE, YOU, AS LICENSEE (AND NOT LICENSOR, ITS SUPPLIERS, DISTRIBU-TORS, DEALERS OR AGENTS), ASSUME THE ENTIRE COST OF ALL NECESSARY CORRECTION, SERVIC-ING, OR REPAIR. b) LICENSOR warrants the disk(s) on which this copy of the Software is recorded or fixed to be free from defects in materials and workmanship, under normal use and service, for a period of ninety (90) days from the date of delivery as evidenced by a copy of the applicable receipt. LICENSOR hereby limits the duration of any implied warranties with respect to the disk(s) to the duration of the express warranty. This limited warranty shall not apply if the disk(s) have been damaged by unreasonable use, accident, negligence, or by any other causes unrelated to defective materials or workmanship. c) LICENSOR does not warrant that the functions contained in the Software will be uninterrupted or error free and Licensee is encouraged to test the Software for Licensee's intended use prior to placing any reliance thereon. All risk of the use of the Software will be on you, as Licensee. d) THE LIMITED WARRANTY SET FORTH ABOVE GIVES YOU SPECIFIC LEGAL RIGHTS AND YOU MAY ALSO HAVE OTHER RIGHTS WHICH VARY FROM STATE TO STATE. SOME STATES DO NOT ALLOW THE LIMITATION OR EXCLUSION OF IMPLIED WARRANTIES OR OF INCIDENTAL OR CONSEQUENTIAL DAMAGES, SO THE LIMITATIONS AND EXCLUSIONS CONCERNING THE SOFTWARE AND RELATED WRITTEN MATERIALS SET FORTH ABOVE MAY NOT APPLY TO YOU.

9. LIMITATION OF REMEDIES. LICENSOR's entire liability and Licensee's exclusive remedy shall be the replacement of any disk(s) not meeting the limited warranty set forth in Section 8 above which is returned to LICENSOR with a copy of the applic-able receipt within the warranty period. Any replacement disk(s)will be warranted for the remainder of the original warranty period or thirty (30) days, whichever is longer.

10. LIMITATION OF LIABILITY. IN NO EVENT WILL LICENSOR, OR ANYONE ELSE INVOLVED IN THE CREATION, PRODUCTION, AND/OR DELIVERY OF THIS SOFTWARE PRODUCT BE LIABLE TO LICENSEE OR ANY OTHER PER-SON OR ENTITY FOR ANY DIRECT, INDIRECT, OR OTHER DAMAGES, INCLUDING, WITHOUT LIMITATION, ANY INTERRUPTION OF SERVICES, LOST PROFITS, LOST SAVINGS, LOSS OF DATA, OR ANY OTHER CONSEQUENTIAL, INCIDEN-TAL, SPECIAL, OR PUNITIVE DAMAGES, ARISING OUT OF THE PURCHASE, USE, INABILITY TO USE, OR OPERATION OF THE SOFTWARE, EVEN IF LICENSOR OR ANY AUTHORIZED LICENSOR DEALER HAS BEEN ADVISED OF THE POSSIBILITY OF SUCH DAMAGES. BY YOUR USE OF THE SOFTWARE, YOU ACKNOWLEDGE THAT THE LIMITATION OF LIABILITY SET FORTH IN THIS LICENSE WAS THE BASIS UPON WHICH THE SOFTWARE WAS OFFERED BY LICENSOR AND YOU ACKNOWLEDGE THAT THE PRICE OF THE SOFTWARE LICENSE WOULD BE HIGHER IN THE ABSENCE OF SUCH LIMITATION. SOME STATES DO NOT ALLOW THE LIMITATION OR EXCLUSION OF LIABILITY FOR INCIDENTAL OR CONSEQUENTIAL DAMAGES SO THE ABOVE LIMITATIONS AND EXCLUSIONS MAY NOT APPLY TO YOU.

11. UPDATES. LICENSOR, at its sole discretion, may periodically issue updates of the Software which you may receive upon request and payment of the applicable update fee in effect from time to time and in such event, all of the provisions of the within License Agreement shall apply to such updates.

12. EXPORT RESTRICTIONS. Licensee agrees not to export or re-export the Soft-ware and accompanying documentation (or any copies thereof) in violation of any applicable U.S. laws or regulations.

13. ENTIRE AGREEMENT. YOU, AS LICENSEE, ACKNOWLEDGE THAT: (i) YOU HAVE READ THIS ENTIRE AGREEMENT AND AGREE TO BE BOUND BY ITS TERMS AND CONDITIONS; (ii) THIS AGREEMENT IS THE COMPLETE AND EXCLUSIVE STATEMENT OF THE UNDERSTANDING BETWEEN THE PARTIES AND SUPERSEDES ANY AND ALL PRIOR ORAL OR WRITTEN COMMUNICATIONS RELATING TO THE SUBJECT MATTER HEREOF; AND (iii) THIS AGREEMENT MAY NOT BE MODIFIED, AMENDED, OR IN ANY WAY ALTERED EXCEPT BY A WRITING SIGNED BY BOTH YOURSELF AND AN OFFICER OR AUTHORIZED REPRESENTATIVE OF LICENSOR.

14. SEVERABILITY. In the event that any provision of this License Agreement is held to be illegal or otherwise unenforceable, such provision shall be deemed to have been deleted from this License Agreement while the remaining provisions of this License Agreement shall be unaffected and shall continue in full force and effect.

15. GOVERNING LAW. This License Agreement shall be governed by the laws of the State of California applicable to agreements wholly to be performed therein and of the United States of America, excluding that body of the law related to conflicts of law. This License Agreement shall not be governed by the United Nations Convention on Contracts for the International Sale of Goods, the application of which is expressly excluded. No waiver of any breach of the provisions of this License Agreement shall be deemed a waiver of any other breach of this License Agreement.

16. RESTRICTED RIGHTS LEGEND. Use, duplication, or disclosure by the Government is subject to restrictions as set forth in subparagraph (c)(1)(ii) of the Rights in Technical Data and Computer Software clause at 48 CFR § 252.227-7013 and DFARS § 252.227-7013 or subparagraphs (c) (1) and (c)(2) of the Commercial Computer Software-Restricted Rights at 48 CFR § 52.227.19, as applicable. Contractor/manufacturer: LICENSOR: LYNDA.COM, LLC, c/o PEACHPIT PRESS, 1249 Eighth Street, Berkeley, CA 94710.